The SA Generals
and the
Rise of Nazism

THE
SA GENERALS
AND THE
RISE OF NAZISM

Bruce Campbell

THE UNIVERSITY PRESS OF KENTUCKY

Publication of this volume was made possible in part by a grant from the National Endowment for the Humanities.

Scholarly publisher for the Commonwealth,
serving Bellarmine College, Berea College, Centre
College of Kentucky, Eastern Kentucky University,
The Filson Club Historical Society, Georgetown College,
Kentucky Historical Society, Kentucky State University,
Morehead State University, Murray State University,
Northern Kentucky University, Transylvania University,
University of Kentucky, University of Louisville,
and Western Kentucky University.

Editorial and Sales Offices: The University Press of Kentucky
663 South Limestone Street, Lexington, Kentucky 40508-4008

02 01 00 99 98   5 4 3 2 1

Library of Congress Catalolging-in-Publication Data

Campbell, Bruce, 1955-
    The SA generals and the rise of Nazism / Bruce Campbell
      p.   cm.
    Includes bibliographical references and index.
    ISBN 0-8131-2047-0 (alk. paper)
    1. Nationalsozialistische Deutsche Arbeiter-Partei. Sturmabteilung.
2. Generals—Germany—Biography. 3. Germany—Politics and
government—1918-1933. 4. National socialism. 5. Germany. Heer—
History. 6. Germany—Military policy. I. Title
DD253.7.C36   1998
943.085—dc21   98-5266

Manufactured in the United States of America

CONTENTS

ILLUSTRATIONS

ACKNOWLEDGMENTS

Modern scholarship is always a collective effort, even in fields such as history where individual researchers are still the norm. Just about the only thing to which an author can still claim exclusive title today are the faults. I cheerfully acknowledge that the shortcomings of this book are all mine, but I equally cheerfully acknowledge the help of the following individuals and organizations.

Pride of place goes to Robert L. Koehl, my doctoral adviser and guiding hand in the early stages of my work. He has been generous with his advice ever since. In this context I also need to thank Hagen Schulze, who was my adviser at the Freie Universität during the three years I spent researching in Berlin. The members of both of their doctoral seminars also deserve my thanks for their help and kind criticism, even though they are too numerous to list here. Jim Strudwick and Wolfgang Pusy will have to stand for many others.

Special thanks go to the staff of the German Academic Exchange Service (DAAD), the National Endowment for the Humanities, and the taxpaying citizens of the German Federal Republic and the United States. Without the generous financial support of the DAAD and the NEH, this book could never have been written. Any loss or diminution of funding for both of these agencies is a major threat to the continuation of scholarship and should be fought by the entire community of thoughtful citizens. Other financial support for this and other projects came from Transylvania University and the David and Betty Jones/Bingham Faculty Development Grants.

The staffs of the many archives and libraries that I used and reused in the course of preparing this book were absolutely essential to the effort. They remained surprisingly helpful and friendly, despite my continued demands. Although I cannot name everyone, special thanks go to Daniel P. Simon, David Marwell, Herr

Eberhard, Herr Pohl, Herr Pix, Frau Wolff, and Frau Grohmann, all of the former Berlin Document Center, Dr. Weiß, Frau Popp, and Frau Emmer of the Institut für Zeitgeschichte, Dr. Henke, Dr. Oldenhage, Herr Verlande, and Frau Loenartz of the Bundesarchiv, Priscilla Neill and the entire staff of the University of Wisconsin-Madison's Memorial Library, Kathleen Bryson of Transylvania University, the staff of the Bibliothèque de Documentation Internationale Contemporaine (Paris), the Bundesarchiv-Militärarchiv (Freiburg), and the libraries of the Freie Universität, Old Dominion University, the College of William and Mary, and the University of California, Berkeley.

The following scholars and individuals (in no particular order) also gave their kind help and support: Alan Steinweiss, Eleanor Hancock, George Browder, Winifried Mogge, Larry Stokes, Rebecca Boehling, Richard Bodek, David Yelton, Anton Kaes, Steve Brockmann, Vibeke Petersen, Glenn Cuomo, Edward Coffmann, John Sharpless, Jürgen Herbst, Jost Hermand, Helmut Anheier, Dr. Lauchs, Dr. Marek, Anthony Vital, Tay Fizdale, Jeff Freyman, Paul Fuller, Joseph Binford, Ingrid Fields, Kathy Brown, Ted Pearson, Gene Mahan, Francis Halzen, Nellie Halzen, Hildegard Glass, Sylvia Klötzer, Maryse Fauvel, Stefan Wilhelmus, Christine Samson, Jütta Diegler, and Tim Morris. I'm sure to have missed more than one person here, so please forgive me if you are not listed.

While I am paying my intellectual debts, I must give special mention to three scholars whom I have never met but who have helped the progress of this book in very real ways. Robert Frank and Andreas Werner have written two important histories of the SA as an organization. My own work would have been much more difficult without theirs to build upon. Mathilde Jamin was kind enough to loan me a copy of her dissertation before it was published, and she provided me with some very useful counsel regarding the study of the SA at the BDC. I also obtained much information and many ideas from her publications, and I am very glad that she, and not I, tackled the difficult question of the social composition of the SA leadership.

Special thanks, too, to the editorial team at the University Press of Kentucky. In this context I particularly need to thank the anonymous readers who critiqued earlier versions of this book. Your help was invaluable, and if I didn't take all your advice, I greatly appreciate it nonetheless.

I must thank my own parents and family on both sides of the Atlantic for their support and love. It is convention to thank one's domestic partner as well, but I find mere language inadequate to do so. I wrote this book, but she put up with it. No one will be happier to see the end of this book and the departure of "my Nazis" from our house than she.

Abbreviations Used in Text

a.D.	außer Dienst (retired)
BDC	Berlin Document Center
d.R.	der Reserve
DAP	Deutsche Arbeiterpartei
DNVP	Deutschnationale Volkspartei
NSDAP	Nationalsozialistische Deutsche Arbeiterpartei
OC	Organisation Consul
OSAF	Oberste SA-Führer/Oberste SA-Führung
SA	Sturmabteilung
SAR	SA-Reserve
SS	Schutzstaffel

Introduction

Who were the Nazis? How could this tiny, obscure party capture power so quickly in Germany, the land of poets and philosophers? How could it grow so fast and yet remain coherent and effective? And how did ordinary human beings become Nazis? Even fifty years later, these are still some of the greatest questions of the twentieth century, and we only have partial answers. This book will move a step closer to a full answer. It studies the lives and careers of the men who occupied the top leadership positions of the paramilitary wing of the Nazi Party, the Sturmabteilung (storm troopers), also known as the SA or Brown Shirts.

Specifically, this book looks at the political and military activities of the 178 men who eventually held one of the three highest ranks in the SA hierarchy on an active basis at any time between 1925 and 1945.[1] Although the titles varied, by 1932 these ranks were Stabschef, Obergruppenführer, and Gruppenführer in descending order.[2] These men built the SA, guided it to victory in 1933, and continued to lead it until they suffered defeat in 1945.

The SA was an extremely important part of the Nazi movement. More than any other single element, it was responsible for the Nazi Party's success in gaining power and intimidating all opposition. The ceaseless activism of the SA (shared by the Nazi Party in general), its imposing presence at meetings, its uniformed public marches, and the terrorism and violence that it practiced against opponents were all critical in transforming the Nazi Party from a small band of fanatics into the largest mass political party in the history of Germany up to that time. The SA was largely responsible for the Janus face of National Socialism, which was so fatally attractive: on the one hand, their uniforms and their marching symbolized the dynamism and discipline of the NSDAP, in contrast to the "somnambulism" of traditional right-wing parties and the "slovenliness" of left-wing parties. This same dynamism further seemed to bear out the NSDAP's claim to represent youth and, by extension, the future. On the other hand, the violence of the SA appealed to the visceral frustrations of many (certainly many males) in a defeated and internally divided Germany, and contrasted with the alleged "laxity" and "weakness" of the democratic parties of the middle.

The key to the SA's success as an organization and to its special value in the political arena was its combination of political mission with military forms and attitudes, creating what it called "political soldiers." This is a new element in political life characteristic of the Weimar Republic and, indeed, of many other European countries in the long truce between the two world wars.[3]

The SA leaders (officers) whose careers are analyzed here were the ones who adapted the various models set by the Imperial Army, the Wehrverbände (paramilitary organizations), and various völkisch (integral German nationalist and usually racist) political organizations to form the SA and who thus invented political soldiering.[4] As will be amply demonstrated in the following pages, they did so based on their own experiences and training. This is why it is so important to study this particular group of men: to understand the SA is to understand that part of the NSDAP which, particularly during the "time of struggle" (Kampfzeit, the common Nazi expression), was most responsible for defining its image and providing much of the dynamism and muscle behind Nazi electoral efforts and Nazi intimidation.[5]

The men in this study produced the world's most effective paramilitary auxiliary, and in doing so, they catapulted the NSDAP into power. Although the reward for this efficiency was the purge of the SA in 1934 and its demotion within the Nazi system, the basic forms and principles of organization created for the SA lived on in its more sinister successor and former sibling, the Schutzstaffel, also known as the SS or Black Shirts. In many ways, the SS merely followed the model developed by the SA's leaders when they "invented" that organization.[6]

The decision to limit this study to the three highest levels of rank found within the SA was made because they were largely responsible for planning, organization, administration, and decision making.[7] They were thus responsible for "setting the tone" in the SA. The next lowest level of rank in the SA, Brigadeführer, largely carried out administrative duties and did not participate in decision making or policy setting in a fundamental sense, and so they are not included.

SA leaders in the Propaganda Ministry, November 1, 1934. Descending the staircase, left to right, are (1) Hans Elard Ludin, (2) Arthur Rakobrandt, (3) Osturmf. Morenga, (4) Johann Heinrich Boehmcker, (5) Joachim Meyer-Quade, (6) Wilhelm Helfer, (7) Heinrich August Schoene, (8) Emil Ketterer, (9) Max Paul Wilhelm Werner Jüttner, (10) Emil Steinhoff, (11) Hans Friedrich, (12) Herbert Robert Gerhard Fust, (13) Hans-Günther von Obernitz, (14) Heinrich August Knickmann, (15) Otto Herzog, (16) Arno Manthey, (17) Otto Schramme, (18) Dietrich Wilhelm Bernhard von Jagow, (19) Adolf-Heinz Beckerle, (20) Arthur Böckenhauer, (21) Gustav Zunkel, (22) Max Otto Luyken, (23) Wilhelm Schepmann, (24) Siegfried Karl Viktor Johannes Kasche, (25) unidentified, (26) Otto Marxer, (27) Viktor Lutze, and (28) Karl-Siegmund Hermann Julius Litzmann. Courtesy of the Bundesarchiv.

Moreover, the three top levels of rank of active duty SA leaders amounts to a very manageable group of 178 individuals. Confining this study to the three top levels of rank in the SA means that it is limited to a small, well-defined, and homogeneous group. In addition, the surviving documents about them are comparatively large in number, comparatively complete (despite some inevitable gaps), sufficiently rich in detail, and sufficiently similar to allow comparison. These practical considerations may seem a bit removed from the historical problems that this book will address, but they are important methodologically.[8]

Certainly, this group of the very highest SA leaders is not necessarily representative of the SA as a whole. It is an important portion of the SA but also a select group. Although the SA claimed to be a particularly egalitarian organization in its class makeup,[9] no hierarchical organization is actually uniform or homogeneous at all levels. Senior leaders are a select group in almost any organization.

Others have tried to make more generalized statements about the SA, but there is still room for more research.[10] The problem with trying to examine the SA as a whole is that its composition varied according to both locality and time, yet the surviving SA records make capturing the nature of these variations very difficult. Given these problems, a viable alternative for social historians is to investigate clearly defined subgroups within the SA for which suitable records are available. This is the approach taken here.[11]

Although this study focuses on the SA elite, the original impulse behind this project was anything but elitist. Even today, specialists writing about the NSDAP have a tendency to proceed as if Adolf Hitler himself were responsible for the organizational success of the SA. There is some truth to this in the sense that Hitler did set broad policy guidelines, and it can serve as a kind of shorthand on a macrolevel, but it is illogical and absurd to credit one man with the design of any organization as large as the SA. My goal has been to draw attention away from Hitler to the group of men who implemented his guidelines and did the real work of creating the SA's organizational structure.[12]

This book began as a study of how the top SA leaders found their way into the Nazi movement. It still discusses this process, but in doing so, it must also pay close attention to the SA's evolution as an organization. In effect, this study is also a new kind of organizational history, which traces the growth and elaboration of the SA through the evolution of its leaders and through the particular skills and experience they brought to the organization. An organization grows and changes not as a function of the set of organizational techniques known to it but rather as a function of the willingness and ability of its members to implement certain organizational methods and forms (and therefore not others). In other words, the SA did not become a mass paramilitary organization simply because a certain set of organizational forms and tools existed; instead, it developed as it did because its leadership consciously made certain decisions and because the forms of organization they chose to use were familiar to them and fit their particular goals and ideological preconceptions. In this sense, no study of an organization is complete without taking the background of its decision makers into account.

Partly in consequence, and unlike nearly all social historical investigations of the Nazi Party or its affiliates, this study will not concentrate on defining and describing class basis or composition. Instead, the focus will be on the military and political activities of these men before they became Nazis and, to a lesser extent, on their careers as SA leaders afterwards. It will trace their evolution and pay particular attention to their voluntary political affiliations. This is a new approach. It is possible because the SA kept thorough records on its leaders. It is necessary because the class basis of the Nazi Party and the SA is now fairly well known, at least in its broad contours.[13] Although this is important to know, it comes nowhere near a full explanation of the Nazi movement. After all, what does knowing the class composition of a given group really tell us? All it truly does is allow us to presume that the individuals in question share the attitudes, status, education, needs, etc., commonly associated with their class[14] and that the group or organization therefore must somehow recognize and reflect these class interests. This is not negligible, because it is sometimes the only available window into the motivations or backgrounds of the group being studied, but in the end, it remains only a set of assumptions.

By looking at the organizations to which the top SA leaders belonged before they joined the Nazi Party, this book adds a new element to our knowledge of who the Nazis were and how they operated. By following the paths these men took into the SA and Nazi Party, it shows as never before the dynamic process of how at least this particular group became Nazis and how they learned how to be Nazis. By looking in particular at the voluntary associations that these men chose to make before they became Nazis, this book can also go beyond what an analysis of class background can tell us about their character and motivation. Finally, by exposing the prior experiences and training of SA leaders, this book can help to explain why the SA took the form it did, how it could be so effective in its tasks despite often difficult circumstances and sometimes vertiginous growth, and how such a complex and effective organization could be built in such a short time.

It is important, however, to note the limits of the approach taken in this book. The question of individual motivation is tricky for historians. Because all the SA's top leaders are now dead, the question of *why* they became Nazis can only be surmised. Examining their voluntary associations and the kinds of organizations that socialized them can certainly help to explain their characters and motivations better than an analysis of their class backgrounds can, but this alone cannot answer the question of individual motivation. Except in very rare cases, the SA and SS personnel records upon which this study is based contain very little of the kind of personal information that would permit an investigator to speak of what motivated a given individual.

This book describes the lives of SA leaders both individually and collectively. In the latter case, it uses very simple descriptive statistics. These statistics are drawn from the analysis of a database containing biographical information about the 178 men in this study, including their organizational activities from 1914 to 1945. For the key period from 1918 to 1935, these activities were recorded in three-month segments. A fuller discussion of the methodology may be found below in chapter 7. Here at the beginning of this study it is useful to point out that, despite the sometimes overwhelming presence of percentages and numbers, this is emphatically and deliberately not a conventional statistical study. It does not involve using a "sample" to describe some larger group through complex mathematical inference; instead, it includes *all* of the SA's top leaders. It also very rarely tries to compare SA leaders with some larger group, such as the German population at large. It is a collective biography that describes a discrete and unique group of individuals in the most efficient way possible, and this means it often uses simple percentages, but nothing more complex than that.

Trying to compare the SA leadership with all Germans in the 1930s would not be very profitable at present. It would only tell us that SA leaders were different from the general population, but it could not tell us much of significance about these differences. The reason is that there is no legitimate basis for comparison. No study exists, for example, that measures the voluntary associations of the entire German population. Comparisons with other, narrower social groups are also still problematic for the same reasons. Studies similar to this one of comparable groups, which would provide a genuinely meaningful basis for comparison, are completely lacking.[15]

The highest SA leaders came from a military background. They continued their military activities by joining the private paramilitary associations that were so characteristic of the Weimar Republic, the so-called Wehrverbände. A significant minority were also völkisch zealots active in political organizations. This common military, paramilitary, and völkisch background led these men into the SA and prepared them for their future role as SA leaders.[16]

They were a homogeneous group, but the practical foundation of their homogeneity was not class or status (although they were homogeneous in this respect as well) so much as it was common experience in the army, Wehrverbände, and völkisch groups. They "spoke the same language," but it was not in its essence the language of a social class. It was the language of the parade ground and the battlefield. Their military training gave them the skills essential to building and running a complex mass organization like the SA. Their domestic military experiences during the German Revolution and especially their civilian experiences in the Wehrverbände taught them that military forms could be applied to civilian problems. Their participation in völkisch parties and organizations and the general influence of those organizations within the Wehrverband milieu gave them an ideology and a set of political goals, culminating in the destruction of the Weimar Republic, an end to the Versailles treaty, and the elimination of socialist, foreign, modernist, and Jewish influence in Germany. Finally, after the failure of the Hitler Putsch, the NSDAP taught them that, although the use of outright military force against the Weimar Republic was not likely to succeed for the moment, their goals could still be pursued with military forms through electoral politics. This is the equation, the recipe for the success of the Nazi Party, as well as the formula for the creation of "political soldiers." The SA leadership were both the inventors of political soldiering and a part of the invention itself. The evolution of these men will be illustrated below.

1

Background

The men examined in this book were participants in an arcane and complex right-wing military and paramilitary subculture that will be foreign to most readers, but its details will be important in the following study. Since the "language" of this subculture is not widely spoken today, the reader might appreciate a short general introduction to the world in which these men lived.

The majority were born into the smug, secure European middle class of the late nineteenth century, a world which even then was in the throes of profound social, cultural, economic, and demographic change. This change was accelerated by the outbreak of the First World War in 1914.

The scale and speed of this process was unprecedented and was not always easy to accept. The men who eventually became the top SA leaders lived in a peculiar postwar subculture that saw itself under attack by change or modernity. This subculture reacted with an aggressive mixture of nostalgia for an idealized past, hatred of the present, and messianic hope for a future that would somehow put to right everything that was seen to be wrong. This caused these men to see themselves as engaged in social war. It allowed them to speak in the name of tradition yet act as revolutionaries, and it allowed them to embrace distinctly modern tools and techniques in their struggle. This was and is a significant contradiction but, unfortunately, one that is still with us.

THE HERITAGE OF THE "OLD ARMY"

If they lived in a larger society marked by "cultural despair"[1] and wrenching modernization, they also came from a very particular social subculture within the German Empire. Nearly all of the men in this study had a military background. Most served in the First World

War, but a large number had already become professional soldiers before 1914. The German army on the eve of the First World War, like most contemporary armies, had firmly embraced modern technology, yet it was also dedicated to tradition.[2] The military in general and officers in particular had tremendous social prestige in Germany. Tradition dictated that the officer corps be kept as socially exclusive as possible. Despite (or because of) the sweeping social and technological changes of the period, the officer corps of the German army and navy at the turn of the century nevertheless still tried to form a corps of men homogeneous in outlook and background and still claimed to represent a moral elite dedicated to serving the emperor and state.[3] The social hierarchy of the Wilhelmine Empire was mirrored in miniature within the armed forces themselves. Some units were more prestigious than others, and there was a deep gulf between professional and reserve officers.

The fact that many men in this study were not only officers but professional (regular, not reserve) officers before the war was very important to them. It also speaks volumes about the way they were socialized as young adults and about how they originally saw themselves fitting into society. No other factor in the background and training of the future top SA leaders is as significant. As a whole, SA leaders defined themselves as military men. What was to change in their lives was not this fact but what they perceived as the proper role of a military man in society.

THE FIRST WORLD WAR AND THE GERMAN REVOLUTION

The exigencies of total war placed great pressure on the social and military structure of Wilhelmine society. It tended to call all existing social hierarchies into question, and it greatly reduced the ability of the nobility and the upper middle class to claim social superiority and special privileges. This leveling effect was felt within the military as well. The high casualty rate among junior officers and the huge increase in the size of the officer corps during the war diluted its social exclusivity, despite extreme attempts by the high command to preserve it. Moreover, combat amply demonstrated that the favored social groups were not necessarily the best equipped to lead men into battle, especially since success in battle was increasingly a function of technological rather than moral prowess.

A new concept of leadership came out of the war, which rejected the Kadavergehorsam (absolute obedience) based on hierarchy and deference to one's superiors in favor of a voluntary subordination based on common ideology, mutual respect, and deference to the personal ability and charisma of a leader. This was a revolutionary element within the army. It threatened the old hierarchy by setting young combat officers against older staff officers, but did not threaten either the military or hierarchical leadership as such. This was emphatically not a democratization of the military, since it still definitely called for the establishment and maintenance of hierarchy and discipline, but it was a populist and a popular concept that distinguished a new generation of officers.

The men in this study were all deeply marked by this new concept of leadership. While the army and navy, which were reestablished as the Reichswehr after the turmoil of the German Revolution, remained largely in the hands of the old-style noble and upper-middle-class officers, the upheaval in the concept of leadership played a strong role within both the armed units formed during the German Revolution and the later paramilitary organizations that were their heirs. This is the reason why there is very little mention in this book of SA "officers." Both the NSDAP and the SA itself rejected the term and consciously chose to use the term *leader* (Führer) instead. This symbolized the self-proclaimed social revolutionary mission of the Nazis and expressed the new definition of leadership that emerged among veterans. It is also the reason why Hitler (the former corporal) could become simply "der Führer," first of the NSDAP and then of all Germany: it expressed his claim to be a new sort of leader who (ostensibly) relied on the power of his innate personality rather than on the force of a formal title or rank.

The German Revolution of 1918-19 (the November Revolution) was only the symbolic manifestation of larger social forces at work that swept away the old Wilhelmine Empire and the entire world of the nineteenth century. It was neither planned nor intended; rather, it was a spontaneous collapse of the old order. Nevertheless, it created a profound crisis of values and identity for large numbers of Germans, and this related directly to the rise of the NSDAP and kindred organizations.

In the resulting power vacuum, a wide range of organizations emerged, some based on older, collapsing institutions, and some new. While the old empire was clearly doomed, the exact form that the future of Germany would take was in no way predetermined. Although Germany turned into a reasonably successful democratic republic after the First World War, the conflict over Germany's proper identity and form implicit in the revolution was never settled. It brought the Weimar Republic constant conflict and ultimately led to its destruction by the combined forces of moderate and radical conservatives who hotly contested the republican definition of a new Germany. The men in this book were all on the front lines of this conflict, and they were among the most responsible for the temporary defeat of the republican ideal in Germany.

The Republic's survival was complicated by the circumstances surrounding its birth. Not only was it born in revolution (however superficial that revolution may have been) but it was burdened with having to sign the Versailles treaty. Worse, the German military leadership, which clearly understood in the fall of 1918 that Germany was facing total and unavoidable military defeat, later ignored or actively assisted in spreading a popular myth which held that Germany had not lost the war militarily but had instead been "stabbed in the back" by profiteers, leftists, and Jews.[4] This famous "stab-in-the-back" legend conveniently freed Germany's military leaders from responsibility for losing the war.[5] It thus served to further delegitimize an already unstable nascent democratic system, and turned thousands, perhaps millions of Germans irreparably against it, particularly those already predisposed to oppose the Republic.

POLITICAL PARTIES AND THE VÖLKISCH MOVEMENT

Political parties dedicated to electoral politics—even if many ultimately rejected democracy and sought to abolish the Republic—dominated and led the political debate in the Weimar Republic. Interestingly, only two parties figure prominently in the backgrounds of the highest SA leaders: the traditional conservative Deutschnationale Volkspartei (German National People's Party, or DNVP) and the NSDAP.

The DNVP was founded in November 1918 as the heir of a number of conservative parties of the Wilhelmine Empire.[6] The fact that it contained so many diverse elements made it hard for the DNVP to coherently define itself. It was a monarchist party, opposed to the democratic system, the Versailles treaty, and the policy of "fulfillment." Although it participated in parliamentary politics, it was never quite comfortable within the Weimar "system" and tended to avoid participation in government coalitions. While its politics were mainly traditional conservative, it tolerated a great deal of sympathy for anti-Semitism in its ranks, and many members condoned a more radical form of conservatism. Although its members came from all classes, the party leadership was particularly sensitive to the interests of big business and big agriculture. Organizationally it was a conventional political party, and yet it maintained close ties to the Stahlhelm, a veterans' association and paramilitary organization. From 1924 to 1928 it was the strongest middle-class party in the Reichstag, but losses in the 1928 election (and a major split in 1929-30) caused it to adopt a more intransigent and antirepublican course under its new chairman, Alfred Hugenberg. Its tactical alliances with the NSDAP in 1929 in the campaign against the Young Plan and in 1931 against the Brüning government (the "Harzburg Front") merely served to legitimize the latter party, while not slowing the DNVP's gradual decline. As this study amply demonstrates, the end result was that DNVP members increasingly migrated to the NSDAP. The DNVP was a major participant in the coalition government that brought Hitler to power as chancellor in 1933. Dreaming that it could "tame" or "use" the Nazis, it was quickly outmaneuvered by them. The party was formally disbanded on June 26, 1933.

The second political party, and the one to which all of the highest SA leaders belonged, is of course the Nationalsozialistische Deutsche Arbeiterpartei, or NSDAP.[7] It presents us with a paradox: even though it eventually became the largest single political party in German history, it began in January 1919 as a tiny sectarian party in the southern German state of Bavaria called the Deutsche Arbeiterpartei (German Workers' Party, or DAP). It existed in the beginning as just one of many tiny splinter groups and parties on the extreme right end of the political spectrum that made up the völkisch movement.

The völkisch movement had its roots in the nineteenth century.[8] This broad and diverse movement had as its common tenants a form of ultranationalist, antidemocratic populism which claimed to represent a kind of integral Germanness. Xenophobic in general, the völkisch movement was particularly identified with a virulent anti-Semitism. It was strongly influenced by the Social Darwinism rampant in European society at the end of the nineteenth century. The völkisch movement embraced such mainstream political positions as the need for a powerful army and a strong state, but individual völkisch thinkers and movements also embraced a wide range of more marginal ideas, which could include such things as nudism, vegetarianism, mysticism, or reincarnation. While völkisch parties or organizations such as the Christlich-soziale Partei (Christian Social Party) of Adolf Stöcker or the separate Christlich-soziale Partei of Karl Lueger in Vienna did occasionally become something like mass movements before the First World War, the organized völkisch movement generally remained small and on the margins of society at that time.

In the atmosphere of revolution, defeat, and despair, the völkisch movement in Germany grew significantly after the war and served to focus the fears and resentments of many Central Europeans. Perhaps just as important, even before the war völkisch ideas had begun to infiltrate mainstream society. The radicalization of the political climate, combined with the earlier gradual acceptance of völkisch ideas by moderate conservatives, allowed for a much closer cooperation between moderate and völkisch (radical) conservatives after the war than had previously been possible.[9]

It is important to emphasize that from the time of its founding in 1919 until about 1927, the NSDAP was just one of many völkisch organizations in Germany and Austria and was seen to be, and generally saw itself to be, just one part of a larger völkisch movement.[10] Although Nazi ideology and policy distinguished itself from that of other contemporary völkisch organizations on a handful of points, it really represented little that was new or original;[11] instead, anyone familiar with the larger völkisch movement would instantly recognize and feel comfortable with most of what the Nazis represented.

The very familiarity of the Nazis to those attracted to völkisch ideology allowed the NSDAP to grow in its early years by gradually absorbing members of other völkisch organizations or their hangers-on. Furthermore, as a minor member of a larger movement, the NSDAP was ensured a safe and congenial, if limited, social space in which to organize and grow in its early years. The NSDAP first absorbed the members of other organizations in this political "niche," which allowed it to reach a certain size and consolidate itself organizationally before it began to take on the much more difficult task of crossing over into the political mainstream, which it had begun to do by 1927. This process can be seen clearly within the top leadership of the SA, and it is therefore not surprising that völkisch groups or parties figure prominently in the backgrounds of many (but by no means all) of the highest SA leaders.

One of the earliest völkisch organizations to achieve national prominence during the German Revolution was the Deutsch-völkischer Schutz- und Trutzbund (German Völkisch Defense and Defiance League).[12] Although it did not have a very tight national organization, and though it only existed from 1919 until 1922, it was extremely important because it served to give a völkisch focus to the great and general resentment, hatred, fear, and disappointment felt by many Germans after the loss of the war and during the upheavals of the revolution. For many of the future top SA leaders, this was their first exposure to völkisch ideas.

A second group of völkisch organizations to which many future SA leaders belonged included both contemporary competitors of the NSDAP, such as the Deutschsoziale Partei (German-Social Party), the Deutschsozialistische Partei (German-Socialist Party), or the Deutschvölkische Freiheitspartei (German Völkisch Freedom Party), or völkisch organizations formed to continue the völkisch movement after the NSDAP and similar organizations were banned in the wake of the failed Beer Hall Putsch, such as the Deutschvölkische Freiheitsbewegung (German Völkisch Freedom Movement), the Nationalsozialistische Freiheitsbewegung (National Socialist Freedom Movement), or the Großdeutsche Volksgemeinschaft (Greater-German National Community).[13] These völkisch organizations are important because they (and the early NSDAP) pioneered many of the tactics and strategies that the Nazis later used so effectively, and they eventually supplied political skills and ideology to the separate but contemporary movement of paramilitary associations, or Wehrverbände.

Although the völkisch element is important in the backgrounds of the higher SA leaders, it is a relatively small element and it functioned more like a catalyst. The military and paramilitary activities of these men are much more important in terms of the number of organizations involved or the length of time devoted to them.

THE PARAMILITARY HERITAGE OF THE REVOLUTION

The collapse that became the German Revolution in November 1918 involved German society in its entirety, but it was perhaps most acute and of greatest consequence in the German armed forces. A naval mutiny in Wilhelmshaven on October 29 began the temporary but near total collapse of the German armed forces. Meanwhile, a political struggle for power broke out within Germany between the moderate social democrats under Friedrich Ebert (who had been handed the reins of government by the last imperial chancellor, Prince Max of Baden) and a collection of more radical socialists who sought to turn Germany into a Soviet-style "council republic" (Räterepublik).

In addition, the power vacuum in eastern Europe caused by the collapse of the Russian, Austro-Hungarian, and German Empires set free the long-held national aspirations of the Baltic peoples, the Poles, and the Czechs, all of whom laid claim to German territory. (Austria faced a similar combination of domestic turmoil and foreign threat.) A certain degree of simple banditry also accompanied the political upheaval.

The Ebert government was thus faced with an acute need for an armed force with which to assert its authority, while the high command was faced with an equally acute need to preserve the future of itself and the armed forces. This led to a deal between the Ebert government and General Groener (then "Erster Quartiermeister" or deputy chief of the general staff and effectively in command of the German army at that point) which was made on the evening of November 10, 1918. Each agreed to support the other.

There was a problem, however. The high command really didn't have much of an armed force at its disposal, since the soldiers returning from the front quickly refused to fight their fellow citizens in the streets. They either waited passively in their barracks for demobilization or, more frequently, simply went home. The high command was thus faced with the task of quickly creating an ad hoc armed force for immediate use before it could really afford to think about rebuilding the armed forces on a permanent basis. Meanwhile, given the collapse of order, other organizations, from bands of citizens interested in protecting their property to political organizations combatting the Ebert government, all set about creating their own armed units. These military and paramilitary forces formed during the revolution played a vital role in the careers and development of future SA leaders. They existed in a confusing variety, and it is important to distinguish between the different kinds.

The army and navy *ordered* the formation of voluntary military units made up of veterans and filled out with hastily trained young men who had not yet been called up to service. These units came to be called Freikorps, or free corps, a term previously used for private or irregular military units formed in the eighteenth and nineteenth centuries, especially those formed in the Germanies at the end of the Napoleonic Wars to throw out the French occupation[14]. While the high command was not the only authority that caused free corps to be formed, the mythology surrounding the free corps[15] even today makes it important to describe them in some detail.

The free corps in general were formed at the initiative and under the direction of the army and navy high command.[16] They were full-time military units under the control of the German government and its representatives. Free corps members were paid, clothed, equipped, and housed at government expense, and they served under regular military discipline. Service in the free corps counted as regular military service in terms of seniority, promotion, decorations, etc.[17] Men, particularly career NCOs and officers, were transferred into and out of individual free corps by the army and navy high commands as a matter of course. On occasion, this even involved transfer of men serving in units in the Baltic who had nominally mutinied.[18] Free corps units were formed by the military as temporary units and were intended to serve only until order was restored and the regular army could be reestablished. As a consequence, most free corps existed for less than six months. The majority were disbanded by June 1919, and the last free corps were disbanded by May and June 1920. Later resurrections of the term (such as in Upper Silesia in 1921) were just that: resurrections of a historical term to provide symbolic continuity, just as had been done in 1918 and 1919 to revive the old tradition of the original free corps of the eighteenth and nineteenth centuries.[19]

A large number of free corps men were transferred into the regular army (the Provisional Reichswehr and later the Reichswehr) or the newly formed state police units called the Sicherheitspolizei. Others were only too happy to return to civilian life. Only a few men who had served in the free corps and who had realistic expectations of continuing a professional military career were forced out of the military by the Treaty of Versailles or their own disloyalty.[20] Such individuals did exist, and their later role as agitators against the Republic was important, but they do not represent the majority of free corps veterans.

Despite these caveats, the free corps were vital to the creation of the later paramilitary subculture from which the future higher SA leaders all came. The occasional savagery of the fighting in which the free corps was involved contributed in a major way to the creation of a postwar political climate in which violence was much more likely than before the war. Most important of all, the free corps were later mythologized and became a symbol of idealism, self-sacrifice, and radical and total engagement in the fight for Germany. Traditional conservatives, radical conservatives of different stripes, and even the Communist Party all tried to co-opt the myth of the free corps for their own purposes. Moreover, the free corps did also serve as a first experiment in the use of military forms and procedures in Germany to solve essentially civilian political problems.[21] Although later organizations under different conditions would elaborate further on this model before it would ultimately become the "political soldiering" of the SA, the free corps did provide an important first step. Also significant, the free corps tended to be a place where many of the most radical and activist elements of the later paramilitary underground came together.[22] The acquaintanceships, friendships, and contacts that were first made in the free corps were the connective tissue that held the later paramilitary subculture of the Weimar Republic together. Although the thesis that the free corps were the "vanguard of Nazism" is no longer tenable today in its simplest version, the free corps are clearly an important (if not necessary) step in the careers of the men who later became the highest leaders of the SA.

The free corps were not the only military or paramilitary units serving under government auspices during the revolution, by any means. Units of both the old Imperial Army and the new army (which would eventually become the Reichswehr) existed side by side. Some of the larger free corps formed units of part-time volunteer reserves called Zeitfreiwilliger, which could be called up quickly in case of renewed revolt or unrest.[23] Many of these were former free corps members, often students, who had returned to their civilian occupations, but they were distinguished from the free corps in that they were part-time organizations. Another armed paramilitary body characteristic of the revolution was a kind of civic guard or citizens militia originally formed spontaneously by middle-class Germans to protect their property. These units were later formed into a national system under government supervision called the Einwohnerwehren (civic guards).[24] They, too, are distinguished by being part-time organizations. Moreover, the Einwohnerwehren were the least "military" and most "civilian" of all the government-sponsored armed organizations in terms of their duties, membership, training, equipment, and leadership.

The Versailles treaty set very strict limits on the size of the armed forces in Germany, and thousands of men who had been career soldiers or who hoped to become career soldiers based on their wartime or free corps service found themselves out on the street. The Einwohnerwehr movement might have served to absorb much of the frustrated martial ardor abroad in German society, but an Allied ultimatum forced the German government to disband it on June 21, 1921.[25]

Some Einwohnerwehr members independently took the movement underground. Several of the more flamboyant free corps leaders such as Gerhard Roßbach, Peter von Heydebreck, or Hermann Ehrhardt had already taken many of their men underground, forming Arbeitsgemeinschaften (labor cooperatives) when the free corps were disbanded in the course of establishing the new Reichswehr. Moreover, there were already a great number of legal, aboveboard veterans' organizations in existence, such as the Stahlhelm. Out of these three wellsprings grew an entire movement of private paramilitary associations collectively called the Wehrverbände (singular, Wehrverband).[26]

THE WEHRVERBÄNDE

In contrast to the free corps, the Reichswehr, and the Einwohnerwehren, the Wehrverbände were strictly private organizations with no overt state influence or control. Moreover, in contrast with the Reichswehr and the free corps, they were part-time organizations with a local power base and relatively decentralized or at least weak organizational structures. They were also strictly voluntary and had no legal way of compelling obedience or secrecy from their members.

Ostensibly, the Wehrverbände existed to maintain the martial will and military skills of the German people. In fact, they also existed as militarized political pressure groups, fighting for everything from a change in the form of national government on down to purely local concerns, although most avoided any direct contact with political parties and opposed electoral politics until at least 1924.

Even this is only half the story. Many, even most, of the Wehrverbände maintained illegal stocks of weapons in case of either a domestic uprising by the leftists or the assault of a foreign enemy, such as Poland. Weapons were hidden both for their usefulness and as a means of circumventing the destruction of surplus weapons stocks mandated by the Versailles treaty. Many of the Wehrverbände enjoyed the covert support of the Reichswehr in these illegal activities. They obtained weapons and training from the Reichswehr, which sought to organize their members into an illegal militia[27] to supplement the military in times of emergency. Furthermore, men were drawn from the Wehrverband milieu by the military to participate in covert operations on behalf of the government, such as sabotage against the French in the Rhineland or opposition to the Polish attempt to seize Upper Silesia in 1921.[28]

The dividing line between the so-called Black Reichswehr (and other army-sponsored covert operations) and the Wehrverbände was fluid and not always clear to the men involved. This led to a curious situation: the German government went behind the backs of many of its own officials and conspired to break its own laws in order to have the benefit of an unofficial reservoir of military talent. Yet many of these same men and organizations that it employed were in fact virulently opposed to that government and actively engaged in conspiracy against it. The German government was then forced to tolerate or even aid in hiding the illegal activities of its protégées, to the great detriment of the democratic system.[29] This even included the government tolerating, ignoring, or even concealing beatings, murders, or other physical intimidation committed by the private organizations employed in covert military preparations. This unofficial system of "justice" was called the Feme and its murders Fememord.[30]

As will be seen below, the Wehrverbände played a crucial role in the backgrounds of most SA leaders. They, and not the free corps, were the place where future leaders truly learned to apply military organization to civil politics and civilian problems. The semiclandestine world of the Wehrverbände was the perfect incubator for future Nazis.

BIRTH OF THE SA

The SA sprang directly out of the Wehrverband milieu, and indeed it functioned as a Wehrverband in its early days. Basic decisions were made in this period about the forms that the SA would take, and these forms were later repeated, even if in modified form. More important, the early years provided Hitler and other Nazi leaders with an example of what could happen if the SA were allowed to become too divorced from the control and the goals of the political party apparatus.

The beginnings of what became the SA are found in the very informal Ordnerdienst (usher service) and Saalschutz (hall defense) established in 1919 on an ad hoc basis to maintain order and fend off outside attacks on meetings of the fledgling Nazi Party in Munich.[31] As the NSDAP began to feel the need for a more organized system of protection for its meetings, and as it began to make more of its own direct attacks on its opponents, it gradually evolved a separate and distinct paramilitary wing, the SA.

The first step in this direction was the collection of a permanent core of members for the Saalschutz Abteilung (hall defense section) of the DAP around Emil Maurice on or shortly after February 24, 1920.[32] Although similar groups were soon founded in other NSDAP party cells,[33] there was no central organization and very little structure at all to the Saalschutz Abteilung. Other party members were still gathered on an ad hoc basis to aid the Saalschutz in its duties whenever the need arose.

It was not until over a year later (August 3, 1921) that the NSDAP felt the need for a more formal and better organized group to protect its meetings. Even then, the new Turn- und Sportabteilung (Gymnastics and Sports Division) hardly went beyond the earlier Saalschutz Abteilung.

By September 17 at the latest, the Turn- and Sportabteilung was being called the Sturmabteilung (SA) on an informal basis. The name was formally awarded to the group after the infamous Battle of the Hofbräuhaus of November 4, 1921, an event which soon assumed mythic proportions within the Party.[34] By this time, small SA groups had already been formed outside Munich, and shortly after the battle, a Munich police intelligence report quoted Hitler as telling the SA that one of its jobs was to disrupt the meetings of groups that the NSDAP opposed.[35]

By the fall of 1921, command of the SA (storm troopers) had been turned over to Hans Ulrich Klintzsch, a young ex-naval officer.[36] Klintzsch was a former member of the Ehrhardt Brigade, and at the time he was named SA commander he was an active member of the shadowy Organisation Consul (OC) and its more aboveground Wehrverband, the Bund Wiking.[37] In fact, Klintzsch and several other members of the OC/Bund Wiking were sent to the NSDAP "on loan" from an infamous putschist and antirepublican conspirator, Captain Hermann Ehrhardt, in order to aid in the organization and training of the fledgling SA. Despite a later parting of the ways, both sides felt in 1921 that they could profit from the arrangement. The NSDAP gained the services of former officers with experience in the formation and organization of conspiratorial paramilitary groups and contacts, through the OC, with the twilight world of the Wehrverbände not only in Munich but throughout Germany and Austria. Klintzsch and the other Ehrhardt men were good organizers who were able to infuse the SA with a different spirit than had the brawling watchmaker, Emil Maurice. Moreover, the acceptance of this outside help shows that, although opportunistic, Hitler and the other Nazi leaders were also interested in seeing the SA develop into something more than just a simple group of muscle-bound ushers to keep order at Party gatherings.

Out of this deliberate association with the Wehrverbände grew a unique form of organization. Partly through the design of the leaders of the NSDAP and partly through contact with its political environment, the SA became a synthesis of several independent political styles current at the time, something that was not quite either a political party or a Wehrverband, but partook of elements of both.

The development of a new style combining military organization with political activism, coupled with increasingly aggressive behavior, began slowly in the late summer and fall of 1921 and gradually picked up speed throughout 1922. More and more SA units were formed outside Munich, such as in Landshut in November 1921. May 1922 saw the creation of enough SA groups outside Munich that guidelines for the formation of a local SA group had to be issued in order to ensure uniform organization and some measure of control by the central party leadership. By August 1922, a year after its official formation, the SA held its first public march in Munich as part of a larger march and demonstration by many Wehrverbände and veterans' groups.[38] This marked the debut of one of the most characteristic and effective SA propaganda tactics—the mass public march.[39] The NSDAP rapidly embarked upon a series of its own marches both within Munich and, for the first time, well beyond. The most famous of these marches, which became with time another of the myths of the Kampfzeit, was the expedition to the Koburger Deutscher Tag (Coburg "German Day") on October 14-15, 1922.[40]

The growing importance of the NSDAP within Munich led to its inclusion in a cartel of conservative and radical groups in November 1922 called the Vereinigte Vaterländische Verbände Bayerns (United Patriotic Organizations of Bavaria, or VVVB). This marked the crest of the political phase of the early SA before it became transformed into a more exclusively military organization. The aggressive tactics that the NSDAP was able to adopt due to the unique character of the SA as half-Wehrverband, half-political movement, gave the NSDAP a high profile in the political environment of Munich. Through this high profile, the NSDAP was able to attract new converts, spread outside Munich and then outside Bavaria, and to attain a certain prestige in right-wing circles. The NSDAP, in significant measure due to the innovative use of the SA, had arrived.[41] Although the SA of late 1922 was not the fully developed organization it became by 1932, and although it may not have been exactly what Hitler had wanted to create, in light of subsequent events Hitler was able to look back on the SA of late 1922 as being the prototype of the militarized mass political organization that he needed.

1923: MILITARIZATION OF THE SA AND FAILED PUTSCH

In January 1923, events occurred outside Bavaria which were to change the SA radically as an organization and to set back the growth of the NSDAP by several years, a setback only partially compensated for by the gain of national notoriety for the Party in the process. On January 11 the French and Belgians invaded and occupied the left bank of the Rhine, in alleged response to German failure to deliver reparations on time. This action radically changed the political climate in Germany and sent the value of the German mark into freefall.

Expectations of further attacks by the French or Poles or both led the army to prepare for active resistance, which included even closer cooperation with the Wehrverbände. Many politicians of all affiliations called for more active measures of resistance, and some dreamed of a new war of liberation that would sweep the French out of Germany and break the shackles of the Versailles treaty. For many, in the face of growing economic hardships caused by runaway inflation, the dream included the destruction of parliamentary democracy and the Weimar system. This situation of external crisis and economic collapse was compounded by a smoldering conflict between Bavaria and the central government over states' rights, and by the formation of left-wing coalition governments in the states of Saxony and Thuringia on Bavaria's northern border.

The change in the political climate caused the NSDAP to alter sharply the course of SA development. Swept along in the general mobilization of the Wehrverbände for national defense, and eager to use the confusion and radicalization of the situation to set off the long-awaited internal battle against the left and against the present government, the SA was transformed into a party army, a pure Wehrverband organized for national defense or civil war or both. Because of this alteration of emphasis, the role of the "first SA" as the pioneers of "political soldiering" was suspended. It would be left to the reestablished SA from 1925 on to make good on the promise first shown in 1921 and 1922.

Hitler was widely respected on the right as a politician, but he was not a military leader. His influence over the SA therefore declined in proportion to the emphasis placed on a narrow military mission and organization for the SA. Whether or not Hitler foresaw this development is immaterial, because there was little he could do to stop it in the general rush to mobilize the Wehrverbände. In early January 1923, Hitler broke with the VVVB over the question of a front of national unity.[42]

A month later, the NSDAP joined the most radical Wehrverbände to form a new cartel, the Arbeitsgemeinschaft der vaterländischen Kampfverbände (Working Group of Patriotic Combat Organizations).[43] The militarization of the SA proceeded apace. At the first National Party Congress of the NSDAP in Munich, January 27-29, 1923, a portion of the SA appeared for the first time in what approached a uniform.[44] Throughout the spring of 1923 the SA was reorganized and given a more military structure, with ranks and unit names changing to parallel those of the army.[45] Military exercises were stepped up. On March 1, 1923, an SA high command was formed, which gradually developed a military staff structure. Several days later, Klintzsch resigned as commander of the SA and became its chief of staff. He was replaced by Hermann Göring, a flamboyant, charismatic, and highly decorated former army officer and flying hero from World War I. Hitler hoped that having such a man at the head of the SA would attract new volunteers and thus help it to expand into a more credible fighting force.[46] An added benefit of this change of command was that it put a party member and Hitler follower at the head of the SA, instead of someone whose first allegiance belonged elsewhere.

After a flurry of activity on the part of the NSDAP and the other members of the Arbeitsgemeinschaft, the summer of 1923 passed relatively quietly, with continued preparation for conflict on the part of the Wehrverbände, Reichswehr, and Bavarian government, but with no major incidents. All parties adopted a waiting policy. Events began to accelerate again only in September. By the fall the economic situation had reached such a point that wide elements of German society were willing to accept almost any solution so long as it promised to bring economic relief, including the violent overthrow of the Republic.[47] The members of the Arbeitsgemeinschaft, under the impact of the economic situation and the strident tones of its own propaganda, were growing increasingly impatient. Moreover, in September they began to grow fearful that either the Reich government or the Bavarian government would take the initiative away from the Wehrverbände and make a putsch on their terms impossible. A series of setbacks all served to put Arbeitsgemeinschaft members on notice that the moment for action might be at hand but was rapidly passing: the NSDAP was banned in the state of Braunschweig on

September 18, 1923,[48] the official end to the policy of passive resistance in the Ruhr was declared on September 26, and the conservative former Bavarian prime minister, Dr. Gustav von Kahr, was appointed general state commissar of Bavaria at the same time as a proclamation of martial law gave him near dictatorial powers. Von Kahr began to take more of a hard line against the Wehrverbände than had previously been the case in Bavaria, while continuing to negotiate with them. Both sides attempted to commit the other to its own plans. Meanwhile, right-wingers in Berlin were making their own plans for a coup in conjunction with the Reichswehr, and they were in loose contact with the Arbeitsgemein-schaft and rather closer contact with von Kahr.

It is within this context that Hitler and the rest of the Wehrverbände with whom he was allied (called the Deutscher Kampfbund, or German Alliance for Struggle, since September 1, 1923) attempted a putsch on the night of November 8, 1923. Weary of the continued talks with other elements of the right and fearful that others might steal their thunder, they made one last desperate and ill-planned attempt to seize the initiative and impose their policies on the Bavarian government. It is unnecessary to recount the details of the putsch itself,[49] except to say that in the end it was a failure. Neither the Bavarian government nor the Reichswehr were ultimately willing to go along with the plans of the Wehrverbände, and alone the Wehrverbände were simply not strong enough to succeed. The putsch ended in disgrace. The NSDAP, SA, and the other Wehrverbände who had participated in the putsch were banned, their leaders were under arrest or in hiding, and their members were scattered.

1924: THE REASSESSMENT OF PUTSCHISM

The period from the failure of the putsch in November 1923 to the reestablishment of the Party and SA in February 1925 was not a happy one for the supporters of National Socialism. The Party, the SA, and most of the organizations closely allied with them were banned and their assets were confiscated. Hitler and the top putsch leaders were in jail. The Bavarian government and the Reichswehr had turned their backs on their former allies, and the leaders of more moderate völkisch and paramilitary groups tried to steal away as many of the former NSDAP supporters for their own groups as they could. The entire völkisch and paramilitary movement was rent with internal divisions and rivalries and subject to careful state scrutiny. National Socialism appeared to be dead, and many of its supporters despaired that the movement could ever be resurrected.

This was hardly a positive development for Hitler in the short term, but the putsch and the trial that followed brought Hitler to the forefront of the völkisch movement, and the failure of the putsch and Hitler's enforced isolation in Landsberg prison brought a thorough reassessment of Party strategy and also the willingness to try out a new strategy that ultimately led to the victory of the Party in 1933. Ironically, the failure of the putsch gave Hitler and his movement a second chance to successfully blend a political party with paramilitary organization.

It would have taken a perceptiveness bordering on the clairvoyant to have predicted the subsequent rise of the NSDAP in 1924. But, in fact, many of the fundamental decisions that laid the groundwork for the future rise of the Party and the rebuilding of the SA grew out of the experiences of this period of forced dormancy. While it was not well understood at the time, what happened in the mid-1920s was a fundamental shift in the political ecology of the Weimar Republic. The old climate—which had favored putschist tactics, large-scale government support for private armies, loose cartels of tiny political movements under jealous and independent leaders, and a general avoidance of participation in the hated parliamentary system—died out, and a new one replaced it.

The change was not total: elements of the old putschist outlook survived into the new era, and many of the later difficulties that the Nazi Party had with the SA can be traced to a preference for military solutions which had not disappeared but had only lain dormant after 1923. Many individuals and organizations, particularly in the Wehrverband movement, either did not notice the change or refused to adapt to it. They struggled on into the mid- and late 1920s, but ultimately they could not survive in the altered environment and so became politically extinct. Later, the refounded NSDAP and SA absorbed many of the individuals left "orphaned" as the Wehrverband movement decayed. Only those individuals and groups who understood that a fundamental change had occurred and that they had to adapt to it were able to survive and prosper.

By having set a national example in the putsch attempt and then by being kept out of the atmosphere of division and jealousy that followed, Hitler was able to leave prison in December 1924 as the only völkisch leader of any stature who was not compromised by bickering with all his rivals.[40] Parallel to this development, countless groups who felt some kinship with NSDAP policies and ideas were made aware of the Party and were unwittingly prepared to join it by its own putsch-inspired myth and the negative example of the ineffectiveness of all the other similar groups under the new conditions. Ironically, the spread of National Socialism to northern Germany, although it had begun before the putsch, gained crucial momentum in the dark days when the Party itself was banned.

One of the most significant developments of this entire period was the increased contact that developed between the Wehrverbände and the völkisch movement. Although organizationally still separate, the völkisch groups and the Wehrverbände became much closer in 1924 because of the völkisch movement's participation in parliamentary politics in the two Reichstag elections of 1924.

Both types of organization often shared the same members.[51] Moreover, they shared many ideological and political ideas and existed in an often uneasy symbiosis within the same general subculture on the far right. For example, they attended each others' meetings and public ceremonies. The Wehrverbände generally volunteered to protect völkisch meetings against disruption by outsiders and, perhaps most significant of all, in the several elections of 1924 they often performed propaganda and campaign duties for the völkisch and conservative parties. At the very least, the exposure to the idea of electoral politics, which came from even a loose association with the völkisch groups, created a new awareness that such a tactic existed as a real possibility and forced even the Wehrverbände to discuss the question. This is true even if the decision of most Wehrverbände in 1924 was not to become directly involved themselves but rather to simply support the conservative and völkisch parties. In many areas this provided the first experience of participation in electoral politics for many individuals who later joined the SA and NSDAP. For many others, it provided the first serious consideration of alternative tactics in the fight against the Republic and all other enemies, especially given the fact that the previously favored approach, an armed putsch, had so recently failed.

Immediately after it became clear that the putsch was a failure, SA members scattered to avoid prosecution. Most of the rank and file returned home, and they either abandoned politics entirely or joined one of the Wehrverbände or völkisch groups that were not banned after the putsch.[52] Some of the more loyal SA members were just able to hold together the remnants of their old SA units under new names.[53] While these diehards managed to keep the faith and even form the core of new SA units to be created after the Party was rebuilt, they were largely isolated from one another by the lack of a central command structure, the difficulties of communication, the need for secrecy, and the lack of effective leadership.

Despite the near total collapse of the SA, a great deal of planning regarding the future SA actually occurred in 1924. Röhm, a former general staff officer and a compulsive organizer, pushed the formulation of plans for the SA (and also for his pet project of a new union of all the Wehrverbände, the Frontbann) that had little basis in reality in 1924 and 1925 but that included many ideas that were later extremely useful in the refounding of the SA and its expansion into a national organization. The later use of these ideas is not always directly traceable back to Röhm, and many of them were simple common sense to anyone with military training. Yet it is incontestable that these ideas were aired at this time within a circle of men who later became important SA leaders.[54]

THE FRONTBANN: STEPFATHER OF THE FUTURE SA

The Frontbann was intended to be a central cartel of all völkisch Wehrverbände, much like the Kampfbund but with more centralized control and organization.[55] It was formally founded on May 31, 1924, although Röhm had apparently been working toward such an organization for some time. Although solidly in the conceptual framework of the older Wehrverband idea and thus not well suited for the changed climate after the Beer Hall Putsch, the Frontbann was at least a larger and more widespread organization than the old SA ever was. Although there was much wrong with the Frontbann, Röhm managed to create a framework within which a large number of programmatically and geographically diverse Wehrverbände could be brought together. This was significant and, in a sense, successful because a serious cartel of northern and southern German, Bavarian, and Austrian organizations was finally formed. For the first time since the days of the Einwohnerwehren, there was a national forum for the cooperation of paramilitary leaders in northern and southern Germany. Had such a national cartel been created in 1923, the outcome of the Beer Hall Putsch might have been quite different.[56]

In turn, although the days of the "pure" Wehrverbände were past and the Frontbann could not possibly succeed in influencing political events or becoming a partner to the Reichswehr, it did provide an organizational basis for the spread of the SA to northern Germany. Also important in this regard was the diffusion of former SA members throughout other Wehrverbände and völkisch groups. The active attempts by the leaders of many of these groups to profit from the banning of the SA by picking up new members aided this development. The NSDAP itself also gave impetus to this process, by ordering all local party group and SA leaders to join other völkisch groups when they couldn't maintain independent underground National Socialist groups.[57] The return home of many northerners who had been living in Munich after the putsch and the cooperation of northern and southern groups through the Frontbann helped to spread individual National Socialists into middle and northern Germany.[58] These men helped to radicalize the groups to which they became attached and to spread faith in the NSDAP to places where it had hardly been known before. As will be shown below, the Frontbann figured in the immediate past of many men who became the highest SA leaders.

Hitler was paroled in December 1924, and in February 1925 he reestablished the Party and SA. Although he offered Röhm the command of the SA, the two could not agree on the relationship between the SA and the Party, nor was Röhm willing to give up his dream of a cartel of all the Wehrverbände. After a final meeting between the two on April 16, 1925, Röhm and Hitler parted company, and on May 1, 1925, Röhm proffered Hitler his resignation as both SA and Frontbann leader. Hitler did not even bother to reply.[59] It would be five more years before Ernst Röhm would be willing to forgo the old Wehrverband dream, albeit temporarily, and head an SA that was an integral part of the NSDAP.

This background made up the collective "memory" or recent experiences of the men in this study. They could have done many things based on these experiences. What they did was build the SA into a new kind of organization synthesizing military forms and civilian political content. The further history of the SA is also the history of their lives and will be described in the following chapters.

2

The Pioneers, 1925-1926

When Hitler walked out of Landsburg Prison shortly before Christmas in December 1924, he seemed to have few prospects. Although the ban on the NSDAP and SA had just been lifted, both organizations had to be completely rebuilt, and Hitler himself was still prohibited from public speaking in nearly all of the German states. He had no choice but to cling strictly to a policy of the utmost legality, for he could be rearrested at any time and returned to finish out his prison sentence if he or a significant number of his followers strayed from the conditions of his parole. Hitler was not even a German citizen and could face deportation at any moment. He was seeking an end to the ban on his public speaking in Bavaria in early 1925, and with his precarious personal situation he was in no mood to run unnecessary risks.[1]

Far worse than this for Hitler was the fact that political conditions no longer favored the growth of radical outsider movements fed by irresponsible and violent demagoguery. Although the anti-Semitic and extremist völkisch organizations had managed to score significant electoral successes in the first half of 1924, they had slipped badly in the second elections that year,[2] and their support continued to wane in 1925 and 1926.

The reason for this lack of support was simple: the reforms initiated by the Stresemann and Marx governments and vigorously backed by the Reichswehr were in the process of restoring economic stability and domestic peace and were even finding a modus vivendi with France and the rest of Germany's former enemies.[3] In short, the Republic had proved that it was strong enough to weather the extreme instability and conflict of 1920-23, and with a return to stability came a corresponding abandonment of support for extremist politics—whether from the electorate or from the government in search of extralegal allies in a time of crisis. The challenge to Hitler and his followers was to rebuild a movement from scratch, at a time when its appeal to the public was minimal and out of a potential stock of supporters who were both demoralized and divided.

It was no simple task, but despite the illogic of his beliefs, Hitler took to the task at hand with exemplary rationality. The movement could not be re-created all at once, so priorities had to be established, and the men beginning to recoalesce around Hitler wisely chose to put the bulk of their energy into reestablishing the political organization, the NSDAP. For the time being they allowed the paramilitary affiliates to go their own way—without, however, ignoring them completely.

The decision to concentrate on the political organization and to delay establishing a central command over the burgeoning local SA groups was in part accidental and in part deliberate. Of course, it made good sense to focus scarce resources where they would do the most good, but it was also a reflection of Hitler's view that the SA was just an auxiliary of the Party, important but not an end unto itself.[4] The potential worth of the SA in a situation where a putsch was (temporarily) out of the question was unproven and unrecognized by most of the political leaders of the NSDAP in 1925. Moreover, the experience of losing control of the SA to the military leaders in 1923 when the SA was converted from a Party troop into a Wehrverband left a bad impression on Hitler and the political leadership of the Party and made them reluctant to allow a potentially rebellious organization to become established until the political apparatus of the Party was firmly in place.[5]

The NSDAP was formally reorganized at a mass meeting in the Munich Hofbräuhaus on February 27, 1925.[6] The day before, the *Völkischer Beobachter,* in its first issue since the ban on its publication was lifted by the Bavarian government, published Hitler's "Fundamental Guidelines for the Reestablishment of the NSDAP."[7] In this document Hitler's two main goals shone through: strict centralization of the rebuilt Party under his personal command, and strict legality.

These "fundamental guidelines" included general instructions for setting up SA as well as Party units, so it is clear that Hitler still intended for the NSDAP to have a paramilitary auxiliary and to rebuild the SA as well as the Party organization. But because his priorities lay elsewhere, the central Party leadership put no real effort into rebuilding the SA until Franz von Pfeffer was appointed Oberster SA-Führer (supreme SA leader, or OSAF) as of November 1, 1926.[8] With the simultaneous collapse of the Frontbann, the SA remained a disparate collection of local groups.[9]

Despite the lack of attention given to the SA by the central Party leadership, SA units rapidly sprang up all over Germany as soon as the Party was reestablished.[10] The circumstances surrounding the founding of individual SA sections varied according to region and locality.[11] In some cases, SA groups that had gone underground in 1923 simply resumed operations.[12] In other cases, entire local Wehrverbände were transformed into SA units, either immediately or gradually.[13] In still other cases, local members of various völkisch and paramilitary groups left them and formed an SA unit. In some of the above cases, indeed, the local SA antedated the Ortsgruppe (local Party chapter).[14] In other cases—probably the majority—no truly separate local SA existed at first: the local SA was simply formed on an ad hoc basis from whatever Party members were available for the protection of a given meeting. But even in this latter case, former members of local Wehrverbände were often very much involved, since they were more willing and able to defend Party meetings and to possess a uniform. In cases where the local SA unit was formed out of an earlier Wehrverband, it might have remained somewhat independent of the local Party leadership, but in general, the practice was just the opposite. The Ortsgruppenleiter (local Party group leader) was often the commander of the local SA unit, and the use and organization of the SA regionally was dominated by the Gauleiter (the head of a Gau, or regional division of the Party). This was reflected in the organization of the SA nationally at the time, since there was actually no provision for any unit beyond the local level, and the highest SA rank then in existence was that of Sturmabteilungsführer (local SA group leader).[15] In some local areas, it was group policy for all Party members to belong to the SA, which then as a matter of course was led by the local Party chapter leader.[16] The result was an SA that was regionally heterogeneous yet widely subordinated to the political activities and leadership of the Party and in large part indistinguishable from the membership at large. This made the rebuilt or "second" SA different from the previous SA of 1923 in three important ways: it was no longer uniquely military, no longer confined to Bavaria, and no longer internally homogeneous.[17]

Despite the many good reasons for the Party to neglect the SA in 1925 and 1926, it was ultimately forced to establish a central leadership for the SA by pressure from local groups and the sheer risk involved in allowing the SA to develop without firm direction. The steady stream of requests from local Party groups for guidance regarding the SA had to be answered, and this took time away from those working to establish the political organization of the Party. More seriously, the unsupervised local groups showed a desire for a more centralized command structure that would allow for the massing of SA units from many local branches when needed, and they proceeded to create such structures independent of central control. Naturally, many of the local SA leaders were former officers, who were accustomed to thinking in terms of larger units and had the kind of military administrative skills needed to establish them.[18] Moreover, the parade of 3,600 to 6,000 SA and SS men at the first Reichsparteitag (national convention) in Weimar in July 1926 showed that there were definite advantages to mass groupings of SA men.[19]

More seriously, the lack of central control over the SA and the great heterogeneity of its units made it possible and even likely that some day a local SA leader would seriously violate the legality policy of the Party, with disastrous consequences for the fledgling Party organization. Almost as dangerous, the lack of strong central control over the SA favored disagreement and rivalry between local SA and Party leaders,[20] and the lack of a command structure to unite the different local and regional SA units favored the use of the SA as a private army and power base by the powerful and jealous regional leaders. These problems could potentially threaten the dominance of Hitler and the central Party leadership in Munich.

The omission of central control over the SA in 1925 and 1926, the allowance of the spontaneous and independent formation of local SA groups without uniform guidelines or planning, and the dangerous usurpation of control over the SA by the Gau leaders and other local Party officials set the stage for later conflicts. The regional and local Party leaders were particularly upset at later having to relinquish control over the SA to a central SA command, and thus to see the SA develop as an organization over which they would have but limited control.[21] Although Hitler's favorite strategy of avoiding a decision until absolutely necessary may have worked in 1925, by the late spring and summer of 1926 it had become increasingly risky.

The Party had already taken steps to formalize the organization of the newly created SS.[22] As a new organization with a very small membership, it was more amenable to central control from Munich and could serve as a counterweight to overly independent SA leaders. This was considered necessary in part because the SA in the north tended to have close ties with potentially dissident Party leaders, such as Gregor Strasser and Joseph Goebbels,[23] and in part because the continued (though diminished) existence of the Frontbann threatened a repeat of the loss of Party control over the SA as in 1923.

These dangers gradually receded, and by May 1926, with the SS fairly well established, the central Party leadership began to hint that it was considering some sort of aggregation of the SA into larger units.[24] In the summer of 1926 (probably after the Party Congress in July), Hitler traveled to Westphalia and spent considerable time discussing the organization of the SA with Franz von Pfeffer, who was the leader of Gau Westfalen. They managed to reach an accord, and in August 1926 von Pfeffer moved to Munich to begin forming a central SA command. In October his appointment was formally announced, and the new supreme SA command took up its duties as of November 1, 1926.[25] The days of neglect and independence were over, and a new period of centralized control and planning began. In a sense, the actual refounding of the SA was marked by the appointment of von Pfeffer, not the spontaneous and unsupervised creation of local SA groups in 1925 and 1926.

The SA, if it were to survive, needed a particular kind of leader in these very early days of the refounded NSDAP. It needed men who had experience in military organization, and who could command respect from the veterans and current members of the Wehrverbände, the SA's natural recruiting ground. The SA also needed men who would become effective parts of the political organization of the NSDAP as well, for this was a time when every Party member wore several hats and the Party could not afford specialists. The SA also required tireless activists, men who could speak well and who had the political skills to unify the faithful, but who were also capable then of putting these faithful into uniform and building a tightly organized paramilitary organization. More than anything else, the new SA also needed self-starters, men who could act independently and who would not easily be discouraged, men with a worldview and a sense of ideological mission equal to that of Hitler himself. It took a special individual with many skills to help Hitler rebuild the SA and NSDAP. Unfortunately for Germany and the world, he found them.

Heinrich Bennecke is a perfect example of the kind of man required to rebuild both the Party and the SA.[26] He was born in Dresden in

1902 to the family of a military physician. Not unusual for the son of a prominent military family, he was imbued with a love of the military and a strong sense of patriotism at a very early age. In 1917, he was already working as a voluntary harvester (Erntehelfer) while most adult males were at the front. Like all young men of his age, he certainly expected to be called to military service one day himself, and given his background and patriotism, he certainly looked forward to it. Yet the war ended suddenly in a disastrous defeat, and Germany experienced a revolution before Bennecke could become a soldier. He could have simply gotten on with his life and career. Instead, he became a political and paramilitary activist and soon joined the NSDAP.

In 1919, only seventeen years of age and still in high school (Gymnasium), he became a member of Zeitfreiwilligenregiment Dresden (Dresden Regiment of Part-Time Volunteers), a unit of temporary local volunteers formed during the German Revolution to provide a reserve force in times of civil unrest. Dresden was the scene of some violence in early 1919, and "order" had to be restored with force through the intervention of Freikorps Görlitz. This may have contributed to Bennecke's radicalization at a young and impressionable age.[27]

Though he saw no real combat yet, in 1919 he did receive military training and an initiation into the male world of the barracks. The military life pleased young Bennecke, for he remained a Zeitfreiwilliger with the Reichswehr into 1920, at which time he was activated during the Kapp Putsch and served in Dresden, Leipzig, and the Vogtland. It pleased him so much that in May 1921 he ran off to Upper Silesia to fight against the Poles in Freikorps Haßfurther, an ad hoc unit formed during the fighting itself. The campaign in Upper Silesia attracted many of the most activist elements of the radical right in Germany, and it served to spread and intensify antidemocratic and völkisch sentiment among those who participated in it due to active recruitment among the men by the anti-Semitic Deutsch-völkischer Schutz- und Trutzbund.[28] Although Bennecke did not become a member of the Schutz- und Trutzbund, he was certainly exposed to its propaganda. Bennecke also saw his first real combat here.

Bennecke's military and political activities did not apparently slow his academic progress. In the same year that he fought in Upper Silesia, he passed his Abitur (university entrance exams) and began studies at the Dresden Technische Hochschule (technical university)

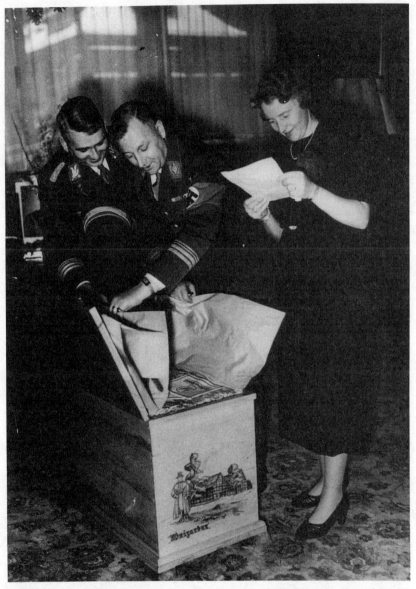

Ogruf. Dr. Heinrich Bennecke (left) giving a handmade wooden chest to Stabschef Viktor Lutze and his wife, December 1938. Courtesy of the Bundesarchiv.

in economics (Volkswirtschaft). In 1922, Bennecke, a proud combat veteran, left home to begin his studies at the university in Munich. He again majored in economics, but this was apparently too tame to occupy all of his time. He became involved in the conspiratorial world of the far right, which soon brought him into contact with the NSDAP. This small extremist party with its Austrian leader appealed to him, and he became a member of both the NSDAP and the SA in May 1922. He remained a loyal member of both organizations (or their surrogates) down to the capitulation of Germany in 1945.

Bennecke quickly distinguished himself and became an adjutant of SA Regiment München. His commitment to the SA was strong enough that he temporarily abandoned his studies to devote all of his time to his (assuredly more exciting) SA duties. Bennecke was certainly not one to stand on the sidelines, especially when things got violent: he participated in both the celebrated Coburg German Day (October 14-15, 1922) and the Hitler Putsch just over a year later. Later he proudly wore the Blutorden (Blood Order) and the Coburger Abzeichen (Coburg Medal) in honor of his participation in these events, two of the most hallowed of all the Nazi Party's decorations. The failure of the putsch and a close brush with the law (he was expelled from Bavaria as an undesirable citizen of another German state) sent Bennecke packing but did little to dampen his activism or his commitment to antidemocratic action.[29]

Upon his arrival home in Dresden he worked as a shop assistant (Handlungsgehilfe) in the paper business. His dedication to the Nazi movement did not weaken, and he was active in surrogate organizations that allowed former SA and NSDAP members to remain together. Unlike many of the other SA leaders in this chapter, he did not become a member of a völkisch organization, but only because he still considered himself to be a member of the banned SA.

Once back in Dresden he quickly joined the Frontbann and became a squad leader (Zugführer), despite his youth and the fact that his only active military service had been his few weeks in Upper Silesia. In May 1925, while still a member of the Frontbann, he was among the first members of the refounded Nazi Party.[30] His early Party membership and subsequent long years of uninterrupted service later brought him the coveted Golden Party Pin (goldenes Parteiabzeichen) and the even rarer Golden Party Service Award (Dienstauszeichnung der NSDAP in Gold).[31] Like many of the men in this chapter, Bennecke had originally joined the NSDAP in Bavaria, but in 1925 he rejoined it north of the Main River, proof that the banning of the NSDAP in 1923 helped spread the Nazi movement northwards as northerners resident in Munich returned home.

Unlike many of the other men in this chapter, Bennecke did not rejoin the SA at the same time at which he rejoined the NSDAP. Instead, he remained a member of the Frontbann for a time until the fall of 1925, when he led his entire Frontbann squad as a unit into the Großdeutsche Jugend (Greater-German Youth), a völkisch youth organization founded in Saxony by Kurt Gruber, which later became the nucleus of the Hitler Youth.[32]

Bennecke remained the Party's youth leader for East Saxony until the end of 1926. In the spring of 1926 he resumed his studies, this time majoring in journalism ("Zeitungskunde") and philosophy at the university in Leipzig. Here he immediately joined the local SA unit. He must have been quite a natural leader, or else the local SA was completely lacking in other leadership material, because in July 1927, at only twenty-five years of age, Bennecke was given command of SA Standarte IV, Leipzig.[33] He remained the leader of the Standarte until August 1929, when he became the adjutant of OSAF-Stellvertreter Mitte (SA district leader for central Germany) in Dresden. By this time he was also editor (Schriftleiter) of the NSDAP party paper in Saxony, the Sächsischer Beobachter (Saxon Observer). He was awarded a doctoral degree in history, journalism, and philosophy in June 1930. This milestone in his young life did not prompt Bennecke to relax a bit. At roughly the same time he also became the commander of SA Brigade V, Dresden, the press representative (Pressewart) of his Gau and a member of the Saxon state parliament (Landtag) for the NSDAP. In his spare time he was a Party speaker.

Bennecke was typical of many of the SA's highest leaders who joined (or rejoined) the SA in 1925 or 1926. He was a natural leader and was active in a string of military and paramilitary organizations from the end of the war on. But he was also very active in the political organization of the Nazi Party and served it in a number of public positions. He could clearly command the respect of the veterans and members of the Wehrverbände, but he could also cooperate with the Party leadership and speak publicly to "civilian" crowds. He was a flexible and tireless activist, equally capable and at home on the parade ground, in parliament, in the press, and in the Party bureaucracy.

From 1930 until the end of the Second World War, Bennecke made a career as a full-time SA leader. The Nazi assumption of power found him in command of SA Untergruppe Dresden (later Brigade

33). In September 1933 he was transferred to the "Chef des Ausbildungswesens" (Chef-AW; "chief of training") organization to become the head of the SA-Hochschulamt (SA office of higher education). This was a politically and militarily sensitive position, for the Chef-AW was designed to funnel young men through a secret and illegal Reichswehr training program, and the Hochschulamt was responsible for coordinating the training of university students.[34] Bennecke's political skills were further demonstrated when he survived the Röhm Purge and was assigned to head the SA's national leadership school (Reichsführerschule) in July 1934.[35] In 1936 he was promoted to head SA Gruppe Pommern, and in late 1944 he was transferred to head SA Gruppe Südmark. Again, this shows both his own leadership qualities and the Nazis desperate search for capable leaders: Gruppe Südmark was in southeast Austria (Carinthia and Styria), hard on the Italian and Yugoslav borders, and by then, practically the front line. Bennecke was no stranger to combat by then, having served with the Wehrmacht as an officer in 1939-41 and again in 1943.

After the war Bennecke became a historian. Incidentally, he wrote one of the standard works on the SA, making him one of the fortunate historians who have been able to write about themselves. Ironically, even after the defeat of Nazism he continued to make a living with the SA.

Thirty-six future top leaders of the SA joined in 1925 and 1926.[36] They came from the Wehrverband tradition but were also broadly committed to the völkisch movement. They were both soldiers and politicians and thus well equipped to blend these two traditions in the creation of the reformed SA. Most of these men were responsible for building the SA in this formative period and almost immediately achieved high rank, while others grew into the second generation of the SA's leadership. Many of these men showed their continuing commitment to the völkisch movement by also becoming some of the earliest leaders of the political organization of the NSDAP (as opposed to the SA), combining paramilitary activism in the SA with political leadership in the Party.

All of the SA's higher leaders had military backgrounds. But the men who joined in 1925-26 differed in some interesting ways from the rest. This first group had the fewest veterans of the First World War: 22 percent did not participate, and 5 percent served in the war but did not see combat.[37] This still means that 72 percent did see combat. Of the veterans, 53.5 percent were officers, and of the officers, 26.6 percent were professional officers.[38] The proportion of former professional officers is striking at first glance, but the high proportion of nonveterans is actually much more significant. The presence of so many nonveterans in the group joining the SA in 1925 and 1926 indicates that there was a substantial subgroup of young but very dedicated activists like Heinrich Bennecke who were not veterans and who had gotten involved in völkisch politics, a Wehrverband, or both during the crisis of 1923 or the dark days of 1924, and they were now continuing their activities within the NSDAP and SA.

The activities of the men in this chapter during the Revolution and in the early 1920s are equally significant. Immediately after the war, one-third were in a free corps,[39] and three were very early members of the Schutz- und Trutzbund and thus already exposed to völkisch ideology.[40] The men in this chapter tended to belong to radical free corps, and several remained active in their free corps until they were officially disbanded, when they often immediately joined Wehrverbände or other paramilitary organizations.[41] A few dedicated individuals participated in the fighting in Upper Silesia in 1921, but this only involved 10 percent of the entire group.[42] An even smaller number of militants were involved in sabotage in the Ruhr against the French and Belgians.[43]

Another significant characteristic of these early SA members is that they had the highest percentage of membership in the pre-putsch SA and NSDAP. Nearly two-thirds had joined either the SA or the NSDAP (or both) by the end of 1923.[44] This is a further sign that this group was strongly committed to the kind of völkisch politics that the NSDAP represented. True believers, they had followed Hitler before the putsch, and they hurried back to carry his banner as soon as he rebuilt the Party.

One man whose career was typical of those of the older military men who joined the SA in 1925 or 1926 is Kurt von Ulrich.[45] He was born in Fulda in 1876, the son of a Prussian general. Young Kurt was brought up to follow in his father's footsteps, but he took a roundabout route into the Prussian officer corps. Instead of entering a military academy at an early age, Kurt remained at home, attended a Gymnasium, and passed his Abitur. He was therefore a man of above-average intelligence, and he apparently continued to study. By 1937 he claimed at least some familiarity with five modern languages and he had attended the military interpreter school to learn at least one of them.

After he finished his Gymnasium education, Kurt von Ulrich entered a prestigious regiment of dragoons in Hesse, in which he was commissioned as an officer and served until the beginning of the First World War, with short absences for training at the Prussian war college (Kriegsakademie) and royal Prussian rifle factory. He served during the war as both a combat and a staff officer. He earned distinction in both activities and ended the war with one wound, the rank of major, and a chestful of medals. After the war he remained in the army until 1920. In that year he left active service as an Oberstleutnant (lieutenant colonel), but continued to work for the army for several months as a civilian official.

Kurt von Ulrich was an early member of the Verband Nationalgesinnter Soldaten (Association of Nationally Minded Soldiers), a right-wing veterans' organization, and in 1924 he joined the more radical National Association of German Officers (Nationalverband Deutscher Offiziere). Sometime before 1925 he was also a member of the German National People's Party (Deutschnationale Volkspartei, DNVP). This was the extent of his political activity until 1925, perhaps because he was trying to establish himself in a new career as an independent salesman and later as a bank official. In 1925 he joined the Stahlhelm and served it until 1927 as a local group leader and then as a district leader. Interestingly, within six months of attaining the latter position in the Stahlhelm, he joined the SA and NSDAP. Although he was still a member of the Stahlhelm and of the National Association of German Officers, he immediately became the Gau SA leader for Hesse-Nassau, and he soon was head of the NSDAP Party cell in Kassel and chairman of the Gau supreme Party court, positions he kept until mid-1927.

Von Ulrich led the SA in Hesse-Nassau until 1928, when he became the commander of all National Socialist paramilitary affiliates in Western Germany, the Oberster SA-Führer Stellvertreter West (literally, the western deputy of the highest SA leader). In 1930 he was made General Inspector of the SA and SS for all of Germany and Austria, a position he held until 1934, when he left active SA service. His career as a leading Nazi was not finished, however. After he left the Party's political administration in 1927, he served as an occasional speaker and from 1930 on as a member of the Reichstag. In 1933, after the NSDAP took power in Germany, von Ulrich was made a Prussian state councilor (Staatsrat) and was named the administrative head (Oberpräsident) of the Prussian province of Saxony. He also became a leader of the German Red Cross.

Although von Ulrich was never a member of a Wehrverband or völkisch Party as many of his fellow SA officers were, he did undergo a gradual process of radicalization in the early 1920s, as his progression through the DNVP and several veterans' organizations to the SA and NSDAP shows. His administrative abilities, his staff training, and even his status as the son of a Prussian general, member of the nobility, and former officer were all important to the NSDAP as it became a major political force in Germany. Although von Ulrich did have some experience in political organizations before joining the NSDAP, his most valuable experience was as a staff officer and administrator.

The activities of these men did not stop with the end of the German Revolution and the failure of the Hitler Putsch. Of the group of thirty-six higher SA leaders who joined in 1925-26, sixteen were not politically active just before joining the SA or the exact nature of their activity is unclear.[46] Of the remainder, several groups stand out as being the springboard to membership in the SA.

First, of all the organizations to which these men belonged in the last quarter of 1924, two-thirds were Wehrverbände or other military associations. Sixteen of the earliest members of the "second SA" came directly from the Wehrverbände.[47] They belonged to a wide range of moderate[48] and radical Wehrverbände, but within this range the Frontbann is clearly the most important. Seven were in the Frontbann,[49] whereas only one other Wehrverband was represented by more than a single man. Almost as important as the Frontbann as a vehicle for joining the SA was, surprisingly, the SA itself; six of the men in this chapter were members of the (illegal and underground) SA at the end of 1924.[50] Together, twelve out of the nineteen whose activities are known were in the SA, the Frontbann, or both.

But the Wehrverbände are only one side of the activities of the men in this chapter; the other side is provided by organizations oriented toward political action. Many were not involved in political activity at all, and none of the 1925-26 SA members were ever moderates or leftists. But a few organizations do stand out as being important in the careers of our group. The most important are völkisch parties or movements: the Nationalsozialistische Freiheitsbewegung (NSFB) with three members, the Großdeutsche Volksgemeinschaft with four members, and the Völkisch-Sozialer Block with six members.[51] Eleven were thus members of one or more of these organizations just before they joined the SA.[52]

In fact, many were in both a Wehrverband and a völkisch political organization, a sign of their commitment to both paramilitary
activity and völkisch ideology. This is concrete proof of the importance of membership in both völkisch and paramilitary organizations
in 1924 for the formation of the NSDAP from 1925 on. All but a
handful were also in more than one organization at the same time or
in rapid succession. Multiple memberships are a common feature of
this group, again an indication that they were strongly committed to
these activities. The men who, in 1924, had learned to blend military organization with a political message were the ones who then
created and built the NSDAP and SA in 1925 and subsequent years.[53]

One other very important factor in the political and military
background of the men in this chapter before 1925 remains to be
discussed. This is membership in the NSDAP before the 1923 putsch
and subsequent banning of the Party. Many members of the group of
1925 and 1926 SA joiners had been members of the NSDAP before
the putsch. Of these men, some joined the first NSDAP as early as
1921, and many more were members by the end of 1922. By the last
quarter of 1923, twenty of the entire group in this chapter had joined
the SA, NSDAP, or both.[54] This is one of the strongest patterns that
emerge in the activities of these men. Many show a pattern of spending little or no time in an organization in 1920-21, then joining the
SA and NSDAP and sticking with it (or a surrogate in some cases,
such as the Frontbann) from then on and rejoining both as soon as
the SA and NSDAP were officially reestablished in 1925.[55] A strong
characteristic of the men who joined the SA in 1925 and 1926, then,
is that they tended to be "true believers," men who became converted to National Socialism at a rather early date and who did not
swerve from that conviction ever again. The higher SA leaders who
joined later often showed a very different development, as will be
demonstrated below.

The earliest members of the SA within its top leadership had a close
relationship to the NSDAP. Every one of the 1925 and 1926 SA men
were Party members. All but two (out of the thirty-one for whom
both dates are known) joined the Party and the SA within six months.[56]
One of these two joined the Party first, and then the SA. All joined
the SA and NSDAP in either the same town or in places close to each
other, suggesting that often the Party branch was in a smaller town
that did not have an SA unit in the early days.[57]

At least on this basis, it cannot be said that this group of SAmen neglected their Party responsibilities or avoided joining the Party out of opposition to "politicians" or for any other reason. Joining both the SA and the Party seems to have been a matter of course for these men, and there is no indication that Party membership was taken less seriously than SA membership at this early stage. This is an important point to make, because it underscores the interpretation that these men were political as well as military activists, and it contradicts attacks against the SA by some members of the NSDAP in the early 1930s, who claimed that many of its leaders deliberately avoided becoming Party members.

The place where the men in this chapter joined the NSDAP in 1925 and 1926 is significant, particularly when compared with the geographical dispersion of the NSDAP before its ban in November 1923. Instead of being dominated by southern German locations, as in the early 1920s, the reverse is true in 1925 and 1926. Of the twenty-six men whose records state where they joined the NSDAP in 1925 or 1926, nineteen (73%) joined north of the Main River. Five of these twenty-six men were also members of the "first" NSDAP and joined it in a known location. Of these five, four joined the Party for the first time in Munich, but rejoined north of the Main River. This demonstrates the very different geographical dispersion of the post-1925 Nazi Party. Of the nineteen who joined the second NSDAP north of the Main, at least nine were members of either the Frontbann, the Völkisch-Sozialer Block, or the NSFB, further proof that these organizations were among the most important agents for the spread of the Party to northern Germany.

The top SA leaders who joined in 1925 or 1926 were not just simple dues-paying members of the NSDAP; they also held positions of leadership. This is not too surprising, given the need for competent leaders. What is surprising is the number of men occupying relatively high Party positions. By the end of 1925, the twenty-two men out of the group in this chapter whose Party ranks were known boasted one Gauleiter (Franz von Pfeffer), one deputy Gauleiter (Viktor Lutze), one Gau staff member (Heinrich Himmler), one leader of a local Party chapter (Wilhelm Stegmann), and three holding one other office within their local group (Wilhelm Dittler, Kurt Günther, and Heinrich Schoene). By the end of 1926, out of the twenty-eight whose Party rank is known, four were deputy Gauleiter, one held an office in the national administration of the Party, three were leaders of local Party chapters, and two more held another office within a local Party group.[58] This shows that there were many who were equally at ease and equally as important leading both the political and paramilitary wings of the Nazi movement. The early joiners among the future highest leaders of the SA were not as a group simple one-dimensional military men with no feeling for politics or civilian affairs. Instead, they were political activists for whom the Party, its ideology, and its success were very important—flesh-and-blood political zealots instead of cardboard soldiers.

If any further proof is needed as to their commitment to the Party and to its ideology, then a quick look at the highest Party rank ever held by these men will dispel any lingering doubts. Six of the thirty-six eventually became Reichsleiter (national leaders),[59] and two of these six were earlier Gauleiter. Nine held positions in either a Gau or on a national Party staff,[60] four were the heads of a Kreis (Party district, equivalent of a county),[61] and three were the heads of a Party cell or local Party chapter.[62] Altogether, twenty-one of the thirty-six men who joined the SA in 1925 or 1926 held some sort of rank within the Party apparatus outside of their SA positions.[63] The men who joined the SA in 1925 or 1926 and who rose to the highest levels of its leadership were true believers, committed equally to the SA and to the Party, who remained active in both to the very end.

Heinrich Schoene presents a good example of an early SA leader who was also active in Party administration.[64] He was born in 1889 in Berlin, the son of a bricklayer and carpenter who later apparently made enough money to buy an estate. He attended a Gymnasium for several years, but transferred to an agricultural school, from which he obtained an Obersekundareife.[65] He worked as an agricultural laborer and then became an agricultural administrator. He did not stay long in this position, however, even though he listed it as his actual profession, and soon he opened up his own building company. He served in the war as an infantryman, messenger, and sergeant. He was wounded and decorated with the Iron Cross Second Class. He did not serve in a free corps or a Wehrverband, and his sole political activity before 1924 was a short membership in the DNVP from 1919 to 1920. Schoene's political activity accelerated in 1924. In that year he joined the Völkisch-Sozialer Block and the NSFB, serving both groups as a local secretary. In April 1925 he joined the SA and NSDAP, becoming a founding member of his local Party cell. From 1925 his Party career paralleled his SA career. In 1926 he became the head of the SA in his town, as well as head of the local Party cell. He was a Party speaker and in 1927 became Kreisleiter. At the same time he

Ogruf. Heinrich Schoene in 1941 or 1942. Schoene wears his Golden Party
Pin, an insignia indicating that he attended the 1928 Nuremberg Party Con-
gress, and a decoration showing that he was wounded in the First World
War. His medals include the Iron Cross Second Class, the Military Service
Cross from the Second World War (Kriegsverdienstkreuz), and a Medal for
War Participants (Ehrenkreuz für Frontkämpfer) from the First World War.
Courtesy of the Bundesarchiv.

led the local Hitler Youth and was adjutant of his SA Gausturm. In 1929 he rose to command the SA Gausturm of his Gau, and very likely left his position in the Party apparatus at this time, although he did not provide the exact date of the latter in his records. His SA career continued upwards, and he became a Gruppenführer in 1932 and an Obergruppenführer in 1934. His services to the Party did not stop, however. He had earlier been a member of the Prussian Provincial Council (Provinzialrat). In 1932 he was elected to the Prussian Landtag for the NSDAP, and in 1933 became a member of the Reichstag. He continued to command an SA Gruppe, and also headed the corresponding administration of the Reichsluftschutzbund (Reich Civil Defense Association) from 1934 to 1939. He was named to several other Prussian administrative organizations, but the height of his career came in 1941, when he was named the general commissar (Generalkommissar) for part of the German-occupied Ukraine. Although this and many of his former positions were technically state positions, it is clear that he obtained them because he was a loyal member of the NSDAP. A successful and influential early SA commander, he was equally as successful and influential as an early Party leader. By 1929 or 1930 his SA duties had taken precedence for a time, but his service to the Party did not stop, and like other high SA leaders, he could be called upon by the Party whenever it needed a leader who was loyal and competent (in that order).

The future highest SA leaders who joined in 1925 and 1926 immediately played important roles. By the end of 1925, at least half of the thirty men who had already joined the SA were officers at some level.[66] Interestingly, the percentage of leaders from this group rises only slowly through the end of 1930, reaching just below 60 percent in that year. This seems strange, given that this is, after all, a group of men who went on to hold one of the three highest ranks in the SA. One answer to this might lie in the ages of the men involved; about a third of the group who joined in 1925 or 1926 were born after 1900 and thus were young even by 1930. Failure to achieve leadership rank by 1930 was due almost always to age. If only those men born in 1900 or before are considered, then fully 75 percent of the men whose rank in the first quarter of 1930 is known were leaders.[67] In fact, all but one of the men who were SA leaders by the end of 1926 are drawn from this group of older men, as might be expected.[68]

Aside from the group of "youngsters," the early members of the SA from our group left their mark. By the end of 1930, eight were in command of Standarten,[69] six were in command of larger units.[70] Dincklage was an OSAF-Stellvertreter (regional commander),[71] von Ulrich was general inspector of the SA, SS, and Hitler Youth, Reschny was the head of the SA in Austria, Himmler was the head of the SS, and von Pfeffer was Oberster SA-Führer. Most of those holding higher rank by this time had, of course, passed through lower ranks such as Sturmführer, which were so crucial to building the SA, especially in its earliest years before larger units existed, and there was a new generation of younger leaders still in lower-level positions.

There were thus two distinct patterns to the early SA careers of the 1925 and 1926 joiners. The first group held command positions immediately and were among the earliest higher leaders of the SA. These are the men who built the SA. The second pattern is characteristic of men who were too young and inexperienced to become leaders right away. These men slowly ripened into leaders within the SA itself, providing the SA with a backbone of capable young men, steeped in the ethos and traditions of the SA and experienced in the ways of the Party. This group provided continuity in later years of high turnover in SA membership among the rank and file, and they were a cadre of young men who could begin to replace the oldest cohort of SA leaders when they died or moved on to other positions outside of the SA.

In summary, the men who joined the SA in 1925 or 1926 were both paramilitary and völkisch activists, true political soldiers long before the term became current in the Party. They were generally members of a Wehrverband and a völkisch political organization immediately before joining the SA in 1925 or 1926, and often this meant that they were pre-putsch SA and Party members. A large number were also members of the Frontbann and of a radical völkisch party such as the NSFB. Some showed a strong history of military activism in free corps, Upper Silesia, and the Ruhr, although many did not have any particular history of political activism at all. In either case they were as strongly committed to the Party as they were to the SA, and they often held office in the Party at the same time that they were in the SA. Many, particularly those old enough to have served in the war, were among the first leaders of the SA, often rising to relatively high rank by the end of 1930, while the younger members of the group tended to remain in much lower ranks until later.

The NSDAP in 1925 and 1926 was a small and struggling organization on the völkisch fringe. Its potential for success was questionable at best, and its later importance was not at all foreseeable. It could only attract and admit the completely committed. Nor could it afford the functional specialization of later years, and all Party members were expected to perform a variety of tasks. This explains the strong commitment to both political and paramilitary activism, both SA and Party leadership of this early cohort. They were the men of the first hour in both the NSDAP and SA, and they served both masters. Their abilities as both paramilitary and political leaders were crucial to the survival of the young (reestablished) NSDAP. Conversely, without the presence and availability of a core group of men skilled in both political and military organization and committed to the radical völkisch principles of the NSDAP, it never could have survived, let alone expanded.

For the Weimar Republic there was a tragic confluence of a large body of men trained in violence and military organization, with widespread alienation of the public and resentment toward the entire postwar political system. These were not a handful of marginalized malcontents or military adventurers, as some historians have characterized the paramilitary activists of the 1920s.[72] Most were well educated, came from middle-class families, and had established careers before the First World War. Although few men entered the SA and NSDAP in 1925 or 1926, there were countless others in the vast rightwing and paramilitary subculture, far too many to simply dismiss as rootless adventurers. At the same time, it is important to recognize that the politically active radical right in Germany in 1925 or 1926 was a relatively small part of the total population. Two things allowed the SA and NSDAP to make the most of these numbers. The first was the ability of the SA to maximize or "multiply" (in the current military jargon) its limited numbers through the use of military or paramilitary forms of organization. This gave the SA and NSDAP a force far beyond their size. The second factor was the ability of the SA (and presumably the NSDAP) to grow like an amoeba by absorbing the members and particularly the leaders of similar but rival organizations. This will be illustrated in the following chapter.

3

The Defectors, 1927-1930

The period from 1927 to 1930 was crucial for the development of the SA and the NSDAP. During this time both organizations became more centralized and developed highly efficient administrative and command structures. Both also grew from marginal, locally based organizations into large, centrally directed national ones. Both did so by absorbing many of the former members of rival right-wing organizations. The two processes of expansion and centralization were in fact related. The leaders necessary to organize and administer both the SA and the NSDAP beyond what had existed in 1926 came as part of the influx of new members who were absorbed from rival groups. This process is graphically illustrated in the careers of the men discussed below.

Between early 1927 and January 1931 the SA transformed itself from a loose collection of isolated activists and Wehrverband remnants into a disciplined national organization of considerable strength. Given the original heterogeneity and disorganization of the early SA and Party in 1925 and 1926, and given the changes in the political climate of Germany since 1923, which had become unsuitable for the formation of paramilitary groups, this was a considerable feat.

The man responsible for this transformation was not Adolf Hitler but retired captain Franz von Pfeffer. More than any other individual, von Pfeffer was responsible for molding the SA into the organization that brought the Nazi Party to power. He may rightly be called the father of the SA and the Party's first political soldier. Yet von Pfeffer did not act alone. He was aided by a corps of capable and committed SA leaders. Without such subordinates, no leader is capable of anything except mere gestures.

"FATHER OF THE SA"

Franz von Pfeffer was born in Düsseldorf in 1888.[1] His father was a Prussian bureaucrat, and he himself chose to become a professional officer in the Prussian army after studying law for a short time. He served on the western front in the First World War in both general staff and combat positions. Ending the war with the rank of captain, he formed a free corps in January 1919 that fought in the Ruhr, Baden, and the Baltic. He was involved in the Kapp Putsch, served in Upper Silesia in 1921, and was a member of various Wehrverbände that evolved out of his free corps. He also had contacts with the Reichswehr, and in 1923 was a member of one of the secret sabotage units operating against the French and Belgians in the Ruhr. By 1924 he was the leader of Gau Ruhr of the Völkisch-Sozialer Block and in contact with Hitler and the NSDAP. In 1925 he led his Gau into the NSDAP and served as Gauleiter and Ruhr SA leader of the NSDAP until 1926.

By all accounts he was a genuine leader, a strong-willed personality of great energy and ability, but of equally great arrogance and independence, who did not lack enemies within the NSDAP because of his ambition and lack of tact.[2] Clearly he was a man who believed he was right and therefore did not like to compromise.[3] Yet it was only through just such a combination of will, ability, and leadership that he was able to transform the SA into a national organization. And despite a certain inflexibility and brutal directness of character, von Pfeffer had learned to adapt to changing conditions and political contexts. By training and sentiment a military man with intimate ties to the old Imperial Army, the free corps, and the conspiratorial, putschist Wehrverbände, he could see beyond the world of guns and uniforms.[4] It is this political side of von Pfeffer which enabled him to create a new form for the SA, different from that of the Wehrverbände and better adapted to current conditions. Critical of the "dilettantism" of the Beer Hall Putsch, he was able to draw the lesson from it that if the "national revolution" were to succeed, what was needed was not a better organized putsch, which was the solution proposed by many who continued to think in exclusively military terms, but rather entirely new tactics. As Gauleiter of the Ruhr he gained the experience necessary to adapt the paramilitary form of the Wehrverband to the substance of a political movement. In this he was aided by Viktor Lutze.[5]

According to von Pfeffer's own testimony, he was appointed su-

Oberster SA-Führer and retired captain Franz von Pfeffer in 1924. Note the whip and his mixture of military and civilian clothing. The photograph is autographed. Courtesy of the Bundesarchiv.

Viktor Lutze (to Hitler's left) in 1931. Lutze wears the early insignia for a Gruppenführer. Courtesy of the Bundesarchiv.

preme SA leader for several reasons. First, as a professional officer and successful free corps leader, he would not permit a repetition of the sloppiness characteristic of the Beer Hall Putsch. Moreover, as a member of the Arbeitsgemeinschaft der Nord- und West-deutschen Gaue (Working Organization of the North and West Districts), he had shown early signs of independence, even rebellion, and his Gau Ruhr was a dangerously large power base. Bringing him to Munich put him in a position where he could be watched, and his oversized Gau Ruhr was broken up.[6] Conversely, the north German Party leaders were suspicious of the Munich leadership and wanted a northerner to take over a key position in Munich in order to guard their interests and bring fresh talent into the central organization. Despite some contrary indications, it is difficult to dispute von Pfeffer's own account,[7] yet the most important reason of all for his selection was simply because Hitler accepted his ideas as to what the SA should be and do.[8] Hitler gave him certain basic guidelines, but von Pfeffer was allowed to decide how these instructions were to be carried out.

Although he was not supposed to begin operations until November 1, 1926, von Pfeffer was ready one month earlier. His first act was to send a letter to all Gauleiter, telling them that he was now

OSAF, explaining his idea of the SA's proper role, announcing that his plans for its reorganization were complete and ready to appear, and asking for their cooperation, particularly in naming suitable candidates for SA leadership in their area.[9] Between November 1 and February 1927, von Pfeffer released a steady stream of orders (SA-Befehle, or SABE). These orders resumed in May 1927 with fundamental regulations (Grundsätzliche Anordnungen der SA, or Grusa).[10]

LAYING THE GROUNDWORK

Von Pfeffer's grand design laid the groundwork for the organization of the SA, which did not change in any fundamental way down to the end of the Third Reich. Essentially he adopted the familiar military-style hierarchy but introduced a great deal of flexibility. This was necessary in order to adapt it to the needs of a voluntary organization which, while attempting to create a centralized, hierarchical structure, in fact had to tolerate a great deal of local autonomy and which depended on the initiative of local leaders for growth.[11] The need to observe the strictest legality and the political mission of supplementing the NSDAP, assigned to him by Hitler, also helped to push von Pfeffer into adapting a military organization to parliamentary politics. His SA was quite different from the old-style Wehrverbände, yet retained those elements which had made the Wehrverbände strong. In particular, he rejected a slavish imitation of the Imperial Army (or the Wehrverbände, for that matter) in favor of a structure that better fit the essentially civilian and domestic arena and that also expressed the völkisch and revolutionary ideals of the early Nazi Party.

The basic building block was the Gruppe (section), whose name was later changed under Röhm to Schar.[12] This was to be a squad of three to thirteen men. Von Pfeffer stipulated that this was to be a permanent group of men who knew each other and who were tied together by personal bonds and associations. This was a sharp break with the practice of the Imperial Army (and indeed, most modern armies), which had treated soldiers as interchangeable parts, arbitrarily thrown together according to height or other outward characteristic.[13] The emphasis on the smallest unit was also very intelligent from the standpoint of the degree of organization present within the Party and SA in 1926 and 1927, since almost any Ortsgruppe (local Party group) could form an SA unit right away. All higher units were formed like building blocks from groups of smaller units. Moreover, the number of subordinate units needed to form a superior one could vary, so that new units could be added as growth demanded, and the creation of larger units could begin from a relatively small base.

The next step after the Schar was the Trupp (platoon or troop). It was made up of several Scharen. Just like the Schar, it was always supposed to remain together as a unit so that its members would form tight personal bonds. Several Trupps made up a Sturm (company),[14] which was the smallest unit to be led by the equivalent of an officer, a Führer, as opposed to a noncommissioned officer, or Unterführer.

Several Stürme then formed a Standarte (regiment), and several Standarten could be united in a Brigade (brigade), although this level of organization remained largely on paper for several years, until the SA increased sufficiently in size. More commonly, several Standarten were grouped together into a Gausturm. Originally nineteen Gaustürme were created.

The boundaries of the Gaustürme as first conceived were deliberately drawn by von Pfeffer so as *not* to coincide with the boundaries of the Party regions, nor did they coincide with either the Wahlkreis (electoral districts) or the Wehrkreis (military recruiting districts) or even the boundaries of the German federal states. Instead, they were drawn to coincide with the Stammesgrenzen (tribal boundaries) of the German Volksgaue (tribal regions or provinces).[15] This attempt to draw organizational consequences from völkisch ideology was also indicative of von Pfeffer's wish to separate the SA from the Party Political Organization as much as possible.

Until 1928, the Gaustürme were the largest SA units actually in existence, and all were directly subordinate to the supreme SA command. In 1928 von Pfeffer introduced a regional level of command between the OSAF and the Gaustürme, in order to facilitate cohesion between Gaustürme. These were the seven regional Oberführer (rank between colonel and brigadier general). In February 1929, their title was changed to OSAF-Stellvertreter (deputy supreme SA leader).[16]

Von Pfeffer made other additions to the SA to give it flexibility in its employment, but also in order to make it as independent as possible from state and public institutions. These additions brought about a growing internal specialization and elaboration, as different types of units were added and as the SA staff and command structure expanded. This included the development of SA liability and life insurance,[17] the establishment of a system of sales outlets for uniforms and equipment (the so-called Reichszeugsmeisterei),[18] and even a plan to purchase large stocks of food conserves in case the regular supply of food was ever cut off.[19] Von Pfeffer also oversaw the formation of special SA communications troops (Nachrichtenstaffeln)[20] and SA motor vehicle troops (Kraftfahrstaffeln) in 1928. Although the motorization effort proceeded slowly, by 1930 the NSDAP, under the auspices of the SA, was able to create the Nationalsozialistische Automobilkorps (National Socialist Automobile Corps) and to order the formation of motorized SA units down to the Standarte and Sturm level.[21] In a similar vein, SA mounted units were formed in 1928 by rural SA members, contributing both to the mobility of the SA and to its attraction for those interested in horses or simply interested in learning to ride.[22] A similar effort in coastal areas was the formation of special SA naval units (Marine-Stürme), first attempted in 1928 and successfully established in 1929.[23]

Other measures were introduced to broaden the appeal and scope of the SA. As early as 1927, von Pfeffer considered forming SA reserves. Although the SA was not yet large enough to support reserve units—in the early days every man was needed regardless of age or infirmity—by 1929 the situation had changed, and in March the SA-Reserve (SAR) was formally established.[24] Its purpose was to allow older men who were physically not up to the day-to-day demands of SA service to participate in a less active capacity and still be available for service on special occasions.

Finally, in June 1930 the SA expanded its medical service. The idea of having SA medical officers was not new; as early as 1923 the SA had recruited doctors, and beginning again in 1927 each Standarte was expected to have a physician. This was expanded in 1930 with the introduction of a medic for each thirty men in local-level units, and the introduction of a chief physician within the supreme SA command.[25] The expansion and elaboration of the SA medical service permitted sympathizing physicians to participate in a professional capacity. More important, the SA was thus assured of prompt medical help "in case of emergency." This was a part of von Pfeffer's long-range plans to make the SA independent of all outside help, but as the street battles in which the SA engaged became increasingly bitter and violent, the expansion of the SA medical services took on a very practical and immediate dimension.

In addition to developing the formal structure of the SA, von Pfeffer was instrumental in giving the SA its own particular identity and its own agenda in the political struggle against the Weimar Republic. Without this new identity, the SA would have remained just another Wehrverband at a time when their day had long passed. But if the new identity that von Pfeffer gave to the SA was the source of its success and thus its utility to the NSDAP, it was also the source of much conflict between the SA and the Party. As the SA became an institution distinct from and often separate from the Political Organization, and as the Political Organization itself became more established, it became clear that von Pfeffer's vision of the SA and Hitler's were actually more divergent than they had appeared to be in 1926. There was ultimately very little difference between what von Pfeffer did as the head of the SA and the proposal from Röhm that Hitler rejected in 1925, save that von Pfeffer's concept for the SA was nonconspiratorial and exclusively National Socialist, whereas Röhm's was not. Nevertheless, both men saw the SA as an organization separate from the Party and independent in its day-to-day workings.[26] Ultimately, the differences between Hitler's concept and von Pfeffer's caused von Pfeffer to resign his post in the fall of 1930. Yet by then he had succeeded so well in giving the SA a solid yet flexible organization and its own distinct identity that the fundamental conflicts between the SA and the Party apparatus did not go away when he did. Rather, they continued to smoulder until the accession to state power gave Hitler the strength to finally confront the problem and force a decision.

After resigning as supreme SA leader in 1930, von Pfeffer remained active as chief of staff of the General Inspector of the SA and SS until April 1933, at which time he left active service but remained an honorary SA officer at the disposal of the SA (SA-Führer zur Verfügung der SA). He later claimed to have run a private diplomatic intelligence agency supported by Reichswehr funds until 1941. He seems to have remained close to the center of power, but his exact activities are not recorded. He fell from favor in 1941, and in November he was expelled from the Party and arrested. He was later released, and at the very end of the Second World War he commanded a Volkssturm division. He survived the war and is known to have lived into the early 1950s at least.

NEW BLOOD

Von Pfeffer had considerable help in organizing the SA. His "officers" included the military and völkisch true believers discussed in the previous chapter, but as the SA grew into a mass national organization and its hierarchy and mission became more and more complex, it needed increasing numbers of new leaders and administrators. A new group entered the SA between 1927 and 1930 and rose to leadership to fill this need. These men are the focus of this chapter.[27]

They were strikingly similar to the men who had already joined the SA, yet they differed in significant ways. They tended not to have quite the same background in völkisch politics as the previous group and to have been more involved in military groups. They were also more likely to come from northern Germany, symptomatic of the spread of the NSDAP out of southern Germany after 1927 to become a truly national organization. Most important, they tended to follow one of several characteristic "paths" into the SA and NSDAP. The men following each path showed a number of similarities not only in their backgrounds but also in their later careers within the Third Reich.

Although they showed some key differences from the 1925-26 group, they shared a basic outlook and a strikingly similar background with the men already in the SA. They also brought with them extremely valuable experience in the nuts and bolts of the kind of paramilitary-political activities in which the SA was engaged. They were thus able to fit into the SA organization very quickly and with a minimum of adjustment. By coming to the SA at this time, they became the backbone of the future, post-1930 expansion of the SA. At the same time, they robbed competing organizations of their skills and numbers, further strengthening the relative position of the SA and NSDAP among its competitors on the far right. Some of these new men were radicals who could no longer find a place in traditionally conservative organizations such as the Stahlhelm. Others were already members of organizations similar to the NSDAP, who gravitated to it simply because they decided that it had a greater potential for success.

A surprisingly high proportion of those joining the SA between 1927 and 1930 were former regular army officers.[28] This is even more remarkable when the men who joined the SA in 1929 or 1930 are considered: close to half were former professional officers.[29] There were also many reserve officers, so that 59 percent of those joining from 1927 to 1930 had been military officers.[30] This is clearly much higher than the percentage of officers in the German adult male population at large[31] and is also higher than the percentage of army veterans among the men in this study who joined the SA in 1925 or 1926.[32] Moreover, the percentages of professional vs. reserve officers in the two groups are nearly reversed: not only were those who joined from 1927 to 1930 more likely to have been officers but they were also more likely to have been professional officers.[33]

This is significant and has several causes. Von Pfeffer was always interested in recruiting former officers. Moreover, by 1930 the SA was particularly interested in recruiting men with the special skills needed to occupy staff positions and lead large bodies of men. Conversely, as the NSDAP and SA grew, they became more attractive to former officers. Greater size meant that the NSDAP and SA could offer the opportunity to put military leadership skills to full use.

A prime example of this is the case of Otto Wagener, who was invited to join the SA in order to develop a central staff structure, a kind of SA general staff, and who immediately became chief of staff.[34] Aside from the fact that he was known to von Pfeffer personally and had impeccable nationalist credentials, Wagener's prime qualification for this post was that he was a former general staff officer in the regular army.[35] While Wagener had been a successful businessman after leaving the service in 1919, many of the professional officers who had remained in the Reichswehr were beginning to retire in the late 1920s. Serving in a staff position within the SA offered them a means of essentially continuing their military careers, offering familiar work as well as a moderate supplement to their pensions, and allowing them to continue to work for what they saw as the national good.[36]

Other former officers had been in rival political and/or paramilitary organizations. Often these were slightly less radical than the NSDAP, since professional officers tended to support traditional conservative organizations. By the late 1920s, some were becoming dissatisfied with the policies of their organizations, and they began to look for something more dynamic, while others, seeing their own organizations stagnating, sought alternatives. Many of them landed in the NSDAP. As we will see below, these processes of "defection" to the NSDAP were important for the entire group of 1927-30 joiners, not just for the former professional officers.

As might be expected, most of the highest SA leaders who joined between 1927 and 1930 were combat veterans of the First World War.[37] They were slightly older and more experienced than the 1925-26 group.[38] Three-quarters had been active in some kind of political or military organization in 1919, during the confusion of the German Revolution, which Ernst von Salomon called *der Nachkrieg* (the post-

Dr. Generalmajor Otto Wagener in 1945, by then a former SA Stabschef. Courtesy of the Bundesarchiv.

war).[39] Just over half of these were in a free corps.[40] Seventeen free corps were listed by the twenty-five men who claimed membership in a free corps in 1919.[41] These are a mix of radical[42] and moderate[43] groups. The three most often cited were Freikorps Ehrhardt (officially, the Second Naval Brigade), the Eiserne Division, and Freikorps Epp, all among the most radical groups. They each had three or more men from the 1927-30 group. Others, each with two members from the group, are Freikorps Maercker and the Loewenfeld Brigade (officially, the First Naval Brigade). What is clear, and what is also a change from the pattern observed in the group joining the SA in 1925 or 1926, is the dominance of north German free corps and the relatively low representation of Bavarian free corps. Only Freikorps Epp and the Freiwillige Sturmabteilung Schlichtingsheim were Bavarian, and the only other south German free corps represented was based in Württemberg. The preponderance of north German free corps reflected the fact that the SA became firmly established in northern Germany between 1927 and 1930. As the SA and NSDAP tended to spread from south to north, many northerners joined after their cousins in the south.

Many men in this chapter were in the army during the revolution,[44] three were in the Grenzschutz,[45] and one was in the police.[46] This considerable range of military activities demonstrates that the free corps were not the only nurturers of future radicalism.

Military activities were not the only choice during the German Revolution: two men were in a radical völkisch association, the Schutz- und Trutzbund, and one of these men was simultaneously in the Grenzschutz.[47] A third belonged to the DNVP and the Stahlhelm, a veterans' association-cum-Wehrverband, and another was briefly a member of the Zentrum (Catholic Center Party).[48] Three were associated with patriotic societies (often with a paramilitary aspect in 1919).[49]

The pattern of activity of the men in this group between 1920 and 1923 was similar to that seen in the previous chapter, with some important differences. The number involved in political or military organizations fell in 1920 and 1921 and rose again in 1922 and again sharply in 1923. Nevertheless, the 1927-30 group generally tended to vary less in its level of activity over time than the 1925-26 group, indicating a more even temperament or mature outlook.[50]

Both the 1925-26 group and the 1927-30 group tended to emphasize paramilitary and military organizations more than political ones in their activities from 1920 to 1923, and the strong activity in radical völkisch groups that characterized a minority of those who joined in 1925 or 1926 was almost completely absent from the 1927-30 group.[51] In 1921 and 1922 a single member of the 1927-30 group belonged to the Schutz- und Trutzbund, and in 1923 one member of the same group joined the Deutschvölkische Freiheitspartei (DVFP), both radical völkisch organizations.[52]

By 1923, ten were members of the NSDAP and eight were members of the early SA.[53] However, the corresponding numbers of the 1925-26 group was much higher, both numerically and as a percentage.[54] Those joining in 1925 or 1926 were more than twice as likely to have been members of the SA or NSDAP before the 1923 putsch.

Activity in nonmilitary political organizations beyond the völkisch fringe was equally low. One member of the 1927-30 group had been a DNVP member since 1920, and two others had belonged for shorter periods.[55] One was a member of the Ostpreußischer Heimatbund, a conservative and regionalist organization in eastern Prussia.[56] All other organizations to which this group belonged were military in nature, the majority being Wehrverbände or the Reichswehr. In almost every case, members of the 1927-30 group outnumbered the 1925-26 group in any given Wehrverband.

The only exceptions to the above rule reflect the shift in geographical focus from the 1925-26 period to the 1927-30 period. Thus, the 1925-26 group outnumbered the later group in such organizations as the Reichskriegsflagge and the Reichsflagge, which were mainly Bavarian Wehrverbände, and in the Bund Olympia and Bund Fredericus, which were Berlin-based Wehrverbände. (Berlin had been an early center of National Socialist activity in northern Germany, dating from before the Beer Hall Putsch.)

Several Wehrverbände that were well represented in the careers of those joining the SA from 1927 to 1930 are completely absent from the backgrounds of those joining in 1925-26, such as the Jungdeutscher Orden (Jungdo) and the Wehrwolf, Bund deutscher Männer.[57] Others are not absent from the 1925-26 group but are much more heavily represented among the 1927-30 group, such as the OC/Bund Wiking, the Stahlhelm, and Bund Oberland.[58] These organizations were strong rivals of the NSDAP and SA, but by 1927 they were slowly beginning to decline. Except for Bund Oberland, they were also mainly north German organizations, so the inroads made by the SA in their membership also reflect its spread northwards.

Also striking is the number of the 1927-30 group who joined the Reichswehr or police in 1920-23. In 1920 this was as high as eighteen (30.5%).[59] Although the absolute numbers fell by 1923, the percentage of those in the Reichswehr or police is still much higher in the 1927-30 group.[60] This is further proof that by the late 1920s, the NSDAP and SA were able to attract conservatives closer to the mainstream than in 1925 or 1926, where the core constituency of the Nazi movement was still on the völkisch fringe.

Roughly the same percentage of both groups fought in Upper Silesia,[61] although all of the Upper Silesian veterans joined the SA by the end of 1929. This is also true of those who actively participated in sabotage actions against the French and Belgians in the Ruhr in 1923, although the percentage is slightly higher in the 1925-26 group.[62]

In summary, the highest SA leaders who joined the SA from 1927 to 1930 tended to come out of north German organizations, and they tended to have been members of either the police/Reichswehr or of Wehrverbände but almost never of political organizations. Some of the north German Wehrverbände were quite radical, like the Wehrwolf, whereas others were comparatively moderate and associated with traditional conservatism, such as the Stahlhelm or the Jungdo. Indeed, army and police veterans must also be counted among the participants in traditional or moderate conservative organizations, at least in the sense that their organizations were dedicated to the preservation of order and the status quo.[63]

Paths into the SA

The year 1923 was marked by high political tension and, consequently, high levels of involvement in political and military organizations for the men in this chapter. Participation began to taper off in mid-1924 as tensions cooled and as the Wehrverbände began to languish. The future highest officers of the SA who did not join it immediately in 1925 or 1926 followed one of several different paths into the SA.

The first path presents a paradox: several men showed no organized activity whatsoever between 1920 and the date when they joined the SA and NSDAP, usually in 1930. This group will be called the "passive activists." This oxymoron was deliberately chosen to describe the paradoxical lack of political experience of men who later rose to command the SA, an organization which prided itself on its extreme political activism.

The second path was also characterized by little organized activity except in crisis periods. These men were active in 1919, again in 1923 (and into the first half of 1924), and then not again until they joined the SA/NSDAP. They tended to join rather late, in 1929 or 1930 (with some exceptions). These are the "sporadic activists."

The men following the next two paths were characterized by more frequent activity, even nearly continuous participation in political or military organizations. The third path led through a chain of organizations, as if the individuals were searching for just the right one.[64] This is the path taken by the "serial activists." The fourth path is that of the "defector." It was followed by men who were active in (and presumably loyal to) a single organization (or several small organizations simultaneously) for a long time before they left to join the SA/NSDAP. Many of these men often did not join the Nazis immediately, but rather were inactive for one to six months first, again suggesting dissatisfaction followed by a period of searching.[65]

The men following the fifth path joined the NSDAP fairly early and only joined the SA a year or more later. This group presumably was attracted to the NSDAP more for its political message and ideology, and only later got involved with its paramilitary auxiliary. Many who followed this path could equally as well have followed Party careers but ended up as SA officers instead, perhaps out of a sense of duty or simply by chance. These men will be called the "Party soldiers."

The Passive Activists

As odd as it might seem, some of the highest leaders of one of the world's most activist and dynamic political movements apparently were not active in paramilitary and political organizations before joining the NSDAP/SA.[66]

The "passive activists" category of this study comprises only seven men, or just over 11 percent of those joining the SA between 1927 and 1930.[67] The reasons for their high SA rank are not always clear and are often very personal. August Burger's skills as a physician explains his rapid rise in rank. Because of their education and skill, physicians are generally accorded officer rank in nearly all armies. The head physician of an SA-Gruppe was accorded the rank of Gruppenführer. Judging from the careers of the early SA doctors, those who joined before 1930 were able to rise to this rank quickly. This was true simply because the SA lacked physicians, so the first to join soon occupied the higher ranks, even with little prior SA service.

Three others also rose to relatively high rank soon after joining.

Ludwig Uhland was promoted quickly due to his skills as a staff officer, since he had served in the army in this capacity and began his SA career in a staff position. Although he began as an SA field commander, Leopold Damian spent much of his SA career as a department head in the central command. Udo von Woyrsch had also been a professional officer, but he had only just been commissioned when the Great War broke out, and he did not possess any extraordinary military or administrative skills. Instead, he joined the SS from the beginning, where the cachet of his nobility, the comparatively greater opportunity for quick promotion within the SS organization, and his utter ruthlessness brought him quick advancement.

For the rest, there seems to be no discernible reason why they would be able to go so far within the SA after years of inactivity. Most of the men in this "passive" category didn't join the NSDAP until 1929 or 1930, and their high SA rank is not attributable to any corresponding high rank in the Party.[68] In fact, all but one joined the SA only after joining the Party, quite in keeping with their earlier reluctance to become involved in paramilitary activity.[69] None of the "passive activists" had any special leadership ability that set them apart. Most were officers in the First World War, but none had an exceptional military career and none ever held an especially high rank.[70] Several may have been promoted out of sheer longevity: three did not became SA-Gruppenführer until the Second World War, when casualties and transfers to other activity gave them an unexpected chance for advancement.

The career of Max Lehmann well represents the passive activists.[71] Friedrich Wilhelm Max Lehmann was born in Cottbus in the Prussian province of Brandenburg in September 1892. His father was a Brenner[72] who died when Max was nineteen. Max attended primary school and then a Handelsschule (a high school concentrating on business skills). He served an apprenticeship as a Kaufmann,[73] then attended a trade school for the textile industry. He lost an eye in combat and was awarded the Iron Cross Second Class, but he did not rise above the rank of private.

He was not active in any sort of political or military organization from 1918 to September 1930, when he joined the NSDAP. Until 1933 he listed his occupation as cloth manufacturer (Tuchfabrikant). He immediately became active in the administration of his local Party group, supervising the Zellenorganisation (factory Party cells) and keeping some of the financial accounts for about a year. This was the end of his service in the Political Organization of the

Party. He also joined the SA in October 1930, beginning as a paymaster with the rank of Sturmbannführer (major), then serving as an adjutant and later as a chief of staff of an Untergruppe. He was promoted to Standartenführer (colonel) and given command of a Standarte in July 1932.

In 1933 he was promoted to the command of a Brigade, which he held until 1937 (still only serving in the SA on a part-time basis), at which time he was transferred to a full-time staff position in the SA central command. It was while serving in this capacity, as head of the Abteilung Organisation und Einsatz (organization and operation department) that he was promoted to Gruppenführer in 1940. In 1944 he was placed on the inactive list, possibly because he returned to his business activities.

From 1933 to 1937 he also served in city government in Cottbus, as was typical of the usurpation of state positions by SA and Party leaders. He did not serve in the Second World War, most likely due to his wounds in the First World War. Lehmann is a good example of a "passive activist." He was politically inactive from the time he left the army at the end of the First World War to the time he joined the SA and NSDAP in the fall of 1930. His subsequent career in the SA was successful, but he never rose as far as more activist colleagues did, and his greatest strengths and most important service to the SA seem to have been administrative in nature. Moreover, the fact that he was exempt from military service gave him a sudden, new value to the SA during the war: he didn't count against the limited number of exemptions from military service granted to the SA by the army, which controlled such matters. While not a complete explanation, it likely contributed to his ability to rise to the rank of Gruppenführer.

The Sporadic Activists

The next path into the SA was followed by those who were active in other political and paramilitary organizations before they joined the NSDAP and SA, but were only intermittently active, during moments of crisis and tension. Eight of the group examined in this chapter followed this basic pattern.[74]

Typically, they began as officers in the First World War.[75] During the 1919 revolution, they were involved in a free corps.[76] After that they were inactive until late 1922 or 1923, when inflation, domestic unrest, and the Franco-Belgian invasion of the Ruhr again spurred them into action.[77] They dropped out of organized activity in

1924 or early 1925, when both the international situation and the domestic situation in Germany cooled.

The next stop in the political careers of the "sporadic activists" was the SA and NSDAP. With one exception, they all joined the NSDAP in 1929 or 1930, as the Weimar Republic again slid into political and economic crisis. This was comparatively late for the men in this chapter.[78] The single exception is Fritz Lauerbach, who joined the Party in August 1925, although he waited until 1928 before joining the SA. He may have joined the Party early due to his membership in a völkisch organization, the Nationalsozialistische Freiheitsbewegung (NSFB), in 1924. The others joined the SA when they joined the Party.[79]

The explanation for the sporadic nature of the activism of this group is that they repeatedly responded to the series of major political crises that plagued the Weimar Republic. Their activism was strong enough to cause them to risk life and limb in a free corps in 1919 and often again later, and it was strong enough to cause them all to become involved repeatedly in right-wing activities, and it was certainly strong enough later to help them rise to high careers in the SA, yet they were not willing or not able to sustain this activism except in times of relative crisis. Of course, each "sporadic activist" often had personal motivations as well.

One explanation lies in a combination of age and social position. Otto Wagener, Ernst Heinrich Schmauser, and Max Luyken were professional officers before the war. Likewise, Friedrich Wilhelm Brückner was a prewar reserve officer. All four were therefore potentially closely tied to the more orderly and law-abiding world of the prewar period. They were also the four oldest "sporadic activists."[80] The combination of age and position led them to exercise some degree of restraint in their activities.

Others simply did not have enough time to become involved in politics unless prompted by a crisis. Fritz Lauerbach was studying medicine until 1920, and was then just establishing a career when the crisis of 1923 occurred. He very likely felt that he simply could not afford the time then, although he joined the NSFB in 1924.

Carl Caspary was also deeply engaged in his studies from 1920 to 1924 and working hard to support himself in his spare time. This limited his activity, although he did find time to become involved in the SA and NSDAP from late 1922 to late 1923.[81] Caspary is, in fact, a typical "sporadic activist."[82] He was born in August 1898 in the village of Illingen in the Saar. His father owned a pharmacy and must have counted as a part of the local village intelligentsia. Carl attended a Realgymnasium (a high school with an emphasis on modern languages and the sciences). At age seventeen, in the second year of the First World War, he left school for the trenches. He did not finish his schooling then, but was able to pass the Abitur after the war.

He served on the eastern and western fronts and was wounded three times. His left hand was crippled. He served in the infantry and later became a pilot. He was decorated for bravery and finished the war as a second lieutenant. His war record as a pilot and infantryman showed that he was a fighter, and his war did not stop with the armistice. In November 1918 he immediately joined a volunteer formation, the Deutsche Schutzdivision. In January 1919 he was badly wounded in the foot in a clash in a Berlin suburb. He must have liked the military life and planned to stay in the army, because he followed his unit into the Reichswehr, only leaving the service in April 1920. In this, he is not typical of the group.

After his free corps service, he attended universities in Munich and Erlangen. He joined a student corps or fraternity, but was not active in politics until late 1922. Typical of the "sporadic activists," he could not sustain his activism in the relative calm of 1921 and 1922. By October 1922 it was a different story. On October 1, he joined both the NSDAP and SA in Erlangen. His military background could be put to good use, and by June 1923 he commanded a battalion of the Nuremberg SA regiment.[83] Despite the subsequent ban on the SA and NSDAP in November 1923, he remained active in both until 1924, when he received a Ph.D. in Volkswirtschaft (economics) and left the university town of Erlangen.

His first job was as a temporary employee in the Reich Finance Ministry, and later he became a economist (Volkswirt) and industrial salesman in a private company. From 1924 to late 1929 he eschewed membership in any political or paramilitary organization, again typical of his group and most likely because of his business activities. But in October 1929 he rejoined the SA and NSDAP in the solid middle-class Berlin neighborhood around the Nollendorfplatz. In Berlin he was active in the Party administration, but was only a member of an SA reserve unit. This changed in 1931, when he moved to Pirmasens in western Germany. Here he was a Party speaker and the propaganda chief of his local Party district (Kreis). He also quickly rose to a position of responsibility on the staff of the local SA Untergruppe, and by July 1932 he was in command of his own SA Standarte.

Caspary became employed full-time by the SA in 1934, at first only as the commander of a Standarte, later of a Brigade. Just after the Anschluß with Austria, he was transferred to head the new SA school in Vienna. In the Second World War he served in the Luftwaffe and again saw combat, rising to the rank of major. In 1942 or 1943 he was apparently released from service for SA duties at the home front. In early 1942 he was promoted to SA Gruppenführer and took over the command of SA Gruppe Kurpfalz. At the very end of the war he was appointed to advise the local Gauleiter for the Volkssturm.[84]

A typical "sporadic activist," Carl Caspary was in a free corps in 1919, then did nothing until 1922, was active in the SA and NSDAP until 1924, then was inactive until 1929, his activity corresponding to periods of domestic crisis in Germany, his inactivity to periods of relative calm. His activist pedigree and his skills were enough to gain him full-time employment with the SA as early as 1934, but he was not promoted to the highest ranks until war cleared the path for advancement.

The Serial Activists

Nine SA leaders who joined between 1927 and 1930 ran through a chain of organizations before ultimately ending up in the NSDAP and SA.[85] They jumped from one organization to another, as if seeking a spiritual home. Alternatively, this moving from one organization to another can be seen as a progression, the development of the individual from a traditionally conservative outlook to a more radical, activist, and völkisch outlook. In this latter case, each organization through which the individual passed actively contributed to the further development of that ideology in a more radical direction.[86] This can be observed in several cases.

Typically, the men in this category go from service in the First World War[87] to service in a free corps,[88] pass through a Wehrverband, then join a political party or a völkisch group, again pass through a Wehrverband or two, and finally join the SA and NSDAP. The order may vary, as may the exact number of Wehrverbände and völkisch organizations, but this basic pattern holds true for 15 percent of the high SA officers who joined between 1927 and 1930.

Aside from service in the Great War and in a free corps, it is difficult to find terms with which to describe the actions of these nine men, since each belonged to his own particular series of organizations in his own particular order. Yet certain organizations do stand out as figuring in the past of more than one member of this category. The most common single organization that these men passed through was the Stahlhelm. Five men in this category belonged to it, all but one before 1924. Four also passed through the Frontbann. Two of these men joined the NSDAP immediately afterwards. Four of the nine also belonged to one or more völkisch organizations, and again, this led two of them to join the NSDAP as their next step.[89] Indeed, five claimed to have been members of the NSDAP or SA in 1922 or 1923. Two of these men were also in other völkisch groups afterwards. Thus, if we include the "first" NSDAP, it can be said that seven of the nine passed through at least one völkisch organization on their way to the post-1925 NSDAP. Three individuals passed through the DNVP, and two passed through the police. At least five of the nine can be said to have progressed in a more radical direction as they changed organizations.

The "serial activists" were all extremely active. Each belonged to at least four political or military organizations before they joined the NSDAP, and many passed through considerably more. All but one joined at least one Wehrverband and at least one nonmilitary political group or party. Although the military/paramilitary organizations dominate, the members of this group were clearly not one-sided militarists. Indeed, their interest in a combination of military and civilian modes of political activity may have been one of the major factors leading them to remain in the NSDAP (as opposed to continuing on to yet another organization), since it combined both in one organization. It also made them resemble the men discussed in the previous chapter much more than the "passive activists" or "sporadic activists" did. Certainly the growing success of the Nazi movement kept them from moving on after joining the NSDAP. It is quite possible that they would have eventually left the NSDAP/SA and continued their search if this had not been the case. Nevertheless, their commitment to Party values should not be doubted; six of the nine joined the NSDAP before 1930, at a time when its later success was by no means guaranteed.

A typical member of the group of "serial activists" is Herbert Fust.[90] He was born in June 1899 in the village of Langenfelde in Pommerania. His father leased and ran a large estate, and he intended to follow in his father's footsteps. He attended a Gymnasium for a short time, then a Realschule (high school with a practical and technical emphasis) from which he graduated with a Sekundareife, a degree which would have entitled him, had he wished, to fulfill his military service obligation as a one-year voluntary officer cadet (a status with some prestige in the Wilhelmine Empire). When Fust finished Realschule, however, the normal peacetime conditions didn't apply, for Germany was at war. Instead of finishing his training as an agricultural administrator, Herbert Fust joined the army. He served at the front for two years in a machine gun company and ended the war as a sergeant. In December 1918 he joined free corps Graf Kanitz in the Baltic, again serving in a machine gun unit, but this time with a promotion to staff sergeant (Unterfeldwebel). His service there ended in May 1919.

The following year, he resumed his career training and spent two years as an agricultural apprentice. He then studied agriculture for two semesters in Munich. There is no evidence that he ever came into contact with the NSDAP at that time. Unlike most of the group, who began their chain of activities much earlier, Herbert did not really participate until 1923. In that year, he joined the Stahlhelm, but remained in it only until 1924. Also in 1923, he joined the Deutschvölkische Freiheitspartei, to which he belonged until 1927. He was working as an agricultural inspector on an estate, and later he became an independent farmer. In 1924 he resumed his paramilitary activities by joining the Frontbann, to which he belonged until 1927, when his local unit was disbanded and the entire Frontbann organization folded.[91]

Fust clearly had a strong desire to continue to belong to a paramilitary organization, since he immediately joined another loosely associated with Gerhard Roßbach, an infamous free corps leader. He remained until late 1930, at which time he joined both the SA and the NSDAP. He did not hold any Party offices, but he served in 1932 first in the Mecklenburg-Schwerin Landtag and then in 1933 in the Reichstag.

He began his SA career as a simple SA-Mann (the lowest SA rank), but within three months Fust was already a Sturmführer (the equivalent of a lieutenant), and by September 1931 he had risen to command his own Standarte. In 1933 he was promoted twice and was given a full-time position in the SA, and in 1936 he was promoted to the rank of Gruppenführer. By this time his experiences in the Kampfzeit (the "period of struggle" before January 30, 1933) had left him depressed and out of control, for in that year his private life was in such a state that he was hauled before the Party court and nearly expelled from the Party. Only direct appeals from the national commander of the SA, Victor Lutze, and the powerful local Gauleiter,

Karl Kaufman, saved him. The sentence was commuted to an official warning.[92]

This brush with the Party court system must have done the trick, for his career continued unabated. He was in command of various SA Gruppen from 1933 until at least 1942, when he was transferred to command Gruppe Hansa. During the Second World War he again served in the army. He reached the rank of first lieutenant in 1940, and by 1942 he had served in France and Africa, where he was wounded and decorated. His fate since 1942 is unknown.

Herbert Fust was a typical "serial activist" because of the string of organizations to which he belonged before finishing in the SA and NSDAP. Although he was not continuously active from 1919 to 1930 (most others were), he did manage to belong to three Wehrverbände and one völkisch political party between 1923 and 1930. Among the group just discussed, he was actually one of the more "stable" members; several managed to belong to five or six organizations during roughly the same time. Within the SA he rose rapidly in rank and was employed full time soon after the NSDAP gained power (and access to state funding). Clearly, he must have been an energetic, ruthless, and dynamic personality to progress so quickly. But the hint of possible instability contained in his boundless serial activism before joining the NSDAP was borne out by his later difficulties in the Party courts and by his dissolute private life. Effective activists are not always stable individuals.

The Defectors

The group of "defectors" is the largest and most important of the highest SA leaders joining the Party between 1927 and 1930. In a way, it is similar to the group of "serial activists." Both groups are characterized by a consistently high level of activity in organized paramilitary or political organizations. The difference is that the "defectors" settled into one (sometimes several) particular organization(s) for a long time instead of skipping regularly from one organization to another. Long-term membership has been defined here as at least two years, but in fact all but two of the seventeen men in this group were members of their organization for at least three years.[93] Presumably, they were loyal until something caused them to become dissatisfied and leave. Roughly half then joined the NSDAP within one year of quitting their former organization, and the rest joined the NSDAP after two or more years.

This group is important for two reasons. It graphically illustrates the process whereby the NSDAP and SA began to attract members of rival right-wing organizations, particularly those more moderate than the NSDAP by 1929 or 1930.[94] Also, while the greatest
numbers of those wooed away from other organizations belonged to
the rank and file, many rival leaders were also won over. This influx
of skilled leaders came mainly in 1929 and 1930, just as the SA was
expanding and consolidating its organization to the point where
skilled leaders, and particularly potential staff officers, were urgently
needed and in short supply.[95]

The value of these men as potential leaders is neatly shown by
the high percentage of former officers. Twelve of the seventeen men
in the group were officers by the end of the First World War.[96] This in
itself is not unusual for the highest SA leaders, for we have already
seen that a great many of the men in previous chapters were former
officers, albeit mainly junior officers. The difference comes here in
the high number of professional officers, in the relatively high rank
of these officers, and in the relatively high number of officers with
general staff experience.[97] Eight of the twelve officers among the "defectors" were prewar professional officers.[98] All but one of these eight
held the rank of captain or higher by 1918, and since several continued their service after the war, by the time they left the army two
were generals, one was a major, and one was a colonel.[99] One was a
member of the elite general staff corps, another served on the Großer
Generalstab (great general staff of the Imperial German Army), and a
third served in the Württemberg Ministry of War. Five served in staff
positions during the war.[100]

Their leadership qualities are also demonstrated by the positions that they later occupied in a Wehrverband or political party. At
least twelve of the seventeen "defectors" occupied leadership positions in other organizations before joining the NSDAP, often rather
high positions.[101] In detail, two were leaders at the national level,[102]
four were leaders at the state level,[103] three were leaders at a lower
regional level,[104] two were leaders at the county level,[105] and one was
a local leader.[106] These men brought considerable leadership skills
into the SA, but the very fact of their defection increased the standing and prestige of the NSDAP. Many of the rank and file of these
organizations soon followed them into the NSDAP.[107]

The organizations from which these men "defected," and the
moment at which they left, depended very much on internal factors
within these organizations.[108] On the whole, the men came from right-

wing Wehrverbände. The only exceptions were the two who "defected" from the armed forces and one who was a member of the DNVP.[109] Only a few Wehrverbände were represented, however.[110] Six "defectors" came from the Stahlhelm,[111] three came from the Jungdeutscher Orden,[112] three came from the OC/Bund Wiking,[113] and two came from the Bund Oberland.[114] These were among the biggest of the Wehrverbände in the Weimar Republic, but it is not their size alone which makes them appear here.

On the whole, those coming from the Wehrverbände did so at a time when the whole concept of paramilitary associations was on the wane, although this must be seen only as a backdrop of general crisis within the Wehrverband movement, and not as a full explanation of why these particular individuals chose to leave and join the NSDAP at this time. Indeed, personal reasons may have played a very large part in their decision to quit and later switch to the NSDAP, and the politics of the local branch of the organization from which they "defected" most certainly did. For example, both of the long-term members of Bund Oberland left it in 1926.[115] This was a time when Bund Oberland was split by internal dissention and was casting about for a new policy to follow that would be appropriate for the contemporary political climate.[116] Likewise, those coming from the Jungdo came in 1926 or 1927, out of disagreement with its policy of rapprochement with France or due to a conflict between the Jungdo branch in Saxony and its central leadership over the question of participation in electoral politics.[117]

Similarly, the former members of the OC/Bund Wiking all left it in 1928. It had already seen many of its members leave since the failure of the Beer Hall Putsch in 1923. In 1926 the Bund Wiking was banned (the OC had already been banned), and Hermann Ehrhardt, its leader, led his men under the protective wing of the Stahlhelm, less out of support for that organization than in the hope of finding a place to hide with a chance of perhaps subverting it for his own ends. By 1926 he had abandoned his former putschism for an outward conversion to electoral politics, and he had also begun to advocate a rapprochement with France, policies which alienated many of his more radical supporters and which generally cost him much sympathy in right-wing circles. In 1928 he quit the Stahlhelm once again and gradually lost much of his influence. This provoked a crisis among his followers.[118]

The Wiking members who left in 1928 may have done so out of a feeling that their beloved "Chief" no longer had a chance of success, and they certainly did so at a time when the organization was languishing.[119] Those who were in the Stahlhelm present only a slight variation on this same theme: two members of this organization left it in 1927, and three left in 1930. In contrast to all other organizations, the majority of those coming from the Stahlhelm joined the NSDAP in the same year that they left that organization.[120] The dates are significant, because by 1927 it was clear that the new Stahlhelm policy of "hinein in den Staat" (literally, "into the state"), announced in October 1926, was a serious effort to gain political influence for the Stahlhelm, and the internal conflict over its exact meaning exacerbated existing divisions within the organization. By 1930 the effects of the Great Depression were being felt, making all political questions in Germany more difficult. By this time, too, Stahlhelm members were confused about its political policy and its relationship to the Republic, and one of its major projects, the referendum against the Young Plan, was a failure.[121] The referendum against the Young Plan had brought cooperation with the NSDAP, however, and it is possible that the contrast between the dynamic and decisive NSDAP and the Stahlhelm caused at least some of the more radical Stahlhelm members to reconsider their loyalty to an organization that increasingly seemed to lack a clear and consistent antirepublican policy.

While many of the organizations out of which the "defectors" came had begun some sort of a compromise with the Republic, the NSDAP was able to stick to a hardline radical position. This made it attractive to radicals who were alienated by the lack of firmness and clarity in their own organizations. The fact that those who left their original organization in 1926, 1927, or 1928 did not join the NSDAP until 1929 or 1930 may be because it was not a clear alternative until it began to have a substantial national impact. On the other hand, it is not surprising that those who were able to recognize the potential of the NSDAP by 1930 subsequently rose to high positions in the Party or, in this case, the SA. They were able to join the SA and NSDAP just at a time when they were gaining momentum and beginning to expand rapidly, offering quick advancement, yet early enough so that they faced relatively little competition for new leadership positions. As we will see, a rather low percentage of the highest leaders of the SA joined after 1930, and nearly all had some sort of special skill that brought them to high rank.

Georg Oberdieck is a good example of a "defector."[122] Born in Hanover in January 1869, the son of a physician, Oberdieck attended a Gymnasium and earned an Abitur before entering Field Artillery Regiment no. 10 of the Royal Prussian Army in 1890 as an officer cadet. In 1891 he was commissioned as a second lieutenant in the regular army. He served in several artillery regiments and on the Großer Generalstab in Berlin, reaching the rank of major. When war broke out he was assigned as the general staff officer of the zeppelin *Viktoria-Luise,* and he later served as a staff officer and a regimental commander. He was wounded twice during the war and highly decorated.[123] He commanded an artillery regiment in the Reichswehr from 1919 to 1920, and left the service in October 1920 as a full colonel. Typical of many of the other "defectors," he was not in a free corps[124] and was not active in a number of organizations. In fact, he loyally served only one organization, the Stahlhelm, to which he belonged from 1924 to 1930. During this time, he occupied the important post of Gauführer (regional leader) of Hannover for one year.[125]

Within two months of leaving the Stahlhelm, Georg Oberdieck had joined the NSDAP, and a month later he joined the SA. After a short period as an ordinary SA-Mann, he rose to command a Sturm and received the rank of Sturmführer, the lowest of the SA officer ranks. After several months he was transferred to a staff position with Gausturm Hannover-South. He remained in staff or SA school positions until September 1939, when he was made acting head of SA Gruppe Niedersachsen, standing in for Max Linsmayer and later Günther Gräntz, who were the actual commanders of the Gruppe but who were serving with the Wehrmacht at the time.[126]

Oberdieck was promoted to Obergruppenführer in early 1944. Although it is not known if he served in the Second World War, his age makes it doubtful. It was more efficient to leave him at home to look after the SA, freeing a younger SA commander for military service. He is typical of many of the skilled administrators and soldiers who joined the SA in the middle years of the Kampfzeit, who were too old or too conservative to lead soldiers physically into street battles, but who were nevertheless able to perform yeoman service by organizing the staffs, doing the planning, and training younger leaders. While much of the shock force of the SA came from young men eager to physically take control of the streets, it should not be forgotten that it took much detailed planning and dedicated training to turn those aggressive young men into a formidable and well-organized Party army.

Oberdieck's "defection" to the NSDAP cost the competing Stahlhelm an important leader, and it surely brought the NSDAP not only Oberdieck's skills but also considerable prestige, at least locally where Oberdieck was known. Although his personal motives can't be determined from the documents at hand, Oberdieck's "defection" in 1930 was clearly a sign of problems within the Stahlhelm and one more milestone on its path to decline.

The Party Soldiers

The final path into the SA between 1927 to 1930 led through the NSDAP. Five men joined the NSDAP in 1925 or 1926 but did not immediately join the SA. Instead, they waited a year or longer. The fact that they did not get involved in the SA immediately leads one to assume that they were first attracted to the ideological or political side of the NSDAP, and only later became interested in the paramilitary activities of the SA. This is a small group, for whom information is often less complete than for the average SA officer in this study.[127] This makes any conclusions drawn about them rather tentative. Nevertheless, three of the five are clearly men who were leaders in the Party organization before joining the SA and who continued to be afterwards.[128] They began as Party activists, joined the SA somewhat later, perhaps out of a sense of duty more than anything else, but nonetheless were active in both organizations in parallel. Then, at a given point, they switched their main efforts to the SA and finally left the Party administration altogether, at least for a significant time.

The reasons why they were forced to make a choice between leadership in the Party and leadership in the SA are clear. By the late 1920s the SA began insisting that SA leaders should devote their full energies to the SA and should not be leaders in the Political Organization of the Party at the same time. The reasons why they joined the SA at all, after first being active in the Party, and why they then made the decision to devote full time to the SA instead of to the Party organization are not as clear and may often have been personal in nature.

It is known that many older veterans did not physically feel up to participating in the SA in the early 1920s, but did participate later, in the early 1930s, when the street battles between the SA and its opponents had reached such a critical point that the Party encouraged every man who could to don SA uniform. Personal advancement may also have seemed easier in the SA. In some places by the late 1920s, the SA was much better organized and much more dynamic than the corresponding local Party organization, and this fact must have had a bearing on any man's decision to opt for the SA. In any case, the above considerations suggest that too sharp a distinction between SA leaders and Party leaders in terms of character or background may not be justified, at least as far as the *Alte Kämpfer* are concerned. The decision to opt for a career in either the Party or the SA may have been as much a matter of chance or local conditions as something that was based on some fundamentally different type of background or character common to SA or Party leaders as a group.

Three of the five "Party soldiers" were veterans of the First World War. None were professional officers, and only two were reserve officers.[129] The two nonveterans were too young to have served. At least two of the five were subsequently in a free corps,[130] and one, Finck von Finckenstein, was active in various paramilitary organizations after that. The rest do not seem to have been particularly active, although this may be a reflection of the lack of information. As far as can be determined, only one member of the group joined the NSDAP before the Beer Hall Putsch in 1923.[131]

Two members of the group joined the NSDAP in 1925, and three joined in 1926. All but one waited at least two years before joining the SA. The sole exception to this is Robert Bergmann, who joined the Party in 1926 and then joined the SA a year later. But even then, he served in the SA for only one year before quitting, and he only rejoined it in 1931.[132]

Three of the five were Ortsgruppenleiter (leaders of a local Party chapter) and then district leaders (Bezirksleiter) in the Party organization before joining the SA, and one of these three was even a business manager in the administration of his Gau.[133] Four of the five subsequently went on to become Reichstag deputies for the Party, and one later resumed his Party career.[134]

All seem to have risen swiftly in the SA hierarchy once they joined. This may have been due to their existing Party seniority and connections, or it might have been due to the fact that they were simply skilled leaders. With the exception of Bergmann, all actually commanded an SA-Gruppe and had considerable other "frontline" command experience with the SA, the point being that they were capable SA leaders and not just Party hacks who owed their ranks to their connections or to their standing in the political administration of the Party. Robert Bergmann, the exception, actually owed his high rank to the fact that he was Ernst Röhm's adjutant while Röhm was

SA chief of staff, and he was chosen for this august position because he had served as Röhm's adjutant in the army during and after the First World War and had even saved Röhm's life.[135] In fairness to Bergmann it should be pointed out that he had commanded a Sturmbann and had been promoted to the rank of Sturmbannführer (roughly equivalent to major in the army) on his own before becoming Röhm's adjutant.

The top leaders of the SA who joined from 1927 to 1930 made a significant contribution to both the NSDAP and the SA. While the top SA leaders who joined in 1925 or 1926 generally played a more important role in the NSDAP and were more often active in völkisch organizations beforehand, the group joining between 1927 and 1930 was also deeply committed to Nazi ideology. Although less active in Party leadership than the group who joined the SA and NSDAP in 1925 or 1926, eighteen members of the 1927-30 group did hold positions of responsibility in the Party apparatus.[136] The greatest number were Kreisleiter (district leaders)[137] or served in the administration of a Gau or at the national level.[138] Moreover, all but two of the ten who served at the Gau or national level did so before 1933. Interestingly, the majority of those who were district Party leaders or who served at the Gau or national level came out of the "defector" or "Party soldier" groups discussed above.[139] This again illustrates the value of the "defectors" as leaders.

The men in this chapter took one of several paths into the SA. Two of these paths were especially significant. These were the "defectors," and "serial activists." Both categories are important in supplying the SA with men who combined leadership ability and experience with drive and activism. The careers of these men vividly illustrate the process whereby the SA (and therefore the NSDAP) grew by absorbing many of its rivals and competitors. It is extremely significant for the growth of both the SA and NSDAP that they were able to attract capable people. It is also significant that these new recruits were so fundamentally similar to the body of SA leaders already in place and that they already possessed the skills necessary to lead a mass paramilitary organization. Without this influx of capable leaders at a time when the SA and NSDAP were expanding, the twin organizations could never have risen to power.

With the steady growth of both the SA and NSDAP and the perfection of their organization, the depression years saw the Nazi movement increasingly capable of acting nationally on a massive scale. During the early 1930s, not only was the scope of SA activities greater than ever before but the degree of violence it engaged in was also far greater. With a basically sound organizational structure in place thanks to the efforts of von Pfeffer and his commanders, the expansion of the scope and violence caused the SA to recruit a variety of specialists into its higher leadership. These men are the subject of the next chapter.

4

The Specialists,
1931-1932

No man is more closely associated with the SA than Ernst Röhm. The SA's contribution to the expansion and success of the Nazi Party in 1931 and 1932 while under his leadership was absolutely crucial to its assumption of power in January 1933. These two years were the most pivotal of the entire Kampfzeit, a time when the NSDAP had to prove to itself and to Germany that it had made the transition from a small sectarian collection of cranks and true believers into a modern mass political party. Two factors gave these critical years a special tension and immediacy for members of the Nazi Party and indeed for anyone engaged in political activity in Germany at this time. The first was the Great Depression and the enormous hardship and suffering that it caused. In 1931, over one-fifth of the German workforce was unemployed, and in 1932 this percentage had risen to almost one-third.[1] The second factor was the increased radicalization and violence of political activity. The two factors were, of course, intimately related. For the SA and NSDAP, the radicalization of political discourse was expressed in two overriding ways: the increase in violence and an all but unbearable acceleration of political activity. In 1931 and 1932 an ever-tightening spiral of electoral campaigns fought on the local, state, and national levels stretched the institutional and personal resources of the SA and NSDAP almost to the breaking point.

The pressure was intense. The growing level of violence, for which the SA was of course not without blame itself, meant that Party members and especially SA members were in constant danger. By the summer of 1932 the level of violence approached a state of latent civil war. The endless electoral campaigns brought increasing success to the NSDAP (at least until the November 1932 Reichstag election) and to that extent helped to keep morale high and ensure a steady stream of converts to the Party. But they also kept the Party and SA working at a fever pitch, and this gradually ate up and wore out not only the savings and physical property of the Party and SA but also the patience and nerves of the members. Sacrifices (and debts) mounted, but even the greatest effort did not bring a majority of votes to the Party, and many began to question the validity of any further pursuit of the legality policy, while others voiced fears that the movement could not continue under the strain. It was within this context that Röhm took command of the SA.

Röhm, the Political Soldier

Ernst Röhm was a soldier.[2] For him this was not an occupation but a way of life. He was straightforward and down to earth, even earthy, and capable of brutality and violence. Yet many contemporaries, even among his opponents, acknowledged that he was one of the few genuinely likable Nazis. He said that he never felt comfortable in civilian clothes, and he led the simple life of a soldier, yet he also acquired a taste for luxury, and in the days after the takeover of power he could be seen riding in his posh limousine or holding lavish banquets for the Berlin diplomatic community. By all accounts he was brave, and he was wounded and decorated in the First World War. Yet his military reputation was that of an extremely competent and energetic staff officer, a capacity in which he served through most of the Great War, during the German Revolution in Freikorps Epp, and later in the Reichswehr. Indeed, for some he was too competent. He seemed to positively delight in complicated decrees and tables of organization that often could not be put into practice with the means at hand. Yet for all his desire to be a soldier and for all his ability as a cool and calculating staff officer, Röhm had thrown away a secure and rewarding career as a professional officer and had been forced to resign from the army due to his ceaseless and illegal political activities in support of the radical nationalist, racist, and above all putschist forces in Munich in 1923. For if Röhm was a soldier, he was also a political soldier, a curious combination of the professional military man— often showing boundless contempt for civilians—and the völkisch politician who was at home in the corridors of the Reichstag or in beery meeting halls.

Röhm was a loyal follower of Adolf Hitler, yet he was never blinded by the myth of the Führer. He was the only high Party leader

SA Stabschef and Captain Ernst Röhm with adjutant (possibly Count Carl du Moulin-Eckart), October 11, 1931, at the time of the founding of the "Harzburg Front." Courtesy of the Bundesarchiv.

who addressed Hitler with the familiar *du* instead of the more formal *Sie*, and he never hesitated to tell Hitler the truth as he saw it—with ultimately tragic results. He also seems to have been much less of a radical anti-Semite than most high Party leaders, and equally as unlikely, he seems to have pursued a genuine policy of rapprochement with France in his brief foray into foreign policy in 1933 and 1934.[3] In the final analysis, Röhm appears a bit theatrical, a Falstaff in a brown shirt, a freebooter out of his time, and a man of sincere if fatally contradictory convictions.

Ernst Röhm was born on November 28, 1887, in Munich. His father was a Bavarian civil servant, and all his life Röhm maintained a romantic but profound attachment to the Bavarian royal house of Wittelsbach. He attended a prestigious Gymnasium and then joined the Bavarian army as an officer cadet. He was commissioned as a second lieutenant in the Royal Bavarian Infantry Regiment no. 10, "Prince Ludwig," in 1908. Just before the war he was promoted to first lieutenant, and in 1917, to captain. He was badly wounded, and his face was permanently disfigured. He later served as an adjutant in the Bavarian Ministry of War, perhaps learning something of politics and parliaments in the process. After this he served as a general staff officer, and in this capacity he joined Freikorps Epp in April 1919, apparently bored with peacetime duty in his home garrison of Ingolstadt and eager to help put down the revolution. He was subsequently taken into the Reichswehr, serving on the staff of the city commandant of Munich and later on the staff of Military District (Wehrkreis) VII.

In both of these latter capacities, Röhm was officially and unofficially engaged in hiding weapons from the Allies that were to be surrendered according to the Versailles treaty, and he was issuing the same weapons to the Einwohnerwehr (citizens' militia) and later the Wehrverbände in Bavaria. Although he was a serving officer in the army, he was also an officer in the Reichsflagge, a Bavarian Wehrverband, and a member of a political party, the DAP (later to become the NSDAP), from 1919 on. Indeed, Röhm overstepped his official duties and responsibilities in the supply and coordination of the various right-wing paramilitary groups to such an extent that he was forced to resign from the Reichswehr in late 1923.

Röhm was a participant in the Beer Hall Putsch and a main defendant in the subsequent trial, but he served little time in jail and no time in prison for the crime of high treason, of which he was so proudly guilty. Continually active in the SA and paramilitary movement in 1924 and 1925, he nominally led the SA for a time and founded the Frontbann, his own creation, which was intended to provide a national cartel of independent Wehrverbände in the grand but by then sadly outdated putschist tradition. He was given the task of leading the SA again in 1925 when it and the Party were rebuilt, but he resigned with bitterness as both head of the SA and the Frontbann when he and Hitler were unable to agree on the SA's proper relationship to the Party. Employed for a time as a book salesman, Röhm eagerly accepted an offer to train the Bolivian army in 1928, happy once again to find employment as a soldier. He remained in Bolivia until Hitler summoned him back to Germany in the late summer or fall of 1930. By this time even he realized that the day of the putschist Wehrverbände was over, and he had accepted the necessity of a legal parliamentary strategy and of subordination of the Party's paramilitary wing to the "politicians."

Yet this last statement still begs the question: Why was Ernst Röhm chosen to lead the SA?[4] On the face of it, Hitler's choice is baffling.[5] Few of his subordinates had shown as much independence and stubborn conviction in their own ideas. Röhm had no compunction about telling Hitler exactly what he thought, even if what he had to say was less than pleasant. Worse, his last dealings with Hitler had been quite unsatisfactory, and they had parted in anger.

Significantly, this had been no trivial personal conflict but a fundamental disagreement over the SA's relationship to the political wing of the Party, and Röhm had supported the outdated and hopelessly inadequate putschist-Wehrverband strategy. Röhm was unconstrained and blunt, and he treated Hitler not as a superior but as an equal. Indeed, their relationship went back to a time when Röhm had clearly been more powerful than Hitler. Some even go so far as to say that he "invented" Hitler,[6] and while this may be an exaggeration, it is safe to say that Hitler and the NSDAP were long dependent on Röhm and other military people who controlled the flow of money and arms in Munich.

Röhm was also a professional officer, with strong ties to the army, the Bavarian officer corps, and the Bavarian royal house. Hitler had ambivalent feelings toward officers in general,[7] and if it was less certain that Röhm shared the lack of political acumen typical of the officer class, it was clear that he had loyalties that might conflict with those toward Hitler and the Party.

He was a problematic figure for another reason. He was a homosexual, which was not acceptable in German society at large and was particularly feared in the conservative, traditional world of the army and the paramilitary associations. Although his homosexuality did not become widely known until some of his private letters were published in 1932, it is highly doubtful that Hitler and others in the Party did not know earlier, especially given Hitler's famous decree on morality, which was issued five weeks after Röhm took office. But even to those who did not know of Röhm's sexual preference, he was suspect. His bluntness and combativeness had brought him many enemies over the years, and the fact that he had "turned his back" on Germany to go to Bolivia and thus had "shirked his responsibilities" in the battle for Germany's "freedom" did not make him any more welcome.

Yet for all his independence, Röhm was completely loyal to Hitler and the NSDAP, and for Hitler, that counted for a great deal. His long relationship with Hitler had created a deep bond between the two men, and because Röhm was a Bavarian and had been a member of the Party as long as Hitler himself, it was likely that the two would share a common outlook and find a common strategy. Moreover, Hitler was in a much stronger position in 1930 than he had been in 1923 or 1925. He was now the head of a strong national movement, and he had ensured that the paramilitary wing of the Party would not dominate it as it had in 1923 and as it had threatened to do in 1925. Röhm returned from Bolivia to a vastly different political situation than he had left, and he was shrewd enough to see that it demanded new tactics. In addition, he himself was in a much weaker position. His absence had left him without a coherent faction of supporters within the Party or elsewhere, and he was out of touch with the situation as it stood.

The fact that Röhm had long been absent from the political scene in Germany was an advantage for Hitler. Aside from some now long out-of-date feuds, Röhm returned as a man uncompromised by the recent conflicts in the SA and Party. His lack of supporters and his sexual orientation isolated him, making him dependent on Hitler and thus more malleable than almost anyone else whom Hitler could have chosen.[8] On the other hand, Röhm was a proven quantity as a leader and administrator. As a former officer, he had the technical knowledge and skills to do the job, and he was not about to tolerate disobedience and poor discipline within the SA. He was also a strong enough personality to make sure that the SA remained under control, a constant concern for Hitler and the leadership of the NSDAP who always feared that the actions of the SA could lead to a ban of the entire Party. The guarantee of SA discipline, combined with Röhm's military background, outlook, and personal contacts, would also make the SA attractive to the Reichswehr, a factor which was taking on added importance at just the time of Röhm's appointment. Above all, remember that Röhm was a political soldier. He shared Hitler's basic goal and outlook, and if he was a soldier first, he had also learned to think like a politician.

COPING WITH SUCCESS

Röhm's tenure as the leader of the SA[9] from its inception until his purge in 1934 was dominated by three great issues: rapid growth of the SA, continued problems of cohesion and discipline, and the question of the relationship between the NSDAP/SA and the state. Röhm's main contribution to the Party in 1931 and 1932 lay in the way in which he helped it to address all three of these issues, just as ultimately his downfall after the Nazis seized power resulted from his failure to address them in a way that was appropriate to new conditions and to Hitler's new policies.

At the time Röhm officially assumed his command on January 5, 1931, the SA had roughly 77,000 members.[10] Within three months the SA had passed the 100,000 mark and was numerically stronger than the Reichswehr for the first time.[11] By December 15, 1931, it had grown to 260,438, more than three times its strength of just one year earlier.[12] In 1932 this figure more than doubled once again.[13] There could be no more vivid proof that Hitler had been persuaded to drop all earlier plans to limit the size of the SA and that he had decided to allow it to develop into a mass organization, parallel to a similar tendency in the Party.[14] One of Röhm's most important achievements for the Party was his mastering of the rapid and unexpected growth of the SA and all of the problems that came with it. These problems were many, because the expansion of the SA and the intensification of the political struggle in which it was engaged were driven by the Great Depression and the immense suffering it caused the German and Austrian people.

On the level of organization, it was a tribute to the soundness of Franz von Pfeffer's original planning that the SA was able to embrace these new members with only a few changes in its basic organization. Röhm immediately discussed abandoning von Pfeffer's equation of rank with position, although this measure did not actually go into effect until the fall of 1931.[15] More important, he created a new unit, the Sturmbann, which came between the Sturm and the Standarte in the hierarchy of SA units. In terms of size, it was identical to the old Standarte (250-600 men). This provided more flexibility to the SA in absorbing ever larger numbers, and it brought the organization of the SA closer to that of the army.[16] The Sturmbann not only provided the SA with greater flexibility to expand but it also was part of an effort to save money for the Party. Since 1923 the NSDAP had awarded an expensive metal and fabric insignia, the "Standarte," to well-established Hundertschaften (the precursor of the Standarte), and the custom continued with the Standarten. By inserting the Sturmbann at the level where an SA unit had been entitled to receive a Standarte, and increasing the size of the Standarte to between 1,000 and 3,000 men, the party was saved the expense of having to award hundreds of new Standarten insignia to keep up with recent expansion.[17] Röhm also introduced the Untergruppe as a replacement of the former Brigade[18] as the next level above the Standarte, and in the cases where size permitted, the Untergruppe was to be coterminous with the Gau boundaries and be called a Gausturm.[19] Above the Untergruppe, Röhm introduced the Gruppe and replaced the five OSAF-Stellvertreter with eleven Gruppenführer, again increasing flexibility and, perhaps more important, decreasing the power of the sometimes rebellious OSAF-Stellvertreter.[20] From February 1931, when these new regulations were first published, to mid-1934, the lower levels of the SA were in almost continuous reorganization and expansion, as Trupps grew into Stürme, Stürme grew into Sturmbanne, Sturmbanne became Standarten, old Standarten subdivided, and new Untergruppen, Brigaden, and Gruppen emerged.

To manage these new units, control them, and do the increasingly complex planning necessary to perform the tasks of the SA given its new size, Röhm also greatly expanded the staff structure of both the SA supreme command (OSAF) and subordinate units. He recruited specialists to fill many of these staff positions. Some of these men were Röhm's old cronies and former Bavarian officers.

In part, the expansion of the SA staff was necessary to enhance the cohesion and discipline of the organization. The necessity of such measures was made plain by the rapid expansion of the SA and by continued outbreaks of poor discipline, not least among the higher leaders of the SA. Efforts at establishing cohesion focused on ensuring that the organizational structure and workings of the SA were as uniform as possible, increasing the training of SA leaders, many of whom by now were not veterans of the First World War, and ensuring that the SA was ideologically uniform and in tune with the Party. These were life-and-death questions in an organization that was undergoing rapid expansion yet lacked capable leaders at lower levels and had barely begun to develop any real cohesion before it was faced with the task of absorbing thousands of new members.[21]

The chronic lack of qualified lower-level leaders was only one of the factors Röhm had to address in order to establish better discipline and control within the SA. He had taken over an organization that was still in the process of changing from a collection of independent regional and local bands into a uniform national unit. Such a transformation was not without conflict, and Röhm inherited all of the resentments associated with it, yet he created a command apparatus capable of consolidating it. Older resentments against the Party organization, the money shortages, and the disagreement about appropriate strategy for the Party had been temporarily suppressed but could erupt at any time. On top of all this, Röhm naturally provoked the usual mistrust and resentment faced by any newcomer replacing an old and respected leader (von Pfeffer, in this case). In the long run, the uniform system of training and indoctrination that he instituted would transform the SA into a relatively homogeneous and disciplined organization, but in the short term, Röhm had to establish his own authority and ensure discipline and a proper working relationship with the Party organization.

After receiving bitter complaints from Walther Stennes, the powerful OSAF-Stellvertreter in eastern Germany,[22] Hitler suddenly removed Stennes from his command and ordered him to meet him in Weimar. Stennes refused.[23] This open attack on Stennes helped Röhm assert his authority. Despite attempts to form a rival organization and the mass resignation of many SA leaders in the east who were loyal to Stennes, the affair passed quickly, with little real damage to the SA. The rebels were quickly isolated and systematically purged from the SA, and a concerted Party and SA effort restored order and never allowed the revolt to spread beyond a fairly narrow group in eastern Germany. After this, there was no chance of effective resistance to Röhm on the part of the other OSAF-Stellvertreter, and they quickly fell into line.

Although the handling of the Stennes affair actually increased resentment and lowered morale within the SA at the time, it established Röhm's authority and formed the basis of his further actions. It also deepened the tensions between the SA and SS, especially in eastern Germany, for the SS had sided with Hitler and against Stennes and his supporters from the beginning of the conflict. The tension between the SA and SS (still both part of the same organization) would be one of the factors leading to the purge of the SA in 1934.

In the spring of 1931, shortly after the Stennes affair had been laid to rest, Röhm announced he was replacing the five (six, if Austria is included) large and powerful OSAF-Stellvertreter regions with ten Gruppen, thus spreading their power among twice the number of SA leaders, and allowing for better control by making each Gruppenführer responsible for a smaller area than before.[24] Although individuals might grumble, after the reorganization Röhm was clearly in control, and the higher SA leaders were all forced to dance to his tune.

By putting himself in complete control of the SA, Röhm was also ensuring that the level of friction between the SA and the Party's Political Organization would drop to a tolerable level. He went to great lengths to ensure a good working relationship. The SA was subordinated to the Party in a clear fashion, and he reiterated the necessity of obtaining permission from the Party (now referred to as the Politische Organisation, or PO, to distinguish it from the SA and other Party affiliates) for any public appearance of any SA unit of Sturm size or above. SA leaders were also required to consult with the local Gauleiter before appointing any subordinate commanders. Röhm was nevertheless careful not to sacrifice any real control over the SA in his campaign to conciliate the PO.[25] Yet it is important to recognize that Röhm could only do so much and that any effort to establish discipline in the SA and ensure cooperation with the PO could only smooth over and cover up fundamental conflicts.

Without the power to compel obedience instead of merely ask for it, no one could guarantee that the SA would remain obedient to anyone. And without a fundamental clarification of the roles of the SA and PO and their relationship to one another, tension and friction between the two organizations would always exist. Röhm could not and did not bring about any definitive resolution of either of these two issues.[26] Just as in the case of the organizational structure of the SA, discipline and relations with the PO were characterized from 1931 to 1934 by constant and often remarkably skillful temporization and ad hoc solutions. It was the ability to do this, particularly in the organizational realm, which was Röhm's major contribution.

As important as Röhm's organizational talents and leadership were, what actually maintained discipline and held friction between the SA and PO to a tolerable level was the fact that the SA and Party were both exceptionally busy in 1931 and 1932 and riding the crest of an extraordinary wave of success. Problems could easily be ignored as long as the SA and Party were kept busy and as long as their efforts seemed to bring progress. Yet, with the mounting pace and level of political conflict in 1932, Röhm was less and less able to control the SA and more concerned with simply keeping it moving in the right direction. Given the conditions under which he had to work, this may have been the best that he could expect, but in any case, the failure to resolve the fundamental issues of discipline and the relationship to the PO would rebound upon Röhm and the SA in 1933 and 1934 after the takeover of power.

During Röhm's early tenure as Stabschef (chief of staff), the NSDAP radically altered its attitude toward the state and its institutions.[27] Since the failure of the Beer Hall Putsch in Munich in 1923, Hitler had strictly prohibited cooperation with state institutions, including the army. A change in the noncooperation policy, fraught as it was with risks for both sides, had great potential benefits for the NSDAP and for the army as well.

The army stood to gain the support of a party whose paramilitary wing was now quite large. The Reichswehr had long been working secretly with organizations like the Stahlhelm on matters of national defense, but they were beginning to be eclipsed by the SA in many areas. This was particularly the case in Germany's eastern border regions and eastern Prussia, where the Reichswehr maintained a covert and illegal defense militia. The change in the NSDAP's policy came at a time when the Reichswehr was expanding this illegal militia system and SA participation was welcomed, albeit with certain reservations.[28]

As for the NSDAP, all levels of the Party agreed that any seizure of power, legal or otherwise, could only be carried out with the acceptance if not support of the Reichswehr. The events of 1923 had shown this without a shadow of a doubt. In this light, the opening toward the Reichswehr was a necessary political chess move if the NSDAP was to be a serious contender for power in Germany. Participation in the national defense and other activities in support of the state was also a way of building bridges to the more traditional conservative parties. As a result, the NSDAP would have more contact with them through these activities and would begin to appear more respectable, perhaps even *regierungsfähig* (capable of forming or participating in a government). Equally as important, it would begin to undermine the greater support that these parties (like the DNVP) enjoyed in government and military circles.[29]

Mass meeting of Stahlhelm (left) and SA, SS, and NSDAP in Bad Harzburg, October 11, 1931, marking the founding of the "Harzburg Front," a loose alliance between the NSDAP and other conservative organizations including the Stahlhelm and DNVP. In the SA group, left to right, are Heinrich Himmler (in black SS cap and tie), Ernst Röhm, two unidentified SA leaders, Adolf Hühnlein (with goggles), and Hermann Göring. Courtesy of the Bundesarchiv.

Röhm, who certainly favored greater cooperation with the Reichswehr, thus gained an additional and highly sensitive area of SA activity to master. As it turned out, despite the modification of the NSDAP's policy at this time and the close cooperation with the Reichswehr that developed in many areas, the issue of the relationship between the two organizations remained problematic. Although it was not foreseeable in 1931 or 1932, this would eventually become the issue over which Röhm would lose his life and the SA would forfeit its preeminent position within the Nazi movement.

Despite the growing support for the SA within the Reichswehr, the rising level of violence in the streets prompted the government of Chancellor Heinrich Brüning to ban the SA on April 13, 1932.[30] The ban was lifted on June 14, 1932, and was supremely ineffective in its stated goal of lessening political violence. The SA had been warned beforehand, possibly by the Reichswehr, and had quickly hidden important documents and equipment.[31] Since the Party itself had not been banned, the SA could easily go underground and carry on as before under the guise of Party work or innocent-sounding sports associations.

The true results of the SA ban were unexpected. It brought the NSDAP a strong wave of sympathy from nearly the entire conservative camp in Germany. It also led to opposition within the Reichswehr, which caused the resignation of the Reichswehr minister, General Wilhelm Groener, and his replacement by his former protegée, General Kurt von Schleicher. In the end, the political fallout of the SA ban served to further the cause of the NSDAP. But the ban had another positive result for the SA in particular.

Although the SA ban did disrupt SA operations somewhat and cost the SA a certain amount of money, it also allowed the SA high command to reorganize at its leisure for the first time since the massive membership expansion had begun in 1930-31. The fiction that the SA had been disbanded and thus needed to be completely rebuilt when the ban was lifted also gave the SA a means of purging its ranks of unsuitable leaders, for all SA leaders had to be "reappointed" or confirmed in their posts when the ban was lifted and the SA was "reestablished."[32] When the reorganization was complete, the SA stood in its final form prior to the Machtergreifung (seizure of power), the culmination of eight years of development, a finely tuned instrument poised to help the NSDAP to gain power.

On the eve of the Machtergreifung in January 1933, the SA boasted 500,000 members and was still growing.[33] The last reorganization had created five Obergruppen as an intermediate level between the OSAF and the Gruppen, designed to coordinate efforts of two or more Gruppen, deal with state agencies on a regional basis, and coordinate training and discipline.[34] It had expanded the number of Gruppen to 18, with 58 Untergruppen and 234 Standarten, guided by 5 inspectorates and a greatly expanded central command. The reorganization had also created the new Gruppenstab zur besonderen Verwendung (Gruppe-staff for special duties), a secret staff unit intended to coordinate general relations and covert military training with the Reichswehr.[35]

THE SPECIALISTS

Like Franz von Pfeffer before him, Ernst Röhm deserves credit for managing the reorganization and expansion of the SA, but he did not do this alone. The SA already had a strong yet flexible organization in place when he took command, as well as a large number of relatively homogeneous and competent officers. By 1931 it was late in the day to join the SA or, for that matter, the NSDAP and expect to rise very far in the ranks. By this time the upper levels of administration were already filled, despite a chronic lack of good leadership at lower levels.[36] Moreover, one would expect that any future additions to the top leadership ranks of either the SA or the Party would come from the next lowest echelons of leadership and not from the outside. This was mainly true, but there was a clearly defined group among those who rose to the top levels of the SA hierarchy who did, in fact, join the SA and often even the NSDAP in the early 1930s.

Forty-six SA leaders joined in 1931 or 1932.[37] In the main, these men were specialists, possessing distinctive skills that the SA needed as it expanded into a mass national organization. Yet though they offered important skills, it was not an accident that these particular individuals joined the SA. Others, sometimes with even better skills, might have been chosen or might have offered their services if professional qualifications were all that mattered. A key factor was that these men also possessed backgrounds in the military, Wehrverbände, and völkisch organizations that closely matched those of the existing highest SA leaders. They were thus able to fit into the organization and work with the SA leaders who were already in place. These men were outsiders, but in a fundamental way they were not strangers, since they shared many experiences and, on this basis, many common attitudes with the existing leadership. Many came to the SA because they knew Ernst Röhm or already had close ties to the NSDAP. Yet most of these men also followed the same "paths" into the SA that were established in the previous chapter.

As might be expected by now, most of the highest SA officers who joined the SA in 1931 and 1932 were combat veterans of the First World War.[38] Many, in fact, had been professional soldiers before the war, the majority of them officers.[39] By 1918, most veterans had been commissioned as officers if they had not already been officers before the war broke out.[40] The rank held by the end of the First World War was higher in this group than in previous groups; almost half of the officers were either captains or majors by 1918.[41] Moreover, a significant number had held a staff position either before or during the war.[42] The presence of so many officers and especially professional officers with staff experience and training in the group that joined the SA in 1931 and 1932 is a sign of the type of skills sought by the SA when they were recruited.

The immediate postwar years of turmoil and revolution saw most of the highest SA leaders who joined in 1931 and 1932 engaged in some sort of military activity. Roughly one-third were still in the regular army through the end of 1919.[43] Several of these same men had earlier served in free corps. Together, roughly one-third of the entire group had served in a free corps,[44] and several others served in limited-term volunteer units (Zeitfreiwilligenverbände) or civic guard units (Einwohnerwehren).[45] Of the free corps, only Freikorps Epp stands out as being represented by more than one member of the group. Fourteen free corps are represented in all, of which two were based in Bavaria.[46] Several men were members of veterans' organizations in 1919 or 1920, usually while they were serving in the army or a free corps, and only a few were members of a political organization.[47] As in previous chapters, the men here were active in a wide range of military organizations during the German Revolution.

This same pattern of activity primarily in paramilitary, military, or veterans' organizations holds true for 1921-23 as well. Although the men in this chapter were active in thirty-three organizations from 1921 to 1923, very few of these organizations are represented more than once. In what will be a familiar pattern by now, most were military or paramilitary—not political—in nature.[48] The organization to which the largest number of the group belonged by the end of 1923 was the Reichswehr,[49] followed closely by the NSDAP.

By the end of 1923 seven members of the group (15.2%) had joined the NSDAP. This is surprising, since these are men who joined the SA at a fairly late date (1931 or 1932), while earlier chapters have shown that members of the pre-putsch NSDAP tended to be quick to (re)join the SA.[50] Eight of the men in this chapter also participated in the Beer Hall Putsch of November 8-9, 1923.[51] In part, these high numbers are due to the fact that there are many Bavarians in this chapter (where the NSDAP was founded), and many of them entered the SA because of their old connections with Röhm and other SA leaders.

The Stahlhelm and the Reichskriegsflagge are two other organizations to which these men belonged in the early 1920s, especially in 1923.[52] In that year, the highest SA leaders who joined the SA in 1931 or 1932 were engaged in military or paramilitary activities, and one-quarter were on the government payroll.

By mid-1924, the level of membership in political or military organizations among the group had dropped dramatically, and many of those who remained active tended to change their affiliation, in part because many organizations had been banned in the wake of the putsch. Although the Wehrverbände remained favored, a significant number of the group became active in political organizations during this time. This was less a blossoming of new interest in politics than a forced switch of allegiance: with one exception, it was the former members of the NSDAP who now became involved in the völkisch groups and parties.[53] The former NSDAP members also tended to join the Frontbann, sometimes in conjunction with a völkisch group or another Wehrverband.[54] This only illustrates the way in which the Frontbann brought together men active in both paramilitary groups and völkisch organizations, former members of the NSDAP, as well as both south and north Germans. The Frontbann was indeed one of the most heavily represented organizations in 1924 among the group, and it ranks only behind the Stahlhelm and the Reichswehr.[55]

From 1925 to 1931, the number of men active in political or paramilitary organizations and the number of different organizations to which they belonged both fell steadily. Over the same period, the number who joined the NSDAP steadily increased. It should be remembered that, although members of this group often joined the Party at an early date, none of them (by definition) joined the SA until 1931 or 1932. Membership in völkisch organizations fell off first, but here, too, it should be kept in mind that very few men in the group were ever engaged in them. By the end of 1927 the two men from this chapter who were members of the Deutsch-Völkische Freiheitsbewegung, the Großdeutsche Arbeiterpartei, and the Tannenberg Bund had quit those organizations.[56] Membership in the Frontbann also fell off very quickly after Ernst Röhm resigned as its leader in 1925. But contrary to the findings in previous chapters, the NSDAP was rarely the next step for the former members of the Frontbann or völkisch organizations in the 1931-32 group.[57] Some went to other organizations, and many others simply dropped out of politics altogether. The organizations that held the loyalty of the largest numbers from the 1931-32 group and that held these loyalties the longest were the Reichswehr and the Stahlhelm.[58] While the Reichswehr was, of course, a profession for the men belonging to it, the Stahlhelm was not, and thus its ability to hold on to more of its members longer shows it to be one of the NSDAP's more effective competitors in the nationalist camp. On the other hand, this also made it a potential source of particularly good leaders, since it had a strong bureaucratic organization much like that of the NSDAP/SA.[59]

PATHS INTO THE SA

Many of the men in the 1931-32 group showed patterns of political and military activity that were remarkably similar to the "paths" followed by the men who joined the SA in 1927-30. This confirms that the patterns of activity found in the careers of the top SA leaders who joined from 1927 to 1930 are in fact significant and characteristic of the top SA leadership as a whole.

While there were strong similarities, there were also slight but notable nuances to the basic patterns that are unique to the men in this chapter. The pattern or path of the "serial activists"[60] is represented by only four individuals in this chapter, whereas the "sporadic activists" are as good as absent.[61] On the other hand, the "defectors," "passive activists," and "party soldiers"[62] are heavily represented in the 1931-32 group, although these "defectors" differ in some respects from those of the preceding chapter.

The Serial Activists

All four "serial activists"[63] joined the SA (or SS) in 1931, and two of the four were field commanders for most of their SA careers, as opposed to being staff specialists.[64] Richard Aster was a good example of a serial activist from the 1931-32 group.[65] He was born in Breslau in 1900, the son of a postal functionary (Postassistent). He attended a Realgymnasium, from which he graduated with an Obersekundareife. After this, he spent two years as an apprentice agricultural official (Landwirtschaftlicher Beamter). He later worked as a traveling salesman for photographic articles and was then employed full time by the SA from April 1932 on.

Although he could have escaped military service because of his age,[66] Aster volunteered for the army in September 1918 and actually managed to reach the front as part of an assault battalion (Sturmbataillon) several weeks before the armistice. His martial ardor was not satisfied by this short exposure to combat, however, and he rapidly volunteered for a series of free corps, serving first in the Grenzschutz in Posen in 1919 and early 1920 and then joining Freikorps Aulock during the Kapp Putsch. The putsch failed, and he found himself in civilian clothes again, but early in 1921 he found an opportunity to serve in Upper Silesia. Here he belonged to the resurrected Freikorps Roßbach. Although young, Aster was a firebrand and a good soldier. By November 1921, he held the rank of sergeant, although he was only twenty-one and commanded older men with more combat experience. He had also been wounded three times, twice while in the Grenzschutz and once again in Upper Silesia.

Typical of many serial activists, Aster was not just a soldier. As early as 1919, while in the Grenzschutz, he joined the Deutsch-Völkischer Schutz- und Trutzbund, and belonged to it until 1922.[67] After the fighting ended in Upper Silesia, he joined an Arbeitsgemein-schaft (work collective) formed out of Freikorps Roßbach. It supported itself by performing labor on the large Junker estates in the east, but its real purpose was to keep Roßbach's men together in anticipation of future military action.[68] After leaving the Arbeitsgemeinschaft, he again engaged in völkisch politics as a member of the Deutschvöl-kische Freiheitsbewegung and of the Großdeutsche Arbeiterpartei. At roughly the same time, he joined the Stahlhelm and led one of its local groups until 1927.

From 1927 until mid-1930, he was politically inactive, but in July 1930 he joined the NSDAP,[69] and in February 1931 he joined the SS. By the end of 1931 he was already an SS Sturmführer (the equivalent of an army lieutenant). In October 1932 he transferred to the SA and gradually rose through the ranks. He was promoted to Standartenführer in November 1934 and to Gruppenführer in 1942. During the war he served in the army, first as a sergeant and then as an officer in an antitank unit. In 1941 he was transferred to the Reich Ministry for the Occupied Eastern Territories.[70] He served in the administration of occupied Estonia and later as the Haupt-kommissar (governor) of that hapless country. He was last reported fighting in "Fortress Breslau" in 1945 and probably did not survive the war.

Aster was typical of the serial activists. He was active in eight organizations between 1919 and 1927, and the organizations with which he was involved included the military, paramilitary, and völkisch political ones. Like most of the serial activists, he got his start in the First World War as a member of the old Imperial Army, continued into the postwar period with a military organization, and then became involved with both paramilitary and völkisch political organizations. Like many, he dropped out of politics in the "good years" between 1925 and 1929 when the Wehrverbände and the völkisch organizations fell on hard times, but then joined the NSDAP and SA (SS) in the very early 1930s. The break between 1925 and 1930 is especially typical of the entire 1931-32 group, not just of the serial activists.

The Defectors

The "defectors" present the largest single block among the 1931-32 group, although the "passive activists" are a close second.[71] Just as in the earlier chapter on the 1927-30 group, remember that, by definition, the "defectors" participated in a single organization for a minimum of two years before joining the SA. In fact, all of the "defectors" in the 1931-32 group belonged to their respective organizations for a minimum of three years and many of them for substantially longer. Nine organizations were involved,[72] and they are very much like those from which the earlier (1927-30) defectors came. All but one (the DNVP) are military or paramilitary organizations. Only the Reichswehr and the Stahlhelm figured in the backgrounds of more than one of the 1931-32 cohort of defectors.

The Reichswehr was the second largest source of defectors, with four men, all of them officers.[73] If the other state-supported organizations are included, such as the police and Grenzschutz,[74] the number rises to six, making state organizations the largest single source of defectors. Clearly, the majority of the men coming from the Reichswehr and police do not represent true defectors in the sense that they were driven to quit the service out of any basic political disagreement with its policies. Rather, most were men who retired honorably from one profession and were now looking for a similar type of occupation.[75] On the other hand, the fact that men leaving the Reichswehr would join an organization that had a very definite political program and that they had previously been forbidden to join as long as they were Reichswehr officers is an indication that they must have been in at least basic ideological agreement with it, not that they were simply interested in a familiar line of work.[76] The degree to which the SA could draw leaders from the officer corps of the elite Reichswehr demonstrates the spread of sympathy with National Socialism that existed by the early 1930s.

The largest category of defectors came from the remnants of the collapsing Wehrverbände. Thus, former leaders of the Frontbann, Organisation Damm, and Bund Oberland came to the SA, and the continued fissures in the Stahlhelm brought another four men, for a total of seven.[77] With experience in similar organizations, these men made ideal SA leaders.

The one factor that sets the defectors in this chapter apart from those in the previous chapter is that the ones here were often inactive between leaving their original organization and joining the

NSDAP/SA. Many of the defectors out of the 1931-32 group were active, loyal members of a political or military organization in the early years of the Republic, and then they temporarily abandoned political activity. After a period of inactivity, often a year or two, they eventually found their way to the NSDAP and SA when the growing crisis caused by the Depression again called the stability of the Republic into question.

Two short biographies will illustrate the careers of representative "defectors." The first is Karl Lucke, a long-term member of a Wehrverband in Baden, and the second is Hans Fuchs, a member of the Bavarian State Police who left it in 1925 and then dropped out of political activity for several years before joining the NSDAP.

Karl Lucke was born in Postdam in 1889.[78] His father was a skilled machine worker (Maschinenmeister). After attending primary school, Lucke found work as a rider or horse exerciser (Bereiter) in the Imperial Stables in Berlin. After three years in this position, he began his military service and volunteered as a professional soldier in the First Baden Dragoons Regiment no. 20 in 1906. He served in another dragoon regiment throughout the First World War, was decorated for bravery, and was retired by his old regiment in October 1919 with the rank of Offizierstellvertreter.[79] As a former professional soldier, he was entitled to and obtained a job as a minor government functionary (rising to the post of Verwaltungsinspektor), a position which he held until 1934 when he became employed full time by the SA. In 1921 he joined Freikorps Damm (also known as Organization Damm), a locally based Wehrverband in Baden that grew out of the Einwohnerwehr (citizens' militia) movement. Lucke participated in this organization until 1928, when it disbanded. He was inactive in 1929, but joined the NSDAP in 1930. He served the Party as an adviser to his Gau on issues relating to government employees. He later served as a member of the Baden Landtag (state parliament) and the Darmstadt City Council. Ten months after becoming a member of the Party, he joined the SA. The SA was beginning to expand, and within three months he was placed in command of a Standarte and promoted to Standartenführer. In 1934 he was given command of a Brigade, and he remained in command of several brigades until 1942. He did not serve in the Second World War, most likely because of his age, but was instead promoted to SA Gruppenführer in 1942, and he commanded two different SA Gruppen, allowing younger SA leaders to serve at the front.

Born in Regensburg in 1877, Johann Baptist Fuchs was the son

The highest SA leaders congratulate Stabschef Viktor Lutze (right) on his fiftieth birthday. Hans Fuchs is the short man in the center of the photo, holding his hat with both hands. Max Jüttner is shaking hands with Lutze. Courtesy of the Bundesarchiv.

of a railway conductor.[80] He was fortunate enough to attend a humanistic Gymnasium. He graduated with the coveted Abitur. After graduating from the Gymnasium, he entered the Bavarian War College (Kriegsschule) and was commissioned as an active officer in 1899. He served in the Bavarian 17th Infantry Regiment until the outbreak of the First World War. He then served in one Prussian unit and several Bavarian units as a brigade adjutant, battalion commander, and general staff officer. He was highly decorated and ended the war as a captain in the general staff corps. After the war he continued his military service, first as chief of staff of Freikorps Bamberg, then as a battalion commander in Wehrregiment München, a unit formed by the Bavarian government to occupy and pacify Munich after its "liberation" from the hands of left-wing rebels in 1919. In November 1919 he was transferred to the Staatliche Polizeiwehr Bayerns (Bavarian state protective police), which later became the Bavarian Landespolizei (state police).[81] He served as a staff officer and district commander in Munich and Ansbach through October 1925, when he was retired as a police major. He also studied law and politics at the

University of Munich between 1923 and 1925. From 1925 until 1931 he worked in business. Throughout this time he was not active in political or military affairs. In early 1931 he joined the NSDAP and SA and immediately took full-time employment in the SA as a staff officer. He left active duty in the SA in 1934 after serving in the Bavarian Interior Ministry. By 1935 he was involved in unspecified Party settlement organizations.

Lucke and Fuchs illustrate different types of defectors. Lucke was a long and loyal member of a paramilitary organization. When that organization folded, he remained inactive for only a short time and then found the NSDAP. Fuchs was a professional soldier and police officer who retired in 1925 after several years of loyal service. He remained politically inactive for six years before he joining the NSDAP. While neither left his organization as the result of a disagreement over politics or for some other voluntary reason, the political character of their decision to join the NSDAP cannot be disputed.

The Passive Activists

Those of the "defectors" who abandoned politics completely for a year or two before joining the NSDAP and SA show some affinity with the "passive activists" of the 1931-32 group. At least fourteen men in this chapter fit the category of passive activists.[82] Five of them ended their activity by the end of 1925, and the rest were inactive for five or more years at any time. In one case, this long inactivity is known to have been imposed by a long prison sentence for the murder of suspected informers while serving in the Black Reichswehr.[83] In some other cases, although no information is given, it may be assumed that a lack of participation in political or military groups was the result of pressing family or job concerns. Nearly half of the passive activists were physicians, for example.[84] But the physicians in the previous chapters were among the most radical and active SA men, so profession alone is not a sufficient explanation for the lack of involvement prior to joining the NSDAP and SA. Given the ability of others to find time for political or paramilitary activity despite active careers or family difficulties, it must be assumed that the majority of the passive activists in this chapter were inactive out of a simple lack of interest or motivation.[85]

A short biography will illustrate the career of a typical passive activist in this chapter. Wilhelm Mörchen was a man who did not engage in any political or military activity after the war until he joined the NSDAP and SA in 1931.[86] Mörchen was born in Erndtebrück, Westphalia, in 1891 to the family of a workshop supervisor (Werkstättenvorsteher). He attended a Realgymnasium and graduated with an Abitur. He then studied medicine. He served a year in the army just before the war broke out, possibly as an Einjähriger Freiwilliger (voluntary officer cadet). He served again from August 1914 to February 1919 in a variety of medical units, and finished the war with the rank of auxiliary field physician (Feldhilfsarzt).[87] He passed his certification exams in 1919 and began work as a state insurance physician (Landesvertrauensarzt).[88] From 1919, when he was demobilized, until February 1931, when he joined the NSDAP, Mörchen was a member of a fraternity (Landsmannschaft) and of a medical association, but he was not a member of any political or paramilitary organization. He joined the SA in February 1931, serving as the doctor for a Sturmbann and later for an Untergruppe. In 1933 he was promoted to Sanitätsgruppenführer and made chief doctor for SA Gruppe Hessen. After 1933 he also served the Party in minor positions in the Office of Social Health (Amt für Volksgesund-heit) and the National Socialist German Association of Physicians. During the Second World War he served as a physician in the Wehrmacht. He was never a very committed political activist, and he clearly owed his high SA rank to his profession. As his work for the Party showed, he was a good soldier who did what was expected of him, but he was not a born leader or a street fighter and would never have attained an equivalent rank in the SA if he had not had his skill as a physician to offer at a time when the SA needed him.

Contrast Mörchen with the only clear "sporadic activist" in this chapter, Paul Holthoff.[89] He was born in 1897 in the village of Filehne in western Prussia, in the area which later became the Polish Corridor. He attended the Gymnasium and entered the army in August 1914. He was soon wounded and became a heavy machine gun specialist. He ended the war as a sergeant after attending two courses for machine gun officers. Soon after the war he joined Freikorps Weickhmann and later Freikorps Libow, both in the Baltic. He was promoted to second lieutenant, but this promotion was never recognized by the Weimar government, which caused him some bitterness. In 1919 he joined the radical nationalist Verband Nationalgesinnter Soldaten, and from 1922 to 1923 he was a member of the equally radical Nationalverband Deutscher Offiziere. He served in the latter as a machine gun instructor, proof that in 1922 and 1923 he and the organization were involved in something far beyond veterans' affairs. He withdrew from political and military activity between 1923 and May 1931, when he joined the SA and the NSDAP.[90] He served in the SA most often as a staff officer, but he also commanded an Untergruppe (later Brigade) for four years. He served with the SA until 1937. In 1938 he became the head of a National Political Educational Institute.[91] It was in this capacity (and simultaneously as a member of the Main Office for Education in the OSAF), that he was promoted to Gruppenführer in 1942.

Mörchen and Holthoff illustrate different kinds of SA leaders whose political mobilization before joining the SA was not terribly consistent. Mörchen wasn't an activist at all, and there appears to be very little in his previous career that would have led him to join the NSDAP. The Great Depression may have sparked a sort of political conversion, but he certainly wasn't directly threatened with unemployment, so the connection between the Depression and his first real engagement in political activity is unclear at best. Whatever the reason, it is clear that if he had not been a medical specialist (a physician), he never would have reached such high rank in the SA. Holthoff is quite different. He had once been active in radical paramilitary and political organizations, and had then dropped out of political activity after the 1923 putsch. It is very possible that he felt the effects of the depression much more directly than Mörchen did, since he omitted to list his occupation on his 1934 SA questionnaire. What is important is not that he was driven to political activity but rather that he chose the NSDAP over other organizations. For him, the decision to join the NSDAP was not a matter of a sudden political conversion. It was a return to a radicalism which he had earlier espoused as a member of two radical veterans' organizations from 1919 to 1923. His experience is more the norm than that of Wilhelm Mörchen.

The fact that the passive activists could still rise to high rank in an organization like the SA despite an earlier lack of interest in political activity prompts two observations. First, there must have been a rather broad and far-reaching identity in outlook between the NSDAP and general conservative and nationalist circles that permitted these men to fit into the SA despite their former inactivity. Second, many of the men involved had specific skills or abilities that were needed enough by the SA to be rewarded with high rank and important position.

The Party Soldiers

In the previous chapter, some of the future higher leaders of the SA fit the pattern of "party soldiers": they joined the NSDAP first and only some months later joined the SA. The case was made that they must have originally been attracted to the NSDAP by its ideological message rather than by the chance of playing soldier in the SA. A similar paradigm can be found in the careers of the men who joined the SA in 1931 or 1932, but the category would have included so many that it would have been difficult to construct other categories that would have had any meaning. Instead, joining first the Party and then the SA is a general characteristic of the entire body of future top SA leaders who joined in 1931 or 1932. Seventy-four percent[92] of the group joined the NSDAP six or more months before joining the SA, and the rest joined the Party and SA at approximately the same time. No member of the 1931-32 group joined the SA more than four months before joining the Party. This suggests that most of 1931-32 SA joiners were attracted to the NSDAP by its ideological message, and they only became involved in the SA once they had become a part of the movement. It also implies—unless one wants to argue that the choice of the NSDAP was essentially random—that a significant number of the members of rival organizations, even those usually considered traditional or moderately conservative in nature, in fact harbored some existing predisposition toward much of the NSDAP's ideology and message. The implication is that the "responsibility" for the rise of National Socialism must be shared across a much broader spectrum of German conservatism than is generally acknowledged.

Their Areas of Expertise

The different paths taken into the SA shed light on the background and thus presumably also on the motives of the men who became the SA's highest leaders, but this still begs the question of why the SA would need to recruit such men in 1931 and 1932. In a nutshell, most who joined the SA in 1931 or 1932 and later became its highest leaders had some special skill to offer that the SA needed. This is why these men were quickly accorded rank and power within the SA over the heads of longtime members. For example, fifteen out of the forty-six in the group entered the SA at the rank of Sturmbannführer (major) or above,[93] and nineteen immediately accepted staff assignments.[94] That this could and did cause resentment within the ranks of SA men who were passed over is understandable, but had to be balanced with the growing need for more specialists as the SA grew into a massive organization with an elaborate command structure.

Although recognizing a need for certain specialists and then recruiting them are rational or "objective" processes, the selection of these particular men had a strong subjective side to it. They were not just any specialists but men who shared common types of training, experience, and attitudes with those SA leaders already in place. Many not only had similar backgrounds but were well known to the SA leadership either personally or by reputation in nationalist circles. Thus, Ernst Röhm himself was selected to head the SA because he was an old and personal friend of Adolf Hitler with ties to the Party that reached back to the very earliest days of its existence.[95] Kurt Kühme, a former Prussian officer, was recommended to Röhm by Walther Stennes, who knew him.[96] The world of the far right during the Weimar Republic was a remarkably small one in the sense that personal ties were very close.

Similarly, Röhm picked former Bavarian professional officers in 1931 and 1932 for various posts in large part because he knew and trusted them. Examples of men who entered the SA in this way abound in 1931 and 1932. They included Karl Schreyer, Josef Seydel, Franz Ritter von Hörauf, and Fritz Ritter von Kraussner.[97] Others, who owed their SA positions to their general reputation in nationalist circles, included Paul Schulz,[98] Walter Luetgebrune,[99] and Hans Peter von Heydebreck.[100] In other words, although these men owed their high rank within the SA in part to their special knowledge and skills, which the SA needed, the reasons for selecting them over others were often highly personal.

The majority of the highest leaders of the SA who joined in 1931 and 1932 can be divided into six categories according to their special skills:[101] officers and military specialists, lawyers, physicians, finance and administrative specialists, Nazi Party officials, and a small miscellaneous category of SS specialists.

Military Specialists

The largest functional category is that of the officers and military specialists. Thirteen men of the total group of forty-six (28.2%) fall into this category.[102] The importance of this group for the SA is apparent. After all, it was organized along military lines, and who better to run such an organization than professional officers, who had the special skills needed to direct large groups of men organized in a military fashion? However, these were no longer just any soldiers, for the SA had plenty of them. What were needed above all were qualified and skilled staff officers who were proficient at solving the kinds of problems that were arising as the SA simultaneously grew in numbers and perfected its organization. The group of former officers here had a very high proportion of men with either staff training, including members of the elite Prussian General Staff Corps,[103] or else relatively high rank, including one general.[104] Not surprisingly, all of these military specialists immediately entered the SA (or SS) in staff or high command positions.[105] Some were selected for more specific reasons. Kurt Kühme, a retired major, had also been director of a sports school for five years.[106] As a result, Kühme was recruited to lead the newly formed SA national leaders' school (Sa-Reichsführer-schule), where his pedagogical and military skills were needed. Hans-Georg Hofmann, on the other hand, was well known to Hitler from the days of the putsch and had been close to the Party since at least 1928. In fact, he later alleged that Hitler had offered him the command of the SA in 1926, a command which he had to refuse at the time because he was engaged in secret work for the Reichswehr.[107] And, of course, there was the most famous military specialist recruited by the SA at this time, Ernst Röhm. Many of the other military specialists were Röhm's friends or former comrades whom he brought into the SA.

Physicians

The second largest functional grouping is that of physicians. Although the SA officially had its own doctors since at least 1927,[108] and unofficially even earlier,[109] the expansion and formalization of the system of SA physicians was given new impetus by the appointment of Dr. Paul Hocheisen to the position of head physician (SA-Reichsartz) in June 1930. The creation of a corps of SA physicians and of a broad hierarchy of SA physicians and medical personnel at all levels of the SA took time[110] and extended well into the period covered by this chapter.

Nine physicians who later were among the highest SA leaders joined in 1931 or 1932.[111] They seem to be of two types. The first (six of the nine) did not engage in much or even any political activity before joining the NSDAP (all but one are passive activists). All were veterans of the First World War. The two "passive activist" physicians who were politically or militarily active at all after the war were only involved for a short time and only in strictly local organizations.[112] Two of the six were employed as physicians by the state or private enterprise instead of being in private practice, suggesting that they were perhaps less successful or ambitious than their colleagues.[113] On the other hand, one was apparently quite successful and worked as a specialist for internal medicine at the University of Bonn.[114] All six were SA physicians attached to "frontline" SA units, and they did not make policy in the SA high command. They were never employed full time by the SA or any other Party organization.

The other three present a different picture.[115] Again, all three were veterans, but two were also quite active in political and military organizations after the war, and the third was a former professional officer in the German Imperial Navy who studied medicine only after retiring. All three seem to have been successful physicians in private practice, and two were specialists. All three occupied high positions as policymakers in the SA high command, and all three held high positions in the Party or state bureaucracies or both.

It is easy to draw a contrast between the majority of only slightly politically active, perhaps less successful frontline SA physicians and the few activist, successful, and highly placed SA and Party "staff" physicians found in the group. The former were promoted to Gruppenführer (and no further) as doctors attached to an SA Gruppe, whereas the latter, while all beginning in "line" positions, rapidly moved on to staff positions and became involved in similar high-level positions as physicians in the Party apparatus. This contrast may be nicely illustrated by looking at the careers of two physicians.

Eberhard Pagels[116] was born in Frankfurt am Oder in 1894 as the son of a physician. He attended a Gymnasium and passed a Kriegsabitur (special wartime college entrance exam) before volunteering for the First World War as an infantryman. He was not decorated, and he ended the war only as a noncommissioned officer. He then studied medicine in Berlin, and for a short time he belonged to a student militia at his university in 1920, the sum total of his organized political activity before he joined the NSDAP. He took over his father's practice but apparently couldn't keep it up, since he later became a police doctor (Polizeiarzt), which was not exactly the fast track to success. He later claimed to have been active in the NSDAP since June 1929 and that he lost his job as a police physician because of "political unreliability," but there is no corroborating evidence in his files, and he did not join the SA and NSDAP officially until July 1931. He began as an SA physician attached to a Sturmbann, the lowest unit with its own doctor. Later he was the physician for an Untergruppe and a Gruppe. He was promoted to medical Gruppenführer in July 1932. Unlike most of his fellows in the group of "line" physicians, he did get involved in the Party apparatus, but only at a relatively low level. He also occupied a few minor positions in city government, the highest of which was on the city council. Although he found himself in the army again during the Second World War, he did not see combat. He died of a heart attack on his way to the front in 1942.

Contrast the career of Pagels with that of Emil Ketterer.[117] He too attended a Gymnasium and then the University of Munich. Unlike Pagels, who was a general practitioner, Ketterer specialized in internal medicine and sports medicine. Ketterer had been an Einjähriger Freiwilliger before the war, and he later served as an officer, ending the war with the rank of Stabsarzt d.R., the equivalent of a captain. He was also highly decorated, being awarded, among other things, the Knight's Cross of the Lion of Zähringen and the Iron Cross Second Class.[118] After the war he was involved in spontaneous resistance to the "reds" in Munich, and he later belonged to the Heimwehr and then to Organisation Lenz (both Wehrverbände). At the beginning of 1923 he joined the NSDAP and soon thereafter the Reichskriegsflagge. He later was awarded the Blutorden in recognition of his participation in the Beer Hall Putsch. In 1924, following a split in the Reichskriegsflagge, he joined the Altreichsflagge, and in April 1925 he again joined the NSDAP, receiving party number 697, which suggests that he might even have attended the Party's founding meeting.[119] He did not officially join the SA until July 1931, but he claimed to have worked with it on an ad hoc basis much earlier. Beginning as a Sturmbann physician like Pagels, in 1933 he was transferred to the SA high command, where he became the chief of staff of the SA's chief of medical services (Chef der Sanitätswesen der SA). Within a few months he succeeded his boss in this position and held it until 1937. In that year he resigned and accepted detached service from the SA as its representative with the Reich leader of physicians (Reichsärzteführer). He also served in the Party as the chief of German sports physicians (Führer der deutschen Sportärzteschaft) and was elected to the Munich City Council.

Administrative and Financial Specialists

The next largest group includes four experts in administration and

SA Sanitätsobergruppenführer and Chef des Sanitätswesens der NSDAP Dr. Emil Ketterer, shown here in Party uniform. Note the saber cuts on his face, a souvenir of his participation in a dueling fraternity. Courtesy of the Bundesarchiv.

financial affairs, although they did not really form as homogeneous a group as the physicians and officers did.[120] By 1930 the Party and SA were chronically short of money, yet their expanding organizations required more and more of it. As a part of his general elaboration and centralization of the SA command structure (and under pressure from the Party to clean up the SA's money management problems), Röhm also instituted a more formal structure for the financial administration of the SA at the Untergruppe and Gruppe level, as well as in the SA high command. This is where the men of this group found their niche. Karl Schreyer is chief among them.[121]

Schreyer was a former Bavarian officer from Röhm's regiment. He had become a businessman after the war, and then had opened a private bank, which unfortunately went bankrupt in 1929 and which brought Schreyer a three-month prison sentence for some rather murky financial dealings.[122] This hardly recommended him as a financial expert or efficient administrator, but what mattered to Röhm was that the man was known to him and knew at least something about money matters. Schreyer entered the SA on February 1, 1931, at the urging of Röhm, and served as the SA's head of administration (Chef des Verwaltungsamtes) until 1934. His financial dealings for the SA were no more transparent than they had been in his business affairs, and he was also compromised as a protegé of Röhm. In the purge of 1934 he was very nearly shot, then expelled from the Party. In 1936 he was sentenced to four years in prison for financial misdeeds while in the SA.

Schreyer's legal problems were not necessarily typical of the other administrative specialists joining in 1931 or 1932, but the rather casual manner in which these men became SA employees was. The main qualifications of another member of the group, Ernst Beißner, were that he had been a state lottery collector. True, he was also an early Party member and had occupied a series of local and district Party positions from 1930 to 1932. He entered the SA at the very beginning of 1931 and rapidly became the head financial administrator for an SA Gruppe, a post which he held until 1940, when he was transferred to the SA central command. This was a lucky break for him, since it kept him out of the army in the Second World War, although he was drafted in 1943 into a local antiaircraft unit. The qualifications of the other two members of the group were similar: one was a former paymaster in the Imperial Navy and an activist in a series of veterans' and völkisch groups, and the other was a former kaufmännischer Angestellter (sales employee) who was also a minor official in the Party administration until he became active in the SA. All four were full-time employees of the SA by 1933.

Party Specialists

The next three categories are all very small, with two or three members each. One group of the highest SA leaders who entered the SA in 1931 or 1932 was made up of men who were high Party officials who were awarded active SA commissions on the basis of their Party position but who were really honorary SA leaders.[123] Röhm began his tour of duty as SA Stabschef just after a period of great tension between the SA and the Party. This tension had died down somewhat by the time he took command, but it clearly still smoldered just below the surface. In order to build bridges to the Party leadership, and especially to the office of the powerful Reich organizational leader,[124] two top leaders of this organization were given nominally active SA rank and the right to wear the SA uniform.[125] The two were Gregor Straßer himself, the Reich organizational leader, and one of his deputies, Paul Schulz. Many others were awarded honorary SA commissions.[126]

Straßer's commission was almost purely honorary, since he never really played any role in the SA after the mid-1920s.[127] On the other hand, Paul Schulz actually did command an SA Gruppe for a very short time. In early 1931, in the wake of the Stennes revolt,[128] he was called in to be the temporary head of SA Gruppe Ost and to help in its purge and reorganization.[129] Schulz was famed as a military and organizational genius, and his great prestige and respect in nationalist circles was useful in limiting the damage after the Stennes incident.

The third high Party official who entered the SA in 1931 or 1932 and who held high (active) SA rank was Willy Liebel. His appointment was also largely honorary, since he was both a high Party official and the mayor of Nuremberg, but he also did command an SA unit and later served in various SA staffs as an adviser on communal and Party questions.[130]

Note that these high Party officials shared some connection to the SA independent of their Party posts, even though the Party position was decisive for their promotion to Gruppenführer or Obergruppenführer. All were also veterans and former officers at that, and all had been involved in Wehrverbände or other paramilitary activities after the war. All but Paul Schulz were also Bavarians, with long ties to the movement.

SA Ogruf. Willy Liebel, Oberbürgermeister of Nuremberg. He is shown here in SA uniform, wearing his chain of office as mayor and decorations from fascist Italy and Hungary. Courtesy of the Bundesarchiv.

Lawyers

Both the Party and the SA were constantly in need of legal advice, primarily because of their violent political activities. As both organizations grew, the establishment of complicated administrative structures with full-time employees, the collection and disbursement of large sums of money, the ownership of large amounts of property, and all the other complications of a major organization created a new need for permanent and systematic legal advice. At the same time, it became financially and organizationally feasible to employ full-time legal council. The two men represented here, Walter Luetgebrune and Hans Frank, were not the only lawyers employed by the SA and Party, but they were the most important, and as such they were awarded high commissions as SA leaders. Hans Frank[131] was the chief lawyer for the NSDAP and head of its legal department from 1929 to 1942, and he had worked for the Party even earlier. In late 1931 he was made the head of the SA legal department as well. Later, as the SA and Party began to develop along separate lines, he was replaced by Walter Luetgebrune.[132] Luetgebrune, who was brought in by Röhm, had not formerly been particularly close to the NSDAP, although he was prominent as the defender of numerous right-wing activists and had even defended Party members on occasion. As a protegé of Röhm and an outsider, he fared poorly in the Röhm Purge. He barely escaped with his life but was expelled from the Party and forced to spend years in obscure poverty.

SS Specialists

Two men entered the SA (or in this case, the SS) in 1931 based solely on their particular expertise but did not fit into any of the categories above. The first is Walter Darré, a professional agronomist and animal breeding specialist who was brought into the SS to head the Rasse- und Siedlungs Hauptamt (race and settlement main office) and who became the SS's resident theoretician on race and agriculture. The second is the infamous Reinhard Heydrich, who was brought into the SS to organize its intelligence operations on the strength of his experience in the navy as a communications officer. Both men had been officers, although Darré was a veteran and a reserve officer, whereas Heydrich had been a professional officer in the Weimar-era Reichsmarine but had not served in the First World War.[133] Both had also been involved in Wehrverbände, yet had not long been members of the NSDAP before joining the SS.[134]

The "Good Soldiers"

A final group of the highest SA leaders might best be called the "good soldiers." It comprises ten men who joined the SA in 1931 or 1932 and who were able to work their way up slowly through the ranks to be promoted to Gruppenführer.[135] All but three of these men were only promoted to the rank of Gruppenführer in the early 1940s, a clear indication that they were not a part of the "first team," but rather were men who worked their way up through the ranks.[136] Indeed, the majority entered the SA at ranks which were the equivalent of enlisted ranks in an army, although some were able to be promoted to the equivalent of officer rank very quickly. Yet this group was quite similar to the rest of the highest leadership corps of the SA in background. All but two of the ten came squarely out of the Wehrverband milieu, all but one were veterans of the First World War, and all of the veterans were officers or noncommissioned officers. It is probable that this group did not rise to higher rank earlier simply because they joined relatively late, but they did manage to work their way to the top.

Ludwig Schmuck is an example of the career of a "good soldier."[137] He was born in Bavaria in 1892, the son of a vocational school director (Gewerbeschuldirektor). He attended a Progymnasium and then a teacher training institute. He became a primary school teacher and later a vocational school teacher like his father. He served as a one-year volunteer in the army before the war and was promoted to lieutenant during the fighting. He was wounded and decorated in the First World War. After the war he joined Freikorps Oberland and remained with it as it became Bund Oberland. In 1923 he joined a splinter group from Bund Oberland, the Bund Blücher and, as he proudly wrote, he once paraded before Adolf Hitler in his capacity as a company commander. In 1923 he joined the Deutsche Werksgemeinde, a völkisch, social-populist group led by Julius Streicher.

After dropping out of political activity in the mid-1920s, he rejoined Bund Oberland in 1927. By 1929 he was dissatisfied again, and in May he joined the NSDAP. He immediately began to serve in district-level posts in the party administration. In 1930 his military background led him to participate in a secret Reichswehr militia, the Feldjägerkorps. This satisfied his martial longings and explains why he did not join the SA until January 1932. He first joined an SA reserve unit and was involved in training new SA men, possibly a reflection of his activities in the secret Reichswehr unit. But in 1933, just before the Nazi assumption of power, he was promoted to Standartenführer and given command of a Standarte in recognition of his loyalty to Gauleiter Streicher in the "Stegmann revolt."[138] This gave him his chance, and within two years he had been promoted to command of a Brigade. Then, almost two years later, his abilities as a teacher gained him command of the SA leadership school in Dresden. His next assignment was to the central SA command, where he was made bureau chief of the Office of Organization and Operations (Amt Organisation und Einsatz). A year later, he was promoted to the rank of Gruppenführer and given command of the Office of Physical Education.

Meanwhile, he continued his relationship with the army and followed a training program for former officers who wished to rejoin the army as reserve officers. He was in the Wehrmacht from 1939 to 1944, where his last post was on the staff of an army group. He left active service in 1944 with the rank of major. Although he was on active military duty at the time, in 1942 he was also finally given command of an SA Gruppe. He only actually assumed command when released from active duty with the army. His fate after the war is unknown. He is a good example of a "good soldier" from within the milieu of the Wehrverbände, a man of clear abilities, who joined the SA rather late, but who still managed, with a bit of luck and ability, to work his way up to the second highest rank that the SA had to offer, the equivalent of a major general.

SA CAREERS OF THE SPECIALISTS

The careers that the men joining in 1931 or 1932 had in the SA are consistent with the picture of them as specialists and technicians. While all attained at least the rank of Gruppenführer by definition, less than one-third were promoted to Obergruppenführer.[139] Of those who did rise this far, close to one-third were promoted only after the Second World War began and the ranks of the existing Obergruppenführer had begun to be thinned out by casualties and transfers to other duties. Yet equally consistent with their positions as specialists, eight became full-time SA employees immediately, and at least three others did so within a year of joining.[140] While this number may seem small, it is actually quite large for the SA, which was chronically short of funds and relied largely on volunteers to lead and staff the organization, at least until 1933, when the state's coffers were suddenly opened to it. Nearly half of the group first served in the SA in a staff position and/or entered as Sturmbannführer (major) or higher.[141]

The highest SA leaders who joined in 1931 or 1932 did not fare well during the Röhm Purge. Many of them carried the stigma of too close an association with Röhm, and five paid for this with their lives.[142] Two others[143] were expelled from the Party and SA and suffered other penalties, and many more were arrested and threatened with prosecution. Although victims were drawn from all categories, no physicians were shot, expelled, or even arrested in the purge. Perhaps this is because their rank was clearly due to their profession, and they were not suspected of being close associates of Röhm.

Yet most of those who survived the Purge continued to have a good relationship with the Party. Fourteen wore the Golden Party Pin,[144] normally denoting those who had a party number under 100,000, but in fact, nine of these were awarded the Golden Party Pin as an honor,[145] even though they had much higher membership numbers and had joined later than the (mid-1928) date when the last party number under 100,000 was awarded.[146] Although many of the experts never played much of a role in the Party administration, some did: one eventually became a Gauleiter,[147] and three others served in some other Gau or Reich staff position.[148] Finally, one was a district party leader (Kreisleiter) and two were local group leaders.[149] Although latecomers to the SA and often to the Party, and although recruited mainly for their specialist knowledge, it is clear that the men in this chapter were also committed National Socialists.

The highest SA leaders who joined in 1931 and 1932 were either good soldiers who slowly worked their way up through the ranks or specialists who had desirable knowledge or skills. But this chapter has shown that there was another element in the equation besides the pure usefulness of the services that these men could provide. Indeed, they may not always have been the most skilled or best-suited men available, but they were all squarely in the nationalist camp and were receptive and favorably disposed to the ideology of the Nazi Party. Moreover, they shared a common background of army, war, Wehrverband, and sometimes völkisch activity with the men who already commanded the SA. In the most extreme cases, they were recruited because of their personal association or friendship with Röhm or some other leading SA commander. The majority also joined the Party before joining the SA, indicating that they were attracted first to its ideological message and not to the prospect of playing soldiers in the SA. Yet equally as important, many were men who had not previously engaged in political or paramilitary activities but were somehow motivated to join the NSDAP and then the SA. They usually did not have profound ties to the völkisch movement and the Nazi Party as did many of those who joined in 1925 or 1926, but they could at least recognize something in the NSDAP or SA that was familiar to them and that they could support.

The majority of these men became committed National Socialists, but first they were all part of a broader conservative nationalist movement that shared much in common with the NSDAP in terms of ideology and belief. This was the prime precondition which then allowed them to either turn to the NSDAP in a moment of national crisis or be drawn into it on the basis of their personal connections to individuals in the Party and SA. The fact that a few were more bound to the SA by personal ties to Röhm than by ties to the Party was a factor causing suspicion, and this eventually led to some of them being killed in the Röhm Purge, but those killed, while significant as individuals, remained a minority. The rest were able to continue in their SA careers and become permanent parts of the SA and Party apparatus.

The selection of many of these experts was haphazard, to say the least, and would seem to bear little relationship to the efficiency and success of the Nazi apparatus. Yet it must be remembered that personal ties counted for a great deal in the Nazi world, and common background greatly facilitated the growth of those ties. While not the most efficient way to choose key administrators, personal contacts did help guarantee loyalty and ideological commitment. It must also be recognized that the NSDAP had an entire right-wing subculture to draw upon for members and leaders that was much larger than itself. If one fellow did not work out, there were many others who had the basic qualifications of common ideology and background who could take his place.

5

The Latecomers,
1933-1934

On January 30, 1933, Adolf Hitler was appointed chancellor of Germany by the president of the Republic, Paul von Hindenburg, in accordance with the Weimar constitution.[1] This was the moment for which every member of the Party had waited so long. After years of struggle, sacrifice, and political impotence, the National Socialist German Workers' Party had legally taken power in Germany. True, it was still a long way from total power. To begin with, the judicial framework of the Weimar Republic endured, and if there were few who supported the Republic, there were many who opposed the Nazis. The National Socialists did not even form the government alone, but were forced to share power in a coalition with traditional conservatives. Field Marshal von Hindenburg still presided as the guardian of the constitution, and at his side stood the most powerful force in Germany, the Reichswehr, which jealously insisted that the form of the law must be obeyed. Yet the cabinet and even the army shared much of Hitler's basic political outlook while lacking the support of a dynamic mass movement, which only Hitler had. This meant that they were likely to acquiesce in many measures taken to "restore order" and were susceptible to being outmaneuvered, since they could not match the Nazis' political guile nor, in the case of the traditional conservatives, could they as easily mobilize large numbers of their supporters in the streets. The Reichswehr did represent an independent center of power within the German state and could seriously challenge the NSDAP, but it had a rather limited political horizon and a relatively short list of demands which, if satisfied, would cause it to lend its support to whatever nationalist or nonsocialist regime happened to be in power. Being forced to share power, being faced with many on the right and on the left who opposed a National Socialist government, and being forced to tread carefully around both von Hindenburg and the army meant that the NSDAP would have to act with great caution in consolidating its power over the state, but this did not prevent it from acting.

Out in the streets, beer halls, shops, factories, villages, and back alleys of Germany, the situation presented itself quite differently to the Party rank and file. They were the ones who had borne hardship, sacrificed property, and even risked death. With Hitler in power, they now felt that the time had come to sweep away the hated product of the November 1918 revolution. All of the frustrations, tensions, and hatreds that had built up during the Party's long struggle for power, especially in the near civil war conditions that had characterized the political debate of 1932, now boiled over. Guided but hardly controlled from the top, the members and supporters of the Nazi Party set out on their own to begin their revolution and crush any and all opposition. At the very forefront of this outbreak stood the SA.[2]

During the spring and summer of 1933, the SA played a crucial role in the consolidation of the new regime. This consisted of several functions. First, the SA served as the power behind the "revolution." It was the SA which gave the words of Hitler and the other Party leaders their force. It was the SA which intimidated the opponents of the new government and which legally or illegally carried out many of the measures that were designed to destroy the old system and consolidate the power of the government and the Party.

Second, the SA served as one of the main vehicles for the Gleichschaltung (coordination) of non-National Socialist political bodies, particularly the remaining Wehrverbände, which were a potential source of opposition. The SA played the same role, with less finesse and less success, in the Gleichschaltung of the police.

Third, the SA brought large numbers of German men into the new order. From the appointment of Hitler as chancellor to the Röhm Purge in June 1934, the SA swelled with a torrent of new members, so that by June 1934 it included roughly 20 percent of all German males over the age of fifteen.[3] Even without making reference to theories of totalitarianism or social atomization,[4] it is clear that by including such a large portion of German society in its ranks the SA had become a wholly new kind of tool for the coordination and indoctrination of an entire society, as well as a power to be reckoned with even apart from the Party.

After having entered the government legally, the Nazis' first task was to consolidate and expand their power. They counted on general agreement and support from the traditional conservatives and on general support and tolerance from wide sections of the German population. Their first overt moves were against the Communists and others on the left. The Nazis could use the police in the states that they controlled, but could neither completely trust them nor count on them to go very far beyond the bounds of legality. The army was unwilling to become actively involved in the conflict unless there was a genuine attempt at a putsch from the left, which there was not, and in any case, the Nazis preferred that the army remain neutral lest it throw its weight behind the traditional conservatives, who resembled army officers in ideology and background. Unhappily for Germany, the Nazi Party possessed its own forces for intimidating or eliminating its enemies.[5]

In a sense, the actions of the SA and SS were simply a continuation of the guerilla war against the opponents of Nazism and against the left in particular which had characterized the last several years of the Weimar Republic. The difference now was that all restraints which had been imposed by both the Party and the state were suddenly removed, and the SA was given free rein to vent its anger on its enemies. Much of this violence was carried out according to orders. Much, too, was illegal but nonetheless encouraged, and some of it was undertaken on purely individual initiative and often for personal reasons. But whatever triggered the violence, whether ordered, permitted, or for private reasons, the key factor was that at the beginning of the "revolution" it was tolerated, encouraged, and used by the Party and its leaders, including the SA leaders. Calculated and spontaneous violence went hand in hand to intimidate any and all possible opposition. It was only later, when the Nazis felt secure enough to come to some sort of a modus vivendi with existing forces in society, that the Party sought to end the spontaneous violence of its members and to return the use of deliberate violence to the agencies of the state, which traditionally have a monopoly on it.[6]

The impressive, near tenfold growth of the SA from 1931 to January 1933 pales when compared with the rate at which the SA grew from January 1933 to June 1934. Over these eighteen months the SA underwent an expansion whose only parallel in all of German history is the equally sudden growth of the NSDAP.

When the Nazis assumed power on January 30, 1933, the SA had roughly 500,000 members.[7] Eight months later, the SA had an estimated 2,500,000 men,[8] and by January 1, 1934, that number had increased to 2,950,000.[9] The maximum size of the SA, estimated at

4.5 million, was reached in June 1934 after it had absorbed large veterans' groups and paramilitary societies.[10]

The SA had to work hard at all levels to assimilate new members. In the final analysis, even the best run and most efficient organization could not completely cope with such massive growth. Add to this the fact that it occurred at a time when the reins of discipline were deliberately being relaxed to encourage "spontaneous" terror in the streets, and the problem for the overstretched SA leadership was clear. Many of the events that led to the purge in 1934 can be traced back to the wild expansion of 1933 and the 1933-34 absorption of competing paramilitary groups. For the SA, the task was made even more difficult by a chronic lack of competent lower and middle-level commanders, by the breadth of the responsibilities that it had undertaken, and by the need to detach SA leaders for other duties.

The SA was especially hampered by the fact that it was not always able to promote lower-level commanders up from the ranks. Many of the competent members who had leadership potential had already been promoted in 1931 and 1932, whereas the pool of rank-and-file members underwent a drastic turnover between 1931 and 1933.[11] This meant that there were actually relatively few rank-and-file members left who had enough experience to merit consideration as leaders or to impress something of the character and spirit of the SA upon the flood of new members. Many, indeed, of the "old" soldiers, especially those who had not yet been promoted to some sort of leadership position, were in fact much less capable than many of the newcomers. As Mathilde Jamin has pointed out, for this reason as well as through sheer numbers alone, the wave of newcomers in 1933 and 1934 threatened to overwhelm the existing structure and character of the SA. She notes that, given the high rate of turnover since 1931, and given the large number of new members, 75 percent of the SA in 1933 had been members of that organization for less than one year.[12] It was understandable, perhaps even inevitable, that problems of discipline, indoctrination, and sheer assimilation would result.

By May 1933, the flood of new members had reached such an extent that the OSAF was forced to raise the minimum strength of SA units at all levels from Sturm (company) to Untergruppe (brigade) because the number of new units that were being formed were surpassing the means of the SA to staff and finance them, and because the SA command wanted to keep the number of its units relatively stable in anticipation of putting them on the state budget.[13] Relatively junior SA leaders were also now allowed to command units at a higher level in the hierarchy than before to give greater flexibility and to make up for a shortage of qualified commanders. May 1933 also saw a major expansion and reorganization of the OSAF staff apparatus. This enabled the SA to better deal with both its expansion *and* the wider scope of its activities after the assumption of power.[14]

By July 1933 the first phase of SA expansion was capped with a complete reorganization, the first since the ban was lifted a year earlier.[15] The most original element of this reorganization was the introduction of Brigaden (brigades) in place of the former Gaustürme. The new Brigaden were no longer coterminous with the Gau boundaries as those of the Gaustürme had been. This gave the SA more flexibility in its geographical organization, but tended to separate it from the Party organization. Moreover, the introduction of the Brigaden later allowed the SA to tie its geographical organization more closely to that of the Reichswehr, an important consideration in view of the far-reaching cooperation that the SA had in mind.

The July-September 1933 reorganization created a total of 8 Obergruppen with 21 Gruppen and 129 new Brigaden. At the Party Congress in 1933, 118 new Standarten insignia were awarded, for a total of 190 officially recognized Standarten.[16] (Compare this with five Obergruppen and eighteen Gruppen with roughly fifty Untergruppen containing seventy-two "official" Standarten in September 1932 after the last complete reorganization.)[17] This increase of three Obergruppen and three Gruppen and the replacement of 50 Untergruppen with 129 Brigaden demonstrates how the SA organization was gradually stretched to accommodate the increases of 1933. Furthermore, it shows how the need also increased for SA leaders at all levels.

The main reason for conducting a major reorganization of the SA in the summer of 1933 was to cope with its swollen membership, but there were other reasons. One, which has been alluded to, was better cooperation with the Reichswehr, particularly in border defense in the east. Another reason, which rapidly took on major significance, was the Gleichschaltung and absorption of competing veterans' and paramilitary groups. This was an important yet generally overlooked step in the expansion and consolidation of power by the NSDAP and in the elimination of all possible rivals.

Although the heyday of the private paramilitary associations in Germany had come and gone in the early 1920s, in 1933 they were still present on the political scene. Although sharing many of the same ideas and enemies as the NSDAP, yet lacking much of the activism, youth, and dynamism of the SA, these groups were at least potential sources of organized opposition to the Nazis and thus by definition a danger. Chief among them was the Stahlhelm, Bund der Frontsoldaten, which had roughly 600,000 members in January 1933. Its size, its strong support for von Papen and the traditional conservatives in the coalition government, and its long-standing ties with the Reichswehr all made it a particular concern.[18] Although there had been occasional clashes and hard feelings between the SA and members of the Stahlhelm before the assumption of power, there had also been much cooperation. Moreover, the NSDAP and the Stahlhelm were even coalition partners and allies in the "government of national regeneration."

Allies and comrades in arms could not simply be banned and broken up like the left-wing Reichsbanner or the industrial unions, so the Nazis were faced with an especially delicate problem if they wanted to eliminate the potential power of the Stahlhelm. This is where the SA came in. Through a series of careful steps, the organizational independence of the Stahlhelm was gradually eliminated so that it could not become a threat. Smaller paramilitary and veterans' organizations were treated the same way, but the process of their absorption was generally much quicker.

The absorption and subordination of rival nationalist paramilitary groups was aided by their leaders' genuine desire to join the "movement of national regeneration" that they saw taking place, knowing full well that the failure of earlier attempts to destroy the "Weimar system" had often resulted from a lack of unity. Personal ambition and a craven desire for personal gain sometimes went hand in hand with this desire for unity.

During the first few months of 1933, relations between the Stahlhelm and the SA were mixed. Although the Stahlhelm provided members for the Hilfspolizei (auxiliary police) and joined with the SA and SS in terrorizing the left,[19] many National Socialists, flushed with victory and eager to settle old scores with the Stahlhelm, began to treat it more like an enemy than an ally. In large part this was due to a certain hubris and arrogance on the part of Nazis, especially the SA. Many SA men equated the Stahlhelm with the *verkalkte Reaktion* (ossified reactionaries) whom they saw as an enemy of the "national revolution" nearly as great as the left. Yet there was some truth in the charges that many opponents of National Socialism had found refuge in the ranks of the Stahlhelm, which also experienced a sudden jump in membership in the first half of 1933.[20] Many in the Stahlhelm reciprocated the SA's suspicion and were not happy with the way the NSDAP began to shoulder aside its former coalition partners.

It was in this atmosphere that Franz Seldte (minister of labor in the coalition government and coleader of the Stahlhelm) suddenly announced that he was joining the Nazi Party and that he was subordinating the entire Stahlhelm to it on April 27, 1933. This was a misguided attempt to curry favor with the Nazis and both enhance his own position as minister and preserve the independence of the Stahlhelm. This announcement surprised and annoyed the leadership of both the NSDAP and the Stahlhelm. It was demoralizing to many conservatives who had hoped that the Stahlhelm would provide a certain counterweight to the SA and NSDAP. After this act, morale in the Stahlhelm leadership plummeted. Some Stahlhelm leaders resigned in frustration, whereas others rushed to emulate Seldte's opportunism and immediately transferred into the SA.[21]

Soon after Seldte's action the process of absorbing the Stahlhelm began. First to be absorbed on June 21, 1933, was its potentially most dangerous unit—the Jungstahlhelm, or Wehrstahlhelm, made up of younger men who often participated in paramilitary sports (Wehrsport, a common euphemism for paramilitary training) or even covert military training.[22] Members of the Stahlhelm were allowed to believe that its autonomy would be preserved as much as possible. This made them more willing to accept what they expected to be only nominal subordination. Then, once subordinated to the SA and thus subject to a degree of control and discipline, the pretense of autonomy was abandoned, and complete absorption was carried out.[23] This pattern, first used with the Wehrstahlhelm, later was used for the rest of the organization.

During talks at a common SA-SS-Stahlhelm leadership meeting in Bad Reichenhall July 1-3, 1933, the entire Stahlhelm was subordinated to the SA and reorganized, although technically it remained independent.[24] Just one month later, the Brigade Ehrhardt, another famous and once powerful paramilitary organization descended from the free corps of the same name, was officially taken over by the SS.[25] In November 1933 Röhm instituted two new subordinate parts of the SA proper that were designed to accommodate most members of the paramilitary and veterans' groups and smooth the consolidation of National Socialist power. These were the SA-Reserve I (SAR I) and the SA-Reserve II (SAR II). While the younger, more "valuable" part of the Stahlhelm had already been taken into the SA proper, the rest of the Stahlhelm was to form the SAR I, where it would supposedly have a reasonable degree of internal autonomy while still being subject to OSAF control and discipline. The SAR II was to be made up of the older and less activist members of the Kyffhäuserbund and less overtly political veterans' groups. Being less important and having only the function of holding these veterans' groups in check until the power of the Nazi regime was consolidated, the organization and formation of the SAR II didn't really proceed beyond the formation of staffs and cadres.[26] Gradually, while preventing any dilution of the regular SA by the influx of Stahlhelm members, the SAR I was tied ever closer to the SA and separated from the Stahlhelm leadership.[27]

By the late fall of 1933 Röhm was confident that his plan was working well and that the Stahlhelm and the other coordinated Wehrverbände were in no position to resist. He then placed increasing pressure on nationalist groups of all stripes who dared to preserve any sort of existence outside of the NSDAP. His demands went so far as to require that the SA have a member on the board of directors of any patriotic organization if SA men were to be allowed to belong to it.[28]

In early 1934 SA attacks, both verbal and physical, increased on the Stahlhelm and its members, both within and outside of the SA. On March 28, 1934, the Stahlhelm was officially transformed into the Nationalsozialistischer Deutscher Frontkämpferbund (National Socialist Veterans' Association, or NSDF), which was to be an affiliate of the NSDAP much like the Nationalsozialistische Betriebs-zellenorganisation (National Socialist Industrial Cell Organization, NSBO) or the Nationalsozialistische Deutscher Juristen-Bund (National Socialist German Association of Jurists, NSDJB). This move was intended to pacify the few remaining conservatives who hoped that the Stahlhelm could have some sort of independent existence and to make a token concession to the aging president, von Hindenburg, who was an honorary member of the Stahlhelm.[29] In practice it had little effect, save that a number of lukewarm members of the SAR I resigned and joined the NSDF. The NSDF slumbered on until the NSDAP, confident of its strength and now supported by the Reichswehr,[30] disbanded it on November 7, 1935.[31]

In the long run, most of the Stahlhelm members who were absorbed into the SA and who swelled its size by nearly a million men[32] did not remain. Most left the SA voluntarily or were eased out by the mid-1930s. This was completely unimportant to the Nazi leadership, even if the size of the SA and the problems caused by SA-Stahlhelm clashes and the alleged instability of the SA in 1934 contributed to the decision to purge the SA in June 1934. Although the expansion in 1933 and 1934 whetted the appetites of Röhm and some of his cronies for a larger policymaking role for the SA,[33] and although some Stahlhelm leaders did remain in SA positions of authority,[34] increasing the SA's size was never actually the point. The main benefit gained from the absorption of the Stahlhelm and other patriotic groups in 1933-34 was that potentially dangerous sources of opposition to the NSDAP and its plans were robbed of their independent organizations and thus of the possibility of actually resisting, all without serious violence or opposition. The coordination of the Stahlhelm and others probably did as much to stabilize the new Nazi regime as any other action of the SA in 1933 or 1934.

By the summer of 1933, the Nazi regime's power had been consolidated to an irreversible point and its strongest enemies had been eliminated. The Law for the Protection of the German People (February 4, 1933) and the Law for the Protection of the People and the State (February 28, 1933) had suspended basic constitutional liberties and proclaimed a state of emergency. The Law for Removing the Distress of the People and Reich (the Enabling Act of March 23, 1933) transferred legislative power to the executive and made the Reichstag simply a rubber stamp. A series of other laws destroyed the independence of the federal states and strengthened the powers of the central government. Finally, beginning in May 1933, all political parties except the NSDAP were banned or dissolved, a process which was then made legal with the Law to Secure the Unity of Party and Reich (December 1, 1933).

At this point the regime confronted several important questions that demanded resolution. What would be the subsequent course of the "national revolution"? Would it become a National Socialist revolution, and if so, just what would that mean? What would be the role of the SA in society, now that the Party's enemies had been silenced or eliminated? What course would the rearmament of Germany take, and what would be the relationship of the Party to the Reichswehr in the process? Hovering over all the others was the question of who would succeed the infirm Paul von Hindenburg. The search for answers to these questions dominated all events and eventually found resolution in the Röhm Purge of June 1934.

By 1933 or 1934 it was very late for anyone to join the SA and expect to rise to a position of importance. Although the Machtergreifung brought a torrent of new members to the SA, the Party, the SS, and all other Party organizations, and the organizational expansion which this brought about caused many low- and medium-ranking members of these organizations to achieve higher rank and greater responsibilities quickly, there were already enough SA leaders in the pipeline to fulfill manpower demands at the very top, and the SA no longer needed to look outside for top talent.[35] The case of the SA was complicated even more by the Röhm Purge, which arrested the expansion of the organization and considerably diminished its overall significance. This further reduced the possibility that newcomers could rise to the very top of the SA hierarchy, since the reduction in size that was ordered after the purge meant that there were more than enough high SA leaders to fill the remaining positions.

Nevertheless, eleven men who only joined the SA in 1933 or 1934 did manage to become Gruppenführer or even Obergruppenführer and thus become part of this study.[36] These eleven men fall into two distinct categories.[37] Two men owed their SA ranks in part to longtime service in the Party and in part to special circumstances. Nine led non-Nazi veterans' and paramilitary groups that were absorbed under the Nazi wing as a part of the Gleichschaltung or elimination of all rival political organizations in Germany. These co-opted members present an interesting case study in the reciprocal relationship between the Nazi Party and other conservative groups. While one or possibly two of these nine men later had differences with the SA, the rest made the transition practically seamlessly. There is an important lesson here in both the differences and similarities between the NSDAP/SA and other conservative organizations.

The smaller group may be dealt with quickly. In the case of Hans Petersen,[38] several reasons combined to bring him to high rank in the SA. He was a retired major with valuable military skills. He had also been a Party member since April 1925. Most important, he was a longtime Party officeholder with valuable contacts.[39] After he had joined the SA and risen to command a Brigade, he also became a high official in the administration of the state of Anhalt, further reason for the SA to encourage his career.

Petersen officially joined the SA in January 1933, just before the takeover of power, at the prompting of his local Gauleiter. His duties were first of a political nature: soon after the Nazi assumption of power he became the SA commissar (SA Sonderkommissar)[40] for the town of Immenstadt and for the district of Sonthofen, as well as the vice mayor of Immenstadt. His next major SA appointment came in

January 1934, when he was appointed head of a department in the SA Reich Leadership School (Reichsführerschule). The name of the department is not known, but very likely it had to do with his expertise in history and military organization. He stayed two years at the school, and from 1935 to 1937 he was also a permanent member of the special verification commissions set up to evaluate and judge the SA leadership in the wake of the Röhm Purge. Up to this point his activities were largely political in nature and obviously related to his close ties to the Party's political apparatus. Surprisingly, in 1936 he was transferred to command an active SA Brigade in Anhalt.

Petersen commanded SA Brigade 39 until 1941, but in 1940 he also became acting head of the SA Gruppe Thuringia while its actual chief was serving in the armed forces. It was in this capacity, and also in recognition of his high position in the state administration of Anhalt, that he was promoted to Gruppenführer. Certainly, the war influenced his promotion. He apparently did serve in the Wehrmacht (again with the rank of major) and won the Iron Cross First and Second Class. Yet he was born in 1885, and as an older man who had already served at the front, he was a likely candidate to be released from active service back to the SA so that a younger SA leader could take his place in the army. He was therefore just the type of man the SA needed to keep the home fires burning. More than this, he was a valuable link with the state and Party administration. Petersen was also named a member of the Reichstag in 1942, and from 1940 to the end of the war he was a lay member of the infamous Volksgerichtshof (Nazi People's Court), even serving as a member of its Besonderer Senat (Extraordinary Senate).

Petersen served as acting head of Gruppe Thüringen until late 1941, then he was transferred to the supreme SA high command. There he headed the personnel office (Personalhauptamt) for the remainder of the war. He was a longtime Party member and activist with strong military skills who gained a midlevel position in the SA by virtue of these two activities, despite joining the SA very late. His later career was clearly influenced by his political position and connections, and he seems to owe at least some of his success to the fact that he was trusted by the Party leadership and could generally work well with them. Nevertheless, it took the war to bring him command of a Gruppe and later of a Hauptamt within the SA central command.

The second case is that of Hans Lukesch.[41] He too was a former professional military man who also joined the Party several years before joining the SA, but his case is not really comparable to Petersen's. Hans Lukesch owed his high rank solely to the extreme disruption of the SA in his native Austria after the abortive putsch of July 1934. Born in 1901, he had been a professional officer and pilot in the Austrian Federal Army from 1925 to 1933. He lost his army commission in 1933 because of his Nazi affiliation. Obviously an aggressive and activist personality, he immediately became a weapons consultant for the Austrian SA. After the putsch, he initially managed to evade arrest, and so became the commander of an Austrian SA Brigade and later even the commander of SA Obergruppe Austria. This lasted until his arrest in 1935, and resumed again for one month in 1938 just before the Anschluß. After Austria became part of the German Reich, however, Lukesch was removed from any active SA command and was shunted off to the inconsequential Reichsarbeitsdienst (Reich Labor Service, or RAD) at a rank considerably below his last SA rank (Brigadeführer). He was not promoted to SA Gruppenführer until 1943 (again, while serving on an inactive basis), when he was also promoted within the RAD to Generalarbeitsführer, the equivalent of Gruppenführer in the SA. He was clearly an expendable, last resort leader for the SA when it was forced underground in Austria in the wake of the failed coup. With the majority of its commanders under arrest or in hiding, the SA was willing to use a brash young leader such as Lukesch who had managed to keep himself out of jail in order to maintain some semblance of an SA organization in Austria. Although he was later paid off with a sinecure in the RAD and an inactive commission in the SA, he was clearly not considered fit to command an SA Gruppe or Obergruppe under normal circumstances.

The second group is far more important. The nine men concerned all came from the leadership of either the Stahlhelm or the Kyffhäuserbund.[42] The Stahlhelm members are the key, since only one member of the Kyffhäuser Bund became a Gruppenführer or Obergruppenführer.

With the information at hand, not much can be said about how these eight men compared with other top Stahlhelm leaders. As of 1933, the eve of their absorption into the SA, three of the eight were Landesführer (leaders at the level of a German state or region).[43] Three were members of the Stahlhelm central leadership,[44] and two of these were also heads of state-level Stahlhelm organizations such as the Gaue of the NSDAP. Two were commanders of Stahlhelm Wehrsport regiments.[45] These were all high positions, but represented only a small portion of the Stahlhelm's central leadership.[46] For example, there were roughly twenty-three Stahlhelm state or regional divisions (Landesverbände),[47] yet only five Landesführer are present here. Even the head of the Stahlhelm, Franz Seldte, is not among the group.[48] Although this might suggest that the former Stahlhelm leaders who rose to the top levels in the SA were not representative, caution is in order. In fact, very few Stahlhelm members were actually taken into the SA at the rank of Gruppenführer or Obergruppenführer, and comparatively few of the others managed to work their way up that far in the SA hierarchy—just like any of the other SA leaders of the same rank. In fact, many more former Stahlhelm leaders would have been present if lower SA ranks had been included in this study. What can be said with certainty, as the remainder of this chapter will demonstrate, is that there was at least a significant minority of former Stahlhelm leaders who were not only willing to work with the SA and NSDAP in a way which allowed them to rise to the very highest levels of rank within the SA, but who were also quite similar in training and experience to the SA leaders already in place.[49] More careful studies of the Stahlhelm leadership will be necessary to confirm these findings, but they suggest that there may have been more similarities between the SA and the Stahlhelm in terms of their leaders than has commonly been realized.

Six of the nine higher SA leaders who came from the Stahlhelm or Kyffhäuserbund were prewar professional officers.[50] Four of the six professional officers were members of the Prussian officer corps, one was a Bavarian, and the sixth was a Württemberger.[51] Most were lieutenants, first lieutenants, or captains when the war broke out, and all saw combat.[52] Five of the six prewar professional officers were taken into the Provisional Reichswehr, but all had left the service by the end of 1920.[53] This might have been due to age if nothing else, since all of the professional officers were born between 1869 and 1888, but on the other hand, even the oldest was only fifty years old in 1919. Moreover, they all had the sort of military background and individual attributes that put them among the most likely to be taken into the Reichswehr.[54] Von Stephani hinted at a likely answer when he mentioned participation in the Kapp Putsch in his files, as did Jüttner, who stated that he was refused admission into the Reichswehr because he was "politically compromised."[55] Whether age or political unreliability was the cause, strong resentment against the Weimar Republic was certainly one result, but the real point is that the Stahlhelm leaders who joined and stayed with the SA shared similar backgrounds and common resentments with their SA comrades.

At least two of the nine were not prewar professional officers but were appointed reserve officers during the war.[56] Like their professional comrades, these two men also saw combat. There is no indication that either of them wanted to remain in the army. On the contrary, both entered the university immediately after the war to prepare for future careers, one as a dentist (Zahnarzt), the other as a teacher.

The activities of these men in 1919 and 1920 are worthy of note. All but one were under arms in those years.[57] One was in the regular army, two were Zeitfreiwilliger,[58] and six were in free corps. This is not unusual, but three of the five free corps members were in fact the commanders.[59] This runs counter to the commonly held notion that there was a special affinity between the extremely radical NSDAP and the equally radical free corps, and it seems surprising that these three former free corps commanders would have been senior leaders in the more moderate Stahlhelm. Yet it must be noted that all three were Prussian officers, whose free corps were formed in northern Germany, and who acted under the close supervision and leadership of the army high command. They were clearly a different breed from the more independent free corps leaders who served in the Baltic or who came out of the German navy. The NSDAP and SA were certainly not alone in being able to attract veterans, even prominent veterans of the free corps movement.

The activities of the coordinated veterans' organization leaders from 1921 to 1933 were much like those of other higher SA leaders, particularly some of those of the 1927-30 group. The major difference is that they did not join the NSDAP and SA.

No one in the group was ever a member of a moderate party, let alone liberal or socialist. Over half the group did belong to a political party or other political organization, but only to traditional or radical conservative ones. This is much like what has already been found in the careers of the other SA leaders who have been discussed up to now. One of the group[60] was a member of the DNVP until 1933, and another was a member for an unspecified time.[61] Given the ties between the Stahlhelm and the DNVP, this is only what one would expect. On the other hand, membership in the DNVP among the other top leaders of the SA, although less frequent, was certainly not uncommon.

Another of the coordinated veterans' leaders was a member of the Nationale Vereinigung through the Kapp Putsch, when it was banned. As a reactionary north German group dedicated to organizing the right in preparation for a putsch, the Nationale Vereinigung fell into the pattern of participation in conservative and radical conservative organizations which is typical of the higher SA leaders.[62] Another led two small conspiratorial organizations, the Schwarze Garde and the Braver Heinrich.[63] One was a leader in the Reichsflagge, a traditional conservative/monarchist Bavarian Wehrverband, and another was a member of the Reichsverband der Baltikumkämpfer, a radical organization of veterans of the free corps in the Baltic.[64] Finally, one was a leader in the Verband Nationalgesinnter Soldaten (Association of Nationally Minded Soldiers), a right-wing veterans' organization.[65] Most of these organizations figure in the backgrounds of the SA leaders already discussed in this book.

What is slightly different in the careers of the Stahlhelm leaders is that they tended not to be involved in Wehrverbände (other than the Stahlhelm) or völkisch groups to the extent that most of the highest SA leaders were. Only one of the nine Stahlhelm or Kyffhäuser leaders in this chapter was in a völkisch organization. Interestingly, the völkisch organization was the early NSDAP, and the individual who belonged to it also belonged to the Stahlhelm and DNVP at the same time.[66] One explanation of these differences is that the Stahlhelm leaders were slightly older than most of the highest SA leaders, and they were more traditional conservatives who did not support the violence of the Wehrverbände. Of course the Stahlhelm, especially in its early years, often functioned as a Wehrverband itself.[67] Note also that two of the group[68] fought in Upper Silesia in 1921, one as a member of the Stahlhelm and one not. Given the above, the seemingly lower participation in Wehrverbände compared with the highest SA leaders is put into perspective, and the differences are reduced to the near absence of participation in völkisch organizations.[69]

The careers of the "coordinated" Stahlhelm leaders can be broken down into two types that were characteristic of many of the other highest SA leaders as well. Four of the eight fall into a pattern much like that followed by the "defectors."[70] They belonged to one organization for a long period without a break before joining a second organization. In this case, the second organization is not the SA but rather the Stahlhelm. This is important, because it shows just how much they resemble their SA counterparts, right down to the paths they followed into their respective organizations. Moreover, two of these three might be called "dual defectors," since they first were absorbed into the Stahlhelm from other organizations, served it loyally, and then were absorbed into the SA.[71]

Here is one example: In the fall of 1927, the Reichsflagge merged with the Stahlhelm, much as the Stahlhelm later merged with the SA, save that in 1927 the Reichsflagge had slightly more say in the matter. Georg Dechant[72] was the Gauführer of the Reichsflagge in Franconia at the time. Since the Stahlhelm was traditionally weak in Bavaria, this brought a great increase in its strength there, and it essentially built on the Reichsflagge organization. Dechant became the Stahlhelm Landesführer for Franconia. In 1933, when the Stahlhelm first began to be absorbed by the SA, Dechant became the leader of the SAR I in Franconia and then of the SAR I Brigade there.[73] He went on to serve the SA in several staff positions and in 1942 became the head of the entire SA Gruppe in Franconia. Although in some ways his career was exceptional, it is nevertheless striking that he could so easily switch from leading one group to leading another. It was as if all that was needed was a change of uniform, and Georg Dechant would serve any master—at least as long as that master stood on the far right.

Three of the other coordinated Stahlhelm leaders had careers very like the "serial activists."[74] They passed through several organizations before they established a stable membership in the Stahlhelm. The assumption is that this pattern is characteristic of a highly activist personality who presumably drifted from one organization to another until he found one that fit his character. This pattern of activity is characteristic of a significant portion of the highest leadership of the SA.

Thomas Girgensohn will serve as an example of a "serial activist" Stahlhelm leader. He was born in the well-to-do Grünewald section of Berlin in 1898.[75] His father was a historian. He entered the army in December 1914, apparently as an officer candidate. He was awarded the Iron Cross, and in 1915, at age seventeen, was wounded, losing his left leg. By this time he was already in command of a company. Despite the gravity of his injury, he did not slow down. In 1917, probably while on convalescent leave, he passed his Abitur exam. He then served in staff positions. At the end of the war he was a lieutenant. Instead of going home for rest and rehabilitation, he immediately joined the assault section of the Baltische Landeswehr, a self-defense organization made up of Germans from the Russian Baltic provinces of Latvia and Estonia, which included a very high percentage of Baltic-German nobles.[76] He became its chief of staff and fought

SA Gruf. and Captain Thomas Girgensohn (seventh from left) with the staff of the Baltische Landeswehr in 1919. He stands between Hans (left) and Heinz (right) von Manteuffel. Courtesy of the Bundesarchiv.

with it until November 1919.[77] He left service with the Baltische Landeswehr as a captain.

Upon his demobilization he began his university studies. This was not, however, the end of his paramilitary activities. In 1920 he joined the Ehrhardt Brigade, although it remains unclear in what capacity. A year later, he was active in the Upper Silesian Selbstschutz (self-defense militia), although he seems to have remained in Berlin. In 1922 he joined the radical Reichsverband der Baltikumkämpfer (Reich Union of Baltic Veterans). He worked in the printing and typesetting trade after he left the university, and remained in the Reichsverband der Baltikumkämpfer until 1928, at which time he joined the Stahlhelm.[78]

In the Stahlhelm, he quickly moved up the hierarchy from simple member to district leader and even commander of a regiment of the Wehrstahlhelm (units of younger Stahlhelm members organized on paramilitary lines, ostensibly for "sports" training). He was taken into the SA in October 1933, and immediately was posted to the staff of the SAR I in Berlin. In 1934 he became employed by the SA full time. He continued to work in staff positions until the end of the Second World War, heading an office (Abteilung) in the OSAF from 1937 to 1942, and heading a division (Amt) in the OSAF from that point until the end of the war. He was promoted to Standartenführer in 1935, Brigadeführer in 1941, and Gruppenführer in 1944.

Girgensohn was clearly an activist. It would be useful to know what effect the loss of a leg had on his motivation, but such information is unfortunately lacking. What is clear is that he, like many of his comrades who joined the SA voluntarily and much earlier, passed through a series of right-wing paramilitary organizations from the time he left military service at the end of the war until he joined the SA. Although like all of the Stahlhelm leaders discussed in this chapter he probably would have remained in the Stahlhelm and never joined the SA if it had not absorbed the Stahlhelm, he did not choose to leave the SA either, as he certainly could have done without difficulty given his handicap. Instead, he continued on in the SA and enjoyed a successful career, rising to a position of authority as if he had never left the Stahlhelm or as if he had been an early member of the SA.

Only two of the eight Stahlhelm leaders in this study entered the SA as active Gruppenführer. Both did so by virtue of their high positions in the Stahlhelm, but also because of the job they were intended to do in the SA. Franz von Stephani was the Bundeshauptmann (literally federal captain) of the Stahlhelm, which made him virtually second in command after Seldte. Hans Elard von Morozowisc was the Bundesbevollmächtigter of the Stahlhelm (federal plenipotentiary) and he headed the Jungstahlhelm.[79] This merited high rank when they were taken into the SA, but the fact that they were awarded *active* rank came from their new duties. Von Morozowisc was given the task of integrating the Wehrstahlhelm (as the Jungstahlhelm was renamed) into the SA. He later became one of Konstantin Hierl's two deputies in the NSDAP's Freiwillige Arbeitsdienst (Voluntary Labor Service, or FAD).[80] Von Stephani was made the titular commander of the SAR I when it was created in late 1933 to bring the Kernstahlhelm (the older members of the Stahlhelm) into an SA organizational framework. Both men thus occupied positions of (ostensible) command within the new SA/Stahlhelm hierarchy. Von Stephani later resigned due to conflicts with Röhm, and von Morozowisc died in an automobile accident.[81]

The remaining six Stahlhelm leaders also entered the SA on an active-duty basis at relatively high rank, but not at the very top. In general, the SA was rather sparing with awards of extremely high rank to the newcomers out of the Stahlhelm. Jüttner, a Stahlhelm Landesführer, entered the SA as a Brigadeführer. The other two Landesführer, von Neufville and Dechant, entered the SA as Standartenführer and Obersturmbannführer, respectively. Möslinger, the Oberquartiermeister (supreme quartermaster) of the Stahlhelm, entered as a Standartenführer, and the two Stahlhelm Regiments-führer, Thomas Girgensohn and Lorenz Ohrt, entered the SA as Sturmbannführer.

They all were eventually promoted to the very highest ranks of the SA in recognition of their abilities, although the war certainly accelerated their progress as a result of high losses of existing Gruppenführer and Obergruppenführer.

Once in the SA, all but two of the eight Stahlhelm leaders went into staff positions. The two exceptions, Lorenz Ohrt and Georg Dechant, held field commands, but the units that they commanded were made up of former Stahlhelm members. There were two very important reasons for this. First, the other six leaders had held staff positions in the Stahlhelm, were competent, and were also getting a little old to be field commanders. Much more important, however, were psychological and political considerations. There had often been conflict between SA and Stahlhelm units in many places during the Kampfzeit, and this increased during 1933 and 1934, when the Stahlhelm was absorbed into the SA. Also, the SA and NSDAP often treated Stahlhelm members as second-class nationalists or danger-ous "reactionaries." There was much ill feeling and even several vio-lent clashes between SA and Stahlhelm units in some areas, although in other areas cooperation was the norm. At any rate, the appoint-ment of former Stahlhelm leaders to command veteran SA men was likely to cause resentment and thus was avoided. At the same time, the SA was not entirely opposed to allowing Stahlhelm men to serve under leaders drawn from that organization, provided that their loy-alty to National Socialism was assured. Although Lorenz Ohrt and Georg Dechant were returned to field commands during the Second World War, even they spent the bulk of their SA service on staffs. This is where the Stahlhelm leaders who were taken into the SA made their greatest contribution.

The career of Lorenz Ohrt is a good example of a Stahlhelm leader who held both staff and field commands in the SA.[82] Ohrt had been commissioned as a lieutenant during the war. He joined the Stahlhelm in 1922, after serving in Zeitfreiwilligenkorps Bahrenfeld in Hamburg from 1919 to 1921. Until 1929 he was just a simple rank-and-file member. In that year he became the leader of a local chapter. In 1932 he left this position to lead a company, a battalion, and then a regiment of Stahlhelm men organized for paramilitary training.

In August 1933 he was absorbed into the SA as a part of the Wehrstahlhelm, and he became the commander of a Standarte in Hamburg composed largely of former Stahlhelm men. In 1935 he was transferred to the staff of SA Gruppe Hansa and later SA Gruppe Nordmark. He remained in staff positions until 1938. During this time he was involved with training and schooling, and for much of the time commanded an SA-Gruppenschule where low-level leaders were trained. In 1938 he was transferred to Gruppe Südmark, where he acted as its chief of staff. In 1941 he was again transferred to the SA high command where he headed an office within Hauptamt Führung (Command Main Office).[83] From 1940 to 1942 he served for very short periods as the acting head of two SA Gruppen. In 1942 he was named head of the Amt Organisation und Einsatz (Office for Organization and Mission), and in 1944 he was promoted to Gruppenführer. Shortly thereafter, he was made the acting wartime head of Gruppe Weichsel, and in 1945 he was named its official commander. Although with this appointment he had reached the acme of his career, it was a rather hollow honor, for by this time he was preoccupied with fighting the Russians in Danzig as a member of the Volkssturm.

Typical of many Stahlhelm leaders taken into the SA, Ohrt quickly occupied important staff positions. Later, as the older antagonisms between the Stahlhelm and the SA were growing dim and the war was beginning to put a strain on the SA command structure, he served temporarily in field commands. Later in the war, he was held fit enough to be awarded a major command of his own. By then, nobody cared whether he had been a Stahlhelm leader or not, for they all had much more important things to worry them.

The relationship of the former Stahlhelm leaders to the NSDAP was much different from that of the other SA leaders. Most had never been active in völkisch politics, and they had little motivation to become involved in Party work when they joined the SA, particularly as their SA duties were more than enough to occupy them at first. Consequently, when many other SA leaders were given positions in the Party administration at the Gau level or below, or were selected for other responsible and politically sensitive assignments, these men were not included.[84] Although they did not ignore their responsibilities to the Party, there was a reluctance on the part of the Party hierarchy to give them politically sensitive positions outside of the SA.

Three joined the Party in 1933, and four joined in 1937 when the moratorium on new Party memberships was lifted.[85] In part this was a function of when they were absorbed into the SA, since the Party moratorium on new members was put into effect on May 1, 1933. Many were not absorbed into the SA until after this date, and there was no real, pressing reason to join the NSDAP before they became members of the SA. Nevertheless, it is significant that those joining in 1933 all became members of the NSDAP before they were absorbed into the SA. This may indicate that these particular individuals were closer to the NSDAP than many other Stahlhelm leaders who waited to join the NSDAP, but is not sufficient by itself to make any generalizations. Interestingly, two of the nine, Max Jüttner and Wilhelm Reinhard, were later honored with the Golden Party Pin, despite the very late date of their Party membership. In general, then, the Stahlhelm leaders who rose to the highest levels of the SA were not very interested in Party affairs, although they did their duty. They were good soldiers, not good politicians.

The Stahlhelm leaders who reached the highest ranks of the SA—whether they decided to stay in the SA or not—were quite similar in background to the men who were already in the SA when they arrived. Both groups shared a strong military and paramilitary background. The Stahlhelm group lacked much involvement in völkisch politics, and showed slightly more involvement in traditional conservative parties than the bulk of their SA comrades, but this was merely a question of degree. Neither groups was involved in moderate or liberal political parties or organizations, both were active militarily in 1919 and 1920, and both later joined the Wehrverband movement.

The Stahlhelm leaders in this study—admittedly a minority of the central leadership core of the Stahlhelm, although the significance of this is debatable—were able to fit into the SA hierarchy with remarkable ease. Only two exceptions were found to this, and of these two, only von Stephani refused out of his own free will to cooperate with the SA.[86] The ease of this transition is striking for men who, after all, were members of a rival organization, and it bears further research. It shows just how important the larger context of the right-wing political and paramilitary organizations was for the SA and NSDAP and just how close they actually could be to the NSDAP, despite all tactical, personal, or even ideological disagreements.

For the transition from one organization to another to be so easy, there had to have been more points of agreement than disagreement between the two groups. These points of commonality were provided not least by the strikingly similar backgrounds of the men involved. The core of their backgrounds was the military experience and the soldierly virtues and attitudes that it taught.

In the case of the Stahlhelm leaders, it must have been quite easy for them to transfer their allegiance to the SA, particularly since by 1933 the SA was in many ways already tied up with the state and the nation. The party to which it belonged dominated the government and soon became the only legal political party. The SA and the Reichswehr teamed up for military training and Grenzschutz, an arrangement which formerly had been shared with many organizations on the right, not least of which was the Stahlhelm. The Stahlhelm men now in the SA only helped cooperate with the army, since they had long-standing contacts with the officer corps and were all former officers themselves. In fact, the men from the Stahlhelm who appear in this chapter later were engaged in many aspects of planning for the SA that involved military matters and cooperation with the Wehrmacht.

What real difference, indeed, was there between a leadership position in the Stahlhelm and in the SA, particularly when the SA's importance to the Party decreased from 1933 on and its obligations to the State increased? The SA and Stahlhelm were and always had been united in many ideological principles: opposition to the Weimar Republic and democratic government, opposition to the Versailles treaty and all it stood for, and support for a strong German state with that most fundamental symbol of sovereignty, a strong national army.[87] The extent of this congruity is best symbolized by one final biography, that of Max Jüttner.

Max Paul Wilhelm Werner Jüttner was born in Saalfeld, Thuringia, in 1888.[88] His father was a self-made man who owned a printing company. Max attended a Realgymnasium, passed his Abitur, and then joined the army, where he became a professional officer in Field Artillery Regiment 55. He was commissioned in 1907 as a second lieutenant and became a captain in 1916. During the First World War he served as an artillery and then as a staff officer, including a

SA Ogruf. and former captain Max Jüttner, 1943. Courtesy of the Bundes-archiv.

posting to the general staff. After the war he served as a leader of a Zeitfreiwilligenverband until 1920, organizing all of the Zeitfrei-willigen units for the Landesjägerkorps.[89] In 1920 he allegedly was refused a position in the Reichswehr due to "political unreliability" and had to leave active service. He left the army in September 1920.

This did not prevent him from continuing to be active in para-military and political organizations. He had already joined the Stahlhelm in 1919, serving in succession as the leader of a local branch, a regional branch, and a state branch. By the early 1930s he was deputy to the Second Bundesführer, Duesterberg. In 1920 he joined the DNVP. In 1921 he went to Upper Silesia to fight the Poles, and in January 1923 he even joined the Nazi Party in Munich, while maintaining his membership in the DNVP and in the Stahlhelm.

In July 1933[90] Jüttner joined the Nazi Party again, and in No-vember he was absorbed into the SA. From December 1933 to 1945 he served in the SA high command, first as an aide in the Führungsamt (Command Office), and from July 1934 on as the head of that office.[91] He also served as an SA liaison to the army. In 1935 he was promoted to Gruppenführer, and in 1937 to Obergruppenführer. In 1939 he was named to the additional post of standing deputy to the chief of staff, and in 1943, when SA Chief of Staff Viktor Lutze died, Jüttner filled in until Wilhelm Schepmann could take his place.

Despite good contacts with the Reichswehr and later Wehrmacht, Jüttner did not serve in the Second World War, in large part because his duties with the SA were considered too important for the war effort. By April 1945, however, with the Third Reich all but defeated and the Allies closing in on Munich, he did fight as the commander of a Volkssturm unit. Jüttner was captured by the Ameri-cans and interned as a high Nazi leader. With SA Chief of Staff Schepmann missing, and the rest of the senior SA Obergruppenführer dead or in hiding, Jüttner was the most senior surviving SA leader. It is symbolic that in Jüttner the soldier, the Stahlhelm leader, and the SA leader had so fused that Jüttner could insist that he was indeed the senior surviving member of the SA and, as such, had to bear full responsibility for the deeds of that organization. In this capacity, former Stahlhelm Landesführer Max Jüttner represented the SA at the Nuremberg war crimes trials.[92]

6

Conclusion

The highest leaders of the SA were a homogeneous group, almost what one could call a corps.[1] They came from the same social class,[2] and they were formed by a common set of military and political experiences and attitudes. Out of a common milieu they then went to the SA and the Nazi Party, their common experiences serving to knit them and the SA into a close and efficient group. This homogeneity adds to our knowledge of the makeup of the Nazi Party, but even more important, it has immediate implications for assessing the significance of the larger paramilitary and right-wing ecology within which the Nazis and so many others like them flourished.

The discovery that the highest officers of the SA were a homogeneous group should not, however, be allowed to conceal from historians the important differences that existed. Diversity and homogeneity are both relative concepts, and the assumption of one should not blind the historian to the importance of the other. This book has also shown that such differences can explain much about the changing nature of the SA and its process of growth and development within the broader right-wing environment of the Weimar Republic. An organization cannot exist completely apart from its members, and vice versa. The evolution of the higher leadership corps of the SA is inevitably also the story of the evolution of the organization itself.

At first glance, the commonalities among these men are the most apparent. The highest SA officers were older[3] and better educated[4] than the rank and file under their command. While there is much truth to the idea that Nazism and fascist movements in general often represent a form of "youth revolt," in the SA this youth revolt was led by older and more experienced leaders.[5] The exact nature of those experiences is the subject of this study. They were concentrated in the very military and political types of activity that best prepared them to form and lead a mass paramilitary organization.

The group was heavily dominated by military specialists who had been trained by and had served in the Imperial Army of the Wilhelmine Empire. Roughly one-third had been professional soldiers before the First World War.[6]

The experience of the First World War only reinforces the point about the military character of the highest SA leaders. At least 76 percent were veterans of the war, and 73 percent had seen combat. Fifty-six percent of combat veterans had been wounded, and 85 percent had been decorated. Nearly all veterans who were not already professional officers before 1914 became reserve officers by 1918.[7] Most served in combat units and were decorated for bravery, but 37 percent served in some sort of staff or administrative position. So the highest SA leaders could be characterized as military specialists both in the use of violence and in its planning. It was no accident that SA regulations and techniques resembled those of the Imperial Army to a remarkable degree. The experience of the First World War marked an entire generation of European males and had profound and lasting effects on the world. Afterwards, the "war generation" took the lead in all movements of social and political renewal, of which Nazism and the SA were but a part. It was not simply a demographic coincidence that so many veterans found their place in the leadership of the SA and of other paramilitary organizations in the Weimar Republic, for they had both the technical skills needed to lead large bodies of men and the political will to do so.

Yet if the highest leaders of the SA were almost exclusively men who were firmly rooted and socialized in the Wilhelmine Empire, and if they were indelibly and profoundly marked by the experience of the First World War, it is equally true that their development did not stop in 1918 and that they were also fundamentally shaped by their actions and experiences after the war.

Nearly all future top SA leaders were politically or militarily active during the revolution and unrest from November 1918 through the end of 1919. While this high level of activity is once again proof that they were a homogeneous group, the exact form of their activity in this period varied. Military types of activity clearly predominated, however. Older scholarship puts particular emphasis on the role of the free corps in molding Nazi attitudes.[8] The reality of the careers of the highest SA leaders was much more complicated. Although a significant number did serve in a free corps,[9] it was not the dominant form of activity during the revolution. Equally if not more important was membership in a range of other organizations, including the new regular army then being formed (which became the Reichswehr), the old Imperial Army (units of which persisted into 1919),[10] local or part-time self-defense organizations,[11] or even (usually short-lived) membership in political parties.[12] Rather than single out the free corps, one must make a more balanced assessment of the postwar influences on and experiences of future Nazis.

After 1920, some of the men in this study abandoned organized political and military activity. Most future SA leaders, however, continued to be active in both paramilitary and political organizations. Of the two, the paramilitary organizations, or Wehrverbände, which arose in 1920 and continued to play a role in German politics until 1933, clearly occupied the greater number of them.[13] These militias played a crucial and largely overlooked role in the formation of many of the forms of action and organization that later became characteristic of the SA. It is these organizations, and not the free corps, which are most similar to the SA and Nazi Party in organization and outlook. Although they were organized along military lines and stressed military knowledge and values, they were still civilian and part-time organizations, rooted in a given locality and class. Most significant of all, they were not organized exclusively for narrow military concerns. From their inception they had a broader political purpose. Activity in one or more of these paramilitary organizations—such as the Reichskriegsflagge, Wehrwolf, or the Jungdeutscher Orden—is one of the most significant factors shared by the greatest number of the highest SA leaders in this study. On this basis alone it must be recognized as one of the most important factors in the formation of men who later joined the Nazi Party. Much further research remains to be done to clarify the influence of the Wehrverbände on the development of both individual future National Socialists and of the Nazi movement as a whole. Even now, however, it is apparent that the Wehrverbände, and not the free corps, were the true "vanguard of Nazism."[14]

A significant minority also became involved in political organizations. While the dominant characteristic of the group is its military character, this should not blind one to the fact that many leaders were also political activists and as such played an important role in the early growth of the NSDAP. This is particularly true of those who were among the first wave to join the SA in 1925 and 1926. Some were members of the DNVP or of some other mainstream conservative political party in the Weimar Republic.[15] More important, a vast proportion of those who were involved in a political organization at all were members of a völkisch political party or organiza-tion.[16] This political experience and even zealotry form the second of the two elements, political and military, in the equation that ulti-mately created the SA. The fusion of paramilitary forms and dyna-mism with the largely völkisch political message of the NSDAP was what made the SA both unique and effective as a political organiza-tion.

Two elements that did not enter into the equation producing the NSDAP to any great extent, and that were completely absent from the careers of the highest SA leaders, were membership in any center or left-wing political party or organization and membership in any confessional or religious organization. With one or two insignifi-cant exceptions, absolutely none of the highest SA leaders in this study ever participated in any organization of this type.[17] The results are clear on this point: the highest SA leaders, to a man, were predis-posed from the beginning in favor of not only secular and conserva-tive political parties but also those on the radical, völkisch fringe. This author has discovered little to explain this apparent predisposi-tion and does not even attempt to address the background of the SA rank and file, which may indeed have been very different. What I can state is that the highest leaders of the SA were drawn from among men who were already clearly situated on the far right of the politi-cal spectrum and who had not been involved in confessional organi-zations. They were certainly not converts from moderate or even left-wing political parties.

The careers of the highest SA leaders evolved or unfolded in a particular way and under particular historical conditions. In a con-crete and fundamental fashion, the model of organization that be-came the SA grew out of the lived experiences of its leadership in their passage from the Wilhelmine Empire into the Third Reich.

Their experiences in the Wilhelmine Empire and in the First World War were largely military in nature, although clearly these military experiences were associated with certain larger but specific types of political socialization as well, such as ideas of duty and obe-dience to the Empire or of comradeship and violence in the war. There is also no "generic" set of military values; those of the Wilhelmine Empire and First World War were embedded in a larger but specific cultural context.

The experiences of these men from 1919 to 1923 were also largely military in nature, although a political and even radical-political com-ponent was increasingly present. In this stage, owing to the common perception on the radical right that politics was somehow corrupt and dirty, whereas military forms of association and organization were somehow straightforward and clean (inherited from the Wilhelmine Empire), the political and paramilitary elements were largely separate. Even if a man belonged to a political group and a paramilitary organization simultaneously, the two activities were still considered separate and distinct. This was true until 1924.

The failure of the Beer Hall Putsch in November 1923, as the last in a series of abortive attempts to overthrow the government of the Weimar Republic by force, and the seeming stabilization of Germany that followed led to the beginning of a fundamental reappraisal of tactics and goals on the radical right. Not all organizations and groups came to the same conclusions, and not all of them embarked on this fundamental reassessment at exactly the same time. The Nazis were among the first, and they developed the most successful new set of tactics. These tactics amounted to the blending of the formerly separate traditions of the paramilitary organizations with those of the völkisch political parties, and they were the joint creation of the future leaders of the SA and of the Party.[18] This fundamental change in the direction of the Nazi Party and SA once they reemerged in 1925 was due less to Hitler's genius, as even many modern historians would seem to imply,[19] and more to the experiences and ideas of individual Nazis in 1924 when the NSDAP was banned and they were members of other paramilitary and völkisch organizations. It was the experience of explaining the failure of the putsch tactic and trying to find more successful methods that led to the fusion of the paramilitary and völkisch traditions and the creation of the new and ultimately successful Nazi Party.[20]

This fusion was mirrored in the activities of most future leaders of the Nazi Party, including the SA leaders who have been studied in this book. In this regard it was also immaterial whether they actually belonged to both paramilitary and völkisch organizations. In the context of 1924, all became aware that the paramilitary organizations could become successful in parliamentary politics when animated by völkisch ideology, as the electoral successes of May 1924 proved. Thus, the new formula so successfully adopted by the NSDAP from 1925 on was the creation of an entire milieu and of countless individuals and not of one man, even though that one man, Adolf Hitler, still played a central role in legitimizing the new tactics and in seeing that they were adopted by the entire party. The new formula was henceforth followed by the SA and the Party in tandem, and indeed, the two organizations were far more closely intertwined in their early years than is commonly recognized today.

From 1925, when the NSDAP and SA were rebuilt, they gradually grew and became more and more important in Germany as political organizations. One of the most important outcomes of this study has been a better understanding of how the process of growth occurred. There were three general stages. In the beginning, the NSDAP/SA was merely one small group among many that existed in the isolated but fertile environment on the far right in the Weimar Republic. The first stage of development was the gradual assertion of the dominance of the NSDAP/SA within this limited ecological niche. In the process of asserting its dominance, the NSDAP and SA absorbed large numbers of leaders and followers from kindred but rival organizations. This made the NSDAP/SA strong enough to begin the second stage of its development, in which it moved to challenge the mainstream national political parties. Here again, large numbers of former supporters of these traditional political parties were absorbed, until the NSDAP/SA became the largest single political party in Germany and thus strong enough to proceed to the third stage of its development in which it assumed control over the government.

Traditionally, accounts of the rise of the Nazi Party have stressed the second stage, when the NSDAP challenged the conventional parties of the center and right and managed to absorb many of their supporters. Few have paid much attention to the crucial first stage, in which the NSDAP grew to dominance among the marginal völkisch organizations. This study emphasizes the importance of the ability of the Nazi Party and SA to absorb members of rival right-wing organizations during this stage and shows just how this process occurred.

The point here is not the common one that the NSDAP was extremely efficient; rather, it is that it could not have existed without the larger ecological niche that supported it.[21] If there had not been a rich variety of organizations occupying the political "habitat" on the right in Weimar, the Nazi Party could never have survived. Had this original environment dried up—or been eliminated—the NSDAP would have perished as well.

The rival organizations that were absorbed and became "extinct" due to the greater success of the NSDAP did not simply supply sheeplike followers who gravitated from one organization to another as if by instinct. Those who switched allegiances had strong ideological motivations. Moreover, the absorption of other radical right-wing organizations by the NSDAP and SA did not bring merely followers. It brought the NSDAP a steady stream of leaders and activists as well. The presence of "defectors" or converts from so many other organizations is proof of this fact. Moreover, as leaders from similar organizations, each of these men brought experiences that were then used to make the NSDAP and SA more effective, while robbing its competitors of just this leadership and experience. The "dying" rival organizations provided capable leaders. Had these organizations not existed, had this transfer of experience and leadership not taken place, the Nazi Party could not have succeeded. In this sense, the Nazi Party was a collective effort not only of every Nazi but of the collective experiences of the members of its environment.

The homogeneity of the higher SA leadership tells a great deal about the political environment on the far right in which the organization developed and also provides the key to understanding how this development was possible at such a rapid rate. Although the top SA leaders came from dissimilar and often competing organizations, these organizations also had much in common. The organizations occupying the far right of the political spectrum together with the NSDAP were rivals and were certainly not identical, but only in the way that members of the same family can be rivals and individuals. To put it another way, there was a remarkable similarity among many leaders and members of the organizations on the far right in the Weimar Republic, which allowed them to be absorbed into the SA leadership without any apparent decline in effectiveness. The fact that rival organizations had a body of members and leaders so much like the existing leaders of the SA meant that absorbing them caused relatively little disruption or "indigestion." National Socialist ideology, the common enemy of the "Weimar system" and the mythic role of Hitler as "Der Führer" integrated them even further and smoothed over any differences that may have existed between them.

Given the above, the slight differences in background among top SA leaders become more important, for they allow us to trace the precise evolution of the organization over time and see the dialectic relationship between the shape of the SA and the experiences or character of its leadership.

Those who joined in 1925 or 1926 did so when the NSDAP was little more than a sect. They were the true and original political soldiers of the Nazi Party. They were the ones who best combined military expertise and experience in paramilitary groups with a singular political radicalism and commitment to völkisch ideology. As pioneers they shaped the SA in their own image, which was a combination of paramilitary and völkisch traditions. They were both soldiers and politicians, and they were equally at home in ideology and in formation. Often they were equally active in the SA and the Party in the early years. It is indicative that all but one of the SA commanders came from within this group.[22] It had the highest percentage of those who had been active in a völkisch organization and the highest percentage of those who had been in the NSDAP or SA before the Beer Hall Putsch. On the other hand, this group had the smallest percentage of former professional officers, former free corps members, and former Wehrverband members.

The next group, those joining from 1927 through 1930, present a mixed picture. Some came out of the Party organization, illustrating that the connection between the SA and NSDAP continued to be closer in this period than is often thought. Others, however, show the ability of the SA and NSDAP to attract activists from other organizations. For some, like the groups of "passive activists" or "sporadic activists," the SA and NSDAP were able to reactivate men whose activism had waned since the revolution and the Beer Hall Putsch. Others, like the "serial activists," progressed from one organization to another, ending up in the SA and NSDAP as a culmination of their military-political careers. Still others best represent the countless members of rival groups who were persuaded to switch allegiances to the NSDAP, providing it and the SA with valuable leadership just as it was beginning to expand.

Similar patterns existed in the body of men in this study who joined the SA in 1931 and 1932. Many were equally "defectors" or "passive activists" or "party soldiers," but above all, those joining in 1931 or 1932 who managed to rise to one of the top ranks in the SA possessed special skills. Yet the fact that these men were specialists does little to explain why they joined or were recruited into the SA. The answer is important. Some had special contacts or relationships with SA leaders who brought them into the SA and into high rank relatively quickly. This is clearest in the case of Ernst Röhm's associates, whom he placed in staff positions within the SA command. Yet the process did not simply involve a handful of men who happened to know Röhm or another SA leader. What actually existed was a more generalized process that awarded advancement to men with special skills and abilities, provided that they also came from a background similar to that of existing SA leaders. The men in this study who joined the SA in 1931 or 1932 had special expertise which the

SA needed and wanted, but they were not chosen at random. Instead, they were men who, by virtue of their background and outlook, could be counted on to mesh well with existing SA leaders.

Further proof of this comes from the men in this study who joined in 1933 or 1934. They were almost exclusively either Party leaders transferring into the SA or former leaders of rival paramilitary organizations that were coordinated and absorbed by the SA after the Nazis took power. At first glance it is indeed surprising that these former rivals could so easily and apparently effortlessly join the SA and continue on as before. The answer to this seeming paradox is that, for all the rivalry between the SA/NSDAP and organizations like the Stahlhelm, the leaders of both lived in the same moral world, shared the same general body of experiences and background, and came from the same radical right-wing political habitat.

Men with many different ideas and backgrounds became SA leaders. What enabled them to work together despite all their differences and personal quarrels was not least the fact that they had participated in many of the same types of activity. It would be rash at this point to attempt to extend this generalization to the rank and file of the SA, but it is interesting to speculate on the importance of the myth of the war experience, the myth of the free corps, and the myth of the old army in legitimizing the leadership of older men for the younger, generationally rebellious SA rank and file. All three kinds of experience were held in high value, even awe by the postwar generation, and this surely allowed them to take direction from an older generation with which they were otherwise in conflict.

Certainly, one of the most important contributions of this study is to redirect attention to the importance of the context, or "habitat," within which the Nazi Party developed. It did not thrive in a vacuum, but instead existed in a complex net of organizations and personal contacts. The same is almost certainly true of the other fascist parties and political organizations that were so common in the interwar period. "Political," after all, means being situated in a social context and acting within the parameters and possibilities of that social context. The history of a prominent or "successful" organization, such as the NSDAP, is also in part the history of all the small, marginal, and "unsuccessful" organizations that existed around it, but all too often this is forgotten. Indeed, while there is much left to know about the interaction of the NSDAP with its political environment, it is still probably the best contextualized of all the fascist parties. Much is still unknown about others. Did they, too, grow out of a wider radical right-wing context, as the NSDAP did? Did they, too, grow by feeding off of their competitors? And if the answer to these questions is no, could the absence of a broader right-wing "ecology" be one reason why few ever succeeded in taking power? Much research remains to be done.

Another implication of this book for future research lies in the way the composition of the membership of political organizations or movements should be studied. What emerges most strikingly from a study of the careers of the highest leaders of the SA is the extreme importance of a process of evolution in their lives. Any explanation for why these men became Nazis and storm troopers that is monocausal, such as the theory that the free corps were the vanguard of Nazism, or that ignores a temporal progression in their activities is wholly inadequate and misleading. It is not enough to use information about individuals that is drawn from one moment in their lives without taking into account the evolution and development of that individual over time and within a given but specific historical context if at all possible. Instead of giving static statements like "most storm troopers came from the war generation," this author's object has been to look at the political development of the highest SA leaders in a dynamic fashion. The nature of these men can only be understood by following them over time and by understanding that individuals change and develop and do not remain static. The concept of change, the entire temporal dimension, is after all at the very foundation of the historical profession, and it is one of the key elements that makes it different from the other social and human sciences.

To return to the context of the Weimar Republic, the findings of this book underscore the fatal consequences of the Republic's failure to create a broad consensus in its own support. For this, the national government itself must bear some of the responsibility insofar as it felt compelled to tolerate and even support the existence of the subculture of right-wing paramilitary and völkisch organizations out of which the Nazi Party gained its early strength. Granted, the institutions and leaders of the Weimar Republic should not be faulted for failing to foresee that the Nazi Party would one day be such a menace while it was still just a tiny handful of true believers. Yet they can and must be criticized for failing to take more vigorous action against the whole subculture of the paramilitary radical right. That this entire demimonde posed a clear threat to the Republic was abundantly clear and often the subject of public and private warnings.[23]

Faced with a clear and present threat to its borders and to domestic law and order (here often by the very people who were used to maintain it) on the one hand, yet bound by its own law (which incorporated the Versailles treaty) on the other hand, the Weimar Republic felt obligated to turn to private organizations and extralegal or even illegal means to fulfill its obligations and policies. Once the Republic broke its own laws, it was forced to tolerate and cover up any and all lawlessness of the private groups used to carry out its policy, regardless of whether the ultimate aims of the Republic and its extragovernmental agents were compatible.[24] Thus the swamp of paramilitary conservatism was not dried but allowed to flourish, spreading its poison throughout the Republic. Many governments today would do well to heed this lesson.

There are other lessons in this book that are applicable to modern groups like the Nazis or SA. Most modern democracies have within them tiny marginal parties or organizations on the far, far right of the political spectrum. Usually these groups espouse or are suspected of espousing the use of violence, and many are organized along paramilitary lines or are associated with separate paramilitary organizations. Thankfully, nearly all of these groups, be they in Germany, France, the United States, Belgium, or some other modern democracy, are decidedly tiny and decidedly marginal. Their danger should not be overstated, but the same was once true of the NSDAP. Given a situation where there are many such groups (such as in the United States today), it should be clear that it is quite possible for many tiny groups to become one large organization in rather short order. The way the SA grew into a mass national organization, as demonstrated in the biographies of even a tiny subset of its leadership, should inoculate anyone against underestimating the danger of any paramilitary organization dedicated to overthrowing the democratic system, however small. The practical lesson to be drawn from this book for those who are engaged in tracking and controlling such organizations today is that they should pay particular attention to the links and ties (however informal or personal) between such organizations, for these are the preconditions for sudden growth.

Perhaps a more difficult lesson can be drawn from this study for the post-cold war era. In this time of military downsizing combined with a newly multipolar world system that seems to favor the eruption of many small wars, revolutions, and "police actions," the uncontrolled spread of military hardware (both sophisticated and simple) is naturally a matter of great concern. The modern rash of small-scale conflict is often born of long-standing hatred (even if many of these "traditions" are, in fact, recent creations), but this hatred is fueled by the ready and almost limitless supply of arms. The prolif-eration of military hardware has even become a matter of domestic concern in many peaceful countries, most notably in the debate over assault weapons in the United States beginning in the mid-1980s or in Australia in the mid-1990s. A lesson from this study of the SA leadership is that it may not be enough to simply monitor and try to restrict the supply of arms in a physical sense. As shown by the men who became SA leaders, the presence of a large body of individuals trained in the organization and use of violence is as dangerous as the presence of the hardware itself. This is a very difficult lesson, for people in a free society cannot be controlled in the same way as hard-ware, and their dangerous knowledge cannot be removed or controlled in the same way as the tools of their trade may be (given the political will to do so). It must also be acknowledged that most of these mili-tary experts are loyal, honorable men and women who risked much and gave exemplary service defending and protecting their countries. They don't deserve suspicion, and yet they have certain skills that could prove quite dangerous indeed. At the very least, the practical lesson from this study is that special attention must be paid to the presence of former (or active) military personnel in any paramilitary organization not tightly under state control, and states might give some thought to limiting not only the amounts of military hardware they produce but also the numbers of men and women they train in their use.

7

Methodology

The information used in this book comes from a variety of sources, but roughly 85 percent comes from personnel files or internal court documents prepared by the SA. Another 10 percent comes from other materials prepared by the NSDAP, contemporary documents such as obituaries in the Nazi Party press, or post facto memoirs. This information was used in its "raw" form about individuals, but it was also summarized to build a database that was used to make statements about the entire group or significant parts of it.

WHO IS IN THE DATABASE: DEFINITION OF SA RANKS

Because the group studied here is defined by rank, and because of the SA's historical development, some further definition of ranks is necessary. The rank of Stabschef is defined to include all of the actual day-to-day commanders of the SA, whether their formal title was Stabschef or Oberster SA-Führer. The reasons for this are found in the development of the SA vis-à-vis the Party. Up until September 2, 1930, the SA had its own commander in chief, called Oberster SA-Führer. When Oberster SA-Führer Franz von Pfeffer resigned his post on August 29, 1930, Adolf Hitler himself assumed the title. He did not assume any of the day-to-day duties of running the SA, however; the chief of staff of the SA (Stabschef), who until then had performed the duties normally associated with a chief of staff in a military organization, took over the actual duties of commander.[1] At the time this had a great symbolic importance, but in practical terms it amounted only to a change in the official designation of the SA's commander. Thus, this study will contain Franz von Pfeffer and Hermann Göring, both Oberster SA-Führer, and Otto Wagener, Viktor Lutze, and Ernst Röhm, all Stabschefs, but not Adolf Hitler. Although a very small group, the Oberster SA-Führer/Stabschefs were naturally of extreme importance in running the SA. Note that they were all former officers, but they were also generally men with high Party positions alongside their SA activities (Lutze, von Pfeffer) or close friends of Hitler (Göring, Röhm).

The SA Gruppenführer and Obergruppenführer are the next two highest SA ranks, the generals of the SA. U.S. army intelligence tables of comparative ranks defined Gruppenführer as the equivalent of major general and the higher Obergruppenführer as the equivalent of lieutenant general.[2] As with the Stabschefs, the holders of the ranks of Gruppenführer and Obergruppenführer are defined rather broadly; they also include anyone who held the earlier rank of OSAF-Stellvertreter (in use between February 8, 1929, and February 20, 1931), which was superseded by the new rank of Gruppenführer.[3] The numbers of Gruppenführer and Obergruppenführer are also relatively small, given the size of the SA, yet they too held positions of great influence. Together, 172 active SA leaders held one of these two ranks.

The emphasis above on active SA leaders is an important distinction. Originally, the SA awarded only functional, not nominal ranks. This meant that the commander of a Standarte (an SA unit much like a modern battalion in size but like a modern regiment in function), for example, held the rank of Standartenführer, but only as long as he actually commanded the Standarte. If he lost or resigned his command, he reverted to being just a simple SA-man. Ranks in the SA were later put on a nominal basis by Ernst Röhm (Stabschef between January 5, 1931, and June 30, 1934), so that they could be held not only by the actual leaders of units but also by leaders in staff positions or even by honorary or inactive SA leaders. This study includes only active SA leaders, not those men who were awarded the rank of Gruppenführer or Obergruppenführer on an honorary basis.

The SS was a subordinate part of the SA until July 1934. Consequently, any SS leader who otherwise met the criteria of selection for this study before June 30, 1934, is included. This is only proper, since there were in fact more similarities than differences between the senior leaders of the SA and those of the SS down through 1934, as this study makes clear. Not only did SA and SS Gruppenführer and Obergruppenführer come from remarkably similar backgrounds before July 1934, but many of them were found to have transferred from the SA to the SS or vice versa at some point in their careers. Among the early leaders of the SA and SS, just who ended up in which organization was often as much a matter of chance as anything else.[4]

The Sample

Most studies of this type use only a small subset, or sample, and then use statistical manipulation to make generalizations about the entire group. This is not the case here. The specialized language of sampling and statistics would technically call even a complete group a "sample," but it is only in this counterintuitive sense that the men analyzed in this book represent one. In fact, all who held one of the three highest ranks in the SA on an active basis (as defined above) are included. No one was left out, and no sophisticated sampling techniques were used. The group analyzed is the highest leadership of the SA without any further qualification. Among other things, this approach has the advantage of avoiding many possible methodological pitfalls concerning the rules to be followed in sample selection and the interpretation of statistical results. Any statistical statements made about this group will be only about the group itself, not some larger whole. There are no inferential statistics, only descriptive ones.

This does not mean that all possible methodological problems have been eliminated. There are certain problems inherent in the types of data used and in the survival of information about the men in this study that must be mentioned. To begin with, it was impossible to collect completely uniform data on every individual. Information was available for some that was not available for others. Many records from the SA and other National Socialist organizations were destroyed in bombing raids on Munich and later in fighting in Bavaria at war's end. This can essentially be considered random and should not affect the validity of any results from this study. A more difficult problem arises from the fact that some records were deliberately destroyed by the Nazis in a more systematic manner. This is particularly true of records pertaining to the victims of the Röhm Purge. Much of this information could be obtained or reconstructed from other sources, since the men affected were all prominent SA leaders and public figures, but the possibility of important gaps must still be recognized. Alas, historical data are often not as perfect as the rules of statistical analysis would require, but this should not stand in the way of making the best use of the most data available. Every attempt has been made to verify any data coming from nonprimary sources and to ensure that the data are as complete as possible. Beyond that, all that can be done is to keep in mind that potential distortions may exist and to point out places where the available data are particularly thin or open to distortion. While this is not ideal, the fact that only descriptive statistics are used makes the situation less problematic.

THE SOURCES

The most important sources for this study are found among the collections of National Socialist documents and records held in the former Berlin Document Center (BDC), now later known as the Bundesarchiv Außenstelle Berlin-Zehlendorf.[5] (For the sake of simplicity, it will be referred to as BDC.) Roughly 90 percent of the information used in this study came from documents in the BDC.

The Berlin Document Center housed a vast collection of biographical Nazi records originally collected by the United States during and after the Second World War for intelligence purposes and later for denazification. After the war, material captured by the British and French was added. The collection remained under U.S. control (specifically, the State Department as a part of the U.S. mission to Berlin)[6] until July 1994, when it was officially returned to the Federal Republic of Germany.[7] The documents themselves were housed in an underground bunker complex topped with what looks like an ordinary house in a wealthy, wooded suburb in the far southwestern part of Berlin. Ironically, the complex originally was built to house a central telephone tapping and domestic intelligence center run by Hermann Göring. Today, only the barbed wire and armed guards disturb the tranquility of the setting in which the BDC sat.

Within the BDC are over twenty-five separate groups or collections of documents, few of which build well-defined homogeneous collections in the normal archival sense. Instead, they usually contain documents from several or even many different provenances and organizations. The exact origin of many documents is impossible to determine with certainty today. Apparently, many former separate collections of documents were simply combined into one large group on the basis of their pertinence to a particular Nazi organization. Nearly all groups of documents have been filed alphabetically. In general, historians using the BDC submit names and dates of birth of the individuals whose records they wish to consult, and the staff of the BDC goes through all twenty-five or more groups of records and presents the visitor with all of the documents in the BDC that relate to a particular individual. (This archaic system was recently computerized through the herculean efforts of the outgoing U.S. director, David Marwell, but until reorganization plans are put into effect by the Bundesarchiv, the complex and often arbitrary internal division of the collections remains.) There is often little or no indication of which group of records a given piece of information or document belongs to within the BDC magazine, and it is only through experience and talking with the BDC staff that information about the different record groups and how they came to be built can be determined. Despite this, several groups of records within the BDC stand out as being particularly useful for this study.

Two groups of SA records exist in the BDC. One is called the Allgemeine Personalakten (general personnel records) or simply AP Akten. This is misleading, since actual personnel records make up only a small part of this group. Those that are present in it include only some SA administrative or medical officers and a handful of active SA-Führer, mostly from southern German SA-Gruppen. There does not seem to be even a full set from any SA-Gruppe. Dominating this collection are the case records of the Sondergericht (special court) der Obersten SA-Führung and its successor, the Disziplinargericht (disciplinary court) der Obersten SA-Führung. Mixed in are older records going back at least as far as 1930, which seem also to have come into the keeping of the Gerichts- und Rechtsamt (SA Court and Legal Department) at a later date, since they mostly document internal investigations, mutinies, etc. All of the records in the AP collection are arranged alphabetically in 777 loose-leaf notebooks of a type common in Germany called Leitz-Ordner. Each notebook contains 400-500 pages.[8]

A larger group of records is called the SA Vorgänge (proceedings). It contains a wide spectrum of materials ranging from a single file card containing hardly more than a name to over 400 pages per individual. Less than twelve pages per individual is certainly the norm. Although the BDC staff considered this to be a group of SA records and the majority of the records do in fact come from the SA, it also contains material from the National Socialist Automobile Corps (NSAK), National Socialist Flying Corps (NSFK), Organisation Todt, and NSDAP, to list just the salient elements.[9] The SA Vorgänge are also filed alphabetically, and they occupy 4,074 Leitz-Ordner. The most important records are the various types of internal SA questionnaires. Most probably once formed a separate collection of personnel files that were centrally stored at SA headquarters in Munich for all SA leaders of the rank of Standartenführer and above. These questionnaires were the backbone of this study.

A third major collection that was frequently consulted was that of SS Offiziers-Akten (SS officer files), a collection of SS personnel files on over 60,000 SS leaders. These dossiers are generally complete, although the collection does not include dossiers from all SS-Führer who ever existed. Other groups of records that were especially helpful include the NSDAP Central Membership Card Files, the so-called Parteikanzlei Korrespondenz (Party Chancellory Correspondence), and records from the Oberstes Parteigericht der NSDAP (Supreme Nazi Party Court) and the Untersuchungs- und Schlichtungsausschuss der NSDAP (Investigation and Mediation Committee).[10]

Another source consulted at both the BDC and the Bundesarchiv in Koblenz is the so-called Schumacher Sammlung (Schumacher Collection). This began as a random assortment of nonbiographical documents that a BDC employee, Herr Schumacher, found in biographical files and brought together for internal use. It was organized topically. This collection eventually occupied several hundred Leitz-Ordner and was later returned to the Bundesarchiv. Duplicate documents and copies of particularly useful materials were kept in the BDC for internal use, and additions were made to the BDC version even after the bulk of the collection was returned to the Federal Republic.[11] The Bundesarchiv recently broke up its Schumacher Collection and reorganized it according to provenance, making any earlier references to the Schumacher Collection in the Bundesarchiv in Koblenz useless. For this reason, when reference has been made here to Schumacher materials, the reference is to the BDC version wherever possible, since it still remains in its "original" form.

Other sources that deserve mention were the eyewitness accounts and other rare contemporary sources at the Institut für Zeitgeschichte in Munich and various government and NSDAP/SA records in the Bundesarchiv and Bundesarchiv-Militärarchiv in Freiburg. These were supplemented with published sources including newspapers (*Völkische Beobachter* and the *SA-Mann*), Reichstag handbooks, contemporary who's who guides such as *Das Deutsche Führerlexikon*,[12] and published officers' seniority lists from the Imperial Army, Reichswehr, and SS.[13]

THE DATABASE

A standardized body of information developed by the author was collected for each individual and later quantified in a database. Usually, the information in the SA questionnaires sufficed to fill in all the individual categories of information, but in many cases, this was supplemented with additional information from one of the other archival sources mentioned above. In very rare cases (such as the case of Ernst Röhm and some others killed in the Röhm Purge), the only information available was from published primary or even secondary sources. All of this information was carefully verified. In all cases where information was missing or could not be verified, it was left blank in the database.

The database was constructed using the popular software package dBase III+. The structure of the database is too long to be reproduced here; it eventually grew to encompass five database files, each with over a hundred pieces of information. Aside from basic biographical information, it includes all of the known organizational activities of the men included from 1914 to 1945. For the crucial period from the end of 1918 to the end of 1935 this information was recorded on a quarterly basis. In this way, the database permitted the activities of the men in question and the changes in those activities over time to be measured. The ability to see both dynamic and static relationships within the data is one of the most distinguishing factors of this study.

All numerical information about groups comes from this database and is not usually cited separately. Any statements or information about individuals is cited in the usual manner, though once again, it almost always comes from the BDC files about that individual.

Originally, the author had intended to do a statistical study on the entire SA. Although this proved impractical, it meant that raw data were collected not only on the 178 individuals in this present study but also on a further 2,500 SA leaders and men of all levels of rank. The records of close to twice that many SA members had to be read in order to collect all this data. Although none of this supplemental data is used directly in this study, it inevitably colors the overall interpretation of the SA, its policies, and its leadership. While each individual file by itself may not have brought any new insights into the makeup of the SA, when taken together they do provide an impression of the personnel politics, makeup, and structure of the SA, at least from 1932 to 1939. All of this information is difficult to quantify or cite individually, but arguably it has played a major role in the author's understanding of the SA and its members and thus in the process whereby many of the conclusions in this study have been reached.

Appendix A

The Organization of the SA

SA ORGANIZATION, 1923

Oberste SA-Führung
Hundertschaft
Zug (3 Gruppen or 23 men)
Gruppe (9 men)

SA ORGANIZATION 1926[1]

Gausturm	(as of fall 1927 there were 18 Gaustürme)
Brigade	(2-5 Standarten)
Standarte	(2-5 Stürme)
Sturm	(2-4 Trupps)
Trupp	(5-8 Gruppen)
Gruppe	(6-12 men)

SA ORGANIZATION 1931[2]

Oberste SA-Führung
Gruppe   (1 or more Untergruppen, not more than 15,000 men)

Untergruppe (Gausturm)
Standarte   (1,000-3,000 men/several Sturmbanne)
Sturmbann   (250-600 men/several Stürme)
Sturm   (70-200 men/2+ Trupps)
Trupp   (20-60 men/3-6 Scharen)
Schar   (4-12 men)
  (formerly Gruppe)

SA ORGANIZATION 1932[3]

OSAF	
Obergruppe	(several Gruppen)
Gruppe	(several Untergruppen, not more than 30,000 men)
Untergruppe	(several Standarten)
Standarte	(several Sturmbanne/1,200-3,000 men)
Sturmbann	(several Stürme/250-600 men)
Sturm	(2+ Trupps/60-150 men)
Trupp	(3 Scharen/up to 50 men)
Schar	(4-16 men)

SA ORGANIZATION 1935[4]

OSAF	
Obergruppe	
Gruppe	
Brigade	(usually 4)
Standarte	(usually 3 plus 2 reserve Standarten)
Sturmbann	(3)
Sturm	(4)

1. SABE 6, "Gliederung" of November 6, 1926, in NSDAP Hauptarchiv, folder 302 (as filmed by the Hoover Institution at the BDC, microfilm roll 16).

2. OSAF I no. 208/31 of February 20, 1931, Erlaß no. 2 Betr: Gliederung der SA in BAK Schumacher Collection, Ordner 404.

3. NSDAP, Oberste SA-Führung, *Dienstvorschrift für die SA der NSDAP*, 2 vols. (Diessen vor München: Jos. Huber, 1932), 28-35.

4. OSAF F no. 220/95geh. of February 27, 1935 (Geheim!) in Schumacher Collection, Ordner 404.

Appendix B

Equivalent Ranks

SA	German Army	U.S. Army
Oberster Sa-Führer		
Stabschef der SA	Generaloberst	General
Obergruppenführer	General	Lieutenant general
Gruppenführer	Generalleutnant	Major general
Brigadeführer	Generalmajor	Brigadier general
Oberführer		
Standartenführer	Oberst	Colonel
Obersturmbannführer	Oberstleutnant	Lieutenant colonel
Sturmbannführer	Major	Major
Hauptsturmführer	Hauptmann	Captain
Obersturmführer	Oberleutnant	First lieutenant
Sturmführer	Leutnant	Lieutenant
Haupttruppführer	Stabsfeldwebel	Sergeant major
Obertruppführer	Oberfeldwebel	Master sergeant
Truppführer	Feldwebel	Technical sergeant
Oberscharführer	Unterfeldwebel	Staff sergeant
Scharführer	Unteroffizier	Sergeant
Rottenführer	Gefreiter	Corporal
Obersturmmann	Obersoldat	Private first class
Sturmmann (SA-Mann)	Soldat	Private

Appendix C

Men Included in This Study

The following 178 men are included in this study. Each occupied one of the top three levels of rank in the SA on an active basis. The names of these ranks changed over time, but from 1932 to 1945 they were Stabschef, Obergruppenführer, and Gruppenführer in descending order. Their biographical information, drawn mainly from SA personnel files, was entered into a database and used to make general statements about the group. See chapter 7 for further information.

* = Indicates that a short biography is found in the text.
Number in parentheses refers to a man's position in the group photo on page 3.

Aster, Richard Arthur *
Bauer, Franz Bernhard August
Beckerle, Adolf-Heinz (19)
Beissner, Ernst Friedrich
Bennecke, Hans Heinrich *
Bergmann, Robert
Bock, Franz
Böckenhauer, Arthur (20)
Boehmcker, Johann Heinrich (4)
Boetel, Erich Hans Jürgen
Börner, Reinhard
Brauneck, Hermann Max-Gustav
Brückner, Friedrich Wilhelm
Buch, Walter
Burger, August
Caspary, Carl *
Czerwinski, Bruno
Daiber, Axel Johannes
Daluege, Kurt Max Franz
Dame, Wilhelm
Damian, Friedrich Leopold
Darré, Walter Richard
Dechant, Georg Hugo *
Detten, Georg von

Diehl, Edmund
Dietrich, Josef (Sepp)
Dincklage, Karl
Dittler, Wilhelm
Dörnemann, Karl Friedrich
Dressler, Albert
Eberstein, Karl Friedrich Freiherr von
Ernst, Karl
Fassbach, Paul
Fenz, Friedrich Josef
Fichte, Ernst Ludwig
Fichte, Werner von
Finck von Finckenstein, Heinrich-Georg Wilhelm Graf
Frank, Hans
Friedrich, Hans (11)
Fuchs, Johann Baptist *
Fust, Herbert Robert Gerhard * (12)
Gaudin, Heinrich Albert Wilhelm
Giesler, Paul
Girgensohn, Thomas Otto Harald *
Gontermann, Leonhard
Gräntz, Günther

Guembel, Otto Karl
Günther, Kurt Wilhelm
Haas, Karl Erwin
Hacker, Elias Gustav Heinrich
Haltern, Friedrich
Hanke, Franz
Hasse, Albert Erich Max
Haug, Gustav Emil Walther
Hayn, Hans
Heiden, Erhard
Heines, Edmund
Heinz, Karl Hermann Rudolf Albert
Heissmeyer, August Friedrich
Heitmüller, Walter Willy August
Helfer, Wilhelm (6)
Helldorf, Wolf Heinrich Graf von
Herzog, Otto (15)
Hess, Ludwig Arthur
Heydebreck, Hans Peter von
Heydrich, Reinhard
Hierl, Konstantin
Himmler, Heinrich
Hocheisen, Paul Friedrich Karl
Hoevel, Walter
Hofmann, Bernhard
Hofmann, Hans-Georg
Holthoff, Paul *
Hörauf, Franz Ritter von
Hühnlein, Adolf
Ivers, Otto Wilhelm Georg
Jagow, Dietrich Wilhelm Bernhard
    von (18)
Jahn, Wilhelm
Jaster, Oscar Martin
Jeckeln, Friedrich
Jensen, Hermann
Jüttner, Max Paul Wilhelm
    Werner * (9)
Kappelmeyer, Eduard
Kasche, Siegfried Karl Viktor
    Johannes (24)
Ketterer, Emil (8)
Killinger, Manfred Freiherr von
Knickmann, Heinrich August (14)
Kob, Adolf Hajo Oltmann
Körner, Karl
Korsemann, Gerret
Kraft, Karl

Krausser, Fritz Ritter von
Krüger, Friedrich Wilhelm
Kühme, Kurt
Lasch, Kurt Arno
Lauerbach, Fritz
Lauterbacher, Hartmann
Lehmann, Friedrich Wilhelm Max *
Lehmann, Hans
Liebel, Willy *
Linsmayer, Max
Litzmann, Karl-Siegmund
    Hermann Julius (28)
Lohmann, Johannes
Lorenz, Werner
Lucke, Karl Friedrich Wilhelm *
Ludin, Hans Elard (1)
Luetgebrune, Walter
Lukesch, Hans Ivo *
Lutze, Viktor (27)
Luyken, Max Otto (22)
Manthey, Arno (16)
Mappes, Georg Friedrich
Marnitz, Meinhard Johannes
Marxer, Otto (26)
May, Franz
Meyer-Quade, Joachim (5)
Michaelis, Rudolf
Mörchen, Wilhelm *
Morozowisc, Hans Elard von
Möslinger, August
Murr, Wilhelm
Neufville, Georg von
Nibbe, Walter
Oberdieck, Georg
Obernitz, Hans-Günther von (13)
Ohrt, Lorenz Karl *
Pagels, Eberhard *
Petersen, Hans *
Pfeffer, Franz von *
Plesch, Kurt Karl Friedrich
Prützmann, Hans-Adolf
Raecke, Horst
Rakobrandt, Arthur (2)
Reimann, Erich Herrmann Julius
Reiner, Rolf
Reinhard, Wilhelm Adolf
Reschny, Hermann
Riecke, Hans-Joachim Ernst

Rigl, Robert Emil
Röhm, Ernst *
Schepmann, Wilhelm (23)
Schirach, Baldur von
Schmauser, Ernst-Heinrich
Schmid, Wilhelm
Schmuck, Ludwig Julius Albert *
Schneider, Albert
Schneider, Georg Karl Friedrich
   Wilhelm
Schneidhuber, August
Schoene, Heinrich August (7)
Schorlemer, Wilhelm Freiherr von
Schormann, Robert August
   Wilhelm
Schragmüller, Konrad
Schramme, Otto (17)
Schreyer, Karl *
Schulz, Paul Gustav
Schulze, Walter
Seidel-Dittmarsch, Siegfried
Seydel, Josef
Späing, Heinz

Stegmann, Wilhelm
Steinhoff, Emil (10)
Stennes, Walter
Stephani, Franz von
Strasser, Gregor
Tschammer und Osten, Hans von
Türk, Oskar
Uhland, Ludwig Adolf Gustav
Ulrich, Kurt Albert Paul Harris von *
Vielstich, Fritz Johann Albert Ernst
Vogel, Hans-Josef
Wagenbauer, Richard
Wagener, Otto *
Wagner, Gerhard
Waldeck-Pyrmont, Josias Georg
   Erbprinz zu
Walter, Otto Max
Weinreich, Hans
Weitzel, Fritz Philip
Wittje, Curt
Woyrsch, Udo von
Zunkel, Gustav (21)

Glossary

Abitur: The most prestigious of several certificates awarded after passing exams at the end of secondary schooling in Germany. Traditionally it allowed entry into the university in any subject.

Abteilung Organisation und Einsatz: Department for Organization and Operation in the OSAF.

Akten: Records, files, dossiers.

Alte Kämpfer: "Old Fighters," members of the NSDAP before it came to power.

Anschluß: The unification of Germany and Austria in 1938.

Arbeitsgemeinschaft: Labor collective. Formed by former members of the free corps as a means of finding employment and remaining together as a (covert) military force.

Arbeitsgemeinschaft der Nord- und West-deutschen Gaue: Working Association of the North and West German Gaue. An informal association of North- and West German Nazi Party leaders, 1925-26.

Arbeitsgemeinschaft der vaterländischen Kampfverbände: Working Group of Patriotic Combat Organizations. A cartel of radical Wehrverbände formed in Munich in 1923 of which the NSDAP was a part.

Berlin Document Center: Major archive of biographical information from the National Socialist period collected by the Allies during and after the war. Under U.S. administration until 1994.

Black Reichswehr: System of illegal military reinforcements formed by the Reichswehr from 1919 to the early 1920s, with the help of the Arbeitsgemeinschaften and the Wehrverbände.

Brigade: SA unit between Gruppe and Standarte.

Brigadeführer: SA, SS, or NSKK brigadier general.

Bund Oberland: A largely Bavarian Wehrverband formed out of the free corps of the same name. The major ally of the NSDAP during the Beer Hall Putsch of 1923.

Bund Wiking: Aboveground Wehrverband formed by Hermann Ehrhardt and led by former members of his free corps.

Bundesarchiv: German Federal Archives, headquarted in Koblenz.

Bundesarchiv-Militärarchiv: Military branch of the German Federal Archives in Freiburg.

Chef des Ausbildungswesens (Chef-AW): A covert organization based on, but separate from, the SA and designed to train young men (mostly students) in military skills, 1933-35.

Deutsche Arbeiterpartei (DAP): German Workers' Party, the original name of the NSDAP. Founded in Munich in January 1919.

Deutsche Arbeitsfront (DAF): The National Socialist Labor Organization.

Deutsche Volkspartei (DVP): German People's Party. A small conservative party in the Weimar Republic just to the left of the DNVP.

Deutscher Kampfbund: German Alliance for Struggle. A cartel of radical organizations including the NSDAP formed September 1, 1923, to force the overthrow of the Weimar Republic.

Deutscher Tag (German Day): A type of nationalist festival often celebrated in the early 1920s.

Deutschnationale Volkspartei (DNVP): German National People's Party. The largest traditional conservative political party in the Weimar Republic.

Deutschsozialistische Partei (DSP): German Socialist Party. A völkisch political organization and sometime rival of the NSDAP.

Deutschvölkische Freiheitsbewegung (DVFB): German Völkisch Freedom Movement. Völkisch organization formed to continue the völkisch movement after the NSDAP and several other similar organizations were banned in the wake of the failed Beer Hall Putsch.

Deutschvölkische Freiheitspartei (DVFP): German Völkisch Freedom Party. A völkisch political organization and sometime competitor of the NSDAP.

Deutschvölkischer Schutz- und Trutzbund: German Völkisch Defense and Defiance League. A radical völkisch organization in the early Weimar Republic.

Disziplinargericht der Obersten SA-Führung: SA Disciplinary Court. An internal SA court system.

Einjähriger Freiwilliger: A type of officer cadet in the German Empire. Young men of good social background were allowed to volunteer as officer cadets for one year in lieu of their obligatory military service, but had to pay for their own equipment and uniforms.

Einwohnerwehr: Part-time civil guard formed in Germany under government auspices during the German Revolution.

Feme: Informal system of "justice" designed to root out suspected informants and maintain the secrecy of the Black Reichswehr and other illegal rearmament measures.

Fememord: A murder committed by the Feme.

Freikorps (Free Corps): Temporary, voluntary military formation formed by the German army and navy during the 1919 revolution.

Freikorps Ehrhardt: One of the largest, most radical, and most important free corps led by Captain Hermann Ehrhardt.

Freikorps Epp: A large Bavarian free corps led by General Franz Ritter von Epp.

Freiwilliger Arbeitsdienst (FAD): Voluntary Labor Service. A state-sponsored but voluntary labor service designed to combat unemployment during the Great Depression in Germany. Ancestor of the compulsory Reich Labor Service (RAD).

Frontbann: A "super" Wehrverband founded in 1924 by a number of nationalist leaders including Ernst Röhm.

Gau: Large regional division of the NSDAP. (The term was used by other organizations as well.)

Gauleiter: Powerful head of a regional division (Gau) of the NSDAP.

Gausturm: An intermediate-level SA unit, usually containing several Standarten and from 1930 to 1933 grouping the SA resources of an entire Gau.

Gerichts- und Rechtsabteilung: The Legal Department within the OSAF, which included a system of internal SA courts.

Gleichschaltung: The "coordination" (takeover or elimination) of private and state organizations by the NSDAP beginning in 1933.

Grenzschutz: 1. Military formations used to defend German borders (especially in the east and northeast) during the German Revolution. 2. Covert Reichswehr system of illegal reinforcements, arms depots, and training designed to slow an eventual enemy attack, particularly in the east. From the early 1920s to the mid-1930s.

Großdeutsche Arbeiterpartei (GDAP): Greater German Labor Party. A small völkisch party.

Großdeutsche Volksgemeinschaft (GDVG): Greater German People's Community. Völkisch organization formed to continue the völkisch movement after the NSDAP and several other similar organizations were banned in the wake of the failed Beer Hall Putsch.

Großer Generalstab: Great General Staff. The general staff of the Imperial Army.

Grundsätzliche Anordnung der SA (Grusa): Fundamental SA regulation. Series of orders issued by von Pfeffer under Hitler's signature, beginning in May 1927. Repeated and interpreted von Pfeffer's earlier SA orders (SABE).

Gruppe: 1. Section. The basic building block of the SA, 1927-31. (Röhm later changed the name to Schar). A group of three to thirteen men. 2. A large regional SA unit.

Gruppenführer (Gruf.): SA, SS, or NSKK major general.

Gruppenstab zur besonderen Verwendung: Gruppe Staff for Special Duties, a secret staff unit within the SA intended to coordinate general relations and especially covert military training with the Reichswehr.

Gymnasium: A type of secondary school in the German-speaking countries designed to prepare its pupils for university study or higher administrative positions.

Handelsschule: A high school that concentrates on business skills.

Heimwehr: An Austrian Wehrverband.

Hilfspolizei: Auxiliary police created from SA, SS, and Stahlhelm members in 1933.

Hundertschaft: Century. The pre-Beer Hall Putsch model for the Standarte.

Institut für Zeitgeschichte (IfZ): Institute for Contemporary History, Munich. A research center.

Jungdeutscher Orden (Jungdo): A Wehrverband.

Jungstahlhelm: Division of the Stahlhelm for young nonveterans.

Kadettenanstalt: A military academy of the Imperial German or Austro-Hungarian army.

Kampfzeit: The "time of struggle," the period from the founding of the Nazi Party to its ascension to power in January 1933.

Kraftfahrstaffeln: SA or SS motor vehicle units.

Kreisleiter: Head of a Nazi Party district, or Kreis, the equivalent of a county.

Kyffhäuserbund: A large German veterans' organization.

Landesführer: A Stahlhelm regional or state leader.

Machtergreifung: The Nazi "seizure of power," January 1933.

Marine-Stürme: SA naval units.

Nachrichtenstaffeln: SA or SS communications troops.

Nationalpolitische Erziehungsanstalt (Napola): National Political Education Institute. A national school for future leaders established by the NSDAP.

Nationalsozialistische Automobilkorps (NSAK): National Socialist Automobile Corps. A Nazi Party organization under the SA for motor vehicle owners and enthusiasts. Ancestor of the NSKK.

Nationalsozialistische Betriebszellenorganisation (NSBO): National Socialist Industrial Cell Organization. A Nazi labor organization.

Nationalsozialistische Deutsche Arbeiterpartei (NSDAP): National Socialist German Workers' Party, also known as the Nazi Party.

Nationalsozialistischer Deutscher Frontkämpferbund (NSDF): National Socialist German Association of Combat Veterans. Formed in March 1934 to replace the Stahlhelm.

Nationalsozialistische Deutscher Juristen-Bund (NSDJB): National Socialist German Association of Jurists. A Nazi Party organization for jurists.

Nationalsozialistische Fliegerkorps (NSFK): National Socialist German Flying Corps. A Nazi Party organization for flying enthusiasts.

Nationalsozialistische Freiheitsbewegung (NSFB): National Socialist Freedom Movement. Organization formed to continue the völkisch movement after the NSDAP and several other similar organizations were banned in the wake of the failed Beer Hall Putsch.

Nationalsozialistische Kraftfahrkorps (NSKK): National Socialist Motor Vehicle Corps. Originally a Nazi Party organization under the SA for motor vehicle enthusiasts, it later became independent.

Nationalverband Deutscher Offiziere: National Union of German Officers. A radical veterans' organization.

Oberführer: SA, SS, and NSKK rank between colonel and brigadier general.

Obergruppenführer (Ogruf.): SA, SS, or NSKK lieutenant general.

Oberste SA-Führer (OSAF): Supreme SA leader.

Oberste SA-Führung (OSAF): The SA high command.

Oberstes Parteigericht der NSDAP (OPG): Supreme Nazi Party Court.

Offizierstellvertreter: A rank created during the First World War in the German army. A noncommissioned officer acting as an officer.

Organisation Consul (OC): An underground organization under the auspices of Hermann Ehrhardt formed by former members of his free corps. Designed to infiltrate and unite the entire Wehrverband and nationalist movement with the goal of overthrowing the Weimar Republic. Classed as a Wehrverband in this study.

Organisation Todt (OT): A paramilitary construction and transport organization formed during the Third Reich.

Ortsgruppenleiter: Head of a local chapter, or Ortsgruppe, of the NSDAP.

OSAF-Stellvertreter: Powerful regional SA commander. First instituted in 1928 and replaced in February 1931 by the position of Gruppenführer.

Personalbogen für Veränderungen und Ergänzungen nach erfollgter Ausfüllung des Personalfragebogens: One of two questionnaires used to supplement the information in the SA-Personalfragebogen.

Personalfragebogen für die Anlegung der SA-Personalakte: Questionnaire used for all SA-Führer from Standartenführer and above and for all full-time SA-Führer of lower rank. This was the most complete SA questionnaire. Used from late 1936 to 1945.

Personalhauptamt: The main office for personnel in the OSAF.

Politische Organisation (PO): The political organization of the NSDAP, in contrast to the paramilitary affiliates, such as the SA.

Rasse- und Siedlungs-Hauptamt: Race and settlement headquarters, a part of the SS high command.

Realschule: A type of secondary school in Germany less prestigious and rigorous than the Gymnasium and designed to prepare pupils for technical or practical occupations.

Reichsarbeitsdienst (RAD): Reich Labor Service. A compulsory labor service formed by the German government during the Third Reich.

Reichsbanner: Left-wing Wehrverband close to the German Social Democratic Party.

Reichsflagge: A mainly Bavarian Wehrverband.

Reichskriegsflagge: A mainly Bavarian Wehrverband formed by a secession from the Reichsflagge.

Reichsluftschutzbund: Reich Civil Defense Association. A semiprivate civil defense association during the Third Reich.

Reichsorganisationsleiter: Reich Leader of Organization. The deputy of Adolf Hitler in charge of Party organization. Position held by Gregor Straßer until his dismissal from the Party in 1932.

Reichsparteitag: The yearly Nazi Party rally in Nuremberg.

Reichszeugsmeisterei: A part of the OSAF maintaining a system of sales outlets for uniforms and equipment of the SA and SS.

Röhm Purge: Purge of the SA leadership June 30 1934. Led to the murder of nearly ninety individuals, including Röhm and a number of top SA leaders. Also known as the "Night of the Long Knives."

SA-Befehl (SABE): SA Orders. Fundamental orders relating to the organization and use of the SA issued by von Pfeffer between November 1, 1926, and February 1927.

SA-Führer-Fragebogen: Questionnaire used for SA-Führer from May 1934 to 1936. Long but not as detailed as the Personalfragebogen.

SA Gruppen-Schule: An SA school for lower-level leaders.

SA-Hochschulamt: A division within the OSAF designed to coordinate SA efforts in the universities and schools of higher learning, particularly covert military training.

SA-Personalbogen für Veränderungen und Ergänzungen nach erfolgter Ausfüllung des Personalfragebogens: One of two questionnaires used to supplement the information in the SA-Personalfragebogen.

SA Reichsführerschule: National school for mid- and upper-level SA leaders.

SA-Reserve (SAR): The SA reserve.

Saalschutz Abteilung: A precursor of the SA founded by Emil Maurice on or shortly after February 24, 1920, in Munich.

Sekundareife: A secondary school degree which allowed a young man to fulfill his military service obligation as a one-year voluntary officer cadet.

Selbstschutz Oberschlesiens (SSOS): Upper Silesian Self-Defense. An armed self-defense organization formed to defend German interests in the contested border region of Upper Silesia.

Schar: Section. The basic building block of the SA. A group of three to thirteen men.

Schumacher Sammlung: Miscellaneous nonbiographical documents first collected in the Berlin Document Center and later transferred to the Bundesarchiv.

Schutz- und Trutzbund (German-Völkisch Defense and Defiance League): One of the earliest völkisch organizations to achieve national prominence during the German Revolution and one of the most radically antisemitic. Founded in 1919 and banned in 1922, although individual gruops hung on illegally for several more years.

Schutzstaffel (SS): Elite paramilitary affiliate of the NSDAP founded in 1925 and later headed by Heinrich Himmler. Administered as part of the SA until 1934, when it became independent and eclipsed the SA in power and importance. First intended to provide bodyguards for Party leaders, it later ran the concentration camps and formed a "fourth branch" of the German armed forces (the Waffen-SS).

Sicherheitspolizei: A kind of militarized police formed in the early Weimar Republic, which absorbed many former soldiers.

Sondergericht der Obersten SA-Führung: A special court system set up to carry out an internal purge of the SA in the wake of the Röhm Purge. Succeeded by the Disziplinargericht der Obersten SA-Führung.

Stabschef: Chief of Staff; actual head of SA from 1930 on.

Stahlhelm: The largest veterans' organization in the Weimar Republic, it also functioned as a Wehrverband. Absorbed by the SA in 1933-34.

Standarte: SA unit between Sturmbann and Brigade.

Standartenführer (Staf.): SA, SS, and NSKK rank between Obersturm-
    bannführer and Oberführer; SA, SS, or NSKK colonel.
Stegmann Revolt: A conflict between the SA Leader of Central
    Franconia, Wilhelm Stegmann, and the Gauleiter of Central
    Franconia, Julius Streicher, in January 1933.
Stennes Revolt: Mutiny of OSAF-Stellvertreter Ost Walther Stennes
    in the spring of 1931.
Sturm: Company. An SA, SS, or NSKK unit made up of several Trupps.
Sturmabteilung (SA): 1. Mass paramilitary affiliate of the Nazi Party.
    Also called Brown Shirts or Stormtroops. 2. Special assault troops
    formed in the Imperial German Army during the First World
    War.
Sturmbann: SA, SS, or NSKK unit containing several Stürme.
Tannenberg Bund: A völkisch organization very close to the
    Wehrverbände, led by former general Eric Ludendorff.
Trupp: Troop. An SA or SS unit made up of several Scharen.
Turn- und Sport Abteilung: Gymnastics and Sports Division. The
    official name of the first SA, founded on August 3, 1921.
Unterführer: Noncommissioned officer in the SA, SS, or NSKK.
Untergruppe: SA unit between Sturm and Gruppe, which became
    the Brigade. Often coterminious with a Gausturm.
Untersuchungs- und Schlichtungsausschuß: Investigation and Me-
    diation Committee of the NSDAP. An internal Nazi Party orga-
    nization formed to arbitrate disputes and investigate problems.
    Later grew into the Nazi Party court system.
Verband Nationalgesinnter Soldaten: Union of Nationally Minded
    Soldiers. A radical veterans' organization.
Vereinigte Vaterländische Verbände Bayerns (VVVB): United Patri-
    otic Organizations of Bavaria. A Bavarian cartel of conservative
    and radical groups formed in November 1922.
völkisch: An adjective denoting an ultranationalist, antidemocratic
    populism that claimed to represent a kind of integral
    Germanness. Xenophobic in general, the völkisch movement
    was particularly identified with a virulent anti-Semitism. It was
    strongly influenced by Social Darwinism.
Völkisch-Sozialer Block: Völkisch-Social Block. A coalition of
    völkisch organizations formed to participate in the Reichstag
    elections in 1924.
Völkischer Beobachter: Völkisch Observer, the official newspaper of
    the Nazi Party.
Volksgerichtshof: Nazi "People's Court." A parallel, extraordinary
    court system used for political crimes.
Volkssturm: Military units formed late in the Second World War as
    part of a program of last-ditch mobilization in Germany. In-

cluded special emphasis on ideological indoctrination, and very
close to the Nazi Party as a result.

Wahlkreis: Electoral district.

Wehrkreis: Military district or region.

Wehrstahlhelm: Division of the Stahlhelm made up of young men
engaged in military sports training.

Wehrwolf: A Wehrverband.

Wehrverband (pl. Wehrverbände): Private paramilitary organization
formed in Germany or Austria between 1919 and 1933.

Zeitfreiwilliger: Part-time volunteer, or reservist, of a free corps or
other military formation during the German Revolution.

Zentrum: The Catholic Center Party in the German Empire and
Weimar Republic.

Notes

Abbreviations Used in Notes

BAK	Bundesarchiv (Koblenz)
BDC	Berlin Document Center
Betr.	Betriff (regarding)
DAP	Deutsche Arbeiterpartei
DNVP	Deutschnationale Volkspartei
DVFB	Deutschvölkische Freiheitsbewegung
DVFP	Deutschvölkische Freiheitspartei
GDAP	Großdeutsche Arbeiterpartei
Gruf.	Gruppenführer
IfZ	Institut für Zeitgeschichte (Institute for Contemporary History)
NS	national socialist/nationalsozialistisch
OPG	Oberstes Parteigericht der NSDAP
OSAF	Oberste SA-Führer/Oberste SA-Führung
SA	Sturmabteilung
SABE	SA-Befehl (order, command)
SAR	SA-Reserve
SS	Schutzstaffel (elite guard)
T&S Abteilung	Turn- und Sport Abteilung
vorl.	provisional grouping of records

Introduction

1. The SA was founded in 1920 but disbanded after the failure of Hitler's Beer Hall Putsch in 1923. It was reestablished in 1925 after the ban was lifted on the NSDAP. For various reasons discussed below, the officers of the first (1920-23) SA are not specifically included in this study unless they were also top leaders of the "second" SA.

2. See appendix for SA ranks and their U.S. equivalents.

3. The creation of "party armies" or of paramilitary organizations is considered characteristic of both genuinely fascist movements and their conservative imitators in the interwar period. See, e.g., Stanley G. Payne, *Fascism: Comparison and Definition* (Madison: University of Wisconsin Press, 1980), esp. 3-21; Peter H. Merkl, "Comparing Fascist Movements," in *Who Were the Fascists? Social Roots of European Fascism*, ed. Stein Ugelvik Larsen, Bernt Hagtvet, and Jan Petter Myklebust (Bergen, Oslo, Tromso:

178 Notes to Pages 2-4

Universitetsforlaget, 1980), 752-83; and Warren E. Williams, "Paramilitarism in Inter-State Relations: The Role of Political Armies in Twentieth-Century European Politics" (Ph.D. diss., University of London, 1965). For the Weimar Republic in particular see James M. Diehl, *Paramilitary Politics in Weimar Germany* (Bloomington: Indiana University Press, 1977); Hans-Joachim Mauch, *Nationalistische Wehrorganisationen in der* Weimarer Republik: Zur Entwicklung und Ideologie des *"Paramilitarismus"* (Frankfurt am Main: Peter Lang, 1982); Richard Bessel, "Militarismus im innenpolitischen Leben der Weimarer Republik: Von den Freikorps zur SA," in *Militär und Militarismus in der Weimarer Republik,* ed. Klaus-Jürgen Müller and Eckardt Opitz (Düsseldorf: Droste, 1978), 193-222; Eve Rosenhaft, "Gewalt in der Politik: Zum Problem des 'Sozialen Militarismus,'" in ibid., 237-60; and Michael Geyer, "Der zur Organisation erhobene Burgfrieden," in ibid., 15-100. For a different approach, which puts paramilitary organizations in the larger context of a crisis of the state in the twentieth century, see Bruce Campbell, "Death Squads: History and Definition," paper presented at the American Historical Association annual meeting, Atlanta, January 1996.

4. See chapter 1 for a more detailed explanation of the "genealogy" of the SA, including such organizations as the Wehrverbände and the völkisch political parties.

5. Moreover, during the Kampfzeit, the SA made up a significant proportion of the total membership of the NSDAP, so even in this sense, the Nazi Party cannot be understood without understanding the SA. According to a priority message from the OSAF Führungsamt to the head of the SA Reichsführerschule (F2 no. 51328) of 3 September 1935 (in Bundesarchiv Koblenz NS23/337), the strength of the SA in January 1933 was 427,538. (It is likely that this figure does not include either the SS or the Austrian SA.) Other sources give a size of 518,977: Andreas Werner, "SA: 'Wehrverband,' 'Parteitruppe,' oder 'Revolutionsarmee'? Studien zur Geschichte der SA und der NSDAP, 1920-1933" (inaugural diss., Friedrich-Alexander-Universität zu Erlangen-Nürnberg, 1964), 551-52. The total membership of the NSDAP on 1 January 1933 was 849,009: NSDAP, Reichsorganisationsleiter, *Parteistatistik* (Munich, 1935), 1:16. Assuming that most SA members were Party members in January 1933 (a fairly safe assumption, despite earlier complaints from some Party officials that this was not the case), and taking the lower figure for SA membership, the SA amounted to approximately half of the total Party membership.

6. It should be pointed out that the SS was a subordinate part of the SA until July 1934; consequently, SS leaders appear in this study if they were of the appropriate ranks before the SS separated from the SA.

7. Another reason for concentrating on this particular group of SA leaders became apparent in the course of research: not only were they the "generals" of the SA but a surprising number were also among the SA's first tactical commanders and actually created its very organization and techniques at the grassroots levels.

8. I have enjoyed the great benefit of being able to use the work of Mathilde Jamin while still in the design and research phase of this book. Not only did she point out these methodological considerations in much greater detail but she came to similar conclusions. See Mathilde Jamin, *Zwischen den Klassen: Zur Sozialstruktur der SA-Führerschaft* (Wuppertal: Peter Hammer, 1984); Mathilde Jamin, "Methodische Konzeption einer

Quantitative Analyse zur sozialen Zusammensetzung der SA," in *Die Nationalsozialisten: Analysen Faschistischer Bewegungen*, Historisch-sozialwissenschaftliche Forschungen 9, ed. Reinhard Mann (Stuttgart: Klett-Cotta, 1980), 84-97; Mathilde Jamin, "Zur Kritik an Michael Katers "Überlegungen über Quantifizierung und NS-Geschichte," in *Geschichte und Gesellschaft* 4 (1978): 536-41; and Richard Bessel and Mathilde Jamin, "Nazis, Workers, and the Uses of Quantitative Evidence," in *Social History* 4 (December 1979): 111-16.

9. The SA even produced the first statistical study of its own leadership to prove this contention. See "Woher kommen unsere SA-Führer? Diese Statistik widerlegt die Behauptung, daß nur frühere Offiziere zu SA-Führern ernannt werden," in *Völkischer Beobachter* (Munich edition), 30 January 1933, suppl., 4.

10. See, e.g., Conan Fischer, *Stormtroopers: A Social, Economic, and Ideological Analysis, 1929-1935* (London: George Allen and Unwin, 1983); Conan Fischer, "The SA of the NSDAP: Social Background and Ideology of the Rank and File in the Early 1930s," *Journal of Contemporary History* 17 (1982): 651-70; Michael H. Kater, "Ansätze zu einer Soziologie der SA bis zur Röhm-Krise," in *Soziale Bewegungen und Politische Verfassung (Industrielle Welt: Schriftenreihe des Arbeitskreises für moderne Sozialgeschichte*, special issue), ed. Ulrich Engelhardt, Völker Sellin, and Horst Sture (Stuttgart: Ernst Klett, 1976), 789-831; Michael H. Kater, "Zum gegenseitigen Verhältnis von SA und SS in der Sozialgeschichte des Nationalsozialismus," *Vierteljahresschrift für Sozial- und Wirtschaftsgeschichte* 62 (1975): 339-79; and Peter H. Merkl, *The Making of a Stormtrooper* (Princeton: Princeton University Press, 1980).

11. Other examples of this approach include Jamin, *Zwischen den Klassen*; Richard Bessel, *Political Violence and the Rise of Nazism: The Storm Troopers in Eastern Germany, 1925-1934* (New Haven: Yale University Press, 1984); and Eric G. Reiche, *The Development of the SA in Nürnberg, 1922-1934* (Cambridge: Cambridge University Press, 1986).

12. Of course, the SA was "made" or "invented" by all of its members, not just the 178 officers at the very top. Yet these top leaders designed the national organization, set the policies, and often even tried out those policies at the grassroots level. Certainly, the question of how those policies were actually perceived and acted upon at the microlevel is an important one, but it is also a separate topic. Remember that the SA was a strictly hierarchical organization designed along military lines. This fact alone limited any potential influence of the rank and file and makes a study of its leadership essential to an understanding of the organization as a whole.

13. See Jürgen W. Falter, *Hitlers Wähler* (Munich: C.H. Beck, 1991); Michael H. Kater, *The Nazi Party: A Social Profile of Members and Leaders, 1919-1945* (Cambridge: Harvard University Press, 1983); Kater, "Ansätze zu einer Soziologie der SA bis zur Röhm-Krise"; Mathilde Jamin, *Zwischen den Klassen*; Conan Fischer, *Stormtroopers*.

14. These putative class attitudes themselves are often only assumptions.

15. Note that *internal* comparisons of the top SA leadership with other subgroups within the SA, such as those performed by Mathilde Jamin in *Zwischen den Klassen*, do make sense at our present level of knowledge. Some studies of the SS have some comparable data, but since the SS was just

a subgroup of the SA before 1934, and since this book on the SA leadership consequently includes SS as well as SA leaders who held one of the top three levels of rank, there is considerable overlap, again making comparison difficult. See Herbert F. Ziegler, *Nazi Germany's New Aristocracy: The SS Leadership, 1925-1939* (Princeton: Princeton University Press, 1989).

16. Motivations based on class, gender, psychology, and personal gain were also present. They should not be minimized, but they cannot be addressed in this study given the limitations of the sources at hand.

1. BACKGROUND

1. The term comes from Fritz Stern, *The Politics of Cultural Despair: A Study in the Rise of the Germanic Ideology* (Berkeley: University of California Press, 1961).

2. See, e.g., Bernd Felix Schulte, *Die deutsche Armee, 1900-1914: Zwischen Beharren und Verändern* (Düsseldorf: Droste, 1977), and Michael Geyer, *Deutsche Rüstungspolitik, 1860-1980* (Frankfurt am Main: Suhrkamp, 1984). For general reviews of the state of research into the German army just before the First World War, see Manfred Messerschmidt, *Militär und Politik in der Bismarckzeit und im Wilhelminischen Deutschland* (Darmstadt: Wissenschaftliche Buchgesellschaft, 1975), and Michael Geyer, "Die Geschichte des deutschen Militärs von 1860-1945: Ein Bericht über die Forschungslage (1945-1975)," in *Die Moderne Deutsche Geschichte in der Internationalen Forschung* (*Geschichte und Gesellschaft*, special issue 4), ed. Hans Ulrich Wehler (Göttingen, 1978), 256-86.

3. On the social makeup of the Imperial officer corps see Karl Demeter, *The German Officer Corps in Society and State, 1650-1945* (London: George Weidenfeld and Nicolson, 1965). On the Imperial Army in general see Gordon A. Craig, *The Politics of the Prussian Army, 1640-1945* (New York: Oxford University Press, 1956); Martin Kitchen, *A Military History of Germany from the Eighteenth Century to the Present Day* (Bloomington: Indiana University Press, 1975); and Militärgeschichtliches Forschungsamt, ed., *Deutsche Militärgeschichte, 1648-1939*, 6 vols. (Herrsching: Manfred Pawlak, 1983).

4. On army control of Germany during the First World War, see Gerald D. Feldmann, *Army, Industry, and Labor in Germany, 1914-1918* (Princeton: Princeton University Press, 1966). For the collapse of the German army in 1918 and the development of the stab-in-the-back myth see the literature cited in Bruno Gebhardt, *Handbuch der Deutschen Geschichte*, 8th ed., vol. 4, *Die Zeit der Weltkriege* (Stuttgart: Union, 1965), 118-19. Among many other more recent treatments, see Hagen Schulze, *Weimar: Deutschland, 1917-1933* (Berlin: Severin und Siedler, 1982), 147-51, 189-90, 200, 206-9.

5. It also had some surface plausibility, for it seemed to confirm the experiences of ordinary Germans and especially ordinary soldiers, who had been told throughout the war that they were winning and who could see that German armies were everywhere deep in enemy territory even at the very end of the war, but who then saw this supposed victory evaporate amid revolution and internal unrest.

6. On the Deutschnationale Volkspartei (DNVP) see Gordon A. Craig, *Germany, 1866-1945* (New York: Oxford University Press, 1978), 506-9; Walter Kaufmann, *Monarchism in the Weimar Republic* (1953; reprint, New

York: Octagon Books, 1973); Wilfried Fest, *Dictionary of German History, 1806-1945* (New York: St. Martin's Press, 1978), 36-37; and Lewis Hertzman, *DNVP: Right-Wing Opposition in the Weimar Republic, 1918-1924* (Lincoln: University of Nebraska Press, 1963).

7. The standard work on the Nazi period is still Karl-Dietrich Bracher's monumental *German Dictatorship* (New York: Praeger, 1970). The standard organizational history of the Nazi Party is Dietrich Orlow, *The History of the Nazi Party, 1919-1945*, 2 vols. (Pittsburgh: University of Pittsburgh Press, 1969, 1973). See also Hans Volz, *Daten der Geschichte der NSDAP*, 7th ed. (Berlin-Leipzig: A.G. Ploetz, 1938).

8. On the völkisch movement in general, see Armim Mohler, Die Konservative Revolution in Deutschland, 1918-1932: Ein *Handbuch*, 2d ed. (Darmstadt: Wissenschaftliche Buchgesellschaft, 1972), 131-38; George L. Mosse, *The Crisis of German Ideology: The Intellectual Origins of the Third Reich* (New York: Grosset and Dunlap, 1964); Peter Pulzer, *The Rise of Political Anti-Semitism in Germany and Austria* (1964; reprint, Cambridge: Harvard University Press, 1988). The best local case study of the evolution of the völkisch movement into the NSDAP is Jürgen Genuneit, *Völkische Radikale in Stuttgart: Zur Vorgeschichte und Frühphase der NSDAP, 1890-1925* (Stuttgart-Bad Cannstatt: Dr. Cantz'sche Druckerei, 1982).

9. Although völkisch ideas did infiltrate mainstream society, German society as a whole was not fundamentally and profoundly anti-Semitic, as a popular myth and some superficial scholarship contend.

10. For example, the official newspaper of the Nazi Party, the *Völkischer Beobachter*, printed a regular column of news from like-minded völkisch organizations entitled "Aus der Bewegung" into the mid-1920s, several years after the refounding of the NSDAP.

11. There was some originality in the Nazi program, such as its focus on workers and the claim that it represented a kind of national German socialism (hence *National-Socialist* German *Workers'* Party), neither of which was ever truly developed. More important, the tactics of the NSDAP, and particularly its decision to engage in electoral politics and take power legally through elections, distinguished it from other völkisch groups and ultimately led to its success. Hitler's most important contribution was not his anti-Semitism but rather his very early realization after the failure of the Beer Hall Putsch in 1923 that electoral politics was a potentially more successful alternative to the armed overthrow of the Weimar Republic, which had been the primary strategy of the antidemocratic and völkisch movements.

12. See Uwe Lohalm, *Völkischer Radikalismus: Die Geschichte des Deutschvölkischen Schutz- und Trutzbundes, 1919-1923* (Hamburg: Leibnitz, 1970); Genuneit, *Völkische Radikale*, 44-64.

13. See Dieter Fricke, ed., *1830-1945: Die Bürgerlichen Parteien in Deutschland*, 2 vols. (Berlin: Europäische Buch, 1968), 1:765-70, 2:668-71; Bracher, *German Dictatorship*, 122-24.

14. There is considerable literature concerning the free corps and the transition from the Imperial Army to the Reichswehr. For a selection see Robert G.L. Waite, *Vanguard of Nazism: The Free Corps Movement in Postwar Germany, 1918-1923* (1952; reprint, New York: W.W. Norton, 1969); Hagen Schulze, *Freikorps und Republik, 1918-1920* (Boppard am Rhine: Harald Boldt, 1969); Hannsjoachim W. Koch, *Der deutsche Bürgerkrieg: Eine Geschichte der deutschen und österreichischen Freikorps, 1918-1923* (Ber-

182 Notes to Pages 15-17

lin: Ullstein, 1978); Craig, *Politics of the Prussian Army*; Harold J. Gordon, *The Reichswehr and the German Republic, 1919-1926* (1957; reprint, New York: Kennikat, 1972); and Francis L. Carsten, *The Reichswehr and Politics, 1918-1933* (Berkeley: University of California Press, 1973). See also Friedrich Wilhelm von Oertzen, *Die deutschen Freikorps* (Munich: F. Bruckmann, 1936); Ernst von Salomon, *Die Geächteten* (1931; reprint, Reinbek bei Hamburg: Rowohlt, 1962); Ernst von Salomon, ed., *Das Buch vom deutschen Freikorpskämpfer* (Berlin: Wilhelm Limpert, 1938); Ernst von Salomon, *Nahe Geschichte: Ein Überblick* (Berlin: Rowohlt, 1936); and Edgar von Schmidt-Pauli, *Geschichte der Freikorps, 1918-1924* (Stuttgart: Robert Lutz Nachf. Otto Schramm, 1936).

15. The mythologizing of the free corps began almost as soon as they were formed. During the Weimar Republic and in the first years of the Third Reich, various groups attempted to gain control over the public perception of the free corps and, as a result, established competing free corps myths. The principal figure in this process was the writer Ernst von Salomon. See Bruce Campbell, "Ernst von Salomon, Self-Fashioning, and the Myth of the Free Corps," paper presented at the German Studies Association annual meeting, Washington, D.C., 9 October 1993.

16. Schulze, *Freikorps*, 26-35. I do not necessarily agree with Schulze's interpretation, which concedes an unwarranted degree of spontaneity in the formation of the first free corps. It is certainly true that some free corps were established without the knowledge of the high command, but they were few in number and quickly brought under the normal command structure. See also Rudolf Absolon, *Die Wehrmacht im Dritten Reich* (Boppard am Rhine: Harald Boldt, 1969-79), 1:22-24, 378-412, 2:32, 179-83, 279.

17. Absolon, op. cit.

18. For example, both Heinz Guderian and Bernhard Ramcke were serving in free corps units in the Baltic when they were ordered home to assume other duties. Both, of course, later became famous generals in the Wehrmacht: Gordon, *Reichswehr*, 80.

19. Interviews with Dr. Gerhard Rose and Karl Krage, June 1989; "Aus Tagebuchblättern der Sturmabteilung Roßbach: Angriff in Oberschlesien," in von Salomon, *Freikorpskämpfer*, 286-88.

20. Examples found in this book include Heinrich Hacker and Arthur Rakobrandt, who were indeed forced out of the Reichswehr, and both Adolf Kob and Oscar Jaster, who voluntarily resigned from the Reichswehr in 1920, even though they had been professional officers before the war. Neither gave a reason for the resignation in his SA file.

21. Note that the argument can be made that the first experience in the use of military forms to solve civilian problems for many men in the paramilitary subculture in the Weimar Republic was in fact in the occupied territories during the First World War. The free corps are thus the first *domestic* experience.

22. This is particularly true for three categories of free corps: (1) the larger free corps which were not disbanded until late in 1919 or early 1920, such as the Ehrhardt Brigade, (2) those free corps who mutinied while serving in the Baltic states, such as the Eiserne Division (actually a collection of smaller free corps), and (3) those free corps which tried to take their men underground in the so-called Arbeitsgemeinschaften, like Freikorps Roßbach and Freikorps von Heydebreck.

23. See Ludwig Maercker, *Vom Kaiserheer zur Reichswehr: Die Geschichte der freiwilligen Landesjägerkorps*, 3d ed. (Leipzig: K.F. Koehler, 1922), 331-32. The Zeitfreiwilligenverbände are scarcely discussed in modern secondary works.

24. David Clay Large, "The Politics of Law and Order: A History of the Bavarian *Einwohnerwehr, 1918-1921*," *Transactions of the American Philosophical Society* 70, no. 2 (1980): 1-87; Horst G.W. Nusser, *Konservative Wehrverbände in Bayern, Preußen, und Österreich, 1918-1933: Mit einer Biographie von Forstrat Georg Escherisch, 1870-1941* (Munich: Nusser, 1973).

25. Nusser, *Konservative Wehrverbände*, 207 and table 22a, 352.

26. Diehl, *Paramilitary Politics*; Peter von Heydebreck, *Wir Wehrwölfe: Erinnerungen eines Freikorps-Führers* (Leipzig: K.F. Koehler, 1931); Gerhard Roßbach, *Mein Weg durch die Zeit: Erinnerungen und Bekenntnisse* (Weilburg-Lahn: Vereinigte Weilburger Buchdruckereien, 1950).

27. Although the Wehrverbände were built into this illegal Reichswehr program, it also had its own units and organizational structure, called the "Black Reichswehr."

28. Absolon, *Die Wehrmacht im Dritten Reich*, 1:35-39; numerous examples of future SA leaders who participated in these activities are presented in the following chapters.

29. Harold J. Gordon, "Politischer Terror und Versailler Abrüstungsklausel in der Weimarer Republik," *Wehrwissenschaftliche Rundschau* 16 (January 1966): 36-54; "Urteil des Schwurgerichts Stettin gegen Heines und Genossen" of 13 March 1929, in Szczecin Provincial State Archives, catalog no. 12171.

30. See Emil Julius Gumbel, *Verschwörer: Beiträge zur* Geschichte und Soziologie der deutschen nationalistischen *Geheimbünde, 1918-1924* (1924; reprint, Heidelberg: Das Wunderhorn, 1979); Emil Julius Gumbel, *Vier Jahre Politischer Mord* (1922; reprint, Heidelberg: Das Wunderhorn, 1980); Walter Luetgebrune, *Wahrheit und Recht für Feme, Schwarze Reichswehr, und Oberleutnant Schulz* (Munich: J.F. Lehmann, 1928); "Urteil des Schwurgerichts Stettin gegen Heines und Genossen" of 13 March 1929, in Szczecin Provincial State Archives, catalog no. 12171.

31. The strong language used by Party speakers and the generally heated atmosphere in Munich in the early 1920s also played a part in the radicalization of political behavior in Munich. See Heinrich Bennecke, *Hitler und die SA* (Munich and Vienna: Günter Olzog, 1962), 25-28; Hans Volz, *Die Geschichte der SA von den Anfängen bis zur Gegenwart* (Berlin: Reimar Hobbing, 1934), 11-12.

32. Volz, *SA*, 11. A list of the first members of this group is given on the same page. Werner's assumption that the founding of this group stood in connection with the disbanding of the Bavarian Einwohnerwehr (Orgesch = Organisation Escherisch) cannot be substantiated. The Orgesch, into which the Bavarian Einwohnerwehren were organized in May 1920, was not dissolved in Bavaria until June 1921: Werner, "SA," 5; on the Orgesch in Bavaria see Nusser, *Konservative Wehrverbände*. Emil Maurice, born 19 January 1897, was a watchmaker in Munich and a member of the Deutsche Arbeiterpartei (DAP) since 1919. He later became an officer in the SS: Erich Stockhorst, *Fünftausend Köpfe: Wer War Was im Dritten Reich* (Velbert and Kettwig: Blick und Bild, 1967), 288.

33. Volz, *NSDAP*, 3.

34. Ibid., 53, pits forty-three members of the T&S Abteilung against eight hundred "Marxists," clearly an impossible feat but typical of the later myths surrounding the battle.

35. Werner, "SA," 25.

36. Information on Klintzsch comes from the following sources: Werner, "SA," 23 and 86-87; Albert Broeren and Manfred von Killinger, eds., *Erinnerungen der Sturmkompagnie* (Schleswig: J. Johannsens, n.d.), 192; "Anklageschrift des Oberreichsanwaltes Ebermayer im Leipziger O.C. Prozess," Bundesarchiv/Militärarchiv, Freiburg, PH26-4, 90.

37. The Organisation Consul (OC) was a conspiratorial organization formed by Captain Hermann Ehrhardt and other officers of his free corps when it was disbanded in 1920. They hoped to unify the splintered Wehrverband movement by infiltrating the paramilitary associations. They then hoped to destroy the Weimar Republic and institute a national dictatorship in Germany, possibly through the ruse of provoking a left-wing uprising. The Bund Wiking was a paramilitary organization built by former members of the Ehrhardt Brigade and controlled by the OC. See Gabriele Krüger, *Die Brigade Ehrhardt* (Hamburg: Leibnitz, 1971), and Howard Stern, "The Organisation Consul," *Journal of Modern History* 35 (March 1963): 20-32.

38. Werner, "SA," 45, 47, 51-53; Volz, *NSDAP,* 6, 53.

39. The effectiveness of this tactic was certainly recognized within the SA itself. See, e.g., OSAF, SABE 3 Staf., "SA und Öffentlichkeit (propaganda)" of 3 November 1926, in Berlin Document Center (hereafter BDC), Schumacher Collection, Ordner 43.

40. Coburg or Koburg (both spellings exist in German) is a city in northeastern Bavaria. A Deutscher Tag was a public celebration of German nationalism commonly staged by right-wing organizations in the 1920s. For the events surrounding the Coburg German Day, see Jürgen Erdmann, *Coburg, Bayern, und das Reich, 1918-1923* (Coburg: A. Rossteutscher, 1969), 92-121. In 1932, at the ten-year anniversary of the expedition, the NSDAP held a mass rally in Coburg and awarded a special medal, the Coburger Abzeichen, to all veterans of the conflict who were still in the Party. This Party decoration ranked only behind the Blood Medal (Blutorden) and the Golden Party Pin (Goldenes Ehrenzeichen der NSDAP) in prestige within the Party. See BDC, Schumacher Collection, Ordner 256, for an official list of 436 recipients of the decoration. See also Dr. Kurt-Gerhard Klietmann, *Deutsche Auszeichnungen: Eine Geschichte der Ehrenzeichen und Medaillen, Erinnerungs- und Verdienstabzeichen des Deutschen Reiches, der deutschen Staaten sowie staatlicher Dienststellen, Organisationen, Verbände, usw. vom 18.-20. Jahrhundert* (Berlin: Verlag "Die Ordenssammlung," 1971), 1:251-52. I am engaged in a separate study of the holders of the Coburger Abzeichen.

41. Of course, the innate talent of Hitler as an orator was also very important, as was help from the Reichswehr and from a number of individuals and organizations on the radical and conservative right.

42. Bennecke, *Hitler und die SA,* 47-48; Schulze, *Weimar,* 249-55.

43. The member organizations of the Arbeitsgemeinschaft were the SA, the Vaterländische Verbände Münchens, Bund Oberland, Reichsflagge, Organisation Niederbayern, and Organisation Lenz. See Volz, *NSDAP,* 6, 54; Werner, "SA," 72-78. Many members of these more radical organizations later joined the post-1925 NSDAP and SA.

44. Previously, the only distinguishing mark for SA members was the swastika armband, although many wore pieces of military attire: Volz, *NSDAP*, 53-54.

45. Volz, *SA*, 13-14; Werner, "SA," 88-91; Bennecke, *Hitler und die SA*, 34-56.

46. Werner, "SA," 84-87; Bennecke, *Hitler und die SA*, 54. The members of the SA high command were Hermann Göring, Adolf Hühnlein, Alfred Hoffmann, Hans Streck, Walter Schulze, Christian Weber, Julius Schreck, and Walter Baldenius.

47. This paragraph is based on Harold J. Gordon, *Hitler and the Beer Hall Putsch* (Princeton: Princeton University Press, 1972), esp. 389-92.

48. Volz, *NSDAP*, 6-7.

49. On the putsch see Gordon, *Putsch*, esp. pt. 2. See also the relevant portions of Werner and Bennecke, *Hitler und die SA*. Gordon and Bennecke stress the role of pressure from the Kampfbund rank and file in sparking the putsch: Gordon, *Putsch*, 321, and Bennecke, *Hitler und die SA*, 103-4.

50. Robert H. Frank, "Hitler and the National Socialist Coalition, 1924-1932" (Ph.D. diss., Johns Hopkins University, 1969), 23; Gordon, *Putsch*, pt. 3, esp. 580-81.

51. This statement is based on the analysis of the biographies of the SA Führer, which are discussed in detail below.

52. Numerous examples of this can be found in the files of SA men in the BDC. See the file of Paul Hirschberg for an example of someone who simply dropped out of political activity, the file of Karl Schaal for someone who joined a legal Wehrverband, and the file of Richard Stock for an example of someone who joined a still-legal völkisch group. Only the rank-and-file members of the Stosstrupp Adolf Hitler were prosecuted in any systematic way. For information on them see Hans Kallenbach, *Mit Adolf Hitler auf Festung Landsberg* (Munich: Kress und Hornung, 1939).

53. For examples see Volz, *SA*, 26, and Werner, "SA," 181-82. Examples are also found in BDC SA files. See, e.g., the files of Adolf Lenk for the Stoßtrupp Adolf Hitler in Munich, those of Arthur Böckenhauer for the SA in Hamburg, or those of Wilhelm Dittler for Ingolstadt.

54. The best example of this is the meeting of the SA leadership in Salzburg of 17-18 May 1924. Aside from the introduction of the brown shirt, which was to become the symbol of the SA, participants discussed such topics as the relationship with other Wehrverbände and parties, the results of the recent Reichstag election, future relations with the Reichswehr, organizational details, and the relationship of the SA to the Party: Werner, "SA," 206ff; Frank, "Hitler and the National Socialist Coalition," 218. The meeting and resulting directives may been seen as representing a halfway point between the old concept of the SA as a purely military Wehrverband and the future concept of the SA as a party organization.

55. Unless otherwise noted, the discussion of the Frontbann is drawn from Frank, "Hitler and the National Socialist Coalition," 209-60; Werner, "SA," 199-232, 245-82; and Volz, *SA*, 28-30.

56. Of course, two preconditions for the formation of this cartel were the example of the failed putsch and the attention that such an attempt brought to the heretofore obscure NSDAP.

57. Werner, "SA," 181-82.

58. See the following chapter for examples of individuals who were a part of this process.

59. Bennecke, *Hitler und die SA*, 116; Volz, *SA*, 30.

2. THE PIONEERS, 1925-1926

1. Volz, *SA*, 32-33.

2. Dietmar Petzina, Werner Abelshauser, and Anselm Faust, eds., *Sozialgeschichtliches Arbeitsbuch*, vol. 3, *Materialien zur Statistik des Deutschen Reiches, 1914-1945* (Munich: C.H. Beck, 1978), 174, table 4.1.

3. Gustav Stresemann was chairman of the Deutsche Volkspartei (DVP), chancellor of Germany in October and November 1923, and foreign minister from October 1923 until his death in 1929. He was the principal architect of the successful German policy of fulfillment. Wilhelm Marx was a member of the Center Party and chancellor from November 1923 to January 1925. Together, he and Stresemann guided Germany out of the crisis of 1923 and into a period of stability.

4. Adolf Hitler, *Mein Kampf* (1925; reprint, Munich: Zentralverlag der NSDAP, Franz Eher, 1943), 599-620.

5. This is a common interpretation. See, e.g., Robert H. Frank, "Hitler and the National Socialist Coalition, 1924-1932" (Ph.D. diss., Johns Hopkins University, 1969), 284-85, or Heinz Höhne, *Order under the Death's Head*, 26.

6. Bennecke, *Hitler und die SA*, 114; Volz, *SA*, 30.

7. "Grundsätzliche Richtlinien für die Neuaufstellung der Nationalsozialistischen Deutschen Arbeiter-Partei," *Völkischer Beobachter*, 26 February 1925, p. 2.

8. Volz, *SA*, 39. Franz von Pfeffer's real name was Pfeffer von Salomon, but he used only the name von Pfeffer beginning in 1918. See Deutscher Offiziersbund, ed., *Ehrenrangliste des ehemaligen deutschen Heeres: Auf Grund der Ranglisten von 1914 mit den inzwischen eingetretenen Veränderungen* (Berlin: E.S. Mittler Sohn, 1926), 148.

9. Werner, "SA," 320-21. In March 1925, Hitler asked Ernst Röhm to head the SA: Frank, "Hitler and the National Socialist Coalition," 275. Röhm desired to see the Frontbann continue to exist as a separate organization, he refused to accept Hitler's demand that it be subordinated to the NSDAP, and he insisted that the SA remain strictly separate from the political organization of the NSDAP. As a result, Röhm and Hitler could not reach an agreement, and Röhm resigned as head of both the SA and the Frontbann on 1 May 1925: Werner, "SA," 305-13; Volz, *SA*, 30.

10. Ironically, the French/Belgian occupation of the Ruhr seems to have given a push to the formation of Nazi Party cells in the occupied and adjoining areas and even helped it to hold together and spread while the Party was officially banned. It is likely that the occupation made many more willing to belong to a radical group like the NSDAP and less willing to tolerate its persecution by German authorities. For example, von Pfeffer claimed to have been made the Gauleiter of Westfalen of the NSDAP in 1924. See Institut für Zeitgeschichte (hereafter IfZ) Zs. (eyewitness report) 177/1; material in the BDC Research Section file on von Pfeffer, and *Das Großdeutsche Reichstag, 1938* (Berlin: R.V. Decker, 1938), 340.

11. Despite the availability of many source materials, no systematic study of the spread of the Party and SA in the early years has been made. Such a study is needed.

12. For examples, see the files of Kurt Günther and Fritz Falkner in the BDC.

13. An example of this is the building of the Berlin SA out of portions of the Berlin Frontbann. See Frank, "Hitler and the National Socialist Coalition," 300-306; Obersturmbannführer Julek Karl von Engelbrechten, *Eine Braune Armee Entsteht: Die Geschichte der Berlin-Brandenburger SA, im Auftrag des Führers der SA Gruppe Berlin-Brandenburg Dietrich von Jagow* (Munich: Eher, 1937), 33-39; and the BDC files of Kurt Daluege. Frank, 294-99, rightly points out the difficulties of determining the exact development of völkisch groups and Wehrverbände into SA units. After the fact, many National Socialists were quite eager to portray the organizations of which they had been members as forerunners or even underground continuations of the SA. Often, only detailed local studies can bring the facts to light. For an exemplary attempt, see Jürgen Genuneit, *Völkische Radikale in Stuttgart.*

14. This was the case for all SA units that went underground after the failure of the Beer Hall Putsch. Examples may be found in the BDC files of Wilhelm Dittler or Heinrich Knickmann.

15. Volz, *SA*, 35, 41.

16. Rudolf Hess, "SA und Partei," in *Nationalsozialistische Monatshefte*, no. 46 (January 1934): 3-4. Other examples are to be found in the BDC SA files: Viktor Lutze was both the Gau SA-Führer and deputy Gauleiter in Gau Rheinland-Nord in 1925, and as late as 1927 this seems to be the case in Plettenberg Westphalia, according to the files of Fritz Bracht.

17. Frank, "Hitler and the National Socialist Coalition," 261.

18. Thus, several Gaue appointed Gau SA-Führer on their own in late 1925 and early 1926 to coordinate the regional use of the SA: Bennecke, *Hitler und die SA*, 125.

19. Frank, "Hitler and the National Socialist Coalition," 209, and Bennecke, *Hitler und die SA*, 127f., give the figure of 6,000. Werner, "SA," 356f., gives the figure of 3,600.

20. Frank, "Hitler and the National Socialist Coalition," 306.

21. Ibid., 346-47. The reluctance of some Gauleiter to relinquish control over the SA in their areas as late as 1930 is illustrated in a letter from OSAF Stellvertreter NW von Fichte to Röhm of 30 March 1931: BDC SA Gerichts- und Rechtsamt Akte [SA Court and Legal Department files] von Fichte. The problem in this case, with Gauleiter Wagner, seems to have continued under von Fichte's successor, Schepmann, until at least 1934. See "Stellungnahme Schepmanns zur 2. Beschuldigungsschrift des OPG von 24.10.34, II Kammer Akt. no. 2624, Zeichen: Bi/Ko" of 6 November 1934, in Oberster Parteigericht [Supreme Party Court] file Schepmann in the BDC.

22. The SS was created in March or April 1925. In September 1925, January 1926, July 1926, and August 1926, a series of orders and guidelines had established, at least on paper, the basic outlines of the organization. See Frank, "Hitler and the National Socialist Coalition," 284-91. In general on the SS, see Heinz Höhne, *Order under the Death's Head*, and especially Robert L. Koehl, *The Black Corps: The Structure and Power Struggles of the Nazi SS* (Madison: University of Wisconsin Press, 1983). The purpose of the SS was to provide a group of dependable bodyguards for Party figures and to

defend meetings. But once the SA was rebuilt, these duties had to be shared. The SS was then given responsibility for tasks that required individuals, not units of SA men. At first one of these tasks was to sell the *Völkischer Beobachter* and the Party brown shirt, but later the SS took on the more sinister intelligence gathering and spying functions.

23. Gregor Strasser was one of the most dynamic leaders of the NSDAP until he was forced out of the Party in 1932. At that time he was head of the Nazi Political Organization (Reichsorganisationsleiter). A proponent of a more social revolutionary and anticapitalist brand of Nazism than Hitler, he was killed in the Röhm Purge. Joseph Goebbels began his Party career close to the social-revolutionary wing of the Nazi Party led by Gregor and Otto Strasser, but he soon fell in behind Hitler and became one of the most important Nazi leaders. He was made district leader of the Party for Berlin Brandenburg in late 1926 and Reich propaganda director in 1929. He committed suicide in Hitler's bunker in 1945.

24. Werner, "SA," 356.

25. Volz, *SA*, 39; Bennecke, *Hitler und die SA*, 128. The announcement was made in the *Völkischer Beobachter* on 29 October 1926.

26. Bennecke's biography is taken from his BDC SA files, particularly his Personalfragebogen (personnel questionnaire) of 18 June 1937 (corrected 8 November 1944), with accompanying Ergänzungsbögen (supplements) and a transcript of his Lebenslauf (curriculum vita). Information was also taken from Stockhorst, *Fünftausend Köpfe*, 51.

27. Gordon, *Reichswehr*, 47. See the background chapter above for an explanation of the Zeitfreiwilliger and other organizations mentioned here.

28. Lohalm, *Völkischer Radikalismus*, 210-37.

29. He had already been fined several times in 1922 and 1923 for illegal distribution of pamphlets and illegal restraint (Freiheitsberaubung), among other things: BDC file Heinrich Bennecke.

30. He was given party number 4 840. BDC file Heinrich Bennecke.

31. The Golden Party Pin was awarded to those who had been Party members without a break since 1 October 1928: Kurt-Gerhard Klietmann, *Deutsche Auszeichnungen*, 2:247-50. The NSDAP service award in gold was for twenty-five years of Party service, although service before 30 January 1933 was counted twice. Very few of the awards in gold were ever given. Awards in bronze (ten years) and silver (fifteen years), which Bennecke also held, were more common: Klietmann, 2:264-66, and "Antrag auf Erwerb der Dienstauszeichnung der NSDAP für (10-15-25) jährige Tätigkeit" in BDC SA file Hans-Georg Hofmann. (Examples of this particular application form abound in the BDC SA files. Hofmann's was chosen purely at random.)

32. To join a youth organization, Bennecke's Frontbann unit must have been made up primarily of very young men like himself. For the early history of the Hitler Jugend, see Arno Klönne, *Jugend im Dritten Reich: Die Hitler-Jugend und ihre Gegner* (Munich: Deutscher Taschenbuchverlag, 1990), 15-19.

33. Given his prior career and in all fairness to the man, he probably was a born leader. Note that in 1927 a Standarte was equivalent in size to the later Sturmbann, yet in terms of importance as a level of command it was still just as important as the later Standarte, which, after all, played a role equivalent to an army regiment. This was a great responsibility for a man of twenty-five.

34. Thilo Vogelsang, "Der Chef des Ausbildungswesens (Chef-AW)," in *Gutachten des Instituts für Zeitgeschichte* (Stuttgart: Deutsche Verlagsanstalt, 1966), 2:146-56.

35. The 1934 Röhm Purge was sparked by false allegations that Ernst Röhm, the head of the SA, was planning a coup. Many high SA leaders were killed or expelled.

36. This is 20.2 percent of all of the 178 Gruppenführer, Obergruppenführer, and Stabschefs. The date of joining the SA could not be determined for twenty. At least three of these very likely joined in 1925 or 1926, but they are not included in this chapter because it cannot be proved that they did so. The following men are included in this chapter: Franz Bauer, Heinrich Bennecke, Franz Bock, Arthur Böckenhauer, Johann Heinrich Böhmcker, Walter Buch, Kurt Daluege, Karl Dincklage, Wilhelm Dittler, Karl Dörnemann, Günther Gräntz, Otto Gümbel, Kurt Günther, Edmund Heines, August Heissmeyer, Walter Heitmueller, Wilhelm Helfer, Ludwig Hess, Heinrich Himmler, Siegfried Kasche, Gerret Korsemann, Kurt Lasch, Viktor Lutze, Rudolf Michaelis, Franz von Pfeffer, Horst Raecke, Hermann Reschny, Wilhelm Schepmann, Baldur von Schirach, Heinrich Schoene, Otto Schramme, Walter Schulze, Heinz Späing, Wilhelm Stegmann, Kurt von Ulrich, and Fritz Weitzel.

37. The following were veterans: Franz Bauer, Arthur Böckenhauer, Johann Heinrich Böhmcker, Walter Buch, Kurt Daluege, Karl Dincklage, Wilhelm Dittler, Otto Gümbel, Kurt Günther, Edmund Heines, August Heissmeyer, Walter Heitmueller, Wilhelm Helfer, Ludwig Hess, Heinrich Himmler, Gerret Korsemann, Kurt Lasch, Viktor Lutze, Rudolf Michaelis, Franz von Pfeffer, Hermann Reschny, Wilhelm Schepmann, Heinrich Schoene, Otto Schramme, Walter Schulze, Heinz Späing, Wilhelm Stegmann, and Kurt von Ulrich. Rudolf Michaelis and Heinrich Himmler were both in the army but did not see combat.

38. By professional I mean active officers as opposed to reserve officers or "Offiziere des Beurlaubtenstandes." Walter Buch, Karl Dincklage, Franz von Pfeffer, and Kurt von Ulrich were professional officers before the war. (Siegfried Kasche, not counted here, was an officer cadet during the war.) Edmund Heines, August Heissmeyer, Gerret Korsemann, Kurt Lasch, Viktor Lutze, Hermann Reschny, Wilhelm Schepmann, Heinrich Schoene, Walter Schulze, Heinz Späing, and Wilhelm Stegmann were reserve officers during the war. Otto Gümbel, not counted here, was a military administrator (Militärbeamter) at a rank corresponding to an officer. Not counting Kasche and Gümbel, 41.6 percent of the group were officers by the end of the First World War.

39. The free corps members include Franz Bauer, Arthur Böckenhauer, Edmund Heines, Heinrich Himmler, Siegfried Kasche, Gerret Korsemann, Rudolf Michaelis, Franz von Pfeffer, Otto Schramme, Walter Schulze, Heinz Späing, and Wilhelm Stegmann. This is 33 percent of the thirty-six, or 52 percent of the twenty-three whose activities during this period are known.

40. Wilhelm Schepmann, Viktor Lutze, and Kurt Daluege. Wilhelm Helfer joined the Schutz- und Trutzbund in 1920 and Arthur Böckenhauer followed in 1922. Five (13.8%) were thus members of the Schutz- und Trutzbund

41. Six remained active in a free corps into the second quarter of 1920; the free corps involved are Ehrhardt, Loewenfeld, Roßbach, and the Eiserne Division.

42. This includes Edmund Heines, Walter Heitmueller, Franz von Pfeffer, and Heinrich Bennecke.

43. Included are von Pfeffer and Schepmann.

44. Twenty-one men in this group (58.3%) were members of the NSDAP by 1923, and sixteen (44.4%) were in the SA. Since not all of these members of the "first" SA were simultaneously Party members, a total of twenty-four members of this group (63.8%) were in either the SA or NSDAP or both by 1923: Franz Bauer, Heinrich Bennecke, Arthur Böckenhauer, Franz Bock, Walter Buch, Kurt Daluege, Wilhelm Dittler, Günther Gräntz, Otto Gümbel, Kurt Günther, Edmund Heines, Walter Heitmueller, Wilhelm Helfer, Ludwig Hess, Heinrich Himmler, Kurt Lasch, Viktor Lutze, Rudolf Michaelis, Hermann Reschny, Wilhelm Schepmann, Otto Schramme, Walter Schulze, Wilhelm Stegmann, and Fritz Weitzel.

45. Information on Kurt Albert Paul Harris von Ulrich is taken from his BDC SA files unless otherwise noted. His Personalfragebogen (personnel questionnaire) of 6 January 1937 and a large file card with a clipped upper left-hand corner from the Oberste SA-Führung (n.d.) were particularly useful. A few minor details came from Stockhorst, *Fünftausend Köpfe*, 428.

46. The activities of four of the sixteen just before joining the SA/NSDAP are not clear from their records.

47. This includes the Stahlhelm, the Nationalverband deutscher Offiziere, and the Reichsverband der Baltikumkämpfer, all veterans' organizations with interests wider than those associated with veterans' organizations today, as well as the Reichswehr and the police.

48. They were considered moderate within the narrow context of the Wehrverbände, which within the broader spectrum of political belief in the Weimar Republic were generally quite radical.

49. They include Heinrich Bennecke, Kurt Daluege, Wilhelm Dittler, Günther Gräntz, Otto Gümbel, Walter Heitmüller, and Ludwig Hess.

50. Arthur Böckenhauer, Wilhelm Dittler, Kurt Günther, Wilhelm Helfer, Viktor Lutze, and Franz von Pfeffer. There is some overlap with the Frontbann members because some underground SA units were also part of the Frontbann.

51. Other political groups represented by one member each are the DNVP, the Deutsch-völkische Freiheitsbewegung, and the Deutsche National-sozialistische Arbeiterpartei (Austrian NSDAP). For further discussion of the völkisch organizations mentioned here, please refer to chapter 1.

52. The individuals were Franz Bock, Arthur Böckenhauer, Wilhelm Dittler, Günther Gräntz, Otto Gümbel, Walter Heitmüller, Ludwig Hess, Siegfried Kasche, Heinrich Schoene, Franz von Pfeffer, and Karl Dincklage—30.5 percent of the entire group of thirty-six or 57.9 percent of the nineteen whose activities are known for certain.

53. An example of an man who was active in both a völkisch organization and the Frontbann is Günther Gräntz. See his BDC SA files.

54. Of the twenty-eight whose activities are known, fifteen were in the SA and eighteen were in the NSDAP by November 1923. They include Heinrich Bennecke, Arthur Böckenhauer, Franz Bock, Walter Buch, Wilhelm Dittler, Günther Gräntz, Otto Gümbel, Kurt Günther, Edmund Heines, Walter Heitmueller, Wilhelm Helfer, Ludwig Hess, Kurt Lasch, Viktor Lutze, Rudolf Michaelis, Hermann Reschny, Wilhelm Schepmann, Walter Schulze, Wilhelm Stegmann, and Fritz Weitzel.

55. It is difficult to quantify this group, since membership depends on

many variables, but examples would be Edmund Heines, Wilhelm Helfer, Viktor Lutze, Günther Gräntz, Arthur Böckenhauer, Walter Heitmueller, Wilhelm Dittler, and Kurt Lasch.

56. When the official dates for joining the SA and NSDAP are within six months of each other, it is safe to say that the individual actually joined both organizations simultaneously. The reasons for this have to do with differences in organization and procedure between the SA and the Party. The major reason is the fact that SA membership at this early date became effective immediately and was determined by the local group. Party membership, on the other hand, was administered centrally. An individual had to apply (and pay) for membership at a local level, but the application was then forwarded to the Gau (although in the very early days it was sometimes sent directly to Munich), and then forwarded periodically to the Party central in Munich as soon as enough applications were collected to make forwarding them worthwhile. Only once the application with the required membership fees had reached Munich and had been accepted and the applicant entered into the central Party card file was a Party number issued and the applicant considered a member of the Party. This process could easily take up to six months and could be delayed further by poor management or deliberate theft of the fees, which were common problems in the early days. Thus, two men in this chapter who actually joined the SA and NSDAP at the same time didn't get official credit for it: Arthur Böckenhauer received a late official date of Party membership due to sloppy bookkeeping either at the Gau or the Reich level: BDC SA file of Arthur Böckenhauer. Walter Schulze joined the Party in 1925, but he moved to an area where there was no local NSDAP group and thus dropped out of sight as far as the Party central was concerned and was forced to apply for a new membership number: BDC SS file of Walter Schulze. See Anton Lingg, *Die Verwaltung der NSDAP* (Munich: Zentralverlag der NSDAP, Franz Eher, 1940); Mathilde Jamin, *Zwischen den Klassen*, 71-73; Hans Buchheim, "Mitgliedschaft bei der NSDAP," in Institut für Zeitgeschichte, *Gutachten des Instituts für Zeitgeschichte* (Munich: Selbstverlag des Instituts für Zeitgeschichte, 1958), 1:313-23; Office of Military Government of the United States for Germany (OMGUS), 7771 Document Center, *Who Was a Nazi? Facts about the Membership Procedure of the Nazi Party* (Berlin: OMGUS, 1947), which is stored in the BDC library.

57. See Jamin, *Zwischen den Klassen*, 72-73. The only exception is Heinrich Bennecke, who joined the SA in Leipzig and the NSDAP in Dresden, but even then, the two cities are only about sixty miles apart. Because he joined the NSDAP first and then the SA several months later, it is likely that the difference in cities is due to a change in residence because he began his studies at the University of Leipzig in 1926. See his BDC SA file.

58. Viktor Lutze, Kurt Daluege, August Heissmeyer and Karl Dincklage, Stellvertretender Gauleiter, Heinrich Himmler, national level official, Heinrich Schoene, Wilhelm Stegmann, and Kurt von Ulrich, Ortsgruppenleiter, and Wilhelm Dittler and Kurt Günther, officials in their Ortsgruppe.

59. The rank Reichsleiter was actually introduced rather late, apparently in the spring of 1933. In June 1933 there were only sixteen in the Party, although the number later increased: Orlow, *Nazi Party*, 2:74. Included are Wilhelm Schepmann, Viktor Lutze, and Franz von Pfeffer as chiefs of the SA, Heinrich Himmler as chief of the SS, Baldur von Schirach as head of the HJ, and Walter Buch as chief judge of the NSDAP.

60. Heinrich Bennecke, Kurt Daluege, Karl Dincklage, Otto Gümbel, August Heissmeyer, Siegfried Kasche, Gerret Korsemann, Walter Schulze, and Kurt von Ulrich.

61. Heinrich Böhmcker, Heinrich Schoene, Heinz Späing, and Wilhelm Stegmann.

62. Karl Dörnemann, Rudolf Michaelis, and Hermann Reschny.

63. Three of the above were Reichsleiter by virtue of the fact that they were the heads of the SA, but each of these three also had held some other Party office earlier.

64. Information on Heinrich August Schoene comes from his BDC SA files unless otherwise noted. The following documents were particularly useful: Schoene's Personalfragebogen (personnel questionnaire) of 1 January 1937, his Personalbogen (n.d.), his Lebenslauf (curriculum vitae) (n.d.), a letter (draft) from the Chef des Hauptamtes Führung to the Hauptamt Verwaltung of 4 December 1942, and a large, green pay card from the Oberste SA-Führung.

65. An Obersekundareife was a certificate of completion of the Obersekunda, the seventh year of secondary school. It was inferior to the Abitur, which was the examination taken at the end of secondary education by those students on the college-preparatory track.

66. The rank and position of only twenty-four are known for 1925, and of these, fifteen were leaders.

67. Twenty-eight of the men in this chapter were born in 1900 or before. (I selected 1900 because it was the last age cohort to be drafted during the First World War.) By the end of the first quarter of 1930, nineteen were SA (or SS) leaders: Franz Bauer, Arthur Böckenhauer, Heinrich Böhmcker, Kurt Daluege, Karl Dincklage, Wilhelm Dittler, Kurt Günther, Wilhelm Helfer, Ludwig Hess, Heinrich Himmler, Kurt Lasch, Viktor Lutze, Franz von Pfeffer, Hermann Reschny, Heinrich Schoene, Otto Schramme, Walter Schulze, Wilhelm Stegmann, and Kurt von Ulrich. The rank of seven could not be determined, and two had temporarily left the SA. (Edmund Heines was in prison, and Walter Buch was by then the head of the Party Investigation and Mediation Committee. Both had previously been SA-Führer and are counted here.)

68. The exception is Heinrich Bennecke.

69. Heinrich Bennecke, Heinrich Böhmcker, Wilhelm Dittler, Kurt Günther, Arthur Hess, Kurt Lasch, Rudolf Michaelis, and Otto Schramme. There were forty-eight officially recognized Standarten by this time: Volz, *SA*, 37-38, 65-66. A Standarte before the reorganization of 1931 had approximately 200-600 men and may be considered the SA equivalent of a regiment (see appendix).

70. Kurt Daluege, Wilhelm Helfer, Wilhelm Schepmann, Heinrich Schoene, Wilhelm Stegmann, and Fritz Weitzel.

71. The five OSAF-Stellvertreter were powerful regional SA commanders.

72. Wolfgang Sauer, "National Socialism, Totalitarianism, or Fascism?" *American Historical Review* 73 (December 1967): 404-24.

3. THE DEFECTORS, 1927-1930

1. This short biography of von Pfeffer is based on the following sources: Institut für Zeitgeschichte Zs. 177, vol. 1 (von Pfeffer); BDC Research Section materials (including copies of various Reichstag handbooks); Stockhorst, *Fünftausend Köpfe*, 322; Bennecke, *Hitler und die SA*, 128; and Volz, *SA* (in IfZ Fa2), which contains numerous marginal comments by von Pfeffer.

2. Bennecke, *Hitler und die SA*, 128-29; Frank, "Hitler and the National Socialist Coalition," 308-10, 343-46; and Werner, "SA," 357. See especially the characterization of von Pfeffer in Henry Ashby Turner Jr., ed., *Hitler aus nächster Nähe* (Frankfurt am Main: Ullstein, 1978).

3. See especially IfZ Zs. 177, Bd. I and the marginal comments in Volz, *SA*.

4. Bennecke, *Hitler und die SA*, 130, even credits von Pfeffer with having greater political experience than Hitler in 1926, which is a slight exaggeration. It may not, however, be an exaggeration to say that von Pfeffer had learned certain lessons and digested past experiences better than Hitler had at that point.

5. Viktor Lutze's contribution should not be underestimated. Lutze was one of the first to understand how to combine soldiering with politics. Among other innovations, he is responsible for the SA's system of ranks and insignia. See *Das Deutsche Führerlexikon, 1934-1935* (Berlin: O. Stollberg, 1934), 294, and the numerous obituary articles in his BDC files.

6. IfZ Zs. 177/1. See especially the interview of von Pfeffer by Dr. H. Krausnick and Dr. Freiherr von Siegle of 20 February 1953. On the Arbeitsgemeinschaft, see Frank, "Hitler and the National Socialist Coalition," 110-59, 308-10, and Joseph Nyomarkay, *Charisma and Factionalism in the Nazi Party* (Minneapolis: University of Minnesota Press, 1967), 71-89.

7. Bennecke, *Hitler und die SA*, 128-30, generally accepts von Pfeffer's version, but Werner, "SA," 356, raises objections.

8. Hitler traveled to Westphalia for long talks with von Pfeffer in the summer of 1926 before his appointment, so they had adequate opportunity to discuss the SA and its mission and to come to an understanding: Volz, *SA*, 39. Briefly, von Pfeffer favored an elite and highly disciplined SA with a strong sense of ideological commitment. He also rejected the purely military approach and organization of the Wehrverbände. These were all things that appealed to Hitler. Yet von Pfeffer also wanted the SA to be strictly independent from the Party hierarchy, and he rejected putschism only for tactical reasons, not out of principle. Both of these latter points proved to be the source of considerable friction later on. See IfZ Zs. 177.

9. Von Pfeffer, Oberster SA-Führer, "An die Herrn Gauleiter!" of 1 October 1926, and OSAF, SABE 1 Sturmf. of 1 November 1926, in BDC, Schumacher Collection, Ordner 403, 86-88.

10. The Grusa, with one or two exceptions, repeated the SABE with minor corrections and changes. The difference between the two classes of orders was really that the Grusa were countersigned by Hitler as chairman of the NSDAP. This had the advantage of reinforcing von Pfeffer's authority vis-à-vis the Gauleiter and other Party leaders, while allowing the Party to distance itself from any lesser orders of an SA leader that might conflict with the law or draw the attention of the authorities: Bennecke, *Hitler und die SA*, 135.

11. Von Pfeffer's basic concept of the differences between the SA and the old army are presented best in SABE 15 "Lenkung von Massen—Militärisches Vorbild" of 19 February 1927, in BDC, Schumacher Collection, Ordner 403. The organizational structure of the SA is taken here from Grusa IV, "Gliederung," of 4 June 1927, in BDC, Schumacher Collection, Ordner 403, 110.

12. *Schar* will be used here to avoid confusion with the large regional level of command also called a Gruppe, which Röhm introduced to replace the OSAF-Stellvertreter regions: Werner, "SA," 535-37.

13. It was also in tribute to the recognition by young combat officers of the First World War of the value and strength of small unit cohesion in building motivation and discipline. Almost all small unit commanders criticized the old army for ignoring this aspect of self-discipline and self-motivation in favor of absolute obedience. Although this recognition is sometimes attributed to the free corps, it does in fact stem from the First World War. The free corps merely provided a forum where young officers were given enough flexibility and freedom to put their ideas into practice.

14. *Sturm*, literally "storm," is translated here as "company" in English, even though the next highest unit after the squad in the American army is the platoon, and only then the company. This is done for two reasons. First, the Sturm functioned more like a company than a platoon tactically. Second, when the SA later, under Röhm, set size limits on its units, the Sturm was given a set size that corresponded more to that of a company than a platoon. The Trupp gradually developed into a platoon size unit, but earlier it resembled a squad in size and use. Note, too, that the term *Sturm* and the other unit names chosen for the SA were deliberately different from those used by the army. The use of equivalent, nonmilitary terms in English would be confusing, so the German terms have been translated into the equivalent English military terms, even though this is technically incorrect.

15. After von Pfeffer's resignation, the Gausturm boundaries were redrawn to correspond to the Gau boundaries of the political organization, which had coincided with the Reichstag electoral districts since 1 October 1928: Volz, *SA*, 45. Von Pfeffer's ideas in this regard were not unique among the right in Germany at the time; such a demand was a part of the *Jungdeutscher Manifest*, written in 1928 by Arthur Mahraun, the leader of the Jungdeutscher Orden. See Klaus Hornung, *Der Jungdeutsche Orden* (Düsseldorf: Droste, 1958), 84.

16. Volz, *SA*, 46.

17. Ibid., 59-60. Werner, "SA," 411-12.

18. Frank, "Hitler and the National Socialist Coalition," 380-81, note 43; Werner, "SA," 415-17.

19. Werner, "SA," 417-18.

20. *Nachrichtenstaffeln* in German may refer to communications units, intelligence units, or both. Although the orders issued to the SA stressed the communications function, von Pfeffer's deep concern with knowing what was happening in the "enemy" camp and scattered references to local intelligence gathering by the SA make it likely that he had both communications and intelligence gathering in mind from the start.

21. Volz, *SA*, 51; Werner, "SA," 405f., 552-55. The NSAK later became the Nationalsozialistische Kraftfahrkorps (National Socialist Motor Corps, or NSKK).

22. Werner, "SA," 407; Volz, *SA*, 54. Mounted units later became a standard part of the SA throughout Germany.

23. See the SA files of Horst Raecke and Wilhelm Boltz in the BDC. See also Volz, *SA*, 54.

24. OSAF, SABE "SA-Reserve (SAR)," 28 March 1929, in BDC, Schumacher Collection, Ordner 403, 113. See also Volz, *SA*, 55; Werner, "SA," 404.

25. Volz, *SA*, 57; Bennecke, *Hitler und die SA*, 148; and the BDC SA files of Dr. Paul Hocheisen and Dr. Walter Schulze.

26. Their common insistence on the independence of the SA was partly to avoid having to share their authority, but also the product of their common socialization as professional officers during the Wilhelmine Empire.

27. The following fifty-nine men are included: Adolf-Heinz Beckerle, Robert Bergmann, Friedrich Wilhelm Brückner, August Burger, Carl Caspary, Friedrich Damian, Edmund Diehl, Sepp Dietrich, Karl Freiherr von Eberstein, Paul Fassbach, Friedrich Fenz, Finck von Finckenstein, Herbert Fust, Leonhard Gontermann, Erich Hasse, Albert Heinz, Wolf Heinrich Graf von Helldorf, Otto Herzog, Paul Hocheisen, Walter Hoevel, Adolf Hühnlein, Bernard Hofmann, Otto Ivers, Dietrich von Jagow, Wilhelm Jahn, Oscar Martin Jaster, Friedrich Jeckeln, Manfred Freiherr von Killinger, Karl Koerner, Karl Kraft, Fritz Lauerbach, Hartmann Lauterbacher, Max Lehmann, Max Linsmayer, Karl-Siegmund Litzmann, Max Luyken, Joachim Meyer-Quade, Georg Oberdieck, Hans-Günther von Obernitz, Hans-Adolf Prützmann, Arthur Rakobrandt, Erich Reimann, Hans-Joachim Riecke, Robert Rigl, Ernst Schmauser, August Schneidhuber, Ludwig Schmuck, Wilhelm Freiherr von Schorlemer, Robert Schormann, Hans von Tschammer und Osten, Oskar Türk, Ludwig Uhland, Fritz Vielstich, Hans-Josef Vogel, Richard Wagenbauer, Otto Wagener, Josias Erbprinz zu Waldeck-Pyrmont, Hans Weinreich, and Udo von Woyrsch.

28. In other words, they were former active officers as opposed to officers of the reserve. Twenty-one men out of the fifty-nine who are the subject of this chapter were former professional officers (35.5%): Paul Hocheisen, Adolf Hühnlein, Dietrich von Jagow, Oscar Martin Jaster, Manfred von Killinger, Karl Kraft, Karl-Siegmund Litzmann, Max Luyken, Georg Oberdieck, Arthur Rakobrandt, Robert Rigl, Ernst Schmauser, August Schneidhuber, Wilhelm Freiherr von Schorlemer, Robert Schormann, Hans von Tschammer und Osten, Ludwig Uhland, Richard Wagenbauer, Otto Wagener, Josias Erbprinz zu Waldeck-Pyrmont, and Udo von Woyrsch.

29. Six out of fourteen men joining in 1929 were former professional officers (42.8%), as were fourteen out of twenty-nine men joining in 1930 (48.2%).

30. Thirty-five of the fifty-nine highest SA leaders who joined the SA from 1927 to 1930.

31. See conclusion, note 6, below.

32. Of the 1925-26 group, 41.6 percent had been officers, as compared with 59 percent in the 1927-30 group.

33. Of the fifteen who joined in 1925-26 who had been officers, 26.6 percent had been active officers and 73.3 percent had been reserve officers. Of those joining from 1927 to 1930 who were former officers, 63 percent had been active officers and 37 percent had been reserve officers.

34. At this time *Stabschef* meant chief of staff and not de facto head of

the SA, as it did after Hitler made himself supreme SA commander in title but not in practice.

35. BDC files Otto Wagener, particularly his supreme Party court file V/760/1936; Turner, *Hitler aus nächster Nähe,* passim, which are actually Wagener's memoirs. See esp. 7-35, where he describes his recruitment for the SA. His convictions are amply detailed in Otto Wagener, *Von der Heimat geächtet* (Stuttgart: C. Belsersche, 1920). See also Stockhorst, *Fünftausend Köpfe,* 434.

36. Examples are Bernard Hofmann and Kurt Kühme (see their BDC SA files). Kühme had been the head of a sports school with ties to the Reichswehr after leaving active service, but the basic principle still applies. Note that from 1927 on, the SA was able to pay a small but growing cadre of its staff and leadership full time. This money came from general Party funds transferred to the SA and from funds raised by the SA through business ventures.

37. Forty-nine of the fifty-nine who joined from 1927 to 1930 served in the war (83%); forty-seven were combat veterans (79.6%). Corresponding figures for the 1925-26 group are 77.7 percent veterans and 72 percent combat veterans.

38. The average year of birth of the 1925-26 joiners was 1895 and ranged from 1874 to 1907, whereas the average year of birth of the 1927-30 group was 1892 and ranged from 1869 to 1909.

39. Forty-five out of the fifty-nine men in this group whose activities are known (76%) were active politically or militarily in 1919.

40. Twenty-five out of forty-five who were active, or 42.3 percent of the total of fifty-nine. They include Robert Bergmann, Friedrich Wilhelm Brückner, Carl Caspary, Karl Freiherr von Eberstein, Friedrich Fenz, Graf Heinrich Finck von Finckenstein, Herbert Fust, Leonhard Gontermann, Wolf Graf von Helldorf, Walter Hoevel, Bernard Hofmann, Adolf Hühnlein, Otto Ivers, Dietrich von Jagow, Karl Kraft, Manfred Freiherr von Killinger, Fritz Lauerbach, Karl-Siegmund Litzmann, Hans-Adolf Prützmann, Arthur Rakobrandt, Hans-Joachim Riecke, Fritz Vielstich, Richard Wagenbauer, Otto Wagener, and Josias Erbprinz zu Waldeck-Pyrmont.

41. This is actually a very small number when the number of possible free corps is considered. My card file contains over 320 different entries, not all of which may have been truly autonomous free corps. Georg Tessin, *Deutsche Verbände und Truppen, 1918-1939* (Osnabrück: Biblio, 1974), 95-99, lists over 356 names of units, some of which may also have not been autonomous free corps. Gordon, *Reichswehr,* 67, states that he has found the names of over 400 free corps, but he lists fewer than this number on 414-20.

42. Ehrhardt, Epp, Eiserne Division, Loewenfeld, Deutsche Legion, Aulock, Lützow, and Garde-Kavallerie-Schützen-Division.

43. Maercker, Württemberg, and Hesse. The missing free corps are the Deutsche Schützendivision, Freiwillige Sturmabteilung Schlichtingsheim, Freikorps Oberbayern, Freikorps Graf Kaunitz, the Ostpreußisches Freikorps, and the Freiwilliges Reservekorps Kowno.

44. Twenty-eight out of fifty-nine (47.4%). Only thirteen (22%) list only army service during the revolution, however; over half of the twenty-eight also served in some other sort of organization, usually a free corps or the Grenzschutz. The army and free corps service overlap, since some men began in a free corps and then transferred to the regular army, others were

technically in regular army units but were assigned to a free corps, and others called their free corps service army service, which it technically was. In assigning men to these different categories, the term they themselves used in their file questionnaires was usually the deciding factor. The only exception was where specific units were named.

45. In the collapse of 1918, volunteers were recruited to protect Germany's eastern border. Those units which actually served in this capacity were termed part of the Grenzschutz or Grenzschutz Ost. (This is to be distinguished from later border protection units also called Grenzschutz.) There is a potential for overlap here: Grenzschutz units were technically in the army, although in 1919 and 1920 they could also have been free corps or other volunteer units. The three men listed here under the Grenzschutz (Erich Hasse, Hans-Joseph Vogel, and Udo von Woyrsch) did not list a free corps. Two others (Arthur Rakobrandt and Otto Wagener) listed both Grenzschutz and one or more free corps.

46. Hans Weinreich.

47. Oscar Jaster and Erich Hasse. Jaster was also in the Karpathendeutscher Partei, and Hasse was also in the Grenzschutz.

48. Karl Freiherr von Eberstein was in the DNVP, and Karl Koerner was in the Zentrum.

49. The three organizations represented were the Stahlhelm (von Eberstein), the Hermannsbund (Friedrich Fenz), and the Vereinigte Vaterländische Verbände Bayerns (Hans-Adolf Prützmann). All three could, with some justification, equally well be considered Wehrverbände at this time.

50. The levels of political, military, or paramilitary activity were as follows:

1925-26 group:	1927-30 group:
1920: 65%	66%
1921: 49%	53%
1922: 64%	56%
1923: 76%	64%

51. Twenty-nine members of this group (49.1%) belonged to at least one Wehrverband, including the Stahlhelm and Selbstschutz Oberschlesiens (SSOS).

52. Erich Hasse was in the Schutz- und Trutzbund, and Herbert Fust was in the DVFP.

53. This actually represents fourteen men (23.7%), since many were members of either the SA or NSDAP but not both. They include Friedrich-Wilhelm Brückner, Carl Caspary, Karl Freiherr von Eberstein, Graf Finck von Finckenstein, Leonhard Gontermann, Wolf Graf von Helldorf, Adolf Hühnlein, Dietrich von Jagow, Wilhelm Jahn, Hans-Günther von Obernitz, Robert Schormann, Fritz Vielstich, Otto Wagener, and Hans Weinreich.

54. By the end of 1923, fifteen members of the 1925-26 group were members of the SA and eighteen were members of the NSDAP. Twenty of the

thirty-seven (54%) were members of either the SA or NSDAP by this time.

55. Edmund Diehl was a longtime member of the DNVP, Karl Freiherr von Eberstein was a member in 1919 and 1920, and Wilhelm Jahn was a member in 1920 only.

56. Arthur Rakobrandt.

57. On the Jungdo see Hornung, *Der Jungdeutsche Orden*; on the Wehrwolf, see Fritz Kloppe, *Der aristokratische Einheitsstaat* (Halle-Saale: Wehrwolf, 1932); and Diehl, *Paramilitary Politics*, 227-41. Arthur Rakobrandt and Manfred von Killinger were in the Wehrwolf; Adolf-Heinz Beckerle, Albert Heinz, Oscar Jaster, Hans von Tschammer und Osten, Friedrich Jeckeln, and Josias Georg Erbprinz zu Waldeck-Pyrmont were Jungdo members.

58. In the 1927-30 group, Wiking: Adolf-Heinz Beckerle, Manfred von Killinger, Hans-Günther von Obernitz, and Fritz Vielstich; Stahlhelm: Karl Freiherr von Eberstein, Herbert Fust, Walter Hoevel, Bernard Hofmann, Wilhelm Jahn, Karl-Siegmund Litzmann, Georg Oberdieck, Arthur Rakobrandt, Erich Reimann, Hans-Josef Vogel, and Hans Weinreich; Bund Oberland: Fritz Vielstich, Sepp Dietrich, and Hans-Joachim Riecke.

59. In the second quarter of 1920, twelve of the fifty-nine (20.3%) were in the Reichswehr, and four (7%) were in the police. In the Reichswehr were Carl Caspary, Friedrich Damian, Paul Fassbach, Walter Hoevel, Dietrich von Jagow, Oscar Jaster, Manfred von Killinger, Georg Oberdieck, Arthur Rakobrandt, August Schneidhuber, Richard Wagenbauer, and Udo von Woyrsch. In the police were Sepp Dietrich, Max Luyken, Hans-Joachim Vogel, and Hans Weinreich. At the same time, only four (11%) of the 1925-26 group were in the Reichswehr, and one (2.7%) was in the police.

60. In 1923, three of the 1927-30 group were in the Reichswehr (Adolf Hühnlein, Erich Reimann, and Robert Rigl), and one was in the police (Hans-Joachim Vogel). By this time none of those who joined the SA in 1925-26 were members of either the police or the Reichswehr.

61. Four of the thirty-six 1925-26 group (11.1%) and eight of the fifty-nine 1927-30 group (13.5%): Karl Freiherr von Eberstein, Friedrich Fenz, Heinrich Graf Finck von Finckenstein, Dietrich von Jagow, Manfred Freiherr von Killinger, Max Luyken, Hans-Adolf Prützmann, and Otto Wagener.

62. Two Ruhr sabotage veterans, von Pfeffer and Schepmann, joined the SA in 1925 (5%). Only one Ruhr-sabotage veteran, Oscar Jaster, joined the SA from 1927 to 1930, and he did so in 1927 (1.6%). Edmund Diehl, who actively fought against the separatist movement in the Rheinland and the Palatinate, and Hartmann Lauterbacher, who claimed to have participated in the fight against the occupation but was only fourteen in 1923, were not included. (Had they been, the percentage of Ruhr sabotage veterans would have jumped to 5 percent, the same as in the 25-26 group.)

63. Of course, the general ideology of an organization, especially one such as the police or the army, does not necessarily have to be shared by all members. In fact, the discrepancy between the ideologies of the organization and the individual may have been one of the main reasons causing members of traditional conservative organizations to defect to the NSDAP from the late 1920s on.

64. This thesis was first advanced by Peter Merkl to explain the careers of a certain group in his sample. See Peter H. Merkl, *Political Violence under the Swastika: 581 Early Nazis* (Princeton: Princeton University Press, 1975), esp. parts 3 and 4, and 678-81.

65. Note that the term *defector* is therefore not to be taken literally; many "defectors" did not immediately join the NSDAP.

66. Each individual who was ultimately included here had, at the very least, an SS-Führerakte (officer personnel file), an SA Personalfragebogen (personal questionnaire), or a Lebenslauf (short autobiography) and an SA Führerfragebogen (officers' questionnaire). These are the most complete and useful types of documents used for this study. See the chapter on methodology for information about the various kinds of SA and SS materials used for the biographies of the SA/SS leaders. Men with weak or incomplete documentation were rigorously excluded from this category, and everything was done to make sure that the "passive activists" were really "passive."

67. Four more men might possibly fit in this category, but they had to be left out because their records were not strong enough for me to be sure that their apparent lack of activity was not due to incomplete information. Those included are August Burger, Friedrich Damian, Karl Koerner, Karl Kraft, Max Lehman, Ludwig Uhland, and Udo von Woyrsch.

68. The earliest to join the Party in the category of the "passive activists" was Karl Kraft, who joined in May 1928.

69. The exception was August Burger, an Austrian, who joined the SA in 1928 but didn't join the Party until 1930. He is one of only a handful of men in this study who joined the SA a significant time before joining the Party. In Burger's case, the delay may have been due in part to poor bookkeeping by his local Party cell or to the more clandestine nature of the NSDAP in Austria.

70. The highest rank was that of captain, held by Ludwig Uhland, a professional officer since 1908.

71. Unless otherwise noted, the biography of Max Lehmann is taken from his BDC SA files. The following documents were particularly useful: his Personalfragebogen of 30 June 1938, the two official supplements, and a large file card from the Oberste SA-Führung with a clipped upper left-hand corner (n.d.).

72. A *Brenner* is either a distiller or an industrial worker tending a kiln or furnace.

73. *Kaufmann* was a very elastic term by the 1930s; it could mean everything from an independent businessman to a store clerk. An apprenticeship as a Kaufmann generally meant on-the-job training as a sales clerk or office worker.

74. These eight were 13.5 percent of the total group of 59 who joined the SA from 1927 to 1930. They were Friedrich Wilhelm Brückner, Carl Caspary, Leonhard Gontermann, Fritz Lauerbach, Max Luyken, Hans-Adolf Prützmann, Ernst Schmauser, and Otto Wagener.

75. Prützmann was too young to serve in the war, although he tried to make up for this later by joining a free corps. Wagener, Luyken, and Schmauser were professional officers, and Brückner was a reserve officer before the war. The others were promoted to reserve officer rank during the war. Lauerbach is included here as a reserve officer, even though his rank, Feldhilfsarzt (auxiliary field physician), actually falls between the categories of commissioned and noncommissioned officers.

76. Lauerbach and Brückner were in Freikorps Epp, Wagener and Gontermann were in Baltic free corps, Prützmann and Caspary were in Central German free corps, and Luyken was in Freikorps Oberschlesien. Only

Schmauser was not in a free corps or otherwise active in 1919.

77. Three joined the NSDAP in 1922 and 1923. Gontermann belonged only to the NSDAP, whereas Caspary and Brückner were also members of the SA. Two others responded differently, joining völkisch groups only in 1924, after the crisis of 1923 was actually over. Thus Schmauser joined the Völkisch-Sozialer Block, and Lauerbach joined the NS-Freiheitsbewegung in that year. Wagener and Prützmann were slight exceptions to the above rule, since they were active in 1921 in addition to 1923-24, and Luyken held a high leadership position in the Orgesch from 1920 to 1925.

78. The date on which Hans-Adolf Prützmann joined the Party is inferred from his Party number, which was 142 290. This indicates a date sometime in the second half of 1929. Carl Caspary joined on 1 October 1929, and had the number 180 713. Paul Hocheisen joined the Party on 1 August 1929 and had the number 145 058, and Ludwig Schmuck, who joined on 1 May 1929, had the number 130 626.

79. Schmauser and Prützmann both joined the SA first, then transferred to the SS approximately a year later.

80. Brückner was born in 1884, Luyken in 1885, Schmauser in 1890, and Wagener in 1888.

81. He even remained a member of the SA until August 1924, when he completed his degree and moved to another city.

82. Unless otherwise noted, the information on Carl Caspary is taken from his BDC SA files. His Personalfragebogen of 1 August 1937 and the two official supplements were particularly useful.

83. Neither his battalion nor the Nuremberg SA regiment were ever as strong as their names would imply.

84. The Volkssturm was a last-ditch mobilization of old men, boys, the sick, and the infirm to resist the Allied invasion of Germany itself in the final days of the war. It had very close ties to the NSDAP to promote ideological enthusiasm.

85. The individuals in this category include Adolf-Heinz Beckerle, Karl Freiherr von Eberstein, Friedrich Fenz, Herbert Fust, Wolf Heinrich Graf von Helldorf, Walter Hoevel, Wilhelm Jahn, Oscar Martin Jaster, and Hans Weinreich.

86. Again, this idea is derived from Peter Merkl. See note 64 in this chapter.

87. The exception is Adolf-Heinz Beckerle, who was born in 1902 and was thus too young to have served in the war. All of the veterans finished the war as officers, except for Herbert Fust, who was a noncommissioned officer. This was likely because of his youth—he was born in 1899—and the fact that he only served for two years. He became an officer in the Second World War. At least one member of the group and possibly two were professional officers before the war.

88. Only Adolf-Heinz Beckerle and Wilhelm Jahn were not in a free corps or similar volunteer unit. On the other hand, two served in radical Baltic free corps.

89. The völkisch organizations include the Deutschvölkischer Offiziersbund (1), the Deutschvölkische Freiheitspartei (2), the Nationalsozialistische Freiheitsbewegung (2), the Deutschvölkischer Freiheitsbewegung (1), the Alldeutscher Verband (1), and the Deutschvölkischer Schutz- und Trutzbund (1). Numbers in parenthesis indicate number of members.

90. Information on Herbert Robert Gerhard Fust comes from his BDC SA file unless otherwise noted. The following documents were particularly useful: Fust's Personalfragebogen of 14 June 1936, with its two official supplements, his curriculum vitae (n.d.), and his SA disciplinary court file F44/M/ 34. He appears as number 12 in the group photo facing page 1.

91. The Frontbann was a dead letter nationally by about mid-1925, following massive defections to the SA and the resignation of its commander, Ernst Röhm. Local groups did exist until 1927, as Fust's case illustrates.

92. The charge was "conduct liable to damage the Party." Fust was accused of taking part in wild, drunken parties, sexual affairs, and public visits to bordellos. He was also accused of submitting abnormally high expenses.

93. Two years may seem short, but it must be remembered that in context it is rather long, since rapid turnover of membership in the paramilitary bands and völkisch movements was the norm. These men were Edmund Diehl, Sepp Dietrich, Albert Heinz, Paul Hocheisen, Bernard Hofmann, Otto Ivers, Dietrich von Jagow, Manfred Freiherr von Killinger, Max Luyken, Georg Oberdieck, Hans-Günther von Obernitz, Arthur Rakobrandt, Erich Reimann, Hans-Joachim Riecke, Robert Rigl, Robert Schormann, and Hans von Tschammer und Osten.

94. The more radical an organization, the earlier its members tended to turn to and be absorbed by the SA and NSDAP.

95. At the time the NSDAP was aware of the great importance of "defectors" from other organizations. See the letter from Philipp Bouhler, NSDAP managing director, to all Gaue and independent Ortsgruppen of the NSDAP of 7 May 1928, in Schumacher Collection, Ordner 374 (transcript).

96. Paul Hocheisen, Bernard Hofmann, Otto Ivers, Dietrich von Jagow, Manfred Freiherr von Killinger, Karl-Siegmund Litzmann, Georg Oberdieck, Hans-Günther von Obernitz, Arthur Rakobrandt, Hans-Joachim Riecke, Robert Rigl, and Hans von Tschammer und Osten. This is 70.5 percent of the total. Note that only two of the seventeen men in this group did not serve in the war, and one of these nonveterans was an naval officer cadet after the war.

97. This means men who were members of the elite general staff corps, a group separate from the main body of the regular officer corps, or who served in the Großer Generalstab. It is quite different from the number of men who had experience in staff planning, which was much larger: Absolon, Wehrmacht, 1:47-48.

98. Paul Hocheisen, Dietrich von Jagow, Manfred Freiherr von Killinger, Karl-Siegmund Litzmann, Georg Oberdieck, Arthur Rakobrandt, Robert Rigl, and Hans von Tschammer und Osten. This is 47 percent of the entire group of seventeen "defectors." A further member of the group, Sepp Dietrich, was a prewar professional NCO. Robert Schormann, another member of the "defector" group who did not serve in the First World War, was later an officer cadet in the navy during the Weimar Republic.

99. The generals were Robert Rigl, a brigadier general in the Austrian Federal Army, and Paul Hocheisen, a major general in the medical corps. The major was Arthur Rakobrandt, a captain who was promoted to major at his retirement. The colonel was Georg Oberdieck, who was a general staff corps major by the end of the war and who was promoted to colonel upon retirement.

100. Georg Oberdieck was a general staff officer, Hans von Tschammer

und Osten served on the great general staff during the war, and Paul Hocheisen served in the Württemberg Ministry of War before the war. Bernard Hofmann, Karl-Siegmund Litzmann, Hans-Günther Obernitz, Arthur Rakobrandt, and Robert Rigl all held staff positions during the war.

101. This count does not include Reichswehr officers, although the Reichswehr is one of the organizations from which members of the "defectors" category are drawn.

102. Hans-Günther von Obernitz was the national business manager (Reichsgeschäftsführer) of Bund Wiking from 1924 to 1926, and Robert Rigl was the chief of staff (Stabsleiter) of the Deutscher Turnerbund.

103. Hans von Tschammer und Osten was the state leader (Großkomtur) of Saxony for the Jungdo; Dietrich von Jagow was the state leader (Landesführer) of the OC/Bund Wiking in Württemberg from 1922 to 1927; Manfred von Killinger was the same for Saxony from 1922 to 1928; Max Luyken was the state business manager (Landesgeschäftsführer) of the Orgesch in Saxony from 1920 to 1925.

104. Georg Oberdieck was the Stahlhelm Gauführer (regional leader) for Hanover for one year sometime between 1924 and 1930; Hans-Joachim Riecke was in charge of all of the central German chapters of the Bund Oberland in 1926 (possibly earlier as well), and Otto Ivers was a deputy regional leader of the Jungdo in the Rheinland between 1925 and 1927.

105. Erich Reimann was a Stahlhelm county youth leader and county treasurer in Altona between 1926 and 1930, and Arthur Rakobrandt was the Stahlhelm and Wehrwolf county leader and also the county business manager of the Ostpreußischer Heimatbund in Kreis Fischhausen (East Prussia) from 1922 to 1927.

106. Albert Heinz was leader of a local Jungdo chapter from 1921 to 1927.

107. Six of the "defectors" also joined the SA immediately as "officers," further proof of their leadership abilities: Sepp Dietrich, Paul Hocheisen, Otto Ivers, Dietrich von Jagow, Manfred Freiherr von Killinger, and Robert Rigl.

108. An exception to this statement must be made regarding the Reichswehr/Reichsmarine. Here the reasons do not lie in internal developments within the military. Rather, they have to do with more personal concerns of the people involved, concerns which may not be political at all. For instance, Paul Hocheisen left the Reichswehr because he retired.

109. Edmund Diehl was a member of the DNVP from 1920 to 1927. Paul Hocheisen retired from the Reichswehr in 1929, and Robert Schormann left the Reichsmarine for unknown reasons in 1930.

110. The "defectors" were members of only six Wehrverbände for a significant period, though they were members of several others for shorter periods.

111. Bernard Hofmann, Dietrich von Jagow, Karl-Siegmund Litzmann, Georg Oberdieck, Arthur Rakobrandt, and Erich Reimann. Rakobrandt was also a member of the Wehrwolf, which loosely affiliated itself with the Stahlhelm in 1924: Volker R. Berghahn, *Der Stahlhelm, Bund der Frontsoldaten, 1918-1935* (Düsseldorf: Droste, 1966), 33. Von Jagow was also a member of the Württembergische Heimatschutz and had been a high leader in the Bund Wiking.

112. Hans von Tschammer und Osten, Otto Ivers, and Albert Heinz.

113. Manfred von Killinger, Dietrich von Jagow, and Hans-Günther von

Obernitz. Killinger had also been in Wehrwolf and Oberland, and von Jagow joined the Stahlhelm for a short time after leaving the Bund Wiking.

114. Sepp Dietrich and Hans-Joachim Riecke.

115. Hans-Joachim Riecke and Sepp Dietrich.

116. Hans Jürgen Kuron, "Freikorps und Bund Oberland" (Ph.D. diss, Friedrich-Alexander University, Erlangen, 1960), 185-96, 204-6.

117. Diehl, *Paramilitary Politics*, 222-27, 234-35; Hornung, *Der Jungdeutsche Orden*, 55. The conflict in Saxony led to the resignation from the Jungdo of its state leader, Hans von Tschammer und Osten, who later joined the NSDAP and is a part of this group.

118. Gabriele Krüger, *Die Brigade Ehrhardt*, 119-23; Berghahn, *Stahlhelm*, 108-9.

119. One follower of Ehrhardt later claimed that von Killinger, the only one of the three here who joined the NSDAP immediately upon leaving the Bund Wiking, was actually sent into the NSDAP by Ehrhardt to be his eyes and ears in that organization and gradually transferred his loyalty to it while he was there. This is unsubstantiated but not implausible, and it is certainly in keeping with Ehrhardt's tactics of sending his men into various competing organizations to influence them and keep an eye on what they were doing: Ernst von Salomon, *Der Fragebogen* (1961; reprint, Reinbek bei Hamburg: Rowohlt, 1991), 113.

120. Only one individual from the Bund Wiking (von Killinger), and one from the Reichswehr (Hocheisen) also joined the NSDAP within one year.

121. Berghahn, *Stahlhelm*, 103-7, 130-31, 143.

122. Unless otherwise noted, information on Georg Oberdieck is taken from a Lebenslauf dated 11 April 1942 in the BDC.

123. He was awarded the Iron Cross First and Second Class and the Knight's Cross First Class with Oak Leaves and Swords of the Order of the Lion of Zähringen.

124. Only seven of the seventeen "defectors" were in a free corps, two on the eastern borders and three in the Ehrhardt Brigade. Three of those in a free corps entered the Provisional Reichswehr and served until 1920, a sign that their free corps service was simply a continuation of their earlier military careers.

125. Due to the independence of the regional chapters of the Stahlhelm, the Gauführer held considerable power and influence over the organization as a whole.

126. Max Linsmayer was killed in action in May 1940 and was replaced by Günther Gräntz.

127. Robert Bergmann, Heinrich Graf Finck von Finckenstein, Otto Herzog, Max Linsmayer, and Joachim Meyer-Quade. A major reason for the sparse nature of the available information on two men in this group, Max Linsmayer and Joachim Meyer-Quade, is the fact that both were killed in action in 1939 and 1940. For some unknown reason, SA records for those killed early in the war are missing, and the only available information consists of collections of obituaries and short biographies prepared and/or collected by the SA press office. Although these are often quite detailed, particularly when friends and colleagues of the deceased in the SA were asked to prepare them, they are not as thorough as the documents commonly found in the SA files.

128. Robert Bergmann, Otto Herzog, and Joachim Meyer-Quade.

129. Robert Bergmann, Heinrich Graf Finck von Finckenstein, and Joachim Meyer-Quade were veterans. The two reserve officers were Finck von Finckenstein and Robert Bergmann. Bergmann had been an einjähriger Freiwilliger before the war, although he was not commissioned until 1915.

130. The two were Finck von Finckenstein (Freiwillige Sturmabteilung Schlichtingsheim and Marine Brigade von Loewenfeld) and Robert Bergmann (Freikorps Epp).

131. Again, the individual is Finck von Finckenstein. Since early Party membership carried great status in the NSDAP, it is highly likely that such information would have been included in an obituary or otherwise figure prominently in any surviving materials on a given individual, so that we can be relatively sure that Finck von Finckenstein was the sole member of the group to have been in the Party up to 1923.

132. When he rejoined the SA, he actually joined the SS, which was a part of the SA at the time, whereas earlier, from 1927 to 1928, he had been a member of the SA proper.

133. Robert Bergmann and Joachim Meyer-Quade were both district leaders, and Otto Herzog was a business manager.

134. The four Reichstag deputies were Joachim Meyer-Quade, Robert Bergmann, Otto Herzog, and Count Finck von Finckenstein. All but the latter were elected deputies before the assumption of power. Robert Bergmann later left the SS and resumed his Party career, but it should be noted that he did not actually leave the SS voluntarily, but was expelled as a result of the Röhm Purge because he had been Röhm's adjutant.

135. IfZ Zs. 827 (Robert Bergmann) and Bergmann's SS Führerakte in the BDC.

136. This is 30.5 percent of the fifty-nine men in this chapter. A "position of responsibility" in the Party is defined as any office at the level of Ortsgruppenleiter and above. The men include Robert Bergmann, Friedrich Wilhelm Brückner, Paul Fassbach, Friedrich Fenz, Erich Hasse, Otto Herzog, Otto Ivers, Dietrich von Jagow, Karl Koerner, Hartmann Lauterbacher, Max Luyken, Joachim Meyer-Quade, Arthur Rakobrandt, Erich Reimann, Hans-Joachim Riecke, Robert Rigl, Robert Schormann, and Otto Wagener.

137. Kreisleiter was the highest Party position held by Joachim Meyer-Quade, Max Luyken, Otto Ivers, Erich Hasse, and Robert Rigl. Several of the others who held higher ranks also served as Kreisleiter.

138. Ten men fell into this latter category: Robert Bergmann (Gau staff, also former Kreisleiter), Friedrich Fenz (a deputy Gauleiter), Otto Herzog (a business manager in a Gau, and also a former district leader), Dietrich von Jagow (a Gau business manager), Otto Wagener (head of the Wirtschafts-politisches Amt in the central Party administration), Karl Koerner (a Gau organization and personnel manager), Hans-Joachim Riecke (a Gau official and after 1933 a Gau inspector), Erich Reimann (a Gau secretary), Robert Schormann (a Gau official after 1933), and Friedrich Wilhelm Brückner (Hitler's adjutant).

139. Three of the five district leaders came from one of these two categories: Otto Ivers, Joachim Meyer-Quade and Robert Rigl. The other two, Erich Hasse and Max Luyken, were "sporadic activists." Six of the ten Gau or national level Party leaders came from one of these two categories: Robert Bergmann, Otto Herzog, Dietrich von Jagow, Erich Reimann, Hans-Joachim Riecke, and Robert Schormann.

4. The Specialists, 1931-1932

1. Petzina et al., *Sozialgeschichtliches Arbeitsbuch*, 3:119, table A, "Arbeitslosigkeit." As Bennecke correctly points out, this figure does not include the potentially large group of the underemployed, nor does it include the dependents (families) of the unemployed or the effect on commerce of the drastic reduction in spending caused by such widespread unemployment: Bennecke, *Hitler und die SA*, 167-71.

2. This short characterization of Röhm is taken from the following sources: Ernst Röhm, *Die Geschichte eines Hochverräters* (Munich: Franz Eher, 1928: this edition is preferable to all subsequent ones); Eleanor Hancock, "Ernst Röhm and the Experience of World War I," *Journal of Military History* 60 (January 1996): 39-60; Bennecke, *Hitler und die SA*, 156-57; Frank, "Hitler and the National Socialist Coalition," 399-408; Werner, "SA," 517-18.

3. The Geneva Disarmament Conference seemed to offer a chance to obtain an increase in the Versailles treaty limits on the size of German armed forces. Röhm sought to obtain such an enlargement and to boost the influence of the SA through his plan to build a militia-based army.

4. The following interpretation generally agrees with that of Eleanor Hancock, who is writing a biography of Röhm. See Hancock, "'Indispensable Outsider'? Ernst Röhm as Chief of Staff of the SA, 1931-1933," paper presented at the annual meeting of the German Studies Association, Seattle, 11 October 1996.

5. In fact, he does not appear to have been the first choice. See Turner, *Hitler aus nächster Nähe*, 138-40.

6. Jean Mabire, *Röhm: L'Homme Qui Inventa Hitler* (Paris: Fayard, 1983).

7. Turner, *Hitler aus nächster Nähe*, 138-40, gives one example of Hitler's reserve, particularly regarding political insight.

8. Frank, "Hitler and the National Socialist Coalition," 457, suggests that Hitler intentionally chose Röhm because his homosexuality would leave him isolated within the Party and thus unable to participate in a fronde against him.

9. Officially, Hitler was the supreme SA leader, whereas Röhm was only his chief of staff (Stabschef), but in fact it was Röhm who set the tone of the organization and who created all but the most fundamental policies.

10. The exact date is from Volz, *SA*, 69. The figure for the strength of the SA is from Werner, "SA," 544. It should be treated as an estimate.

11. Werner, "SA," 544-45. This had more of a symbolic meaning than anything else, since the SA could not be compared to the Reichswehr in terms of training, discipline, or equipment.

12. OSAF Ib no. 316/32 of 1 January 1932 in the Bundesarchiv in Koblenz (hereafter abbreviated as BAK) NS23/vorl. 123; OSAF, part 1 of 1 February 1932, in BAK, Schumacher Collection, Ordner 415. Werner, "SA," 550-51, gives a January 1932 figure of 290,941.

13. A Schnellbrief (priority message) from the OSAF Führungsamt to the head of the SA Reichsführerschule (F2 no. 51328) of 3 September 1935 (in BAK NS23/337), puts the strength of the SA in January 1933 at 427,538. (It is likely that this figure does not include either the SS or the Austrian SA.) Werner, "SA," 551-52 gives a slightly different figure of 518,977. For the

sake of comparison, note that the size of the SA on 1 January 1935 was 3,543,099: NSDAP, Reichsorganisationsleiter, *Parteistatistik* (Munich: Hauptorganisationsamt, Amt Statistik, 1935), 3:70-71. As Bennecke rightly points out, this figure is likely well under the spring 1934 maximum size of the SA: Bennecke, *Hitler und die SA*, 214.

14. Alleged plans to radically decrease the size of the SA as a means of subordinating it to the political organization had played a role in the first Stennes incident and the resignation of von Pfeffer. See Walter Stennes, *Wie es zur Stennes-Aktion kam!* (Berlin: Hausdruck von Walther Stennes, n.d.), 2 (in IfZ Fa3); Werner, "SA," 465.

15. Volz, *NSDAP*, 58; Frank, "Hitler and the National Socialist Coalition," 413-15. The only organizational benefit of this change was that it paved the way for a larger (even top-heavy) staff structure. On the other hand, it was tidier for Röhm and other former soldiers, and it provided a means of promoting SA leaders to reward them without necessarily giving them a higher command.

16. The Sturmbann corresponded to a battalion in the German army. Frank, "Hitler and the National Socialist Coalition," 412, argues that this similarity was not coincidental but a product of a deliberate militarization of the SA under Röhm.

17. Frank, "Hitler and the National Socialist Coalition," 418-19. In general, on the introduction of the Sturmbann, see Frank "Hitler and the National Socialist Coalition," 412-19, Bennecke, *Hitler und die SA*, 160, Werner, "SA," 535ff., Volz, *SA*, 71-72.

18. Röhm later reintroduced the Brigade as an intermediate level between the Standarte and the Gruppe.

19. Frank, "Hitler and the National Socialist Coalition," 535ff.; Bennecke, *Hitler und die SA*, 160. Aside from helping the SA cope with greater numbers, this particular reform went a long way toward establishing better relations between the SA and the local Gauleiter, since under von Pfeffer, the Gausturm lines were deliberately drawn so as to ignore Gau boundaries.

20. Werner, "SA," 535ff.; Frank, "Hitler and the National Socialist Coalition," 429; Bennecke, *Hitler und die SA*, 160. The most openly rebellious OSAF-Stellvertreter was Walther Stennes, but they were all very strong and independent personalities and all had made decisions at odds with the central SA leadership in the past.

21. The chronic lack of lower-level leaders resulted in considerable effort being put into the development of SA schools. These included not only the national Reichsführerschule but also schools for leaders in each SA Gruppe, the so-called SA-Führerschulen (originally SA-Führer Vor-Schulen). See Frank, "Hitler and the National Socialist Coalition," 422-29; Werner, "SA," 555-62; BDC SA file Kurt Kühme; Standartenführer Späing, "Erziehungswesen und SA-Führervorschulen," in *Der SA-Mann*, no. 6 of February 1932, 4.

22. OSAF-Stellvertreter Ost Ia. no. 1161/31. St/v.B. to Röhm of 28 February 1931 in *Stennes-Aktion*, and passim; Werner, "SA," 525-29.

23. Information on the so-called Stennes Putsch has been taken from the following sources: OSAF Gerichts- und Rechtsamt file on the Stennes Putsch in the BDC; Frank, "Hitler and the National Socialist Coalition," 477-504; Werner, "SA," 524-34; Nyomarkay, *Charisma and Factionalism*, 120-21; *Wie es zur Stennes-Aktion kam!*

24. Frank, "Hitler and the National Socialist Coalition," 435-36; Volz, *SA*, 72. Note that Stennes was the only OSAF-Stellvertreter who was actually deposed. Of the five remaining OSAF-Stellvertreter, four became Gruppenführer and one became the inspector general of the SA and SS, so that not the individuals personally but only their overly powerful positions were actually under attack.

25. Frank, "Hitler and the National Socialist Coalition," 455-76.

26. Frank in particular credits Röhm with truly disciplining the SA, which is an exaggeration at best. See, e.g., ibid., 399, 411.

27. See the extended discussions of this in Bennecke, *Hitler und die SA*, 157-59; Heinrich Bennecke, *Die Reichswehr und der "Röhm-Putsch"* (Munich und Vienna: Günter Olzog, 1964), 13-16; Frank, "Hitler and the National Socialist Coalition," 515-30.

28. Absolon, *Wehrmacht*, 1:35-39.

29. Frank, "Hitler and the National Socialist Coalition," 507-15.

30. On the SA ban, see the following: Bennecke, *Hitler und die SA*, 182; Werner, "SA," 576-77; Karl-Dietrich Bracher, *Die Auflösung der Weimarer Republik* (1955; reprint, Königstein/Ts.-Düsseldorf: Athenäum Droste, 1978), 424-38; Erich Eyck, *A History of the Weimar Republic*, vol. 2, *From the Locarno Conference to Hitler's Seizure of Power* (New York: Atheneum, 1970), 362-77.

31. Bennecke, *Hitler und die SA*, 182, states that it was the Reichswehr which warned the SA, although he supplies little concrete proof. On the other hand, as a high SA leader he was in a position to have known at the time. It is clear that the SA was forewarned: Engelbrechten, *Braune Armee*, 239-40.

32. OSAF IIa no. 1549/32, Neuaufstellung der SA und SS: Führerbefehl no. 1 of 1 July 1932, in BDC, Schumacher Collection, Ordner 404.

33. See note 13 above.

34. OSAF 2420/32, Führerbefehl no. 2 of 9 September 1932, in BDC, Schumacher Collection, Ordner 410; Werner, "SA," 541ff.

35. Werner, "SA," 551-52; OSAF IIa no. 1549/32, Neuaufstellung der SA und SS: Führerbefehl no. 1 of 1 July 1932; OSAF 2420/32, Führerbefehl no. 2 of 9 September 1932; OSAF 3520/32, Führerbefehl no. 3 of 29 November 1932, all in BDC, Schumacher Collection, Ordner 410; On the Gruppenstab z.b.V., see Bennecke, *Reichswehr*; Absolon, *Wehrmacht*, 1:35-134, 4:28-29.

36. For example, 68 percent of all Stabschefs, Obergruppenführer, and Gruppenführer had already joined the SA before 1931.

37. They included Richard Aster, Ernst Beißner, Reinhard Boerner, Hermann Brauneck, Bruno Czerwinski, Axel Daiber, Walter Darré, Ludwig Fichte, Hans Frank, Hans Friedrich, Hans Fuchs, Paul Giesler, Karl Haas, Heinrich Hacker, Walther Haug, Hans Peter von Heydebreck, Reinhard Heydrich, Franz Ritter von Hörauf, Hans-Georg Hofmann, Paul Holthoff, Emil Ketterer, Adolf Kob, Fritz Ritter von Krausser, Friedrich-Wilhelm Krüger, Kurt Kühme, Hans Lehmann, Willy Liebel, Werner Lorenz, Walter Luetgebrune, Karl Lucke, Hans Ludin, Georg Mappes, Meinhardt Marnitz, Wilhelm Mörchen, Eberhard Pagels, Kurt Plesch, Ernst Röhm, Wilhelm Schmid, Ludwig Schmuck, Albert Schneider, Karl Schreyer, Paul Schulz, Siegfried Seidel-Dittmarsch, Josef Seydel, Gregor Strasser, and Otto Walter.

38. Only five out of forty-six (10.8%) were not war veterans. They are Ernst Beißner, Reinhard Heydrich, Hans Ludin, Walter Luetgebrune, and

Meinhardt Marnitz. Four of these five were too young to have been in the war. Luetgebrune was thirty-five when war broke out, but did not serve for reasons unknown. Axel Daiber, Hans Frank, and Georg Mappes served in the war, but did not see combat.

39. Of the forty-four for whom this information is known, twenty-one (47.7%) were professional soldiers. Seventeen were professional officers (Hermann Brauneck, Hans Friedrich, Hans Fuchs, Karl Haas, Hans-Peter von Heydebreck, Reinhard Heydrich, Franz Ritter von Hörauf, Hans-Georg Hofmann, Adolf Kob, Franz Ritter von Krausser, Friedrich-Wilhelm Krüger, Kurt Kühme, Hans Ludin, Ernst Röhm, Karl Schreyer, Siegfried Seidel-Dittmarsch, and Josef Seydel), three were professional enlisted men (Werner Lorenz, Karl Lucke, and Paul Schulz) and one (Kurt Plesch) was a professional military official (Militärbeamter). Note that Reinhard Heydrich and Hans Ludin began their careers as professional officers in the Reichswehr, not in the Imperial Army.

40. At least thirty-two of the forty-one who served in the war were officers by the end of 1918. This is 69.5 percent of the entire group of forty-six, or 78 percent of the veterans. Karl Lucke, a professional soldier, was an Offizierstellvertreter, meaning that he fulfilled the duties of an officer but was not considered a member of the officer corps.

41. Of the thirty-two who were officers, ten were captains (Reinhard Boerner, Hans Fuchs, Hans-Peter von Heydebreck, Emil Ketterer, Adolf Kob, Fritz Ritter von Krausser, Ernst Röhm, Wilhelm Schmid, Siegfried Seidel-Dittmarsch, and Josef Seydel) and four were majors (Karl Haas, Franz Ritter von Hörauf, Hans-Georg Hofmann, and Kurt Kühme) or the equivalents in the navy. Since many continued their service after the war, the final ranks of the officers in the group were even higher.

42. At least fourteen of the forty-one veterans (34%) served in some sort of staff position. Reinhard Boerner, Hermann Brauneck, Friedrich-Wilhelm Krüger, Hans Lehmann, and Paul Schulz served as adjutants or orderly officers. Hans Fuchs, Heinrich Hacker, Hans-Peter von Heydebreck, Hans-Georg Hofmann, and Adolf Kob served in regimental or divisional staffs. Franz Ritter von Hörauf served on a corps staff, Ernst Röhm in the Bavarian Ministry of War, Siegfried Seidel-Dittmarsch at the army level and in the Prussian Ministry of War, and Hans Fuchs in the general staff corps.

43. "Regular army" means (in contrast to the various types of temporary volunteer units created during the revolution) units of the old Imperial Army that were not yet demobilized or units of the embryo Provisional Reichswehr. Veterans of the regular army included Hans Friedrich, Karl Haas, Franz Ritter von Hörauf, Hans-Georg Hofmann, Adolf Kob, Fritz Ritter von Krausser, Werner Lorenz, Karl Lucke, Kurt Plesch, Ernst Röhm, Wilhelm Schmid, Paul Schulz, and Siegfried Seidel-Dittmarsch.

44. At the most, in the first quarter of 1919, sixteen of the group served in a free corps: Hans Friedrich, Hans Fuchs, Hans-Peter von Heydebreck, Reinhard Heydrich, Hans-Georg Hofmann, Franz Ritter von Hörauf, Paul Holthoff, Fritz Ritter von Krausser, Friedrich-Wilhelm Krüger, Kurt Kühme, Wilhelm Schmid, Gregor Strasser, Ernst Röhm, Karl Schreyer, Paul Schulz, and Josef Seydel. Note, however, that some of these men were assigned to their particular free corps as professional officers by the army high command. An example is Franz Ritter von Hörauf, who was sent to be the general staff officer of Freikorps Epp.

45. One member of the group was in an Einwohnerwehr (Emil Ketterer) and a second in a Zeitfreiwilligenverband (Ludwig Fichte) without also serving in a free corps or the army. A further individual (Eberhard Pagels) was a member of a Studentenwehr (armed student company), but only in 1920.

46. Ten men in this chapter served in Freikorps Epp, although not all served in it at the same time (Hans Frank, Franz Ritter von Hörauf, Hans-Georg Hofmann, Fritz Ritter von Krausser, Ernst Röhm, Wilhelm Schmid, Karl Schreyer, Josef Seydel, Gregor Strasser, and Otto Walter). The other Bavarian unit was Freikorps Bamberg (Hans Fuchs). Hans Fuchs also served in Wehrregiment München, which was formed by the Hoffmann government to maintain order in Munich and was not properly a free corps. The other free corps include the Eiserne Division, the Baltische Landeswehr, the Eiserne Torpedobootsflotille, Freikorps von Lettow-Vorbeck, Weickhmann, Libow, Schlesien, Halle, Eulenberg, Lützow, and von Heydebreck.

47. Five (10.8%) were members of a völkisch organization in 1919 or 1920: three in the Deutsch-Völkischer Schutz-und Trutzbund (Richard Aster, Reinhard Heydrich, and Kurt Plesch) and two in the NSDAP, one of which was earlier a member of the Thule Gesellschaft (Hans Frank and Ernst Röhm). Three were members of nonvölkisch political organizations: one of the DNVP (Adolf Kob), one of the DDP (Reinhard Boerner), and one of the Deutsch-Nationaler Jugendbund, really a youth group but associated with the DNVP (Reinhard Heydrich). Three were members of veterans' groups: one was a member of the Stahlhelm (Walther Haug), two were members of the Verband Nationalgesinnter Soldaten (Paul Holthoff and Gregor Strasser), and one was a member of the Deutsche Offiziersbund (Kurt Plesch) and later of the Nationalverband Deutscher Offiziere. Finally, one man was a member of the Organisation von Pflugh-Hartung (Heinrich Hacker), a secret society founded to prevent, through murder if necessary, the surrender to the Allies of Germans accused of war crimes.

48. Very few nonmilitary organizations are found in the backgrounds of these men: three individuals belonged to the Deutsch-Völkische Schutz-und Trutzbund in 1921 (Richard Aster, Reinhard Heydrich, Kurt Plesch), one each belonged to the DNVP (Adolf Kob) and the DDP (Reinhard Boerner), one belonged to the Deutsche Pfadfinder, a kind of boy-scout organization (Hans Ludin), one belonged to the Deutsch-Völkische Jugendschaft, a völkisch youth group (Reinhard Heydrich), and one belonged to the Technische Nothilfe, a state-sponsored disaster relief/civil defense organization that could even be included among the paramilitary organizations (Meinhardt Marnitz).

49. Seven members of the group of 1931-32 SA joiners were in the Reichswehr in 1922 and 1923 (Karl Haas, Reinhard Heydrich, Franz Ritter von Hörauf, Hans-Georg Hofmann, Fritz Ritter von Krausser, Kurt Plesch, and Ernst Röhm) and six were in it in 1921 (in addition to the above—and minus Reinhard Heydrich-Wilhelm Schmid and Siegfried Seidel-Dittmarsch). Two served in the illegal Black Reichswehr from 1921 to 1923 (Hans Lehmann and Paul Schulz). Those who were members of the police might also be included with the Reichswehr, since both were state organizations. Two members of the group were in the police from 1921 to 1923 (Hans Fuchs and Adolf Kob). So 15.2 percent of the group were members of the Reichswehr in 1923; this figure rises to 23.9 percent if the members of the Black Reichswehr and the police are included.

50. Only two members of the group were members of the NSDAP in

1921 and 1922 (Hans Frank and Ernst Röhm), meaning that five joined in 1923 (Heinrich Hacker, Emil Ketterer, Wilhelm Schmid, Josef Seydel, and Gregor Strasser).

51. The eight were Hans Frank, Hans Fuchs, Emil Ketterer, Fritz Ritter von Krausser, Ernst Röhm, Wilhelm Schmid, Josef Seydel, and Gregor Strasser. All but Strasser and possibly Frank were later awarded the Blutorden in memory of their participation in the putsch. See the BDC files of the above and Klaus D. Patzwall, ed., *Der Blutorden der NSDAP* (Hamburg: Militaria-Archiv Klaus D. Patzwall, 1985). Hans-Georg Hofmann was also eventually awarded the Blutorden, but his role during the putsch is not clear.

52. Two members of our group were in the Stahlhelm in 1921 (Walther Haug and Kurt Plesch), three in 1922 (Hans Friedrich, in addition to Haug and Plesch), and five by the end of 1923 (Walter Darré and Heinrich Hacker, in addition to the others). The Reichskriegsflagge, which was only founded in 1923 as a fission from the Reichsflagge, had three members from our group by the end of 1923 (Fritz Ritter von Krausser, Ernst Röhm, and Josef Seydel). Three members of the group were also in the Reichsflagge (Willy Liebel, Ernst Röhm, Josef Seydel). The only other organization which had more than one member from the group by the end of 1923 was the SA (Hans Frank, Gregor Strasser).

53. Four men in the group were members of a total of five völkisch organizations by mid-1924. Three of these men were former NSDAP members (Heinrich Hacker, Ernst Röhm, and Gregor Strasser). The one non-Party member now active in völkisch politics was Richard Aster, who had earlier been a member of the Deutsch-Völkische Schutz- und Trutzbund while serving in the Grenzschutz in 1919.

54. Three of the six early PGs were members of the Frontbann. They were Ernst Röhm, Josef Seydel, and Heinrich Hacker.

55. The Frontbann was represented by four members of the 1931-32 group (the three mentioned in note 55 above, plus Fritz Ritter von Krausser), the Stahlhelm by six (Richard Aster, Walter Darré, Hans Friedrich, Heinrich Hacker, Walther Haug, and Kurt Plesch), and the Reichswehr by five (Karl Haas, Reinhard Heydrich, Franz Ritter von Hörauf, Hans-Georg Hofmann, and Hans Ludin), although the number continued to drop through 1924 and 1925 due to repercussions from the putsch. One member of the group was also in the police in 1924 (Hans Fuchs).

56. Richard Aster was a member of both the DVFB and the GDAP; Adolf Kob was a member of the Tannenberg Bund.

57. Of the six members of the Frontbann or of a völkisch organization in 1924, only Heinrich Hacker and Gregor Strasser joined the NSDAP in 1925 or 1926, and Hacker left the NSDAP again in 1925 or early 1926 and did not rejoin until 1929.

58. At least four members of the 1931-32 group were members of the Stahlhelm in 1925: Richard Aster, Walter Darré, Hans Friedrich, and Walther Haug. One other, Paul Giesler, was a member of the Stahlhelm by 1927 and very possibly earlier. By 1930, Hans Friedrich and Walther Haug were still members, and Franz Ritter von Hörauf had joined. All left the Stahlhelm by the end of 1930. The Reichswehr was represented by four members of the group between 1925 and 1930 (Karl Haas, Reinhard Heydrich, Hans-Georg Hofmann, and Hans Ludin), but they, too, left by the end of 1930.

59. See, e.g., Heinrich Hildebrandt and Walter Kettner, eds., *Stahlhelm*

Handbuch, 4th ed. (Berlin: Stahlhelm, 1931).

60. See chapter 3 above. "Serial activists" are defined above as men who were members of several organizations in succession. They seem to drift from one organization to another, as if searching for one that really expressed their interests and desires.

61. The "sporadic activists" were characterized by little organized activity except in crisis periods. These men were typically active in 1919, again in 1923, and then not again until they joined the SA/NSDAP. Paul Holthoff is the only member of the group who fits this model unambiguously; Kurt Kühme and Fritz Ritter von Krausser come close, but their involvement with the Reichswehr makes their inclusion in the category problematic. As a result, the "sporadic activists" will not be discussed in detail in this chapter.

62. The "passive activists" were men who were involved in very little or no organized political activity at all from 1920 until they joined the SA and NSDAP. The "defectors" were loyal members of a single organization (or a small number of organizations simultaneously) for a long time who then quit and "defected" to the NSDAP. The "Party soldiers" characteristically joined the NSDAP relatively early but did not then join the SA until a year or more had passed. Most of these men were also active in the political organization of the Party, and could have made a career in the Party apparatus as easily as they did in the SA. See the previous chapter for an elaboration of these models.

63. The four are Richard Aster, Heinrich Hacker, Adolf Kob, and Emil Ketterer.

64. Emil Ketterer was a physician and was automatically exempt from field command, although his career was also mostly in higher staffs of the SA as an administrator, not as a "frontline" SA physician.

65. Information on Aster is taken from his BDC files unless otherwise noted. His Personalfragebogen (personnel questionnaire) of 20 September 1937, with its supplements and a transcript of his Lebenslauf (curriculum vitae) were particularly useful.

66. Although the class of 1900 was the last to be eligible for the draft in Germany, not all young men from this class were called up. See Absolon, *Wehrmacht,* 1:8, esp. 8n. 45.

67. The organization was banned in that year in nearly all German states. Note also that the S&T Bund made a deliberate effort to recruit soldiers in the Grenzschutz and in the free corps in 1919. See Lohalm, *Völkischer Radikalismus,* 215-22, 246-51.

68. Roßbach, *Mein Weg durch die Zeit,* 64, 73-74; Waite, *Vanguard of Nazism,* 191-96, 137-38, and 188-91; Diehl, *Paramilitary Politics,* 78, esp. 78nn. 6 and 7.

69. His official membership date was June 1931, however.

70. The best study on the German occupation of the East is still Alexander Dallin, *German Rule in Russia, 1941-1945: A Study of Occupational Policies* (London: Macmillan, 1957).

71. There were sixteen clear "defectors" in all, although because many of the men in this chapter connected to Ernst Röhm have incomplete records, the category is potentially larger. They are Walter Darré, Hans Friedrich, Hans Fuchs, Paul Giesler, Karl Haas, Walther Haug, Reinhard Heydrich, Hans-Georg Hofmann, Hans Lehmann, Karl Lucke, Hans Ludin, Meinhard Marnitz, Kurt Plesch, Ludwig Schmuck, Josef Seydel, and Otto Walter.

72. They are Freikorps and Bund Oberland, the Stahlhelm, Freikorps Damm, the Frontbann, the Einwohnerwehr Danzig, the DNVP, the Reichswehr, the police, and the "Black Reichswehr"/ secret Reichswehr Grenzschutz.

73. These men are Karl Haas, Reinhard Heydrich, Hans-Georg Hofmann, and Hans Ludin. Note that Karl Haas was not actually a member of the Reichswehr but, rather, an officer in the Austrian Federal Army. Franz Ritter von Hörauf and Fritz Ritter von Krausser probably could be added, but there is not enough information in their files to be sure. Even Ernst Röhm might well have been included, since he also "defected" from the army—albeit the Bolivian army.

74. Hans Lehmann was a battalion commander in the Grenzschutz in Jüterbog, and Hans Fuchs was an officer in the Bavarian Landespolizei. Both men entered their respective organizations as a direct result of their prior service in the Imperial Army. This mid-Weimar era Grenzschutz was an army-sponsored secret militia designed to supplement the army in time of war. Its main task was to slow down any enemy advance into Germany to allow time for mobilization and the preparation of a counterattack by regular army troops. It was similar in mission, but organizationally quite distinct from the Grenzschutz established during the German Revolution. See Absolon, *Wehrmacht*, 1:35-39; and Carsten, *Reichswehr and Politics*, 147-52, 220-32, 265-75, 350-56.

75. It may be argued that men like Karl Haas or Hans Ludin, who engaged in political activities that led to their dismissal from the service, are actually ideologically motivated true defectors in the usual sense of the word.

76. Reichswehr members were forbidden to belong to any political party: Absolon, *Wehrmacht*, 1:74-76.

77. Ludwig Schmuck came from Bund Oberland, where he was a local group leader. Josef Seydel had been the second-in-command of the Frontbann, and Karl Lucke came from Organisation Damm. Walter Darré, Hans Friedrich, Walther Haug, and Kurt Plesch all came from the Stahlhelm.

78. Information on Karl Lucke is taken from his BDC SA files unless otherwise noted. The following were particularly useful: his Personalfragebogen of 15 June 1939, his Lebenslauf, "Bericht des Führers der SA-Brigade 2250 (Offenbach) Oberführer Lucke, über seine Verhaftung" (n.d.), "Meldung [report] des Obertruppführers Erich Rebentisch" of 10 July 1934, and Personalstammkarte (green) for 1944 and 1945.

79. See Absolon, *Wehrmacht*, 2:175-79, for an explanation of the peculiar rank of Offizierstellvertreter.

80. All information on Fuchs is taken from his SA files in the BDC unless otherwise noted. His Personalfragebogen of 14 January 1937 was particularly helpful.

81. The Bavarian Landespolizei was a paramilitary police force intended to maintain domestic law and order in situations that were beyond the capability of local city police. It was organized along military lines and armed with a variety of light infantry weapons, including heavy machine guns, armored cars, and mortars. It was later absorbed into the Wehrmacht. It and the similar Bereitschaftspolizei (readiness police) or "Grüne Polizei" ("green police," after their characteristic uniforms which were green, in contrast to the blue of the normal city police) elsewhere were under state, as opposed to federal, control. See Gordon, *Putsch*, 120-21, 124-28, and Georg Tessin,

Deutsche Verbände und Truppen, 3:459-68. In general, see Jürgen Siggemann, *Die kasernierte Polizei und das Problem der inneren Sicherheit in der Weimarer Republik: Eine Studie zum Auf- und Ausbau des innerstaatlichen Sicherheitssystems in Deutschland, 1918-1933* (Frankfurt am Main: R.G. Fischer, 1980).

82. They were Ernst Beißner, Reinhard Boerner, Hermann Brauneck, Bruno Czerwinski, Axel Daiber, Ludwig Fichte, Friedrich-Wilhelm Krüger, Werner Lorenz, Georg Mappes, Wilhelm Mörchen, Eberhard Pagels, Albert Schneider, Paul Schulz, and Siegfried Seidel-Dittmarsch. The fourteen make up 30.4 percent of the entire 1931-32 group, and may be even higher if several individuals are included whose files are sketchy or incomplete. Readers may note that Johann Fuchs could have been included in this category, since he left the police in 1925. He is classed as a "defector" and not as a "passive activist" due to his long membership in the police.

83. The individual is the infamous Oberleutnant Paul Schulz. Given his character, it is likely that he would have appeared in another category had he not spent time in prison. He was a leading organizer of the illegal "Black Reichswehr" in Prussia. He became a close associate of Gregor Strasser in the NSDAP, and they left the Party at the same time. Schulz was later shot in the Röhm Purge and left for dead. He escaped Germany and worked as a businessman during the Second World War. He was responsible for saving a large number of Jews and other targets of the Nazi regime at considerable risk of his own life. See Paul Schulz, "Meine Erschiessung am 30. Juni 1934" (privately published, 1948; in IfZ F57); and Paul Schulz, "Rettungen und Hilfeleistungen an Verfolgten 1933-45 durch Oberlt. a.D. Paul Schulz" (privately published, 1967; IfZ Zs. A52).

84. The six physicians are Hermann Brauneck, Bruno Czerwinski, Axel Daiber, Wilhelm Mörchen, Eberhard Pagels, and Albert Schneider.

85. Curiously, three of the "passive activists" joined the SS, not the SA. They were Friedrich-Wilhelm Krüger, Werner Lorenz, and Siegfried Seidel-Dittmarsch.

86. Information on Wilhelm Mörchen is taken from his BDC SA files unless otherwise noted. His Personalfragebogen of 12 October 1937 and its supplements were particularly useful.

87. A Feldhilfsarzt ranked similarly to a Feldwebelleutnant; both were technically noncommissioned officers who were given the responsibilities and many of the privileges of officers. The rank was reserved for medical students who were advanced in their studies but who had not yet passed their medical board examination. See Absolon, *Wehrmacht*, 2:50.

88. A Vertrauensarzt was responsible for verifying insurance claims for long-term disability compensation and similar duties connected with health insurance and worker's compensation.

89. The information on Paul Holthoff has been taken from his SA files in the BDC and Eric Stockhorst, *Fünftausend Köpfe*, 206, unless otherwise noted. Among his BDC materials, the following were particularly useful: his SA-Führer-Fragebogen (SA leader's questionnaire) of 1 November 1934, a large file card with a clipped left-hand corner from the OSAF (n.d.), and the two supplements to his Personalfragebogen.

90. He officially joined the SA roughly one month before joining the Party. This is not typical of either the smaller group of "passive activists" or of the larger group of 1931-32 SA joiners among the highest SA leaders. It

may actually be due to a lag in Party bookkeeping, since the men in this
chapter typically joined the NSDAP first, and only then the SA. See 18-19
below.

91. The Nationalpolitische Erziehungsanstalten (Napola) were special
Party schools that were intended to train a future governing elite. They
emphasized ideological training. See Horst Überhorst, ed., *Elite für die
Diktatur: Die Nationalpolitischen Erziehungsanstalten, 1933-1945. Ein
Dokumentarbericht* (Düsseldorf: Droste, 1969).

92. In other words, thirty-four individuals out of the forty-six in the
category of 1931-32 SA joiners.

93. The men are Walter Darré, Hans Frank, Hans Fuchs, Paul Giesler,
Karl Haas, Hans-Peter von Heydebreck, Franz Ritter von Hörauf, Hans-Georg
Hofmann, Kurt Kühme, Werner Lorenz, Hans Ludin, Ernst Röhm, Karl
Schreyer, Josef Seydel, and Gregor Strasser. This is 32.6 percent of the group
of forty-six. This number would be higher yet if men were included who
reached the rank of Sturmbannführer or higher within six months of joining
the SA, or if the physicians were included.

94. They are Ernst Beißner, Walter Darré, Hans Frank, Hans Fuchs, Karl
Haas, Hans-Peter von Heydebreck, Franz Ritter von Hörauf, Hans-Georg
Hofmann, Adolf Kob, Friedrich-Wilhelm Krüger, Kurt Kühme, Hans Ludin,
Walter Luetgebrune, Ernst Röhm, Karl Schreyer, Paul Schulz, Siegfried Seidel-
Dittmarsch, Josef Seydel, and Gregor Strasser. The nineteen are 41.3 percent
of the total group of 46.

95. Turner, *Hitler aus nächster Nähe,* 195. Note that in Röhm's case,
the fact that he was a known quantity outweighed Hitler's earlier disagreements with him and rumors of his homosexuality: ibid., 197-201.

96. BDC files of Kurt Kühme and "Akt no. 49 Meuterei Stennes," in the
BDC SA Allgemeine Personalakten.

97. Schreyer and von Hörauf came from Röhm's regiment, and von Hörauf
later served with Röhm in the staff of Free Corps Epp. Although the majority
of these men were recruited by Röhm for their military skills, note that
Emil Ketterer, a physician, and Karl Schreyer, who was recruited specifically to handle SA finances and who was a former banker, were both also
former Bavarian officers whom Röhm had known for a considerable time.
See IfZ Zs. 357/2, Interrogation of Karl Schreyer on 28 May 1947 by the
Counterintelligence Corps, and IfZ Sp2/1, Spruchkammer Akten des Grafen
du Moulin-Eckart; BDC files of Josef Seydel, Franz Ritter von Hörauf, Emil
Ketterer, and Fritz Ritter von Krausser. See also Gordon, *Putsch,* 346, and
Gordon, *Reichswehr,* 245. Others who were well known to Röhm but not
necessarily recruited by him directly were Hans-Georg Hofmann and Wilhelm
Schmid.

98. The infamous "Feme Schulz" and organizer of the Black Reichswehr
in Brandenburg. BDC files on Paul Schulz, and Walter Luetgebrune, *Wahrheit
und Recht für Feme, Schwarze Reichswehr, und Oberleutnant Schulz*
(Munich: J.F. Lehmann, 1928).

99. Luetgebrune gained a great deal of notoriety in defending a series of
celebrated right-wing activists. See Rudolf Heydeloff, "Staranwalt der
Rechtsextremisten: Walter Luetgebrune in der Weimarer Republik," in
Vierteljahreshefte für Zeitgeschichte 32 (July 1984): 373-421. See also von
Salomon, *Fragebogen,* 271-77, 430-34.

100. Information on von Heydebreck is scanty. What is clear is that he

was one of the most celebrated free corps leaders and nationalist activists in the Weimar Republic, who had a strong following above all in Silesia and eastern Germany. See von Heydebreck, *Wir Wehrwölfe*, and Stockhorst, *Fünftausend Köpfe*, 195-96.

101. To put it another way, 71.7 percent of the forty-six future highest SA leaders who joined the SA in 1931 or 1932 fall into one of six functional categories.

102. They include Hans Fuchs, Karl Haas, Hans-Peter von Heydebreck, Franz Ritter von Hörauf, Hans-Georg Hofmann, Adolf Kob, Fritz Ritter von Krausser, Kurt Kühme, Hans Ludin, Ernst Röhm, Wilhelm Schmid, Siegfried Seidel-Dittmarsch, and Josef Seydel.

103. At least eight of the thirteen had staff experience: Hans Fuchs, Hans-Peter von Heydebreck, Franz Ritter von Hörauf, Hans-Georg Hofmann, Adolf Kob, Fritz Ritter von Krausser, Hans Ludin, and Siegfried Seidel-Dittmarsch. Adolf Kob was a member of the Prussian general staff corps, Röhm and Seidel-Dittmarsch served in staffs in the Bavarian and Prussian War Ministries, while von Hörauf had experience at the corps level. On the other hand, two of the seven, Hans Ludin and Peter von Heydebreck, served only briefly with staffs. Not included with the seven staff experts are Fritz Ritter von Krausser, Wilhelm Schmid, and Josef Seydel, all Bavarian captains whose records are too incomplete to reveal any staff training which they may have had.

104. Kurt Kühme left the Reichswehr as a major, Hans-Georg Hofmann left as a colonel, and Karl Haas left the Austrian Federal Army as a brigadier general (Generalmajor).

105. Due to a lack of information, this could not be verified for Wilhelm Schmid, but he is the only possible exception.

106. BDC files Kurt Kühme; "Akt no. 49 Meuterei Stennes," BDC; Stockhorst, *Fünftausend Köpfe*, 255; Frank, "Hitler and the National Socialist Coalition," 424.

107. See his BDC SA files, especially "Das militärische und politische Werden des Staatssekretärs SA-Obergruppenführer Hofmann in der Nachkriegszeit," Franz Ritter von Epp, 1938.

108. Werner, "SA," 407.

109. BDC SA files of Emil Ketterer and Walter Schulze.

110. For example, the SA-Führerbefehle, the official orders announcing promotions, appointments, and other changes in command and personnel did not carry a separate rubric for physicians until February 1932. See OSAF IIa no. 430/32, Führerbefehl no. 7 of 10 February 1932, in BDC, Schumacher Collection, Ordner 410.

111. Hermann Brauneck, Bruno Czerwinski, Axel Daiber, Walther Haug, Emil Ketterer, Wilhelm Mörchen, Eberhard Pagels, Albert Schneider, and Otto Walter.

112. The two were Axel Daiber, who was a member of the Grenzschutz in his home province of West Prussia until he was forced to leave, and Eberhard Pagels, who was a member of a Studentenwehr (student militia) in Greifswald, where he was studying medicine, in 1920. Walther Haug is an exception here, since he was a member of the Stahlhelm from 1919 to 1931.

113. Wilhelm Mörchen and Eberhard Pagels.

114. Albert Schneider.

115. Hermann Brauneck, Emil Ketterer, and Otto Walter.

116. Information on Dr. Eberhard Pagels is taken from his SA BDC files. His obituary from the *Frankfurter Oder-Zeitung* of 23 March 1942 and his curriculum vitae, both in his BDC SA file, were particularly helpful.

117. Information on Dr. Emil Ketterer is taken from his BDC SA files, especially his SA Führer-Fragebogen (SA leader's questionnaire) of 22 May 1935, and his SA Personalbogen (n.d.), and "SA Sanitätsgruppenführer Dr. Ketterer," in the *Völkischer Beobachter* (Munich edition), 19 November 1934.

118. The Knight's Cross of the Order of the Lion of Zäringen was awarded by the Grand Duke of Baden. It was the third highest military order awarded by the Grand Duchy of Baden. The Knight's Cross was the lowest of the five levels of the order and was awarded 7,549 times in the First World War. See Klietmann, *Pour le Mérite und Tapferkeitsmedaille* (Berlin: Verlag "die Ordenssammlung," 1966), 6-7.

119. The founding meeting of the NSDAP occurred on 27 February 1925 in Munich. Although Ketterer gave 14 April 1925 as his official date of membership, it is possible that he applied for membership in February, but was only issued a Party number by the overworked Party office in April. His number is certainly extraordinarily low.

120. Ernst Beißner, Karl Lucke, Kurt Plesch, and Karl Schreyer.

121. Information on Schreyer, as well as coming from his BDC files, has been taken mainly from IfZ Zs. 357/2, Interrogation of Karl Schreyer of 28 May 1947 by the Counterintelligence Corps, and IfZ Sp2/1, Spruchkammer Akten des Grafen du Moulin-Eckart.

122. He was convicted in 1930 under article 240, paragraph 1 of the Commercial Statutes for illegal futures transactions (Termingeschäfte).

123. They are included here because they did technically hold their SA ranks on an active basis. There were also eighty-eight honorary Gruppenführer and Obergruppenführer who are not included in this study.

124. The Reich leader of organization (Reichsorganisationsleiter) was responsible for the entire administration of the Nazi Party aside from propaganda, treasury, and Party affiliates. Gregor Strasser was the holder of this office when Röhm was given the administration of the SA. He may fairly be termed the second most powerful man in the entire Nazi Party.

125. A third, Konstantin Hierl, was not included in this chapter because the exact date when he began his association with the SA is unclear, but he was also one of the members of the staff or the Reichsorganisationsleiter who became active SA Gruppenführer at this time.

126. Although these men received *active* SA commissions, a similar policy was applied to the award of honorary or inactive SA commissions, which were granted by Röhm both as a means of honoring former SA leaders who had to leave active service, and as a means of building bridges to the Party. Most of these more numerous honorary commissions went to Party officials who had some previous connection with the SA and who were veterans and who had been active in either Wehrverbände or völkisch organizations in the early 1920s. Information on the honorary SA leaders was taken from the BDC files of eighty-eight honorary SA Gruppenführer or Obergruppenführer.

127. He had of course been an SA commander and early SA organizer in Landshut before the Beer Hall Putsch in 1923. See Peter Stachura, *Gregor Strasser and the Rise of Nazism* (London: George Allen and Unwin, 1983).

128. Walter Stennes was the OSAF-Stellvertreter Ost, or head of the SA

in eastern Germany. There were actually two Stennes crises: the first was a threat by Stennes and several of his subordinates in August 1930 to resign and suspend any SA activities if SA leaders were not included among the Party members proposed for election to the Reichstag. The second was more serious: Fearing a threat to the legality policy of the NSDAP, Hitler removed Stennes from his post on 31 March 1931. Stennes thereupon left the NSDAP and SA and took a fairly large number of his subordinate officers and men with him. His attempts to found a countermovement to the SA and NSDAP failed, yet the crisis was a major threat to Party unity.

129. BDC Research Section file on Schulz; Akte des Obersten Parteigerichts and Parteikanzlei Korrespondenz Paul Schulz, both in the BDC.

130. Information on Liebel comes from his BDC SA file (particularly his curriculum vitae of 7 April 1942 and a pink file card recording his entitlement to the Dienstauszeichnung der NSDAP) and from Stockhorst, *Fünftausend Köpfe*, 270.

131. Information on Frank comes from Stockhorst, *Fünftausend Köpfe*, 140; Joachim Fest, *Das Gesicht des Dritten Reiches: Profile einer Totalitärian Herrschaft*, 7th ed. (Munich: R. Piper, 1980), 286-99; John Dornberg, *Munich 1923: The Story of Hitler's First Grab for Power* (New York: Harper and Row, 1982), 345; *Das Deutsche Führerlexikon*, 129, and Rudolf Glandeck Freiherr von Sebottendorf, *Bevor Hitler Kam: Urkundliches aus der Frühzeit der Nationalistischen Bewegung* (Munich: Grassinger, 1933), 234.

132. Information on Luetgebrune is taken from Heydeloff, "Staranwalt," passim, and von Salomon, *Fragebogen*, 430-44.

133. Heydrich might arguably have been included in the category of "military specialist," as was Hans Ludin, the other Reichswehr officer without experience in the Imperial Army.

134. Darré had been a member of the Stahlhelm from 1923 to 1928, and Heydrich had been a member of several organizations, including two free corps, the Orgesch and the Deutsch-Völkische Schutz- und Trutzbund. See their respective SS Führerakten in the BDC. In addition, on Darré see Stockhorst, *Fünftausend Köpfe*, 98 and *Das Deutsche Führerlexikon*, 21-22.

135. The men were Meinhardt Marnitz, Reinhard Boerner, Hans Lehmann, Karl Lucke, Paul Giesler, Hans Friedrich, Richard Aster, Paul Holthoff, Heinrich Hacker, and Ludwig Schmuck. Only one of these men was promoted further, and only on an honorary basis. This was Paul Giesler, who originally transferred into the SA from the political apparatus of the Party. He was later drafted by the Party to become a Gauleiter in 1941. Only then was he promoted to (honorary) Obergruppenführer.

136. The three exceptions were Hans Friedrich (Gruf. 1933), Paul Giesler (Gruf. 1937), and Ludwig Schmuck (Gruf. 1939). Two of these three entered the SA at ranks equivalent to officer rank, which gave them an advantage over most of the other "good soldiers."

137. Information of Ludwig Schmuck has been taken from his BDC SA files, and in particular his Personalfragebogen of 6 March 1937 with its later supplements and "SA-Gruppenführer Schmuck" in the *Bayreuther Kurier* of 4 November 1942.

138. The Stegmann Revolt was a conflict between the SA Leader of Central Franconia, Wilhelm Stegmann and the Gauleiter of Central Franconia, Julius Streicher. It ended with Stegmann's mutiny and the resignation or expulsion of a significant portion of the SA under Stegmann's command. See

the BDC files on Wilhelm Stegmann and Eric G. Reiche, *The Development of the SA in Nürnberg, 1922-1934* (Cambridge: Cambridge University Press, 1986), 146-72.

139. Fifteen of the forty-six were eventually promoted to Obergruppenführer, and Ernst Röhm was of course the chief of staff and actual head of the SA. They were Hermann Brauneck, Hans Frank, Hans Fuchs, Paul Giesler, Franz Ritter von Hörauf, Hans-Georg Hofmann, Emil Ketterer, Adolf Kob, Fritz Ritter von Krausser, Friedrich-Wilhelm Krüger, Kurt Kühme, Willy Liebel, Werner Lorenz, Hans Ludin, and Georg Mappes. Together, only 34.7 percent of the group went beyond Gruppenführer. Note that Ketterer was a Sanitäts-Obergruppenführer, and Mappes was a Verwaltungs-Obergruppenführer.

140. Hans Fuchs, Karl Haas, Franz Ritter von Hörauf, Kurt Kühme, Hans Ludin Ernst Röhm, Karl Schreyer, and Josef Seydel immediately, Richard Aster, Reinhard Heydrich, and Adolf Kob within one year. Exact dates for full-time SA employment are lacking for many of the men in this group, and the true number is certainly much higher.

141. Twenty (43.4%) began in staff positions: Ernst Beißner, Walter Darré, Hans Frank, Hans Fuchs, Karl Haas, Hans-Peter von Heydebreck, Franz Ritter von Hörauf, Hans-Georg Hofmann, Adolf Kob, Friedrich-Wilhelm Krüger, Kurt Kühme, Hans Ludin, Walter Luetgebrune, Ernst Röhm, Karl Schreyer, Wilhelm Schmid, Paul Schulz, Josef Seydel, and Gregor Strasser. Twenty (43.4%) entered as Sturmbannführer or higher: Ernst Beißner, Walter Darré, Hans Frank, Hans Fuchs, Paul Giesler, Karl Haas, Heinrich Hacker, Hans-Peter von Heydebreck, Hans-Georg Hofmann, Franz Ritter von Hörauf, Fritz Ritter von Krausser, Kurt Kühme, Hans Ludin, Walter Luetgebrune, Ernst Röhm, Wilhelm Schmid, Karl Schreyer, Paul Schulz, Josef Seydel, and Gregor Strasser. Note that this does not include the eight SA medical officers who entered at Sturmbannführer or higher; counting them, the percentage is 60.8 percent.

142. Paul Schulz was also shot, but he managed to escape and tell the tale. See Paul Schulz, "Meine Erschiessung am 30. Juni 1934"; see also Heinz Höhne, *Mordsache Röhm: Hitlers Durchbruch zur Alleinherrschaft, 1933-1934* (Hamburg: Spiegel/Rowohlt, 1984), 7-22. Those shot from this group were Röhm himself, Gregor Strasser, Wilhelm Schmid, Peter von Heydebreck, and Fritz Ritter von Krausser. A list of those shot in the Röhm Purge may be found in Bennecke, *Reichswehr*, 87-88. See also Karl Martin Graß, "Edgar Jung, Papenkreis, und Röhmkrise, 1933/34" (Ph.D. diss., Rupprecht-Karl-Universität at Heidelberg, 1966), 292-95.

143. Luetgebrune and Schreyer.

144. Ernst Beißner, Walter Darré, Paul Giesler, Heinrich Hacker, Reinhard Heydrich, Hans-Georg Hofmann, Emil Ketterer, Adolf Kob, Friedrich-Wilhelm Krüger, Kurt Kühme, Willy Liebel, Werner Lorenz, Georg Mappes, and Gregor Strasser.

145. Walter Darré, Reinhard Heydrich, Hans-Georg Hofmann, Adolf Kob, Friedrich-Wilhelm Krüger, Kurt Kühme, Werner Lorenz, Georg Mappes, and Gregor Strasser.

146. Jamin, *Zwischen den Klassen*, 74-76; Klietmann, *Deutsche Auszeichnungen*, 247-50; Buchheim, "Mitgliedschaft bei der NSDAP," in *Gutachten*, 1:313-22.

147. Paul Giesler.

148. Willy Liebel, Paul Schulz, and Otto Walter.

149. Kreisleiter: Ernst Beißner, Ortsgruppenleiter: Hans Ludin and Georg Mappes. Of course, several, including Gregor Straßer or Hans Frank, even owed their high SA rank to their Party position in the first place, even though they were nominally "active" SA leaders.

5. THE LATECOMERS, 1933-1934

1. The classic studies on the Machtergreifung include Bracher, *Die Auflösung der Weimarer Republik*; Karl-Dietrich Bracher, Wolfgang Sauer, and Gerhard Schulz, *Die nationalsozialistische Machtergreifung* (1962; reprint, Frankfurt am Main: Ullstein, 1974). For more recent views see Karl Dietrich Erdmann and Hagen Schulze, eds., *Weimar, Selbstpreisgabe einer Demokratie: Eine Bilanz Heute* (Düsseldorf: Droste, 1980); Volker Rittberger, ed., *1933: Wie die Republik der Diktatur Erlag* (Stuttgart: W. Kohlhammer, 1983).

2. Although the SA plays a role in all of the more politically oriented accounts of the Nazi assumption of power, and there is a considerable body of literature dealing with the purge of Ernst Röhm and the SA in 1934 that includes events of early 1933, very little research has been done specifically on the SA in this period. The best histories of the SA such as Bennecke, *Hitler und die SA*, Werner, or Frank all stop with the Machtergreifung or else gloss over many of the developments of 1933 and 1934 that do not directly concern the purge.

3. This estimate is based on the following figures: 23,737,000 German males of age 15 or more in 1923 (Petzina et al., *Arbeitsbuch*, 3:28) and 4,300,000 members of the SA in 1934, derived from adding the figure for the SAR II as of 1 January 1935 (roughly 1,400,000; from *Parteistatistik*, 3:76, cited in Mathilde Jamin, "Zur Rolle der SA im nationalsozialistischen Herrschaftssystem," in *Der "Führerstaat": Mythos und Realität*, ed. Gerhard Hirschfeld and Lothar Kettenacker [Stuttgart: Klett-Cotta, 1981], 334) to the figure for the strength of the SA and SAR I in August 1934 (roughly 2,900,000; from "SA Stärkemeldung" [Report of Effective Strength], BAK, Schumacher Collection, Ordner 415, cited in Jamin, "Rolle," 334.) Note that this is only a rough estimate, however, since the exact strength of the entire SA in the early summer of 1934 is unclear. If anything, the above estimate for the size of the SA is on the small side, since the size of the SAR II decreased between the time of the putsch and 1 January 1935.

4. See, e.g., Hannah Arendt, *The Origins of Totalitarianism* (1951; reprint, New York: World, 1958); Reinhard Bendix, "Social Stratification and Social Power," *American Political Science Review*, no. 46 (1952): 357-75; William S. Kornhauser, *The Politics of Mass Society* (Glencoe, Ill.: Free Press, 1959). For a critique of the "mass society" hypothesis, see Bernt Hagtvet, "The Theory of Mass Society and the Collapse of the Weimar Republic: A Re-Examination," in *Who Were the Fascists? The Social Roots of European Fascism*, ed. Stein Ugelvik Larsen, Bernt Hagtvet, and Jan Petter Myklebust (Bergen, Oslo, Tromso: Universitetsforlaget, 1980), 66-117, and Jürgen Falter, *Hitlers Wähler* (Munich: C.H. Beck, 1991).

5. As long as measures were being directed against the left, the Stahlhelm, which supported the conservative-Nazi coalition, was also used. The sup-

pression of civil rights and violent repression of dissent that characterized the consolidation of power in 1933-34 was in no way the sole responsibility of the Nazi Party, even though it did take the lead in these actions.

6. See Bruce Campbell, "The SA after the Röhm Purge," *Journal of Contemporary History* 28 (1993): 659-74. Note that the distinction between "calculated" and "spontaneous" violence is somewhat misleading; the "spontaneous" violence was in fact quite calculated and encouraged by the NSDAP leadership (in its new role as masters of the state). Indeed, an organization like the SA existed only to institutionalize and manipulate "spontaneous" violence.

7. A Schnellbrief (priority message) from the OSAF Führungsamt to the head of the SA Reichsführerschule (F2 no. 51328) of 3 September 1935 (in BAK NS23/337) gives a figure of 427,538 for the SA proper for January 1933. To this must be added roughly 27,000 Motor-SA, 24,500 SS, and 25,000 SA-Anwärter, as reported in OSAF, sec. 1, "Gesamtstärke [general strength] der SA nach 15.10.32. Septembermeldung" of 14 November 1932, in BAK NS23/vorl. 124.

8. Kater, "Ansätze zu einer Soziologie der SA," 799.

9. OSAF F no. 4513 betr: Neugliederung der SA of 27 March 1934, in BAK, Schumacher Collection, Ordner 404.

10. Kater, "Ansätze zu einer Soziologie der SA," 799.

11. Jamin, "Rolle," 332. Little is known in any systematic way about why this turnover occurred. Disagreement with the Nazis' political course was a factor in some cases, but so was lack of interest or simple exhaustion.

12. Ibid. See also the letter to the SA Gerichts-und Rechtsamt from Wilhelm Frhr. von Schorlemer of 14 July 1935, in his SA Disziplinarverfahren Akte (Aktenz. Sch 38/L/35) in the BDC, for an example of resentment against newcomers, even from a high SA leader.

13. OSAF I no. 1209/33 betr: Kopfstärken der SA: Neuaufstellungen von SA-Einheiten of 24 May 1933. SA units were ultimately not put on the state budget directly, but large lump sums for the SA were provided by the Ministry of the Interior from April to June 1934: Jamin, "Rolle," 340.

14. Compare OSAF Qu. no. 3386/32, Diensteinteilung im Stabe der Obersten SA-Führung of 1932 (after the July 1932 refounding of the SA at the lifting of the SA ban), with the schematic diagram attached to OSAF C. no. 1077/33 of 20 May 1933, both in BAK, Schumacher Collection, Ordner 404.

15. OSAF Erlaß no. 2 of 7 July 1933, and OSAF Ch. no. 1350/33, Verfügung betr: Neugliederung der SA of 7 July 1933, both in BAK, Schumacher Collection, Ordner 404.

16. Many more Standarten actually existed but had not yet been awarded an official insignia: SA-Gruf. Max Jüttner, "Standarten des Aufbruchs und der Treue," *Nationalsozialistische Korrespondenz*, 28 August 1935, 4a; OSAF Ch. no. 1350/33, Verfügung betr: Neugliederung der SA of 7 July 1933, in BAK, Schumacher Collection, Ordner 404; OSAF II no. 1328/33, Führerbefehl no. 15 of 1 July 1933, in BDC, Schumacher Collection, Ordner 410. The new Brigade level, generally announced in Ch. no. 1350/33 of 7 July 1933, was set down in specific terms in the Verfügung betr: SA-Gliederung of 15 September 1933, as cited in "Die Organisation der Obersten SA-Führung von 5.1.1931—20.4.1944 einschliesslich Rangliste" von Dr. Horst Heinrich, in BAK NS23/438. Because of the way in which the Brigaden were numbered,

it seems likely that the number of Brigaden that were called for in July had already been increased by about one-third by September.

17. Again, many more Standarte actually existed at this time but had not yet been formally awarded an insignia. These flags or standards were formally awarded to new SA units in great ceremonies usually held at Party congresses. It marked the official recognition and establishment of a new SA or SS Standarte, but of course these units actually existed long before they were awarded their insignia. This was often largely a financial matter: the insignia of a Standarte was very expensive, so before the NSDAP gained access to state coffers, it tended to wait as long as it could before awarding them: OSAF Ia no. 1549/32, Neuaufstellung (new formation) der SA und SS: Führerbefehl no. 1 of 1 July 1932; OSAF 2420/32, Führerbefehl no. 2 of 9 September 1932; OSAF no. 3520/32, Führerbefehl no. 3 of 29 November 1932, all in BDC, Schumacher Collection, Ordner 410; SA-Gruf. Max Jüttner, "Standarten des Aufbruchs und der Treue," *Nationalsozialistische Korrespondenz*, 28 August 1935, 4a; OSAF Ch. no. 1568/32, Verordnung of 6 July 1932, in BAK, Schumacher Collection, Ordner 404; OSAF Qu no. 2410/32, Verfügung betr: Obergruppen of 9 September 1932, in BAK, Schumacher Collection, Ordner 404.

18. Other major Wehrverbände which were also absorbed by the SA (SS) include the Wehrwolf and the Brigade Ehrhardt. Berghahn, *Stahlhelm*, 250-51; Alois Klotzbücher, "Der politische Weg des Stahlhelms, Bund der Frontsoldaten in der Weimarer Republik: Ein Beitrag zur Geschichte der Nationalen Opposition, 1918-1933" (Ph.D. diss., Universität Erlangen, 1964), 49.

19. Berghahn, *Stahlhelm*, 151-253.

20. Ibid., 251-52, 263-72; Klotzbücher, "Der politische Weg," 263-67.

21. Klotzbücher, "Der politische Weg," 287-99; Berghahn, *Stahlhelm*, 245-74.

22. On the Wehrstahlhelm, see Berghahn, *Stahlhelm*, 267-69. By January 1934, 310,000 members of the Wehrstahlhelm were taken into the SA proper: Klotzbücher, "Der politische Weg," 49.

23. Klotzbücher, "Der politische Weg," 299-301. The dates given in the text are the official ones; the process actually proceeded more slowly. See, e.g., the BDC files of Erich Wiethaus and Friedrich Lüth.

24. Klotzbücher, "Der politische Weg," 301-2.

25. OSAF Ch. no. 1456/33 betr: Eingliederung der Brigade Ehrhardt of 10 August 1933. See von Salomon, *Fragebogen*, 423-28, for an account of the formal ceremony for the entry of the Brigade Ehrhardt into the SS, which throws light on the reluctance with which the absorption of the proud and independent paramilitary associations into the SA and SS was often made.

26. OSAF Ch. no. 2273 betr: Organisation der SAR II of 12 February 1934, in BDC, Schumacher Collection, Ordner 407.

27. OSAF Ch. no. 569/34 betr: SAR I of 25 January 1934; OSAF P2 no. 4592/34 betr: Stellenbesetzung der SAR I of 5 March 1934, both in BAK, Schumacher Collection, Ordner 407.

28. Only the strictly nonpolitical regimental veterans' associations were specifically exempted from his attacks. See OSAF Ch/Z1 no. 2254/34 betr: Vereine und Clubs of 26 February 1934, in BDC, Schumacher Collection, Ordner 415; OSAF Ch. no. 569/34 betr: SAR I of 25 January 1934, in BDC, Schumacher Collection, Ordner 407.

29. Dual membership in the NSDF and the SAR I was allowed, but those

members of the SAR I who wished would be allowed to resign and join the NSDF. See the analysis in Graß, "Edgar Jung," 105-9.

30. With the introduction of conscription in March 1935, the army no longer had need of the paramilitary and veterans' organizations as a covert source of manpower, and army support for any sort of preservation of the Stahlhelm evaporated.

31. Klotzbücher, "Der politische Weg," 306-9.

32. Ibid., 49.

33. See OSAF Ch. no. 800/33 betr: Aufnahme (enrollment) in die SA of 20 March 1933, in BAK, Schumacher Collection, Ordner 407.

34. Max Jüttner is a good example. See his BDC files.

35. The SS presents one case where some individuals who entered late were able to rise to high rank, but many of them were specialists, and the expansion of the SS after the takeover of power was particularly great.

36. A twelfth man, Franz May, joined the SA even later, in 1938. He is not included in this chapter because he represents a special case and because he joined so late. In brief, he was a leader of the Freiwilliger Schutzdienst of the Sudeten German Party in Czechoslovakia. He was unable to officially join the NSDAP and SA until the Sudetenland had been annexed to Germany, although he worked for German army intelligence much earlier. Upon annexation he was immediately appointed to head the newly formed SA Gruppe in the Sudetenland.

37. The men are George Dechant, Thomas Girgensohn, Max Jüttner, Hans Lukesch, August Moeslinger, Hans Elard von Morozowisc, Georg von Neufville, Lorenz Ohrt, Hans Petersen, Wilhelm Reinhard, and Franz von Stephani.

38. Material on Hans Petersen is taken from Records of the U.S. Nuremberg War Crimes Trials Interrogations, 1946-49, National Archives, microfilm pub. M1019, roll 52, interrogation of Hans Petersen of 22 October 1946, as well as from his BDC files (particularly his curriculum vitae) and from Stockhorst, Fünftausend Köpfe, 320-21.

39. He was county organization leader of the south Bavarian county of Sonthofen from 1925 until 1933 and a Party speaker.

40. The SA Sonderkommissare were appointed in 1933 in Bavaria to represent and protect the interests of the SA in local and regional offices of the civil administration. The SA was particularly interested in securing jobs for its many unemployed members.

41. Information about Hans Lukesch comes from his BDC files, especially from his Personalfragebogen of 1 May 1938 and its two supplements. See also Stockhorst, Fünftausend Köpfe, 280.

42. Georg Dechant, Thomas Girgensohn, Max Jüttner, August Möslinger, Hans Elard von Morozowisc, Georg Freiherr von Neufville, Lorenz Ohrt, Wilhelm Reinhard, and Franz von Stephani. They will be treated as one group in the following analysis, unless otherwise noted.

43. Georg Dechant, Landesführer Franken, Max Jüttner, Landesführer Mitteldeutschland, and Georg von Neufville, Landesführer Württemberg und Baden.

44. Franz von Stephani, Bundeshauptmann of the Stahlhelm and also Oberstlandesführer Großberlin, Hans von Morozowisc, the leader of the Wehrstahlhelm and also Oberlandesführer Brandenburg and Braunschweig, and August Möslinger, the Oberquartiermeister of the Stahlhelm.

45. Thomas Girgensohn in Berlin and Lorenz Ohrt in Hamburg. A Wehrsport regiment seems to have been similar to an SA Standarte in terms of size. On the Wehrsport units, see Berghahn, *Stahlhelm*, 134ff. and 193ff., and Klotzbücher, "Der politische Weg," 211, 213ff.

46. The Stahlhelm (after about 1927) was headed by its first and second Bundesführer. Below them were the Bundesrat, made up of the first and second Bundesführer and five leaders of Landesverbände chosen by the two leaders. Below it was the Vorstandsversammlung, made up of all of the Landesführer and the leaders of the independent Gaue [regions], plus individual members enjoying the special trust of the leadership and elected by the Landesführer. Beside the Bundesführer and Bundesrat for the day-to-day administration of the organization was the Bundesamt, a staff and administrative structure organized on a general staff model. It contained numerous offices and departments under three main divisions for politics, organization, and finances. Although the two Bundesführer and the Bundesrat made up the actual leadership, a great deal of power lay in the hands of the Landesführer, since they had autonomy in their areas and together elected the two Bundesführer every three years. The core leadership of the Stahlhelm would therefore be the Bundesführer, Landesführer, and the heads of the most important offices in the Bundesamt, roughly thirty to forty men. See Berghahn, *Stahlhelm*, 283-84 and 285, and Hildebrandt and Kettner, eds., *Stahlhelm Handbuch*, 76.

47. See the table in Berghahn, *Stahlhelm*, 287, of *Landesverbände* as of 1931.

48. Leadership of the Stahlhelm was shared from 1927 to early 1933 by Franz Seldte and Theodor Duesterberg, the first and second Bundesführer of the Stahlhelm. But in early 1933, shortly before he subordinated the Stahlhelm to the NSDAP, Seldte forced Duesterberg to resign. Therefore, there was only one Bundesführer of the Stahlhelm at the time it was absorbed into the SA. See Berghahn, *Stahlhelm*, 257-63. Even though Seldte was presented with the rank of SA Obergruppenführer in recognition of his subordination of the Stahlhelm to the NSDAP, this was only an honorary commission, and he never actually served as an active SA leader. See Der Oberste SA-Führer II no. 1411/33, Führerbefehl no. 16 of 1 August 1933, in BDC, Schumacher Collection, Ordner 410.

49. Technically, members of the Stahlhelm were given a choice whether or not to join the SA, but for the Stahlhelm leaders this was not a genuine alternative when the Stahlhelm was *first* being absorbed into the SA and its future status within that organization was unclear. Immediate refusal would have been tantamount to open resistance to the Nazis and could have jeopardized any future concessions to the Stahlhelm and the expected (but, as far as the SA was concerned, never seriously intended) autonomy for it within the SA. Moreover, resignation or refusal at this stage of the game for a Stahlhelm leader would have meant relinquishing any control or influence over events and over the Stahlhelm in the future. All of the former Stahlhelm members had ample opportunity to quit the SA without penalty once their absorption was complete. At the latest, the forced cutbacks in the SA in the wake of the Röhm Purge gave any SA member an unblemished pretext to leave.

50. It is possibly true for one more individual, Thomas Girgensohn.

51. Jüttner, von Stephani, von Morozowisc, and von Neufville were the

Prussians, Möslinger was the Bavarian, and Reinhard was the Württemberger.
52. Wilhelm Reinhard was already a major when the war broke out. It is possible that August Möslinger was, too, although the evidence suggests that he was a captain.
53. Max Jüttner, August Möslinger, Georg von Neufville, Wilhelm Reinhard, and Franz von Stephani. It is not clear whether Thomas Girgensohn was an officer in the regular army or the reserves, but because he lost a leg in the war, he could not possibly have been taken into the Reichswehr.
54. Von Stephani was a noble originally commissioned in an elite guards regiment. Von Neufville was also noble, and he, Wilhelm Reinhard, and Max Jüttner all had general staff experience. Reinhard, in addition, had been awarded the Pour le Mérite, Germany's highest military decoration in the First World War. All six had also served actively in the German Revolution.
55. On Stephani see Berghahn, *Stahlhelm*, 40, 268; Stockhorst, *Fünftausend Köpfe*, 412; Deutscher Offiziersbund, ed., *Ehrenrangliste des ehemaligen deutschen Heeres*, 190, 127, 1015; and Franz von Stephani, "Der Sturm auf das Vorwärtsgebäude am 10 Januar 1919," in *Das Buch vom deutschen Freikorpskämpfer*, ed. Ernst von Salomon (Berlin: Wilhelm Limpert, 1938), 39-40. On Max Jüttner see his BDC files and IfZ Zs. 251/1-2. Von Neufville may also have participated in the Kapp Putsch.
56. Both Georg Dechant and Lorenz Ohrt were given commissions as reserve officer during the war.
57. The exception is von Morozowisc, due to a lack of information.
58. August Möslinger was in the regular army, and Lorenz Ohrt and Max Jüttner were Zeitfreiwilliger. Jüttner is also included as a member of a free corps, since he was not only a member of a Zeitfreiwilligenverband but he actually commanded a unit as a part of the Landesjägerkorps, the core of which was made up of Freikorps Maercker and two other free corps. He listed both in his SA records. See Tessin, *Deutsche Verbände und Truppen*, 59-60; BDC files of Max Jüttner.
59. Georg Dechant, Thomas Girgensohn, Max Jüttner, and Hans Petersen were members of Freikorps, and three others were free corps commanders: Wilhelm Reinhard was the commander of Freikorps Reinhard, Georg von Neufville was the commander of Freikorps von Neufville, and Franz von Stephani was the commander of Freikorps Potsdam.
60. Max Jüttner.
61. Hans von Morozowisc.
62. On the Nationale Vereinigung see Dieter Fricke, ed., *1830-1945: Die Bürgerlichen Parteien in Deutschland*, 2 vols. (Berlin: Europäische Buch, 1968), 2:339-40.
63. Little is known about these two groups, and they must have been quite small. Georg von Neufville led them.
64. Georg Dechant was in the Reichsflagge, and Thomas Girgensohn was in the Reichsverband der Baltikumkämpfer.
65. Franz von Stephani.
66. The individual was Max Jüttner.
67. Berghahn, *Stahlhelm*, 13-54; Klotzbücher, "Der politische Weg," 1-30.
68. Max Jüttner and Thomas Girgensohn.
69. Not that even among the highest SA leaders, only a minority (though a sizable one, especially among the 1925-26 group) were members of a völkisch organization.

70. Georg Dechant, Thomas Girgensohn, Lorenz Ohrt, and Franz von Stephani.

71. The two are Georg Dechant, a Reichsflagge leader in Franconia, and Franz von Stephani, a leader of the Verband Nationalgesinnter Soldaten. See Klotzbücher, "Der politische Weg," 31-33, for a description of the way the Stahlhelm absorbed many smaller organizations.

72. Information on Georg Dechant is taken from his BDC files, especially his Personalfragebogen of 7 June 1937. He was born in Franconia in 1893. His father was a head forest administrator (Oberforstverwalter). He became a teacher, although he apparently did not exercise his profession for very long. He served in the First World War from 1914 to 1918, was wounded, decorated, and commissioned as an officer. When he returned, he served in Freikorps Epp and later the Transitional Reichswehr (Übergangsheer) until December 1919. In 1920 he joined the Reichsflagge and from 1922 to 1933 he was a full-time paid employee of the Reichsflagge and later of the Stahlhelm. He served in the Second World War, but only in a local flak unit so that he could continue his SA duties. He rose to the rank of captain in the Luftwaffe. His fate after the war is not known.

73. There were occasional difficulties between Stahlhelm members and Party/SA members in Franconia in early 1934, just as there were elsewhere. Dechant apparently worked hard to end such difficulties and cooperate with the Nazis. See Der Sonderbevollmächtigte für Ober-, Mittel- und Unterfranken (von Obernitz) 1026/34 an den Sonderbevollmächtigten für das Land Bayern Obergruppenführer Fuchs of 15 February 1934, betr: Verhältnisse in Koburg, in BDC SA files Hans Fuchs.

74. The three are Max Jüttner, Thomas Girgensohn, and Georg von Neufville.

75. Information on Thomas Girgensohn is taken from his BDC files, especially his Personalfragebogen of 9 December 1937 and its two supplements, a large OSAF file card with a clipped upper left-hand corner (n.d.), and a large blue card recording wages and benefits payments for the years 1942-44.

76. See Alfred Fletcher, "Die Baltische Landeswehr," in Baltische Blätter 12 (March 1929): 69-71; Baltischer Landeswehrverein, ed., Die Baltische Landeswehr im Befreiungskampf gegen den Bolschewismus: Ein Gedenkbuch (Riga: G. Löffler, 1929).

77. He later married Freiin von Loudon, the daughter of one of the Baltic-German noble families from Latvia.

78. It is possible that the entire organization was absorbed into the Stahlhelm at this time, as many similar organizations already had been, but this is conjecture.

79. Both Bundeshauptmann and Bundesbevollmächtiger were relatively new positions in the Stahlhelm hierarchy due to its reorganization in 1933. Compare the 1931 Stahlhelm Handbuch with the organizational chart of the Bundesamt of the Stahlhelm in BAK, Schumacher Collection, Ordner 470, n.d. (sometime after Duesterberg's resignation on 26 April 1933). The Jungstahlhelm was made up of young men of German background ages seventeen to twenty-three: Hildebrandt and Kettner, Stahlhelm Handbuch, 117.

80. Konstantin Hierl was a former professional officer who joined the NSDAP in 1927. He occupied a high position in the Party bureaucracy as its "Reich Leader of Organization II" from 1929 to 1933. He then became a

state secretary for the Voluntary Labor Service (Freiwillige Arbeitsdienst, FAD) in the Ministry of Labor, and later the head of the compulsory Reich Labor Service (Reichsarbeitsdienst, RAD), which absorbed the FAD. Although the labor service later declined in importance, in the early 1930s it was of great importance to the Nazis, who needed to gain public support through concrete amelioration of the unemployment problem.

81. Berghahn, *Stahlhelm*, 267-68.

82. Information on Lorenz Ohrt comes from his BDC files, particularly from his Personalfragebogen of 2 March 1937, and from a large OSAF file card with a clipped upper left-hand corner.

83. While moving up in his SA career, Ohrt also served on active duty with the Wehrmacht. After completing training exercises in 1934 and 1936, he was commissioned as a first lieutenant of the reserve in 1937 and as captain in 1940. He saw combat with the Wehrmacht and was awarded the Iron Cross First and Second Class. He was later promoted to major.

84. The sole exception was Georg Dechant, who did have a minor position in the Deutsche Arbeitsfront but not in the Party administration proper.

85. Max Jüttner, Georg von Neufville, and Lorenz Ohrt all joined the Party in 1933. Georg Dechant, Thomas Girgensohn, August Möslinger, and Wilhelm Reinhard joined in 1937. Only two never joined the NSDAP. Von Morozowisc also might have joined later had he not been killed in an accident in 1934. The case of the other, von Stephani, is unclear, and it is possible that he did later join the Party after he resigned from the SA.

86. To be fair, it should be emphasized that von Morozowisc had had his disagreements with the SA leadership and might have left the SA if he hadn't died in an accident. Wilhelm Reinhard, the head of the Kyffhäuserbund, left the SA when the SAR II, of which the Kyffhäuserbund had been a part, was disbanded, but, sensing where the real center of power had gravitated, immediately joined the SS, and so cannot be considered to have left the SA out of any ideological disagreement with National Socialism.

87. Much of the Stahlhelm could also agree with the SA on the equally fundamental point of anti-Semitism: Berghahn, *Stahlhelm*, 65-67.

88. Information on Jüttner comes from his BDC files, especially his Personalfragebogen of 22 February 1937 and its two supplements, his curriculum vitae, and IfZ Zs. 251/1-2 (Max Jüttner).

89. See the background chapter for information on the Zeitfreiwilliger. The Landesjägerkorps was a free corps formed and led by General Maercker from 1918 to June 1919. It was subsequently absorbed into the Reichswehr and was one of the most reliable and disciplined of all the free corps. See Tessin, *Deutsche Verbände und Truppen*, 59-60, 120, 177-78; Waite, *Vanguard of Nazism*, 185; and Gen. Ludwig R. Maercker, *Vom Kaiserheer zur Reichswehr: Geschichte der freiwilligen Landesjägerkorps*, 3d ed. (Leipzig: Koehler, 1922).

90. This was Jüttner's official date of Party membership. Since it is after the 1 May 1933 moratorium on Party membership, it is likely that he applied for membership earlier and suffered the inevitable delay in processing.

91. In November 1937 the Führungsamt was elevated to be a Hauptamt (main office) within the Oberste SA Führung.

92. The SA was tried as an organization by the International Military Tribunal at the Trial of German Major War Criminals in Nuremberg in 1945 and 1946. Max Jüttner was called to testify as a witness for the defense as

the senior surviving SA leader available to the court. See International Military Tribunal, *The* Trial of the German Major War Criminals: Proceedings of the *International Military Tribunal Sitting at Nuremberg, Germany*, pt. 21: *9th August, 1946 to 21st August, 1946* (London: His Majesty's Stationery Office, 1949), 153-226.

6. Conclusion

1. Note that the term *corps* is used here only in reference to the SA leaders included in this study and not in reference either to the totality of the SA leadership or to the SA as a whole. This issue is addressed for the SS by Robert L. Koehl in "Was There an SS Officer Corps?" unpublished paper, Citadel Symposium on Hitler and National Socialism, proceedings, 24-25 April 1980, Charleston, S.C., 1981. In many ways, the highest officers of the SA were more homogeneous than the better known SS officer corps of the late 1930s.

2. Jamin, *Zwischen den Klassen*.

3. They were born between 1869 and 1907; the average year of birth was 1890.

4. It is clear that the highest SA leaders were an extremely well educated group by the standards of their day. For example, 15.7 percent of the 178 highest SA leaders held a doctorate (Ph.D., J.D., or M.D.) and a further 24.7 percent had studied at the university level (including the Technische Hochschulen; the category includes incomplete university study, those holding a diploma, and all Rechtsanwälte [lawyers]). No study of the level of education of the SA as a whole has been done, nor is such a study likely in the near future.

5. David Schoenbaum, *Hitler's Social Revolution: Class and Status in Nazi Germany, 1933-1939* (Garden City, N.Y.: Anchor Books, 1967), 17, 41; Merkl, *Political Violence*, 289; Merkl, *Stormtrooper*, 411-45.

6. Reliable information is available for 157 of the 179 men in this study. At least 58 were prewar professional soldiers (officers and enlisted men). Many more served one year in the army as voluntary officer cadets (Einjähriger Freiwilliger) or were members of the corps of cadets before the First World War, so that the number influenced by the spirit of the officer corps is actually greater. This is, of course, much greater than the percentage of professional soldiers in the male population of Germany before the war. In 1910 (the last prewar census) the German Empire had 32,040,166 male inhabitants: *Statistisches Jahrbuch für das deutsche Reich* 42 (1921/22): 2. In 1914, there were 30,739 officers and 105,856 noncommissioned officers in the army and 3,899 officers and 4,069 noncommissioned and warrant officers in the navy (Deckoffiziere), for an approximate 144,563 professional soldiers and enlisted men (this number is almost certainly slightly higher than the true number of professional military personnel): *Statistisches Jahrbuch für das deutsche Reich* 45 (1926): 445. This would mean that theoretically .45 percent of German men were professional soldiers just before the First World War. It should be noted that three of the professional soldiers among the highest SA leaders studied here were, in fact, Austrians and not citizens of the German Empire in 1914.

7. At least 135 of the 178 served in the First World War; 111 of the 140

for whom this information is known were commissioned as officers by the end of 1918 (79.2%). Remember that the raw data used in this study was taken primarily from SA personnel files. Although generally informative, they sometimes lack specific information, such as the exact date of a commission.

8. The classic statement of this thesis is Waite, *Vanguard of Nazism.* Koch, *Der deutsche Bürgerkrieg,* is a more recent restatement of essentially the same thesis.

9. Seventy-four out of the 177 men (41.8%) for whom this could be determined were in a free corps in 1919.

10. In 1919, 67 (37.6%) of the 179 were in the army, 9 (5%) were serving in Grenzschutz or border protection units under army command, and 4 (2.2%) were in the police. Note that the army and Grenzschutz categories specifically exclude free corps.

11. In 1919, 5 (2.8%) of the 178 highest SA leaders in this study served in a citizens' militia and 4 (2.2%) were Zeitfreiwilliger.

12. In 1919, five members of the group (2.8%) belonged to a political party, excluding the NSDAP. The figure including the NSDAP is only eight (4.5%). The short-term nature of many of these early Party memberships is explained with the supposition that the men involved were searching for some sort of a response or affiliation appropriate to the changed conditions of the postwar era. Inexperienced in democracy, many soon abandoned these original Party memberships, either for affiliation with more radical organizations or for temporary inactivity.

13. Of the 174 highest SA leaders for whom information exists, 58 (33.3%) were in a Wehrverband between 1921 and 1927. If the Stahlhelm is included as a Wehrverband, this figure rises to 72 (41.3%).

14. Interestingly, the men joining in 1925 or 1926 had the lowest percentage of both free corps and Wehrverband membership (33%). Free corps membership rose in the 1927-30 group (42.3%), dipped slightly in the 1931-32 group (34.7%), and rose sharply in the 1933-34 group (63.7%). Wehrverband membership followed a similar pattern, as shown in figures for 1925-26 (44.4%), 1927-30 (49.1%), 1931-32 (45.6%), and 1933-34 (90%).

15. Eight (4.5%) of the 178 had been members of the DNVP or DDP. Note that membership was often of relatively short duration, suggesting that the future SA leaders were dissatisfied with the style and program of the more conventional conservative parties.

16. Of the 178 highest SA leaders, 27 (15.2%) had been members in a völkisch political party. This was 77 percent of the thirty-five who had been in any sort of a political party.

17. The single exception was Reinhard Boerner, who belonged to the DDP from 1919 to 1921.

18. This idea first appeared in Frank, "Hitler and the National Socialist Coalition." Whereas Frank looks at this from a perspective of relations between the SA and the Party organization and thus stresses coalition and alliance, I wish to stress the blending of the two strains within the experiences of the SA leaders. The new formula for success that resulted from this blending was the creation of both the SA leaders and those of the political organization of the NSDAP together. Had it been otherwise, the two groups could never have cooperated as effectively as they did, despite all internal quarrels.

19. An overemphasis on Hitler is still encountered in many German history textbooks: see, e.g., Dietrich Orlow, *A History of Modern Germany*, 2d ed. (Englewood Cliffs, N.J.: Prentice Hall, 1991), 159-60; Alan Bullock, *Hitler: A Study in Tyranny* (New York: Bantam Books, 1961), 101; Volker R. Berghahn, *Modern Germany*, 2d ed. (Cambridge: Cambridge University Press, 1987), 110-12; Craig, *Germany, 1866-1945*, 544-49. This is also true of more specialized studies (see, e.g., Orlow, *Nazi Party*, 1:52ff.; Bracher, *German Dictatorship*, 128-31) as well as popular historical works (see John Tolland, *Adolf Hitler* [New York: Ballantine Books, 1977], 252-53, 279-87, 294-301).

20. Frank, "Hitler and the National Socialist Coalition," esp. 205-7, 438-39. Frank stresses the inherent instability of the relationship between the SA and NSDAP, which he characterizes as an alliance. In contrast, the stress in the argument here is rather on the fusion that took place in terms of tactics.

21. This is not to portray the Nazi assumption of power as some sort of natural or organic occurrence. It was the product of flesh-and-blood human beings, motivated by ideology and self-interest and responding to a situation produced by long-term social and economic forces.

22. Even Ernst Röhm (technically the sole exception, since he only joined the SA in 1930) could be included in this category, given his previous membership in the Party and his activities in völkisch groups and the paramilitary Frontbann in 1924 and early 1925.

23. The clearest voice warning of the dangers of the Wehrverband-völkisch subculture was that of Emil Julius Gumbel. Unfortunately, his voice and countless others went unheeded. For a sample of his works see Gumbel, *Verschwörer: Beiträge zur* Geschichte und Soziologie der deutschen nationalistischen *Geheimbünde, 1918-1924* (1924; reprint, Heidelberg: Das Wunderhorn, 1979); Gumbel, *Deutschlands Geheime Rüstung?* (Berlin: Liga für Menschenrechte, 1925); Gumbel, *Vier Jahre Politischer Mord* (1922; reprint, Heidelberg: Das Wunderhorn, 1980). For a recent assessment of Gumbel, see the forthcoming book by Arthur Brenner.

24. Harold J. Gordon, "Politischer Terror und Versailler Abrüstungsklausel in der Weimarer Republik," *Wehrwissenschaftliche Rundschau* 16 (January 1966): 36-54.

7. METHODOLOGY

1. Partei und Oberster SA-Führer, "An die gesamte SA und SS" of 2 September 1930 (signed Adolf Hitler), and OSAF, "Abschied," of 29 August 1930 (signed von Pfeffer), both in BDC, Schumacher Collection, Ordner 403; NSDAP, Oberster SA-Führung, *Dienstvorschrift für die SA der NSDAP* (Diessen vor München: Jos. C. Huber, 1932), 1:35. See also Werner, "SA," 465-70, 486-87; and Bennecke, *Hitler und die SA*, 149-55.

2. War Department, Technical Manual E 30-451, *Handbook on German Military Forces*, 15 March 1945 (Washington: Government Printing Office, 1945; facsimile ed., Military Press, 1970), I-6 (fig. 1) and III-25 (fig. 5).

3. Werner, "SA," 445-48.

4. This is not true for the SS after July 1934, of course. After the SS became independent from the SA, it embarked on a tremendous expansion in terms of both numbers and its functional duties. For the SS after 1934, see

Robert L. Koehl, *The Black Corps: The Structure and Power Struggles of the Nazi SS* (Madison: University of Wisconsin Press, 1983); and Heinz Höhne, *The Order under the Death's Head: The Story of Hitler's SS* (1966; reprint, New York: Ballantine Books, 1977).

5. A guide to the BDC's collections was published in a very limited edition just before it was transferred to the administration of the German Federal Republic. It should appear in a more accessible form shortly. See also George C. Browder, "Problems and Potentials of the Berlin Document Center," in *Central European History* 5 (1972): 362-80; Office of the Military Government of the United States in Germany (OMGUS), 7771 Document Center, *Who Was a Nazi? Facts about the Membership Procedure of the Nazi Party* (Berlin: OMGUS, 1947).

6. OMGUS, and verbal information from Daniel P. Simon, director of the BDC, and his staff, 1982-84.

7. This transfer did not occur without some controversy. See Gerald Posner, "Secrets from the Files," in the *New Yorker*, 14 March 1994, 39-47; Geoffrey J. Giles, chair, "German Studies Association Archives Committee Annual Report 1994," MS, 26 September 1994. A panel at the 1994 German Studies Association annual conference entitled "The Transfer of the Berlin Document Center to German Control: Implications for Scholars" served to clear the air a little, but controversy continues. Microfilm copies of all BDC materials are now available to scholars through the National Archives branch in College Park, Maryland.

8. The above information is based on my personal experience with these documents, including a tour of the magazine where the records were actually kept. It is corroborated by Jamin, *Zwischen den Klassen*, 50-54. Note that Jamin gives a total of 776 Ordner in the Allgemeine Personalakten. I have seen the last Ordner in the collection, which bears the number 777, and I am not aware that any number was skipped or that two files were later combined, but this is certainly possible. Jamin was able to actually consult every single file in the collection, whereas I used less than half.

9. Browder estimates that the two SA collections contain 260,366 names. I estimate that only about 85 percent of those named were actually SA members. Most of the non-SA names and records are contained in the SA-Vorgänge." Browder's total must only be considered approximate for several reasons, notably because a small percentage of individuals have records in both groups. See Browder, "Problems and Potentials of the BDC," 369.

10. Browder, "Problems and Potentials of the BDC," 366-68. BDC staff members confirmed Browder's count of 60,000 SS personnel files.

11. Conversation with Herrn Eberhardt of the BDC, 1983.

12. *Das Deutsche Führerlexikon, 1934-1935* (Berlin: Otto Stollberg, 1934.

13. Various SS officers' seniority lists (Dienstalterslisten) were used in the BDC, including Stellenbesetzung im Reichsheer vom 16. Mai 1920, 1. Oktober 1920, *1. Oktober 1921* (reprint, Osnabrück: Biblio Verlag, 1968), and Deutsche Offiziersbund, ed., *Ehrenrangliste des ehemaligen deutschen Heeres: Auf Grund der Ranglisten von 1914 mit den inzwischen eingetretenen Veränderungen* (Berlin: E.S. Mittler and Sohn, 1926).

Bibliography

I. Primary Sources

Bibliothèque de Documentation Internationale Contemporaine

Bundesarchiv, Koblenz (BAK)
Sammlung Schumacher, Ordner 219-21, 256 I and II, 313, 374, 377-
  79, 400, 402-9, 414, 415, 422-24, 470, 471, 494
NS23 SA
NS26 NSDAP Hauptarchiv
NSD NSDAP Publications
R2 Reichsfinanzministerium
R18 Reichsministerium des Innern
R43II Reichskanzlei
Kleine Erwerbungen 653-2

Bundesarchiv/Militärarchiv, Freiburg
RH53-7 Akten des Wehrkreiskommando VII
RH61 Nachkriegskämpfe
RM6 Admiralität: Militärpolitische Berichte
RM33 II Marine Brigade
RM122 II Marine Brigade
PH26 Freikorps/Nachkriegskämpfe
N70 Nachlaß von Kleist

Bundesarchiv, Potsdam
5.07   Reichskommissariat für die Ueberwachung der Oeffentlichen
        Ordnung
61Sta1 Der Stahlhelm, Bund der Frontsoldaten
61Re2 Reichsverband der Baltikumkämpfer Landesverband Mittel-
        deutschland

Berlin Document Center (BDC)
SA Allgemeine Personalakten
"SA Vorgänge"
Akten des Obersten Parteigerichts der NSDAP bzw. des Unter-
    suchungs- und Schlichtungsausschusses der NSDAP
Parteikanzlei Korrespondenz
Sammlung Schumacher, Ordner 256, 313, 336, 374, 402-410, 414-
    417
SS-Führerakten
Rasse- und Siedlungshauptamt Akten
Research Abteilung Akten
Zentralkartei der NSDAP

Geheimes Staatsarchiv Preußischer Kulturbesitz Berlin-Dahlem
B31C. Rep 92 (NL Daluege). Zeitgeschichtliche Sammlung.
XX HA Rep. 1; 2, I; 2, II
Rep 240 (Staatsarchiv Königsberg, Gauarchiv Ostpreußen) /22; /31

Institut für Zeitgeschichte
Zeugenschriftum: Zs37; Zs44; Zs145/I; Zs177/I-II; Zs251/I-II; Zs317/
    I; Zs319; Zs349; Zs357/I-II; Zs827; Zs924; Zs1147/I; Zs1473;
    Zs1491/I-II; Zs1495; Zs1546; Zs1615; Zs1682; Zs1685; Zs1849;
    Zs1945; Zs1949; Zs3137
Db15.02; Db20.20; Db52.02; Db52.22; Db52.24; Db52.26; Db52.29;
    Db52.30; Db52.39; Db52.41
F7. F28. F56. F58. F92. Fa2. Fa3. Fa7. Fa74. Fa90/1. Fa107/2. Fa152.
    Fa153. Fa 199/28. F92. 2FG 1619/54. ED1/2-5. ED4. ED33. ED60/
    1; /4; /7. ED106/102. ED168. MS28-28e. MS130. Sp2/1.

Szczecin Provincial State Archives
Regierung Stettin 8911; 10191; 10486; 12078; 12079; 12080; 12140;
    12145; 12144; 12171; 12172; 12176; 12177
Oberprasidium vom Pommern 3612

U.S. National Archives
Records of the U.S. Nürnberg War Crimes Trials Interrogations, 1946-
    1949, Microfilm publication M1019, roll 52

NSDAP Hauptarchiv: Microfilm rolls 16-17

Other: Interview with L.S., June 1989

II. CONTEMPORARY SOURCES

... *wurde die SA eingesetzt: Politische Soldaten erzählen von wenig beachteten Frontabschnitten unserer Zeit.* Kampfschriften der Obersten SA-Führung, vol. 11. Munich: Franz Eher, 1938.

Anacker, Heinrich. *Die Trommel: SA Gedichte.* Munich: Zentralverlag der NSDAP, 1936.

Baltischer Landeswehrverein, ed. *Die Baltische Landeswehr im Befreiungskampf gegen den Bolschewismus: Ein Gedenkbuch.* Riga: G. Löffler, 1929.

Bayer, Sturmführer Dr. Ernst. *Die SA: Geschichte, Arbeit, Zweck und Organisation der Sturmabteilung des Führers und der Obersten SA-Führung.* Heft 21 der Schriften der deutschen Hochschule für Politik. Berlin: Junker und Dünnhaupt, 1938.

Bildnisse der Mitglieder des Preußischen Landtags. III Wahlperiode (von 1928 ab). Stand am 25. Oktober 1928. 1928.

Bischoff, Major a. D. Josef. *Die Letzte Front: Geschichte der Eisernen Division im Baltikum 1919.* Berlin: Schützen, 1935.

Bley, Wulf, ed. *Revolutionen der Weltgeschichte: Zwei Jahrtausende Revolutionen und Bürgerkriege.* Munich: Justin Moser, 1933.

Braeuner, Eugen, ed. *Sturmführerbuch: Dienstkontrollbuch für Sturmführer.* Bochem-Langendreer: F.A. Grimmerthal, 1934.

Brammer, Karl. *Das politische Erlebnis des Rathenau-Prozesses.* Berlin: Verlag für Sozialwissenschaft, 1922.

Die Braunhemden im Reichstag: Die Nationalsozialistische Reichstagsfraktion 1932, VII Wahlperiode, mit Abbildungen und Personalangaben der Mitglieder. Munich: Franz Eher, 1933.

Brauns, Lt. d.R. a.D. *Maschinengewehr Scharf-Schützen Abteilung 22.* Erinnerungsblätter dt. Regimenter, no. 81. Bearbeitet nach dem amtlichen quellenmaterial sowie persönlichen Erinnerungen und Aufzeichnungen. Berlin/Oldenburg i.O.: Stalling, 1923.

Bredow, Klaus. *Hitlerrast: Die Blittragödie des 30. Juni 1934. Ablauf, Vorgeschichte, und Hintergründe.* Saarbrücken: Volksstimme, 1935.

Buchrucker, Bruno Ernst. *Im Schatten Seeckt's: Die Geschichte der "Schwarzen Reichswehr."* Berlin: Kampf, 1928.

Das Deutsche Führerlexikon, 1934-1935. Berlin: O. Stollberg, 1934.

Deutscher Offiziersbund, ed. *Ehrenrangliste des ehemaligen deutschen Heeres: Auf Grund der Ranglisten von 1914 mit den inzwischen eingetretenen Veränderungen.* Berlin: E.S. Mittler Sohn, 1926.

Deutschland Erwacht, Werden, Kampf, und Sieg der NSDAP. Hamburg: Cigaretten-Bilderdienst, 1933.

Ecke, Maj. a.D. and Karge, Geh. Kanzlei-Inspektor im Marine-Kabinet. *Das deutsche Reichsheer und die Kaiserliche Marine. Nebst Anhang: die Kaiserlichen Schutztruppen für Deutsch-Ostafrika,*

Deutsch-Südwestafrika und Kamerun. Lehr und Nachschlag-buch der Organisation des deutschen Heer- und Marinewesens. Vol. 10, finished 9 June 1899. Kassel: Gebr. Gotthelft, 1899.

Ehrenthal, Günther. *Die deutschen Jugendbünde: Ein Handbuch ihrer Organisation und ihrer Bestrebungen.* Berlin: Zentral, 1929.

Engelbrechten, Obersturmbannführer Julek Karl von. *Eine Braune Armee Entsteht: Die Geschichte der Berlin-Brandenburger SA, im Auftrag des Führers der SA Gruppe Berlin-Brandenburg Dietrich von Jagow.* Munich: Franz Eher, 1937.

Engelbrechten, Julek Karl von and Volz, Hans. *Wir Wandern durch das Nationalsozialistische Berlin.* Munich: Franz Eher, 1937.

Forschungsanstalt für Kriegs- und Heeresgeschichte. *Darstellungen aus den Nachkriegskämpfen deutscher Truppen und Freikorps.* Vol. 2, *Der Feldzug im Baltikum bis zur zweiten Einnahme von Riga, Januar bis Mai 1919.* Berlin: E.S. Mittler and Sohn, 1937.

Forschungsanstalt für Kriegs- und Heeresgeschichte. *Darstellungen aus den Nachkriegskämpfen deutscher Truppen und Freikorps.* Vol. 4, *Die Niederwerfung der Räteherrschaft in Bayern 1919.* Berlin: E.S. Mittler and Sohn, 1939.

Frank, Walter. *Franz Ritter von Epp: Der Weg eines deutschen Soldaten.* Hamburg: Hanseatische, 1934.

Freksa, Friedrich, ed. *Kapitän Ehrhardt: Abenteuer und Schicksale, nacherzählt von ***.* Berlin: August Scherl, 1924.

Great Britain, General Staff. *Handbook of the German Army in War, April 1918.* Reprinted as *German Army Handbook, April 1918.* London: Arms and Armour Press, 1977.

Grote, Hans-Henning Freiherr von, and Herbert Erb. *Konstantin Hierl: Der Mann und Sein Werk.* Berlin: Brunnen, 1934.

Gruss, Helmuth. *Die deutschen Sturmbataillone im Weltkrieg: Aufbau und Verwendung.* Berlin: Junker and Dünnhaupt, 1939.

Gumbel, Emil Julius. *Vier Jahre Politischer Mord.* 1922, 1924. Heidelberg: Das Wunderhorn, 1980.

Gumbel, Emil Julius. *Verschwörer: Beiträge zur Geschichte und Soziologie der deutschen nationalistischen Geheimbünde 1918-1924.* 1924. Heidelberg: Das Wunderhorn, 1979.

Gumbel, Emil Julius. *Deutschlands Geheime Rüstung?* Berlin: Liga für Menschenrechte, 1925.

Handbuch der SA. Berlin: Offene Worte, 1939.

Handbuch für den Preußischen Landtag 1925. Berlin: Reichs-druckerei, n.d.

Hartenstein. *Der Kampfeinsatz der Schutzpolizei bei Inneren Unruhen.* Charlottenburg: Offene Worte, 1926.

Heinz, Friedrich Wilhelm, ed. *Die Nation Greift An. Geschichte und Kritik des soldatischen Nationalismus.* Berlin: Das Reich, 1933.
Hess, Rudolf. "SA und Partei." *NS-Monatshefte,* no. 46 (January 1934): 3-4.
Heydebreck, Peter von. *Wir Wehrwölfe: Erinnerungen eines Freikorps-Führers.* Leipzig: K.F. Koehler, 1931.
Hildebrandt, Heinrich, and Walter Kettner, eds. *Stahlhelm Handbuch.* 3d and 4th eds. Berlin: Stahlhelm, 1929, 1931.
Himmler, Heinrich. "Die Aufgabe der SS." *NS-Monatshefte,* no. 46, pp. 10-11.
Hinkel, Hans, and Wulf Bley. *Kabinett Hitler!* Berlin-Schöneberg: Drei-Kultur-Wacht, 1933.
Hirschfeld, Dr. Magnus, and Andreas Gaspar. *Sittengeschichte des Ersten Weltkrieges.* 1929. Hanau: Müller and Kiepenheuer, n.d.
Hitler, Adolf. *Mein Kampf,* 1925, 1927. Munich: Franz Eher, 1943.
Hoffmann, Heinrich. *Das Braune Herr: 100 Bilddokumente: Leben, Kampf und Sieg der SA und SS.* Berlin: "Zeitgeschichte," 1932.
Hotzel, Kurt, ed. *Deutscher Aufstand: Die Revolution des Nach-krieges.* Stuttgart: W. Kohlhammer, 1934.
Jünger, Ernst, ed. *Der Kampf um das Reich.* 2d ed. Essen: Deutsche Vertriebsstelle "Rhein und Ruhr" Wilhelm Kamp, n.d.
———. *Krieg und Krieger.* Berlin: Junker und Dunnhaupt, 1930.
Kallenbach, Hans. *Mit Adolf Hitler auf Festung Landsberg.* Munich: Kress und Hornung, 1939.
Kern, Fritz. *Das Kappsche Abenteuer: Eindrücke und Feststellungen.* Leipzig: K.F. Koehler (Abt. Grenzboten), 1920.
Kienast, E., ed. *Handbuch für den Preußischen Landtag: Ausgabe für die 4. Wahlperiode (von 1932 ab).* Berlin: R. von Decker's Verlag G. Schenck, 1932.
Killinger, Manfred Freiherr von. "SA Männer--Landsknechte!" *Der SA-Mann* 5 (February 1932): 4.
———. *Die SA in Wort und Bild.* Leipzig: R. Kittler, 1933.
———. *Kampf um Oberschlesien 1921: Bisher unveröffentlichte aufzeichnungen des Führers der "Abteilung von Killinger" genannt "Sturmkompagnie Koppe."* Leipzig: K.F. Koehler, 1934.
———. *Der Klaubetermann: Eine Lebensgeschichte.* Munich: Franz Eher, 1936.
———. *Ernstes und Heiteres aus dem Putschleben.* Munich: Franz Eher, 1939 (7. Aufl.).
———. *Das Waren Kerle.* Soldaten, Kameraden! Vol. 68. Munich: Franz Eher, 1944.
———. *Erinnerungen der Sturmkompagnie.* Schleswig: F. Johannsens Buchdruckerei, Johs. Ibbeken, n.d.

Klähn, Friedrich Joachim. *Sturm 138: Ernstes und viel Heiteres aus dem SA-Leben*. Leipzig: Schaufuß, 1934.

————. *Wille und Vollendung: Auftrag und Durchführung der kulturellen Dienstgestaltung in der SA*. (*Der Appell*, vol. 1). Munich: Zentralverlag der NSDAP, n.d.

Kloppe, Fritz. *Der aristokratische Einheitsstaat*. Halle-Saale: Wehrwolf, 1932.

Koch, Karl W.H. *Das Ehrenbuch der SA*. Düsseldorf: Floeder, 1934.

Lingg, Anton. *Die Verwaltung der NSDAP*. Munich: Franz Eher, 1940.

Lohmann, Heinz. *SA räumt auf! Aus der Kampfzeit der Bewegung*. Hamburg: Hanseatische, 1935.

Ludin, Hanns. *SA.--Marschierendes Volk*. Munich: Franz Eher, 1939.

Luetgebruene, Walter. *Wahrheit und Recht für Feme: Schwarze Reichswehr und Oberleutnant Schulz*. Munich: J.F. Lehmann, 1928.

Maercker, Gen. Ludwig R. *Vom Kaiserheer zur Reichswehr: Geschichte der freiwilligen Landesjägerkorps*. 3d ed. Leipzig: Koehler, 1922.

Mahraun, Artur. *Das Jungdeutsche Manifest*. Berlin: Jungdeutscher, 1928.

Nationalsozialistischer Deutscher Frontkämpferbund (Stahlhelm). *Der NSDFB (Stahlhelm): Geschichte, Wesen und Aufgabe des Frontsoldatenbundes*. Berlin: Freiheitsverlag, 1935.

Naziführer sehen Dich an: 73 Biographien aus dem Dritten Reich. Paris: Editions du Carrefour, 1934.

NSDAP: Unsere Führer im Bild. Vol. 1. Leipzig: Willy Rebentisch, 1931.

NSDAP, der Oberste SA-Führer. *Allgemeine Dienstordnung (ADO) für die SA*. Diessen vor München: Jos. Huber, 1933.

NSDAP, Oberste SA-Führung. *Anzugs-Ordnung für die SA*. Diessen von München: J.C. Huber, n.d.

NSDAP, Oberste SA-Führung. *Dienstvorschrift für die SA der NSDAP*. 2 vols. Diessen vor München: Jos. Huber, 1932.

NSDAP, Oberste SA-Fuhrung, Ausbildungsabteilung. *Der Exerzierdienst der SA*. Munich: Oberster SA-Führung, 1935.

NSDAP, Oberste SA-Führung, Führungsamt. *Exerziervorschrift für die SA*. Vol. 1, *Fußexerzieren*. Munich: Oberster SA-Führung, 1937.

NSDAP, Oberste SA-Führer. *Warnungsbuch Nr. 2*. Munich, 1 January 1935. Nur für den Dienstgebrauch!

NSDAP, Reichsorganisationsleiter. *Organisationsbuch der NSDAP*. Munich: Franz Eher, 1943.

NSDAP, Reichsorganisationsleiter. *Partei-Statistik. Stand:1935*. 4

vols. Munich, printed manuscript. Reichsorganisationsleiter der NSDAP, Hauptorganisationsamt, Reichsamt für Statistik, 1935

NSDAP, Reichsschatzmeister der NSDAP. *Anordnungen, Anweisungen, Bekanntgaben, Verfügungen 26.7.26-1934.* Munich, n.d.

NSDAP, Stellvertreter des Führers. *Anordnungen des Stellvertreters des Führers.Zusammenstellung aller bis zum 31. März 1937 erlassenen und noch gültigen.* Munich: Franz Eher, 1937.

NSDAP, Oberste SA-Führung. *Handbuch der SA.* Berlin: Offene Wort, 1939.

NSDAP, Reichsleitung, Reichsschatzmeister. *Rundschreiben des Reichsschatzmeisters 26.7.26-31.12.34.* Munich, 1935.

NSDAP, Oberste SA-Führung, *Ausbildungsrichtlinien für 1939.* Vol. 1. N.p., n.d.

NSDAP, Oberste SA-Führung. *Dienstvorschrift für die SA der NSDAP (SADV) (Entwurf).* Diessen vor München: J.C. Huber, 1931.

NSDAP, der Führer. *Entwurf der Dienst-Vorschrift für die PO der NSDAP.* Munich, 1932.

NSDAP. *Unsere Führer im Bild.* Vol. 1. Leipzig: Willy Rebentisch, 1931.

Oberland in Oberschlesien: Auf Grund eigener Berichterstattung bearbeitet von Verlag "die deutschen Baumeister" München. Munich: Lindauer, n.d.

Oertzen, Friedrich Wilhelm von. *Die deutschen Freikorps.* Munich: F. Bruckmann, 1936.

Posse, Ernst H. *Die politischen Kampfbünde Deutschlands.* Berlin: Junker and Dünnhaupt, 1930.

Rehm, SA-Hauptsturmführer. *Geschichte der SA.* Sonderdruck 4 der Zeitschrift *Die SA.* Munich: Franz Eher, 1941.

Reichel, F.C.H., ed. *Westermanns Deutscher Reichsatlas.* Braunschweig: Georg Westermann, n.d.

Reichstag III Wahlperiode 1936. *Verzeichnis der Mitglieder des Reichstages und der Reichsregierung.* Berlin [?], 20 May 1936.

Reichswehrministerium, Heeres-Personal-Amt. *Rangliste des deutschen Reichsheeres mit der Dielstalterisliste sämtlicher Offiziere nach dem Stande vom 1. Mai 1928.* Berlin: E.S. Mittler and Sohn, 1928.

Reinhard, Wilhelm. *Der NS-Reichskriegerbund.* Schriften der Hochschule für Politik 29. Berlin: Junker and Dünnhaupt, 1939.

Röhm, Ernst. *Die Geschichte eines Hochverräters.* Munich: Franz Eher, 1928.

———. "SA und deutsche Revolution." *NS-Monatshefte* 4, no. 39 (June 1933): 251-53.

––––––. *Pourquoi les SA. Discours Pronouncé le 7. Dèc. 1933 à Berlin, Devant le Corps Diplomatique.* Berlin: Liebheit and Thiesen, 1933.

––––––. "Die braunen Bataillone der deutschen Revolution." *NS-Monatshefte* 5, no. 46 (1934): 5-9.

––––––. "Warum SA?" *NS-Monatshefte* 5, no. 46 (1934): 11-20.

Roßbach, Gerhard. *Die Sturmabteilung Roßbach als Grenzschutz in Westpreußen.* Kolberg: Victor Burmann, 1919.

Der SA-Mann.

Salomon, Ernst von. *Die Geächteten.* 1931. Reinbek bei Hamburg: Rowohlt, 1962.

––––––. *Nahe Geschichte: Ein Ueberblick.* Berlin: Rowohlt, 1936.

––––––, ed. *Das Buch vom deutschen Freikorpskämpfer.* Berlin: Wilhelm Limpert, 1938.

Schauwecker, Franz, ed. *Das Frontbuch: Die deutsche Seele im Weltkrieg.* Halle (Saale): Heinrich Diekmann, 1927.

Schmidt. *Die Kriegsstammrolle und ihre Führung, mit einem Anhang: Verfahren bei Sterbefällen und bei Vermittten, nach amtlichen Quellen Zusammengestellt.* 9th ed. Oldenburg i. Gr.: G. Stalling, 1918.

Schmidt-Pauli, Edgar von. *Geschichte der Freikorps 1918-1924.* Stuttgart: Robert Lutz Nachf. Otto Schramm, 1936.

Schönstedt, Walter. *Auf der Flucht Erschossen: Ein SA-Roman 1933.* Basel: Universum Bücherei, 1934.

Schulz, Oberleutnant Paul, ed. *Femeprozesse und Schwarze Reichswehr: Vortrag des Rechtsanwalts Prof. Dr. Grimm, Essen-Münster, im Plenarsaal des ehem. preussischen Herrenhauses zu Berlin, gehalten am 29. Januar 1929.* Munich: Lehmann, [1929].

Schulzebeer, Herbert. *Standarte "X": Tagebücher einer Landstandarte.* Leipzig: K.F. Koehler, 1934.

Schwede-Coburg, Franz. *Kampf um Coburg.* Munich: Franz Eher, 1939.

Schwerin, Eberhard Graf von. *Königl. Preuß Sturm-Bataillon Nr.5 (Rohr).nach der Erinnerungen aufgezeichnet unter Zuhilfenahme des Tagebuches von Herrn Oberstlt. a.D. Rohr.* Aus Deutschlands großer Zeit Vol. 116. Zeulenroda i. Th.: Shorn, 1939.

Sebottendorff, Rudolf von. *Bevor Hitler Kam.* Munich, 1933.

Seidel, Ernst, ed. *Kampfgenossen des Fürhers: Hitler und die Männer seiner Bewegung. Ein Bilderwerk.* Linz a.d. Donau: NSP, 1933.

Snyckers, Hans. *SA-Wehrmannschaften--Wehrbereites Volk.* Munich: Franz Eher, 1940.

––––––. *Tagebuch eines Sturmführers.* Munich: Franz Eher, 1941.

Der Stahlhelm, Bund der Frontsoldaten. *Der Stahlhelm: Erinnerungen und Bilder.* 2 vols. Berlin: Stahlhelm, 1932, 1933.

Stahlhelm Handbuch. 3d ed. Magdeburg: Stahlhelmverlag, 1929.

Stahlhelm Handbuch. 4th ed. Magdeburg: Stahlhelmverlag, 1931.

Stellenbesetzung im Reichsheer von 16. Mai 1920, 1. Oktober 1920 und 1. Oktober 1921. Bibliotheca Rerum Militarium, vol. 15, reprint of originals, 1920-1921. Osnabrück: Biblio, 1968.

Stelzner, Fritz. *Schicksal SA.* Munich: Franz Eher, 1936.

Stennes, Walther, ed. *Wie es zur Stennes-Aktion kam!* Berlin: Hausdruck Walther Stennes, n.d.

Stephan, Karl. *Der Todeskampf der Ostmark 1918-1919: Die Geschichte eines Grenzschutzbataillons.* 3d ed. Schneidemühl: Comenius, 1933.

Strasser, Otto. *Der deutsche Bartholomäusnacht.* 3d ed. Zürich: Reso, 1935.

Sturm 33, Hans Maikowski. Berlin: NS-Druck und Verlag, 1933.

Sturm, H. *Erlebnisse eines Kriegsfreiwilligen mit Nutzanwendungen für die deutsche Jugend.* Leipzig-Berlin: B.G. Teubner, 1915.

Die Uniformen und Abzeichen der SA, SS, HJ, des Stahlhelm, Brigade Ehrhardt, Amtswalter, Abgeordnete, NSBO, NSKK. Berlin: Traditionsverlag Rolf and Co., n.d. (facsimile reprint)

Volck, Herbert. *Rebellen um Ehre.* Berlin: Brunnen, 1932.

Völkische Beobachter

Volkmann, Maj. a.D. "Die sozialen Mißtände im Heer während des Weltkriegs." *Wissen und Wehr*, February 1929, 65-81, and March 1929, 152-67.

Volz, Hans. *Die Geschichte der SA von den Anfängen bis zur Gegenwart.* Berlin: Reimar Hobbing, 1934.

———. *Daten der Geschichte der NSDAP.* Berlin: A.G. Ploetz, 1938.

Von Oertzen, K.L. "Alter und Ueberalter." *Wissen und Wehr*, December 1932, 520-54.

Wagener, Otto Wilhelm Heinrich. *Von der Heimat geächtet: Im Auftrage der Deutschen Legion.* Stuttgart: C. Belsersche, 1920.

Warnecke, Karl Joachim. "Rechtliche Entwicklung und Stellung der Nationalsozialistischen Sturmabteilung (SA)." Inaugural diss., Universität Göttingen, 1935.

Weissbuch über die Erschiessungen des 30. Juni. Paris: Editions du Carrefour, 1934.

Wollenberg, Klaus-Werner. "Meine Baltikum-Erinnerungen." Berlin, handwritten manuscript, 1922.

III. Modern Secondary Sources

Abraham, David. *The Collapse of the Weimar Republic: Political Economy and Crisis.* 2d ed. New York: Holmes and Meier, 1986.

Abrams, Philip. *Historical Sociology.* Ithaca, N.Y.: Cornell University Press, 1982.

Absolon, Rudolf. *Die Wehrmacht im Dritten Reich.* 4 vols. Schriften des Bundesarchivs 16. Boppard am Rhine: Harald Boldt, 1969-79.

Ager, VerKuilen. *Freikorps Insignia.* Rochester, N.Y.: Privately printed, 1979.

Albertini, Lt. d.R. von. "Politik und Kriegführung in der deutschen Kriegstheorie von Clausewitz bis Ludendorff." *Schweizerische Monatsschrift für Offiziere aller Waffen: Organ für Kriegswissenschaft* 59 (January/February/March 1947): 11-29, 33-45, 78-91.

Allen, William Sheridan. *The Nazi Seizure of Power: The Experience of a Single German Town 1930-1935.* New York: Franklin Watts, 1973.

———. "Farewell to Class Analysis in the Rise of Nazism: Comment." *Central European History* 17 (March 1984): 54-62.

Auerbach, Hellmuth. "Hitlers politische Lehrjahre und die Münchener Gesellschaft 1919-1923." *Vierteljahreshefte für Zeitgeschichte* 25 (January 1977): 1-45.

Ayçoberry, Pierre. *The Nazi Question: An Essay on the Interpretations of National Socialism (1922-1975).* New York: Pantheon Books, 1981.

Bartov, Omer. "The Barbarisation of Warfare: German Officers and Men on the Eastern Front, 1941-1945." *Jahrbuch des Instituts für Deutsche Geschichte,* vol. 13, ed. Walter Grab, 306-39. Tel Aviv: Institut für Deutsche Geschichte, 1984.

———. *The Eastern Front, 1941-1945: German Troops and the Barbarization of Warfare.* New York: St. Martin's Press, 1986.

———. "Indoctrination and Motivation in the Wehrmacht: The Importance of the Unquantifiable." *Journal of Strategic Studies* 9 (March 1986): 16-34.

———. *Hitler's Army: Soldiers, Nazis, and War in the Third Reich.* New York: Oxford University Press, 1991.

Bender, Roger James. *The Luftwaffe.* Palo Alto: DD Associates, 1972.

Bennecke, Heinrich. *Hitler und die SA.* Munich and Vienna: Günter Olzog, 1962.

———. *Die Reichswehr und der "Röhm-Putsch"* Beiheft 2 der Zweimonatsschrift *Politische Studien.* Munich and Vienna: Günter Olzog, 1964.

Bennett, Edward W. *German Rearmament and the West, 1932-1933.* Princeton: Princeton University Press, 1979.

Berghahn, Volker R. *Der Stahlhelm, Bund der Frontsoldaten, 1918-1935.* Beiträge zur Geschichte des Parlamentarismus und der politischen Parteien 33. Düsseldorf: Droste, 1966.

Berghahn, Volker R., ed. *Militarismus.* Cologne: Kiepenheuer and Witsch, 1975.

Bessel, Richard. "Militarismus im innenpolitischen Leben der Weimarer Republik: Von den Freikorps zur SA." In *Militär und Militarismus in der Weimarer Republik,* ed. Klaus-Jürgen Müller and Eckardt Opitz, 193-222. Düsseldorf: Droste, 1978.

———. "The Rise of the NSDAP and the Myth of Nazi Propaganda." *Wiener Library Bulletin* 33, nos. 51 and 52 (1980): 20-29.

———. *Political Violence and the Rise of Nazism: The Storm Troopers in Eastern Germany, 1925-1934.* New Haven: Yale University Press, 1984.

———. "Violence as Propaganda: The Role of the Stormtroopers in the Rise of National Socialism." In *The Formation of the Nazi Constituency, 1919-1933,* ed. Thomas Childers, 131-46. Totowa, N.J.: Barnes and Noble, 1986.

———. *Germany after the First World War.* Oxford: Clarendon Press, 1993.

Bessel, Richard, and Mathilde Jamin. "Nazis, Workers, and the Uses of Quantitative Evidence." *Social History* 4 (January 1979): 111-16.

Bird, Keith W. *Weimar, the German Naval Officer Corps, and the Rise of National Socialism.* Amsterdam: B.R. Grüner, 1977.

Birn, Ruth Bettina. *Die Höheren SS- und Polizeiführer: Himmlers Vertreter im Reich und in den besetzten Gebieten.* Düsseldorf: Droste, 1986.

Black, Peter R. *Ernst Kaltenbrunner: Ideological Soldier of the Third Reich.* Princeton, N.J.: Princeton University Press, 1984.

Blackbourn, David, and Geoff Eley. *The Peculiarities of German History: Bourgeois Society and Politics in Nineteenth-Century Germany.* Oxford: Oxford University Press, 1985.

Bloch, Charles. *Die SA und die Krise des NS-Regimes 1934.* Frankfurt a/M.: Shurkamp, 1970.

Boberach, Heinz. "Das Schriftgut der staatlichen Verwaltung, der Wehrmacht und der NSDAP aus der Zeit von 1933-1945." *Der Archivar* 22 (1969): 137-57.

Boberach, Heinz, and Hans Booms. *Aus der Arbeit des Bundesarchivs: Beiträge zum Archivwesen, zur Quellenkunde und Zeitgeschichte.* Schriften des Bundesarchivs 25. Boppard a/R: Boldt, 1977.

Bracher, Karl-Dietrich. *The German Dictatorship.* New York: Praeger, 1970.

———. *Die Auflösung der Weimarer Republik.* 1955. Reprint, Königstein/Ts.-Düsseldorf: Athenäum Droste, 1978.

Bradley, Dermont, and Ulrich Marwedel, eds. *Militärgeschichte, Militärwissenschaft und Konfliktforschung. Festschrift für Werner Hahlweg.* Osnabrück: Biblio, 1977.

Broszat, Martin. "Soziale Motivation und Führer-Bindung des Nationalsozialismus." *Vierteljahreshefte für Zeitgeschichte* 18 (1970): 392-409.

———. *The Hitler State: The Foundation and Development of the Internal Structure of the Third Reich.* London: Longman, 1981.

———. *Kommandant in Auschwitz: Autobiographische Aufzeichnungen des Rudolf Höss.* Munich: Deutscher Taschenbuch, 1983.

———. "Zur Struktur der NS-Massenbewegung", in: *Vierteljahreshefte für Zeitgeschichte* 31, no. 1 (1983): 52-76.

Browder, George C. "Problems and Potentals of the Berlin Document Center." *Central European History* 5 (1972): 362-80.

———. *Foundations of the Nazi Police State: The Formation of Sipo and SD.* Lexington: University of Kentucky Press, 1990.

Browning, Christopher R. *Ordinary Men: Reserve Police Battalion 101 and the Final Solution in Poland.* New York: HarperCollins, 1992.

Bucher, Peter. *Der Reichswehrprozeß: Der Hochverrat der Ulmer Reichswehroffiziere 1929/1930.* Boppard a/R: Harald Boldt, 1967.

Buchheim, Hans. "Mitgliedschaft bei der NSDAP." In *Gutachten des Instituts für Zeitgeschichte,* 1:313-22. Munich: Selbstverlag des Instituts für Zeitgeschichte, 1958.

Buchheim, Hans, Martin Broszat, Hans-Adolf Jacobsen, and Krausnick, Helmut. *Anatomie des SS-Staates.* 2 vols. Munich: Deutscher Taschenbuch, 1967.

Burleigh, Michael, and Wolfgang Wippermann. *The Racial State: Germany, 1933-1945.* Cambridge: Cambridge University Press, 1991.

Büsch, Otto. ed. *Wählerbewegung in der europäischen Geschichte: Ergebnisse einer Konferenz.* Einzelveröffentlichungen der Historischen Kommission zu Berlin. Berlin: Colloquium, 1980.

Campbell, Bruce. "The SA after the Röhm Purge." *Journal of Contemporary History* 28 (1993): 659-74.

Carsten, Francis L. *The Reichswehr and Politics, 1918-1933.* 1966. Reprint, Berkeley: University of California Press, 1973.

Childers, Thomas. "The Social Bases of the National Socialist Vote." *Journal of Contemporary History* 11 (October 1976): 17-42.

———. *The Nazi Voter: The Social Foundations of Fascism in Germany, 1919-1933*. Chapel Hill: University of North Carolina Press, 1983.

———. "Who, Indeed, Did Vote for Hitler?" *Central European History* 17 (March 1984): 45-53.

———, ed. *The Formation of the Nazi Constituency, 1919-1933*. Totowa, N.J.: Barnes and Noble, 1986.

Childers, Thomas, and Jane Caplan, eds. *Reevaluating the Third Reich*. New York: Holmes and Meier, 1993.

Chorley, Katharine. *Armies and the Art of Revolution*. Boston: Beacon Press, 1973.

Cocks, Geoffrey, and Konrad Jarausch, eds. *German Professions 1800-1950*. Oxford: Oxford University Press, 1990.

Craig, Gordon A. *The Politics of the Prussian Army, 1640-1945*. New York: Oxford University Press, 1956.

———. *Germany, 1866-1945*. New York: Oxford University Press, 1978.

Darmberg, John. *Munich 1923: The Story of Hitler's First Grab for Power*. New York: Harper and Row, 1982.

Davis, Brian Leigh. *German Uniforms of the Third Reich, 1933-1945*. New York: Arco, 1980.

Deak, Istvan. *Beyond Nationalism: A Social and Political History of the Hapsburg Officer Corps, 1848-1918*. Oxford: Oxford University Press, 1990.

Deist, Wilhelm. *The Wehrmacht and German Rearmament*. Toronto: University of Toronto Press, 1987.

Demeter, Karl. *Das deutsche Offizierskorps in Gesellschaft und Staat 1650-1945*. Frankfurt a/M: Bernard and Graefe Verlag für Wehrwissen, 1962.

———. *The German Officer Corps in Society and State, 1650-1945*. London: George Weidenfeld and Nicolson, 1965.

Deutsches Marine Institut, ed. *Seemacht und Geschichte: Festschrift zum 80. Geburtstag von Friedrich Ruge*. Bonn-Bad Godesberg: MOV, 1975.

Diehl, James M. *Paramilitary Politics in Weimar Germany*. Bloomington: Indiana University Press, 1977.

Dobert, Eitel Wolf. *Convert to Freedom*. New York, 1940.

Dornberg, John. *Munich 1923: The Story of Hitler's First Grab for Power*. New York: Harper and Row, 1982.

Drage, Charles. *The Amiable Prussian*. London: Anthony Blond, 1958.

Dülffer, Jost, and Karl Holl, eds. *Bereit zum Krieg: Kriegsmentalität im wilhelminischen Deutschland 1890-1914*. Göttingen: Vandenhoeck and Ruprecht, 1986.

Eksteins, Modris. *Rites of Spring: The Great War and the Birth of the Modern Age.* New York: Anchor Books, 1989.

Eley, Geoff. *Reshaping the German Right: Radical Nationalism and Political Change after Bismarck.* Ann Arbor: University of Michigan Press, 1980.

————. *From Unification to Nazism: Reinterpreting the German Past.* Boston: Allen and Unwin, 1986.

Ellis, John. *Armies in Revolution.* New York: Oxford University Press, 1974.

Englehardt, Ulrich, Volker Sellin, and Horst Stuke, eds. *Soziale Bewegung und Politische Verfassung. Werner Conze zum 31.12.75.* Stuttgart: Klett, 1976.

Erdmann, Jürgen. *Coburg, Bayern, und das Reich, 1918-1923.* Coburg: A. Rossteutscher, 1969.

Erdmann, Karl Dietrich, and Hagen Schulze, eds. *Weimar, Selbstpreisgabe einer Demokratie: Eine Bilanz Heute.* Düsseldorf: Droste, 1980.

Esler, Anthony, ed. *The Youth Revolution: The Conflict of Generations in Modern History.* Lexington, Mass.: D.C. Heath, 1974.

Evans, Richard J. *Rethinking German History: Nineteenth-Century Germany and the Origins of the Third Reich.* Boston: Allen and Unwin, 1987.

Eyck, Erich. *A History of the Weimar Republik.* 2 vols. New York: Atheneum, 1970.

Falter, Jurgen W. "Wer verhalf der NSDAP zum Sieg? Neuere Forschungsergebnisse zur parteipolitischen und sozialen Hintergrund der NSDAP-Wähler 1924-1933." *Aus Politik und Zeitgeschichte,* 14 July 1979, 3-21.

————. "Wählerbewegungen zur NSDAP 1924-1933. Methodische Probleme—Empirisch abgesicherte Erkenntnisse—Offene Fragen." In *Wählerbewegung in der europäischen Geschichte: Ergebnisse einer Konferenz,* ed. Otto Büsch, 159-202. Einzelveröffentlichungen der Historischen Kommission zu Berlin. Berlin: Colloquium, 1980.

————. *Hitlers Wähler.* Munich: C.H. Beck, 1991.

Falter, Jürgen W., Thomas Lindenberger, and Siegfried Schumann, eds. *Wahlen und Abstimmungen in der Weimarer Republik: Material zum Wahlverhalten, 1919-1933.* Munich: C.H. Beck, 1986.

Fest, Joachim, *Das Gesicht des Dritten Reiches: Profile einer Totalitären Herrschaft.* 7th ed. Munich: R. Piper, 1980.

Finker, Kurt, "Die militaristischen Wehrberbände in der Weimarer Republik. Ein Beitrag zur strategie und Taktik der deutschen

Großbourgeoisie", *Zeitschrift für Geschichtswissenschaft* 14, no. 3 (1966): 357-77.

Fischer, Conan. "The Occupational Background of the SA's Rank and File Membership during the Depression Years, 1929 to Mid-1934." In *The Shaping of the Nazi State*, ed. Peter D. Stachura, 131-59. London: Croom Helm, 1978.

Fischer, Conan. "The SA of the NSDAP: Social Background and Ideology of the Rank and File in the Early 1930s." *Journal of Contemporary History* 17 (1982): 651-70.

———. *Stormtroopers: A Social, Economic, and Ideological Analysis, 1929-1935*. London: George Allen and Unwin, 1983.

Fischer, Conan, and Carolyn Hicks. "Problems of Research: Statistics and the Historian: The Occupational Profile of the SA of the NSDAP." *Social History* 5 (January 1980): 131-38.

Foertsch, Hermann. *Schuld und Verhängnis. Die Fritsch-Krise im Frühjahr 1938 als Wendepunkt in der Geschichte der NS Zeit*. Stuttgart: Deutsche Verlagsanstalt, 1951.

Forstmeier, Friedrich. "Zur Rolle der Marine im Kapp-Putsch." In *Seemacht und Geschichte: Festschrift zum 80. Geburtstag von Friedrich Ruge*, ed. Deutsches Marine Institut, 51-80. Bonn-Bad Godesberg: MOV, 1975.

Frank, Robert H. "Hitler and the National Socialist Coalition, 1924-1932." Ph.D. diss., Johns Hopkins University, 1969.

Franz-Willing, Georg. *Die Hitlerbewegung: Der Ursprung 1919-1922*. Hamburg: R. v. Decker's Verlag G. Schenck, 1962.

Frei, Norbert. *National Socialist Rule in Germany: The Führer State, 1933-1945*. 1987. Oxford: Blackwell, 1993.

Fricke, Dieter, ed. *1830-1945: Die Bürgerlichen Parteien in Deutschland*. 2 vols. Berlin: Das Europäische Buch, 1968.

Fussel, Paul. *The Great War in Modern Memory*. Oxford: Oxford University Press, 1975.

Gallo, Max. *The Night of the Long Knives*. Trans. Liley Emmet. New York: Harper & Row, 1972.

Genuneit, Jürgen. *Völkische Radikale in Stuttgart: Zur Vorgeschichte und Frühphase der NSDAP, 1890-1925*. Stuttgart-Bad Cannstadt: Dr. Cantz'sche Druckerei, 1982.

Geyer, Michael. "Die Geschichte des deutschen Militärs von 1860-1945: Ein Bericht über die Forschungslage (1945-1975)." In *Die Moderne Deutsche Geschichte in der Internationalen Forschung* (*Geschichte und Gesellschaft*, special issue 4), ed. Hans Ulrich Wehler, 256-86. Göttingen, 1978.

Geyer, Michael. *Deutsche Rüstungspolitik, 1860-1980*. Frankfurt am Main: Suhrkamp, 1984.

Gillis, John R., ed. *The Militarization of the Western World*. New Brunswick: Rutgers University Press, 1989.

Gordon, Harold J. *Die Reichswehr und die Weimarer Republik 1919-1926*. Frankfurt am Main: Verlag für Wehrwesen Bernard & Graefe, 1959.

———. "Politischer Terror und Versailler Abrüstungsklausel in der Weimarer Republik." *Wehrwissenschaftliche Rundschau* 16 (January 1966): 36-54.

———. *The Reichswehr and the German Republic, 1919-1926*. 1957. New York: Kennikat, 1972.

———. *Hitler and the Beer Hall Putsch*. Princeton: Princeton University Press, 1972.

Graml, Hermann, *Der 9. November 1938 "Reichskristallnacht."* (Schriftenreihe der Bundeszentrale für Heimatdienst, vol. 2). 1955.

Graß, Karl Martin. "Edgar Jung, Papenkreis, und Röhmkrise, 1933/34." Ph.D. diss., Rupprecht-Karl-Universität at Heidelberg, 1966.

Grill, Johnpeter Horst. "The Nazi Party in Baden 1920-1945." Ph.D. diss., University of Michigan, 1975.

Gundelach, Ulrich. "Der Nationale Wehrgedanke in der Weimarer Republik." Ph.D. diss., Bonn, 1977.

Hagtuet, Bernt, Stein U. Larsen, and Jan Myklebust, eds. *Who Were the Fascists? New Perspectives on the Social Roots of European Fascism*. Oslo: Universitetsforlaget, 1980.

Halcomb, Jill. *The SA: A Historical Perspective*. Overland Park, Kans.: Crown/Agincourt, 1985.

Hambrecht, Rainer. *Der Aufstieg der NSDAP in Mittel- und Oberfranken, 1925-1933*. Nürnberger Werkstücke zur Stadt- und Landesgeschichte, vol. 17. Nuremberg: Dissertationsdruckerei HOGL, 1976.

Hamilton, Richard F. *Who Voted for Hitler?* Princeton: Princeton University Press, 1982.

———. "Braunschweig 1932: Further Evidence on the Support for National Socialism." *Central European History* 17 (March 1984): 3-36.

———. "Reply to Commentators." *Central European History* 17 (March 1984): 72-85.

Hancock, Eleanor, "'Only the Real, the True, the Masculine Held Its Value': Ernst Röhm, Masculinity, and Male Homosexuality." Manuscript, 1993.

———. "Ernst Röhm and the Experience of World War I." *Journal of Military History* 60 (January 1996): 39-60.

———. "'Indispensible Outsider'? Ernst Röhm as Chief of Staff of the SA, 1931-1933." Paper presented at the annual meeting of the German Studies Association, Seattle, 11 October 1996.

Handourtzel, Rémy. "Sur les trajectoires individuelles dans la vie politique." *Sources: Travaux Historiques*, no. 3/4 (*la Biographie*, 1985): 88-92.

Hatheway, Jay. "The Pre-1920 Origins of the National Socialist German Worker's Party." *Journal of Contemporary History* 29 (1994): 443-62.

Heiber, Helmut, ed. *Das Tagebuch von Joseph Goebbels 1925/1926.* Stuttgart: Deutsche Verlags-Anstalt, n.d.

Hennig, Eike. *Bürgerliche Gesellschaft und Faschismus in Deutschland: Ein Forschungsbericht.* Frankfurt am Main: Shurkamp, 1977.

Herff, Jeffrey. *Reactionary Modernism: Technology, Culture, and Politics in the Weimar and the Third Reich.* Cambridge: Cambridge University Press, 1984.

Hermann, Carl Hans. *Deutsche Militärgeschichte.* Frankfurt am Main: Bernard and Graefe, 1966.

Herwig, Holger H. *The German Naval Officer Corps: A Social and Political History, 1890-1918.* Oxford: Oxford University Press, 1973.

Heydeloff, Rudolf. "Staranwalt der Rechtsextremisten. Walter Luetgebrune in der Weimarer Republik." *Vierteljahreshefte für Zeitgeschichte* 32 (July 1984): 373-421.

Hirschfeld, Gerhard, and Lothar Kettenacker, eds. *Der "Führerstaat": Mythos und Realität. Studien zur Struktur und Politik des Dritten Reiches.* Stuttgart: Klett-Cotta, 1981.

Hofer, Walter, Deouard Calic, Karl Stephan, and Friedrich Zipfer, eds. *Der Reichstagsbrand: Eine Wissenschaftliche Dokumentation.* 2 vols. Berlin: Arani, 1972.

Höhne, Heinz. *The Order under the Death's Head: The Story of Hitler's SS.* 1966. New York: Ballantine Books, 1977.

———. *Mordsache Röhm: Hitlers Durchbruch sur Alleinherrschaft, 1933-1934.* Hamburg: Spiegel/Rowohlt, 1984.

Holborn, Hajo, ed. *Republic to Reich: The Making of the Nazi Revolution.* New York: Random House/Pantheon, 1972.

Hornung, Klaus. *Der Jungdeutsche Orden.* Düsseldorf: Droste, 1958.

International Military Tribunal. *The Trial of the German Major War Criminals: Proceedings of the International Military Tribunal Sitting at Nuremberg, Germany,* pt. 21: *9th August, 1946 to 21st August, 1946.* London: His Majesty's Stationery Office, 1949.

Institut für Zeitgeschichte. *Gutachten des Instituts für Zeitge-*

schichte. Vol. 1. Munich: Selbstverlag des Instituts für Zeitgeschichte, 1958.

————. *Gutachten des Instituts für Zeitgeschichte.* Vol. 2. Stuttgart:
Deutsche Verlagsanstalt, 1966.

Jablonsky, David. "Röhm and Hitler: The Continuity of Political-
Military Discord." *Journal of Contemporary History* 23 (1988):
367-86.

Jacobsen, Hans-Adolf. *Nationalsozialistische Außenpolitik 1933-
1938.* Frankfurt am Main: Alfred Metzner, 1968.

Jaeger, Harald. "Problematik und Aussagewert der überlieferung-
sgestörten Schriftgutbestände der NS-Zeit." *Der Archivar* 28,
no. 3 (1975): 275-92.

Jäger, Herbert, Gerhard Schmidtchen, and Lieselotte Süllwold.
Lebenslaufanalysen. Opladen, 1981.

Jamin, Mathilde. "Zur Sozialstruktur des Nationalsozialismus."
Politische Vierteljahresschrift 19 (1978): 88-91.

————. "Zur Kritik an Michael Katers "Überlegungen über Quantifizierung und NS-Geschichte." *Geschichte und Gesellschaft* 4
(1978): 536-41.

————. "Methodische Konzeption einer Quantitative Analyse zur
sozialen Zusammensetzung der SA." In *Die Nationalsozialisten:
Analysen Faschistischer Bewegungen,* Historisch-sozialwissenschaftliche Forschungen 9, ed. Reinhard Mann, 84-97. Stuttgart:
Klett-Cotta, 1980.

————. Zur Rolle der SA im nationalsozialistischen Herr-
schaftssystem." In *Der "Führerstaat": Mythos und Realität,*
Studien zur Struktur und Politik des Dritten Reiches, ed.
Gerhard Hirschfeld and Lothar Kettenacker, 329-60. Stuttgart:
Klett-Cotta, 1981.

————. *Zwischen den Klassen: Zur Sozialstruktur der SA-Führerschaft.* Wuppertal: Peter Hammer, 1984.

Janowitz, Morris. *The Professional Soldier. A Social and Political
Portrait.* 1960. New York: Free Press, 1971.

John, Hartmut. *Das Reserveoffizierkorps im deutschen Kaiserreich
1890-1914.* Campus Forschung, vol. 224. Frankfurt am Main:
Campus, 1981.

Jovy, Ernst Michael. "Deutsche Jugendbewegung und Nationalsozialismus: Versuch einer Klärung ihrer Zusammenhänge und
Gegensätze." Ph.D. diss., Universität Köln, 1953.

Kaelble, Hartmut, "Chancenungleichheit und akademische
Ausbildung in Deutschland 1910-1960." *Geschichte und
Gesellschaft* 1, no. 1 (1975): 121-49.

Kater, Michael H. "Zur Soziographie der Frühen NSDAP."
Vierteljahreshefte für Zeitgeschichte 19 (April 1971): 125-37.

———. "Zum gegenseitigen Verhältnis von SA und SS in der Sozialgeschichte des Nationalsozialismus." *Vierteljahresschrift für Sozial- und Wirtschaftsgeschichte* 62 (1975): 339-79.

———. "Ansätze zu einer Soziologie der SA bis zur Röhm-Krise." In *Soziale Bewegungen und Politische Verfassung*, ed. Ulrich Engelhardt, Volker Sellin, and Horst Sture, 789-831. Stuttgart: Klett, 1976.

———. "Quantifizierung und NS-Geschichte. Methodologische Ueberlegungen über Grenzen und Möglichkeiten einer EDV-Analyse der NSDAP Sozialstruktur." *Geschichte und Gesellschaft* 3 (1977): 453-84.

———. *The Nazi Party: A Social Profile of Members and Leaders 1919-1945*. Cambridge: Harvard University Press, 1983.

———. "Generationskonflikte als Entwicklungsfaktor in der NS-Bewegung vor 1933." *Geschichte und Gesellschaft* 11, no. 2 (1985): 217-43.

———. "Hitler's Early Doctors: Nazi Physicians in Predepression Germany." *Journal of Modern History* 59 (March 1987): 25-52.

———. *Doctors under Hitler*. Chapel Hill: University of North Carolina Press, 1989.

Kershaw, Ian. *The Nazi Dictatorship: Problems and Perspectives of Interpretation*. London: Edward Arnold, 1989.

Kissenkotter, Udo. *Gregor Strasser und die NSDAP*. Stuttgart: Deutsche, 1979.

Kitchen, Martin. *The German Officer Corps, 1890-1914*. Oxford: Clarendon Press, 1968.

———. *A Military History of Germany from the Eighteenth Century to the Present Day*. Bloomington: Indiana University Press, 1975.

Klietmann, Kurt-Gerhard. *Pour le Mérite und Tapferkeitsmedaille*. Berlin: Verlag "die Ordenssammlung," 1966.

———. *Deutsche Auszeichnungen: Eine Geschichte der Ehrenzeichen und Medaillen, Erinnerungs- und Verdienstabzeichen des Deutschen Reiches, der deutschen Staaten sowie staatlicher Dienststellen, Organisationen, Verbände, usw. vom 18.-20. Jahrhundert*. 2 vols. Berlin: Verlag "die Ordenssammlung," 1971.

Klotzbücher, Alois. "Der politische Weg des Stahlhelms, Bund der Frontsoldaten in der Weimarer Republik: Ein Beitrag zur Geschichte der Nationalen Opposition, 1918-1933." Ph.D. diss., Universität Erlangen, 1964.

Koch, Hannsjoachim W. *Der deutsche Bürgerkrieg: Eine Geschichte der deutschen und österreichischen Freikorps, 1918-1923*. Berlin: Ullstein, 1978.

Koehl, Robert L. "Was There an SS Officer Corps?" Unpublished pa-

per, Citadel Symposium on Hitler and National Socialism, pro-
ceedings 24-25 April 1980. Charleston S.C., 1981.
————. *The Black Corps: The Structure and Power Struggles of the
Nazi SS.* Madison: University of Wisconsin Press, 1983.
Köhler, Henning. *Arbeitsdienst in Deutschland. Pläne und
Verwirklichungsformen bis zur Einführung der Arbeits-
dienstpflicht im Jahre 1935.* (Schriften zur Wirtschafts- und
Sozialgeschichte, vol. 10). Berlin: Duncker & Humblot, n.d.
König, René. *Handbuch der empirischen Sozialforschung, Band 9:
Organisation. Militär.* Munich: Deutscher Taschenbuchverlag,
1977.
Kopetzky, Helmut. *In den Tod—Hurra! Deutsche Jugend-Regimenter
im Ersten Weltkrieg: Ein historischer Tatsachenbericht über
Langemarck.* Cologne: Paul Rugenstein, 1981.
Koshar, Rudy. "From *Stammtisch* to Party: Nazi Joiners and the Con-
tradictions of Grass Roots Fascism in Weimar Germany." *Jour-
nal of Modern History* 59 (March 1987): 1-24.
————, ed. *Splintered Classes: Politics and the Lower Middle Class
in Interwar Europe.* New York: Holmes and Meier, 1990.
Krabbe, Wolfgang R., ed. *Politische Jugend in der Weimarer Republik.*
Bochum: Universitätsverlag Dr. N. Brockmeyer, 1993.
Krausnick, Helmut. "Der 30.Juni 1934. Bedeutung--Hintergründe--
Verlauf." *Aus Politik und Zeitgeschichte,* 30 June 1954, 317-
24.
Krüger, Gabriele. *Die Brigade Ehrhardt.* Hamburger Beiträge zur
Zeitgeschichte, vol. 7. Hamburg: Leibnitz, 1971.
Kühn, Dieter. *Luftkrieg als Abenteuer. Kampfschrift.* Reihe Hanser,
no. 180. Munich-Vienna: Carl Hanser, 1975.
Kuron, Hans Jürgen. "Freikorps und Bund Oberland." Ph.D. diss.,
Friedrich-Alexander-Universität zu Erlangen, 1960.
Laffan, Michael, ed. *The Burden of German History, 1919-1945: Es-
says for the Goethe Institute.* London: Methuen, 1988.
Laqueur, Walter Z. *Young Germany: A History of the German Youth
Movement.* New York: Basic Books, 1962.
Laqueur, Walter, ed. *Fascism, a Reader's Guide: Analyses, Interpre-
tations, Bibliography.* Berkeley: University of California Press,
1976.
Laqueur, Walter, and George Mosse, eds. *International Fascism, 1920-
1945.* New York: Harper & Row, 1966.
Large, David Clay. "The Politics of Law and Order: A History of the
Bavarian *Einwohnerwehr,* 1918-1921." In *Transactions of the
American Philosophical Society* 70, no. 2 (1980): 1-87.
Lasswell, Harold D., and Daniel Lerner, eds. *World Revolutionary*

Elites: Studies in Coercive Ideological Movements. Cambridge: MIT Press, 1965.

Leed, Eric J. *No Man's Land.* Cambridge: Cambridge University Press, 1979.

Levine, Herbert S. *Hitler's Free City: A History of the Nazi Party in Danzig, 1925-39.* Chicago: University of Chicage Press, 1973.

Liang, Hsi-Huey. *The Berlin Police Force in the Weimar Republic.* Berkeley: University of California Press, 1970.

Loewenberg, Peter. "The Psychohistorical Origins of the Nazi Youth Cohort." *American Historical Review* 76 (December 1971): 1457-1502.

Lohalm, Uwe. *Völkischer Radikalismus: Die Geschichte des Deutschvölkischen Schutz- und Trutzbundes, 1919-1923.* Hamburg: Leibnitz, 1970.

Longerich, Peter. *Die braunen Bataillone: Geschichte der SA.* Munich: C.H. Beck, 1989.

Mabire, Jean. *Röhm: L'Homme Qui Inventa Hitler.* Paris: Fayard, 1983.

McInnes, Colin, and G.D. Sheffield, eds. *Warfare in the Twentieth Century: Theory and Practice.* London: Unwin Hyman, 1988.

Madden, Paul. "Some Social Characteristics of Early Nazi Party Members, 1919-1923." *Central European History* 15 (March 1982): 34-56.

Mallebrein, Wolfram. *Konstantin Hierl: Schöpfer und Gestalter des Reichsarbeitsdienstes.* Hannover, 1971.

Mann, Reinhard, ed. *Die Nationalsozialisten: Analysen Faschistischer Bewegungen.* Historisch- sozialwissenschaftliche Forschungen 9. Stuttgart: Klett-Cotta, 1980.

Manvell, Roger, and Heinrich Fraenkel. *Heinrich Himmler.* London: Heinemann, 1965.

Martin, Bernd. "Zur Tauglichkeit eines übergreifenden Faschismusbegriffs: Ein Vergleich zwischen Japan, Italien, und Deutschland." *Vierteljahreshefte für Zeitgeschichte* 29 (1981): 48-73.

Martin, Bernd, ed. *Die deutsche Beraterschaft in China, 1927-1938: Militär-Wirtschaft-Außenpolitik.* Düsseldorf: Droste, 1981.

Martini, Winfried. "Zelle 474." *Der Monat* 9 (June 1957): 180ff.

Maschmann, Melita. *Fazit: Mein Weg in der Hitler-Jugend.* 1963. Munich: Deutsche Taschenbuchverlag, 1979.

Maser, Werner. *Die Frühgeschichte der NSDAP: Hitlers Weg bis 1924.* Frankfurt am Main: Athenäum, 1965.

———. *Der Sturm auf die Republik: Frühgeschichte der NSDAP.* Frankfurt am Main: Ullstein, 1981.

Mau, Hermann. "Die Zweite Revolution—der 30. Juni 1934." *Vierteljahreshefte für Zeitgeschichte* 1 (1953): 119-37.

Mauch, Hans-Joachim. "Nationalistische Wehrorganisationen in der Weimarer Republik: Zur Entwicklung und Ideologie des 'Paramilitarismus.'" Ph.D. diss., Technische Hochschule Aachen, 1982.

Mayer, Arno J. *Dynamics of Counterrevolution in Europe, 1870-1956: An Analytic Framework.* New York: Harper & Row, 1971.

Merkl, Peter H. *Political Violence under the Swastika: 581 Early Nazis.* Princeton: Princeton University Press, 1975.

————. *The Making of a Stormtrooper.* Princeton: Princeton University Press, 1980.

Mertens, Lothar. "Das Privileg des Einjähr-Freiwilligen Militärdienstes im Kaiserreich und seine gesellschaftliche Bedeutung: Zum Stand der Forschung." *Militärgeschichtliche Mitteilungen* 39, no. 1 (1986): 59-66.

Messerschmidt, Manfred. *Militär und Politik in der Bismarckzeit und im Wilhelminischen Deutschland.* Erträge der Forschung, vol. 43. Darmstadt: Wissenschaftliche Buchgesellschaft, 1975.

Michalka, Wolfgang, and Gottfried Niedhart, eds. *Die Ungeliebte Republik: Dokumente zur Innen- und Aussenpolitik Weimars 1918-1933.* Munich: Deutscher Taschenbuch, 1980.

Militärgeschichtliches Forschungsamt. *Deutsche Militärgeschichte, 1648-1939.* 6 vols. Herrsching: Manfred Pawlak, 1983.

Mohler, Armin. *Die Konservative Revolution in Deutschland, 1918-1932: Ein Handbuch.* 2d ed. Darmstadt: Wissenschaftliche Buchgesellschaft, 1972.

Mommsen, Hans. "Der Reichstagsbrand und seine politische Folgen." *Vierteljahreshefte für Zeitgeschichte* 12 (October 1964): 351-413.

Mommsen, Wolfgang J., and Gerhard Hirschfeld, eds. *Social Protest, Violence, and Terror in Nineteenth- and Twentieth-Century Europe.* New York: St. Martin's, 1982.

Mosse, George L. *The Crisis of German Ideology: The Intellectual Origins of the Third Reich.* New York: Grosset and Dunlap, 1964.

————. *Germans and Jews: The Right, the Left, and the Search for a "Third Force" in Pre-Nazi Germany.* New York: Grosset & Dunlap, 1970.

————. *The Nationalization of the Masses: Political Symbolism and Mass Movements in Germany from the Napoleonic Wars through the Third Reich.* New York: New Americazn Library, 1975.

————. *Nationalism and Sexuality: Middle-Class Morality and Sexual Norms in Modern Europe.* Madison: University of Wisconsin Press, 1985.

————. "Two World Wars and the Myth of the War Experience." *Journal of Contemporary History* 21 (1986): 491-513.

————. *Masses and Man: Nationalist and Fascist Perceptions of Reality.* Detroit: Wayne State University Press, 1987.

————. *Fallen Soldiers: Reshaping the Memory of the World Wars.* Oxford: Oxford University Press, 1990.

Mühlberger, Detlef. "The Sociology of the NSDAP: The Question of Working-Class Membership." *Journal of Contemporary History* 15 (July 1980): 493-512.

————. *The Social Basis of European Fascist Movements.* London: Croom Helm, 1987.

————. *Hitler's Followers: Studies in the Sociology of the Nazi Movement.* London: Routledge, 1991.

Müller, Klaus-Jürgen. "Dokumentation: Reichswehr und "Röhm-Affäre: Aus den Akten des Wehrkreiskommandos (bayr.) VII." *Militärgeschichtliche Mitteilungen* 7, no. 1 (1968): 107-44.

————. *Armee, Politik, und Gesellschaft in Deutschland, 1933-1945: Studien zum Verhältnis von Armee und NS-System.* Paderbord: Schöningh, 1979.

Müller, Klaus-Jürgen, and Eckardt Opitz, eds. *Militär und Militarismus in der Weimarer Republik: Beiträge eines internationalen Symposiums an der Hochschule der Bundes-wehr Hamburg am 5. und 6. Mai 1977.* Düsseldorf: Droste, 1978.

Nusser, Horst G.W. *Konservative Wehrverbände in Bayern, Preußen, und Österreich, 1918-1933: Mit einer Biographie von Forstrat Georg Escherisch, 1870-1941.* 2 vols. Munich: Nusser, 1973.

Nyomarkay, Joseph. *Charisma and Factionalism in the Nazi Party.* Minneapolis: University of Minnesota Press, 1967.

Office of the Military Government of the United States in Germany (OMGUS), 7771 Document Center. *Who Was a Nazi? Facts about the Membership Procedure of the Nazi Party.* Berlin: OMGUS, 1947.

Orlow, Dietrich. *The History of the Nazi Party, 1919-1945.* 2 vols. Pittsburgh: University of Pittsburgh Press, 1969, 1973.

Patzewall, Klaus D. *Der Blutorden der NSDAP.* Hamburg: Verlag Militaria-Archiv Klaus D. Patzwall, 1985.

Pauley, Bruce F. *Hitler and the Forgotten Nazis: A History of Austrian National Socialism.* Chapel Hill: University of North Carolina Press, 1981.

Payne, Stanley G. *Fascism: Comparison and Definition.* Madison: University of Wisconsin Press, 1980.

Perlmutter, Amos. *The Military and Politics in Modern Times.* New Haven: Yale University Press, 1977.

Peukert, Detlev. *Inside Nazi Germany: Conformity, Opposition, and*

Racism in Everyday Life. New Haven: Yale University Press, 1987.

Peukert, Detlev, and Jürgen Reulecke. Die Reihen fast geschlossen: Beiträge zur Geschichte des Alltags unterem Nationalsozialismus. Wuppertal, 1981.

Picker, Dr. Henry. Hitlers Tischgespräche im Führerhauptquartier 1941-1942. Stuttgart: Seewald, 1963.

Pusey, Wolfgang. "Idealismus und Terror. Eine mentalitätsgeschichtliche Untersuchung des sog. Freikorps-Geistes. (Entwurf)." Manuscript, Freie Universität Berlin, 1984.

Pusey, Wolfgang. "Der Weg vom Innersten ins Aeußerste." Manuscript, Berlin, 1984.

Rang und Organisationsliste der NSDAP mit Gliederungen, angeschlossenen Verbänden und betreuten Organisationen. Stuttgart: W. Kohlhammer, 1947.

Rau, Friedrich. "Die höheren Reichswehr Führer in der Weimarer Zeit: Charakteristische Beispiele sozialer Herkunft und bestimmter Ausleseprinzipien." Master's thesis, Freie Universität Berlin, 1966.

———. "Personalpolitik und Organisation in der vorläufigen Reichswehr." Ph.D. diss., Universität München, 1972.

Reiche, Eric G. "The Development of the SA in Nuremberg, 1922 to 1934." Ph.D. diss., University of Delaware, 1972.

———. "From 'Spontaneous' to Legal Terror: SA Police and the Judiciary in Nürnberg 1933-34." European Studies Review 9 (April 1979): 237-64.

———. The Development of the SA in Nürnberg, 1922-1934. Cambridge: Cambridge University Press, 1986.

Ringer, Fritz K. "Bildung, Wirtschaft, und Gesellschaft in Deutschland, 1800-1960." Geschichte und Gesellschaft 6, no. 1 (1980): 5-35.

Rittberger, Volker, ed. 1933: Wie die Republik der Diktatur Erlag. Stuttgart: W. Kohlhammer, 1983.

Ritter, Gerhard A., and Susanne Miller, eds. Die deutsche Revolution 1918-1919: Dokumente. 2d ed. Frankfurt am Main: Fischer Taschenbuch, 1983.

Rosenberg, Arthur. Imperial Germany: The Birth of the German Republic, 1871-1918. 1928. Boston: Beacon Press, 1964.

Rosenhaft, Eve. Beating the Fascists? The German Communists and Political Violence, 1928-1933. Cambridge: Cambridge University Press, 1983.

Roßbach, Gerhard. Mein Weg durch die Zeit: Erinnerungen und Bekenntnisse. Weilburg-Lahn: Vereinigte Weilburger Buchdruckereien, 1950.

Rumpf, Maria Regina. "Die lebensalterliche Verteilung des Mitgliederzuganges zur NSDAP vor 1933 aufgezeigt an einer Großstadt und einem Landkreis: Ein Beitrag zum Generationsproblem." Ph.D. diss., Ruprecht-Karl Universität, Heidelberg, 1951.

Rust, Eric C. *Naval Officers under Hitler: The Story of Crew 34.* New York: Praeger, 1991.

Salomon, Ernst von. *Der Fragebogen.* 1961. Reinbek bei Hamburg: Rowohlt, 1991.

Saul, Klaus. "Der Kampf um die Jugend zwischen Volksschule und Kaserne: Ein Beitrag zur "Jugendpflege" im Wilhelminischen Reich, 1890-1914." *Militärgeschichtliche Mitteilungen* 10, no. 1 (1971): 97-143.

Schieder, Wolfgang, ed. *Faschismus als soziale Bewegung.* 1976. Göttingen: Vandenhoeck & Ruprecht, 1983.

Schoenbaum, David. *Hitler's Social Revolution: Class and Status in Nazi Germany, 1933-1939.* Garden City, N.Y.: Anchor Books, 1967.

Schottelius, Herbert, and Wilhelm Diest, eds. *Marine und Marinepolitik im kaiserlichen Deutschland, 1871-1914.* Düsseldorf: Droste, 1972.

Schulte, Bernd Felix. *Die deutsche Armee, 1900-1914: Zwischen Beharren und Verändern.* Düsseldorf: Droste, 1977.

Schulz, Paul. "Meine Erschiessung am 30. Juni 1934." Privately published, 1948.

———. "Rettungen und Hilfeleistungen an Verfolgten, 1933-1945, durch Oberlt. a.D. Paul Schulz." Privately published, 1967.

Schulze, Hagen. *Freikorps und Republik, 1918-1920.* Militärgeschichtliche Studien 8. Boppard am Rhine: Harald Boldt, 1969.

———. *Weimar: Deutschland, 1917-1933.* Berlin: Severin und Siedler, 1982.

Schwarz, Max, *M.d.R. Biographisches Handbuch der Reichstage.* Hanover: Verlag f. Literatur und Zeitgeschen, 1965.

Seidler, Franz W. "Das Nationalsozialistische Kraftfahrkorps und die Organisation Todt im Zweiten Weltkrieg." *Vierteljahreshefte für Zeitgeschichte* 32, no. 4 (December 1984): 625-36.

Showalter, Dennis E. "Army and Society in Imperial Germany: The Pains of Modernization." *Journal of Contemporary History* 18 (October 1983): 583-618.

Siggemann, Jürgen. *Die kasernierte Polizei und das Problem der inneren Sicherheit in der Weimarer Republik: Eine Studie zum Auf- und Ausbau des innerstaatlichen Sicherheitssystems in Deutschland, 1918-1933.* Frankfurt am Main: R.G. Fischer, 1980.

Smelser, Ronald, and Rainer Zitelmann, eds. *The Nazi Elite.* New York: New York University Press, 1993.

Smith, Bradley F. *Heinrich Himmler: A Nazi in the Making, 1900-1926.* Stanford: Hoover Institution Press, 1971.

Sontheimer, Kurt. *Antidemokratisches Denken in der Weimarer Republik.* Munich: Deutsche Taschenbuch, 1978.

Speier, Hans. *German White-Collar Workers and the Rise of Hitler.* 1977. New Haven: Yale University Press, 1986.

Spires, David N. *Image and Reality: The Making of the German Officer, 1921-1933.* Westport, Conn.: Greenwood Press, 1984.

Stachura, Peter D. "Who Were the Nazis? A Socio-Political Analysis of the National Socialist *Machtübernahme.*" *European Studies Review* 11 (July 1981): 293-324.

Stachura, Peter D., ed. *The Nazi Machtergreigung.* London, 1983.

Steger, Bernd. *Berufssoldaten oder Prätorianer: Die Einflußnahme des bayerischen Offizierskorps auf die Innenpolitik in Bayern und im Reich 1918-1924.* Frankfurt am Main: Rita G. Fischer, 1980.

Steinbach, Lothar. *Ein Volk, ein Reich, ein Glaube? Ehemalige Nationalsozialisten und Zeitzeugen berichten über ihr Leben in Dritten Reich.* Bonn: J.H.W. Dietz, 1983.

Stern, Fritz. *The Politics of Cultural Despair: A Study in the Rise of the Germanic Ideology.* Berkeley: University of California Press, 1961.

Stern, Howard. "The Organisation Consul." *Journal of Modern History* 35 (March 1963): 20-32.

Stockhorst, Erich. *Fünftausend Köpfe: Wer War Was im Dritten Reich.* Velbert and Kettwig: Blick and Bild, 1967.

Stokes, Lawrence D. "Heinrich Böhmcker." In Gesellschaft für Schleswig-Holsteinische Geschichte und des Vereins für Lübeckische Geschichte und Altertumskunde, *Biographisches Lexikon für Schleswig-Holstein und Lübeck,* 9:61-65. Neumünster: Karl Wachholtz, 1991.

Striesow, Jan. *Die Deutschnationale Volkspartei und die Völkisch-Radikalen, 1918-1922.* 2 vols. Frankfurt am Main: Haag und Herchen Verlag, 1981.

Stumpf, Reinhard. "Die Luftwaffe als drittes Heer: Die Luftwaffen-Erdkampfverbände und das Problem der Sonderheere 1933 bis 1945." In *Soziale Bewegung und Politische Verfassung. Werner Conze zum 31.12.75,* ed. Ulrich Englehardt, Volker Sellin, and Horst Stucke, 857-94. Stuttgart: Klett, 1976.

Stürmer, Michael, ed. *Die Weimarer Republik: Belagerte Civitas.* 2d ed. Königstein/Ts.: Athenäum Taschenbücher, 1985.

Tessin, Georg. *Deutsche Verbände und Truppen, 1918-1939.* Osnabrück: Biblio, 1974.

Thamer, Hans-Ulrich, and Wolfgang Wippermann. *Faschistische und Neofaschistische Bewegungen.* Erträge der Forschung 72. Darmstadt: Wissenschaftliche Buchgesellschaft, 1977.

Theweleit, Klaus. *Männerphantasien.* 2 vols. Reinbek bei Hamburg: Rowohlt Taschenbuch, 1980.

Tobias, Fritz. *Der Reichstagbrand, Legende, und Wirklichkeit.* Rastatt, 1962.

Treziak, Ulrike, *Deutsche Jugendbewegung am Ende der Weimarer Republik. Zum Verhältnis von Bündischer Jugend und Nationalsozialismus.* Quellen und Beiträge zur Geschichte der Jugendbewegung, vol. 28. Frankfurt am Main: Dipa, 1986.

Turner, Henry A. Jr., ed. *Nazism and the Third Reich.* New York: New Viewpoints/Franklin Watts, 1972.

———. *Hitler aus nächster Nähe.* Frankfurt am Main: Ullstein, 1978.

U.S. War Department, *TM-E 30-451 Handbook on German Military Forces 15 March 1945* (Restricted). Washington, D.C.: U.S. Government Printing Office, 1945; facsimile reprint, Military Press, 1970.

Vagts, Alfred. *A History of Militarism.* 1937. Meridian Books, 1959.

Vogelsang, Thilo. "Neue Dokumente zur Geschichte der Reichswehr 1930-1933." *Vierteljahreshefte für Zeitgeschichte* 2, no. 4 (October 1954): 397-436.

Wachenbruch, Hans Joachim. "Der Dritte Man hört mit." *Der Fortschritt* 5, nos. 8 & 9.

Waite, Robert G.L. *Vanguard of Nazism: The Free Corps Movement in Postwar Germany, 1918-1923.* 1952. Reprint, New York: W.W. Norton, 1969.

Ward, Stephen R., ed. *The War Generation.* Port Washington, N.Y.: Kennikat Press, 1975.

Weber, Hermann. *Die Wandlung des deutschen Kommunismus.* 2 vols. Frankfurt am Main: Europäischer, 1969.

Wegner, Bernd. *Hitlers Politische Soldaten: Die Waffen-SS 1933-1945. Studien zu Leitbild, Struktur und Funktion einer Nationalsozialistischen Elite.* Paderborn: Ferdinand Schöningh, 1982.

Wehler, Hans-Ulrich. *Das Deutsche Kaiserreich, 1871-1918.* Kleine Vandenhoeck-Reihe/Deutsche Geschichte 9. Göttingen: Vandenhoeck & Ruprecht, 1973.

———, ed. *Eckart Kehr, der Primat der Innenpolitik: Gesammelte Aufsätze zur preußisch-deutschen Sozialgeschichte im 19. und 20. Jahrhundert.* 1965, 1970. Frankfurt am Main: Ullstein, 1976.

Werner, Andreas. "SA: 'Wehrverband,' 'Parteitruppe,' oder 'Revolutionsarmee'? Studien zur Geschichte der SA und der

NSDAP, 1920-1933." Inaugural diss., Friedrich-Alexander-Universität zu Erlangen-Nürnberg, 1964.

Whalen, Robert Weldon. *Bitter Wounds: German Victims of the Great War, 1914-1939.* Ithaca: Cornell University Press, 1984.

Willems, Emilio. *Der Preußisch deutsche Militärismus: Ein Kulturkomplex im sozialen Wandel.* Cologne: Verlag Wissenschaft und Politik, 1984

Williams, Warren E. "Paramilitarism in Inter-State Relations: The Role of Political Armies in Twentieth-Century European Politics." Ph.D. diss., London, 1965.

Wippermann, Wolfgang. *Europäischer Faschismus im Vergleich, 1922-1982.* Frankfurt am Main: Shurkamp, 1983.

Wistrich, Robert. *Who's Who in Nazi Germany.* New York: Bonanza Books, 1984.

Wohl, Robert. *The Generation of 1914.* Cambridge: Harvard University Press, 1979.

Wolfe, Robert, ed. *Captured German and Related Records: A National Archives Conference.* National Archives conferences, vol. 3. Athens: Ohio University Press, 1974.

Zabel, Jürgen-K. "Jugend und Militär. Zur Sozialgeschichte militärischer Erziehungsinstitutionen in Deutschland." *Aus Politik und Zeitgeschichte,* 28 July 1979, 23-40.

Zaika, Siegfried. "Preußische Polizeiformationen bis 1933: Ein Beitrag zur historischen Konfliktforschung." In *Militärgeschichte, Militärwissenschaft, und Konfliktforschung: Festschrift für Werner Hahlweg,* ed. Dermont Bradley and Ulrich Marwedel, 475-83. Osnabrück: Biblio, 1977.

Ziegler, Herbert F. *Nazi Germany's New Aristocracy: The SS Leadership, 1925-1939.* Princeton: Princeton University Press, 1989.

Zuricher, Louis A., and Gwyn Harries-Jenkins, eds. *Supplementary Military Forces: Reserves, Militias, Auxiliaries.* Sage Research Progress Series on War, Revolution and Peacekeeping, vol. 8. Beverly Hills: Sage, 1978.

Index

*Indicates men with short biographies in the text. Numbers in parentheses after names refer to the group photo on page 3.